ROBERT G. CALDWELL, Ph.D., University of Pennsylvania, is Professor of Criminology at the University of Iowa. A member of the Virginia State Bar, his professional affiliations include the National Council on Crime and Delinquency, American Correctional Association, the American Society of Criminology, and the International Society of Criminology. Dr. Caldwell also served for many years as a consultant in criminology for the Iowa Board of Control. He is the author of *Criminology*, also published by The Ronald Press Company.


JAMES A. BLACK, Ph.D., University of Iowa, is Associate Professor and Head of the Department of Sociology at the University of Tennessee. Dr. Black is the author of numerous scholarly papers and of articles and reviews for the professional journals.

# JUVENILE DELINQUENCY

**ROBERT G. CALDWELL**
UNIVERSITY OF IOWA

**JAMES A. BLACK**
UNIVERSITY OF TENNESSEE

THE RONALD PRESS COMPANY · NEW YORK

*HV*
*9104*
*. C248*

Library of Congress Catalog Card Number: 79-153805
PRINTED IN THE UNITED STATES OF AMERICA

*To LaMerle and Cindy*

# Preface

The major objective of this textbook is to provide a definitive, carefully balanced, and well-integrated view of juvenile delinquency in contemporary America. The general socio-legal framework within which the subject is discussed is charted early. We begin with a clear-cut definition of juvenile delinquency as a legal concept and proceed to an examination of delinquency as a social problem. To illustrate how this framework can be applied to particular types of delinquency and, at the same time, provide materials related to timely and significant adolescent problems, the issues of juvenile drinking and drug abuse are examined.

Relying on the most recent data available, a statistical overview of the amount of delinquency is next presented, along with an assessment of the various methods for measuring the extent to which delinquency prevails in American society.

After carefully examining the trend toward viewing delinquency from a typological perspective, causes of delinquency are considered. In addition to evaluating theories, concepts, and empirical findings, numerous actual case-study situations are included which focus around major sets of causal factors.

In view of the complexity of the problem, we have chosen to employ a broad frame of reference covering the full range of pertinent theories, discussing their strengths and weaknesses, and arriving at whatever conclusions are justified in the light of existing knowledge. This approach is interdisciplinary, drawing upon the contributions of many fields, including those of biology, anthropology, sociology, psychology, psychiatry, medicine, and law.

Although juvenile delinquency is recognized as a world-wide problem, the treatment in this text is focused primarily on the American framework. It is felt that a better understanding of its manifestations here will provide deeper insights into its nature and growth elsewhere.

The book concludes with what we believe to be a carefully balanced analysis of the dimensions of delinquency control. Not only are crucial social and legal issues in the sentencing and correctional setting explicitly dealt with, but specific recommendations for improving these agencies are made.

Many sources have been drawn upon in the preparation of this text, and we have acknowledged our indebtedness. Even so, we wish to express again our appreciation to the many persons and organizations that have assisted us in our work. We especially thank Miss Eula Van Meter and Mrs. Margaret Garrett for their expert checking and typing of the manuscript.

ROBERT G. CALDWELL
JAMES A. BLACK

Iowa City, Iowa
Knoxville, Tennessee
July 1971

# Contents

I

# THE PROBLEM

# 1

# The Meaning of Juvenile Delinquency

## THE STUDY OF JUVENILE DELINQUENCY

One out of every nine children in the United States—one out of every six male children—will be referred to the juvenile court in connection with some delinquent act (other than a traffic offense) before his eighteenth birthday. Furthermore, of all the persons arrested in the United States during 1969 (not including traffic offenders), about 39 per cent were under 21 and about 26 per cent were under 18.

And the situation has been getting worse. In fact, the number of juveniles who have been arrested has sharply increased during recent years, and more and more young people are becoming involved in serious crimes. From 1960 to 1969, for example, the number of juveniles arrested for serious crimes increased 90 per cent.

Do these figures surprise you—perhaps alarm you? They have alarmed the leaders of our country, especially since studies indicate that many adult offenders begin their criminal careers by acts of delinquency.[1]

This, for example, is what happened to Mike, who began his criminal career in a large eastern city. When he was six years old, he and several companions pilfered fruit and candy from a neighborhood store. Apprehended, they were held overnight in a detention home and then released. Several months later, Mike was arrested with three older boys as they were caught in the act of shoplifting. His companions were held for the juvenile court, but he was again released. During the next ten years, Mike committed a number of increasingly serious acts of delinquency,

[1] Federal Bureau of Investigation, *Uniform Crime Reports, 1969*, pp. 110, 115; The President's Commission on Law Enforcement and Administration of Justice, *The Challenge of Crime in a Free Society* (Washington, D.C.: U.S. Government Printing Office, 1967), pp. 46, 55, 56.

including running away from home, truancy, vandalism, larceny, breaking and entering, robbery, and assault and battery. Several times he was placed on probation; once he was committed to a training school; but usually he was released to his parents. At the age of sixteen he was traveling with a gang of older boys and, with several of them, he was arrested for breaking and entering. This time he spent three years in the state training school, from which he was released on parole. Mike soon violated his parole, stole several cars, and committed a series of armed robberies, for which he was taken into custody, convicted, and committed to the state reformatory, where he remained for eighteen months. Again he was paroled, and again he violated his parole. Along with several companions, he stole cars, robbed filling stations and supermarkets, and raped two women. Trapped in a hotel room, he shot it out with the police, killing one officer and seriously wounding several others. For this, Mike was convicted of first-degree murder and executed.

"A tragic, wasted life," you say. Yes, but Mike's record is not only one of his crimes and failures, but also one of the neglect, inadequacies, and incompetence of those who might have helped him to become a useful and law-abiding citizen.

Jim was more fortunate. On the way to the same tragic end, he was guided into a responsible, happy life by wise and skillful counseling. After having committed a number of acts of vandalism and larceny, Jim, at the age of fifteen, killed the owner of a grocery store and took his day's receipts. For this, he was sentenced for life to the state penitentiary. There the warden became interested in Jim and assisted him in securing a high-school education. When Jim was twenty-five, he was paroled and given permission to take the entrance examinations at the state university. He passed these with high grades and was admitted to the college of engineering. An excellent student, he graduated with honors and eventually married and became a partner in a prosperous engineering firm.

It is true that Jim's case is an unusual one, and no competent student of the problem contends that all delinquents can be converted into law-abiding citizens; but there is general agreement that we can greatly improve our work with juveniles and thereby significantly reduce the rates of delinquency and crime in the United States. This view has been emphasized by the report of the President's Commission on Law Enforcement and Administration of Justice, which explains that studies show the importance of juvenile delinquency as a forerunner of adult crime, and that the recidivism rates for young offenders are higher than those for any other age group.[2]

[2] The President's Commission on Law Enforcement and Administration of Justice, pp. 46, 55.

It is not difficult, therefore, to understand why the President's Commission believes that America's best hope for the reduction of its crime problem lies in the lowering of its juvenile delinquency and youth crime. On the one hand, youth is apparently responsible for a substantial and increasingly disproportionate part of the national crime problem. On the other hand, however, preventive and correctional programs directed toward young people seem to hold greater promise of success than do those dealing with adults. A child's habits are not so firmly fixed as those of adults; his attitudes, not so hardened; his reticulum of social relationships, not so complex and entangling; his goals, not so well established. Besides, the community is more interested, sympathetic, understanding, compassionate, and hopeful in children's cases than in those of adults; and, insist criminologists, a study of juvenile delinquency may well provide insights which will prove helpful in the rehabilitation of adult offenders.

Certainly, Americans cannot afford to let today's juvenile delinquency and restlessness take care of themselves. The problem demands the intelligent action of every neighborhood, every community, every state; and intelligent action can come only with a better understanding of the nature and causes of the problem. It should be clear, then, why the study of juvenile delinquency has become so important in our modern society.

## HISTORICAL PERSPECTIVE

The term "juvenile delinquency" is relatively new—coming into general usage in the United States only within the past century. However, the problem of providing collective or public care, protection, guidance, and discipline for children, an integral part of which is what we now call juvenile delinquency, is an ancient one, extending back through all cultures and all historical periods to the very beginnings of human society. The customs and rituals of primitive man and the laws of the ancient world attest to its antiquity. The severe punishment of refractory children, for example, was possible under the Mosaic Code and the early Roman law, but, in all probability, the patriarchal family system, buttressed by a home economy, hallowed customs, and religious traditions, made the use of this punishment necessary in only exceptional cases. Moreover, pagan Rome did not ignore its destitute, wayward, and dependent children, but instead sought to protect and guide them by the establishment of orphanages, asylums, and schools.

Even so, early Christianity became the major force in the salvaging of the helpless, the unfortunate, and the poor and in the creation of foundling homes and asylums for abandoned children. As feudalism declined and governments confiscated the monasteries, new steps had to be taken to handle the problems of the poor and the distressed; and in England, from the time of the Black Death in 1348 until the reign of Queen Elizabeth, the roots of local responsibility gradually developed, and the period culminated in the passage of the Poor Laws in 1601, which charged the parishes with providing for the needy.[3]

In Rome, Pope Clement XI opened the famous Hospice of Saint Michael for errant boys in 1703. Although this institution stressed education, the life of the inmate was a hard one. While working together at spinning and knitting, the juvenile offenders, chained by one foot and subject to a strict rule of silence, listened to the reading of religious tracts, and the unfortunate youth who incurred the displeasure of his keepers might receive a flogging.[4]

In the meantime, England was transporting her troublesome children to her colonies, sending them into the naval service, and putting them, along with adults, into jails, houses of correction, workhouses, and prisons. Although private societies were organized to care for unfortunate juveniles—the Philanthropic Society of London, founded in 1788, being the pioneer in this work—no provision was made for a public institution for juveniles until the passage of the Parkhurst Act in 1838.[5] During the early years of her history, America tended to follow in the footsteps of the mother country, committing her juvenile offenders to jails and prisons and indenturing her destitute, neglected, and dependent children or sending them to almshouses. The first institution for juvenile delinquents in the United States—the New York House of Refuge—was opened in 1825, under the direction of the Society for Reformation of Juvenile Delinquents. It was not until 1847, however, when Massachusetts opened a reform school for boys at Westborough, that the United States established a strictly public institution for juvenile delinquents. A few years later, in 1853, the foster-home movement originated in New York with the organization of the Children's Aid Society, which specialized in the placement of destitute and deserted children and sent thousands of them into the farms and small towns of the Middle West. These and similar developments in the fields of education, welfare, and correction charac-

[3] Charles Loring Brace, *The Dangerous Classes of New York; and Twenty Years' Work Among Them* (New York: Wynkoop and Hallenbeck, Publishers, 1872), pp. 14–22.

[4] Max Grünhut, *Penal Reform* (London: Oxford University Press, 1948), p. 21; Negley K. Teeters and John Otto Reinemann, *The Challenge of Delinquency* (Englewood Cliffs, N.J.: Prentice-Hall, Inc., 1950), p. 44.

[5] Enoch Cobb Wines, *State of Prisons* (Cambridge, Mass.: University Press, John Wilson and Son, 1880), pp. 75–77; Edmund F. DuCane, *The Punishment and Prevention of Crime* (London: Macmillan and Co., 1885), pp. 202, 203.

terized the nineteenth century in the United States as the public assumed more and more responsibility in the care, protection, and discipline of children, and the trend reached a high point with the establishment of the juvenile court in Chicago, Illinois, in 1899.[6]

"Why have you presented this brief historical sketch?" you may ask. The answer, of course, is that it is so easy to believe that the problem which we now call juvenile delinquency is an entirely modern one. The reporting and dramatizing of delinquency and the crimes of youthful offenders by television, radio, moving pictures, and newspapers, and the unprecedented publicity about these problems generated by forums, conferences, and legislative investigations and reports, have helped to create this impression. Yet history reminds us that violence and brutality characterized the frontier and early cities of the United States, and that even then many writers were condemning the behavior of America's children. Here, for example, is an item published by the *St. Paul Dispatch* in 1898: "The bad boy of America has no counterpart in any other part of the world. . . . His language is slang and profanity, his amusement is violence, his education a blank, and his name a terror to society." [7]

Thus, children have not suddenly become "little monsters." Many children have troubled and alarmed their elders. What we have been witnessing is the great increase of an old problem and the expansion of society's efforts to cope with it; but then, when one considers the turmoil and confusion of the modern world, one may well wonder why today's children are not worse.

## POINTS OF VIEW

Since delinquency is an old problem, it is not surprising that many points of view regarding its nature and causes have been advanced. A brief consideration of some of these will help to indicate that the problem is also a complex one.

### The Classical School

In 1764 the Italian Cesare Beccaria published his famous *Essay on Crimes and Punishments*, which provided the starting point for the classical school of criminal law and criminology. Although the primary purpose of the classical school was the improvement of the criminal law and procedure, it also carried with it the belief in the existence of a free

---

[6] Robert G. Caldwell, *Criminology* (New York: The Ronald Press Co., 1965), pp. 386, 512; Teeters and Reinemann, pp. 74–81.

[7] Quoted by The Commission on Juvenile Delinquency, Adult Crime, and Corrections in *Anti-Social Behavior and Its Control in Minnesota*, a Report to the 1957 Legislature, pp. 14, 15.

will and the moral responsibility of the individual. The violator of the law, therefore, was a *willful offender*. Since this school also assumed that man exercised his will in terms of a balancing of pleasure and pain and directed his behavior toward securing the greatest net total of pleasure, it advocated that a definite penalty should be attached to every crime and invariably inflicted so that every would-be offender might take the penalty into consideration in his calculation of pains and pleasures that would result from his violation of the law.

Through the application of the principles of the classical school great reforms were introduced into the criminal law and the courts,[8] but it exaggerated the role of reason and underestimated the importance of habit, emotions, and the social factors in human affairs. Modifications gradually crept into the practice of the classical school, which, for example, began to exempt young children and lunatics from punishment on the ground that they were unable to calculate pleasures and pains intelligently. This modified approach is sometimes called the neoclassical school of criminology.

## Biological Views

The positive school of criminology was inaugurated in 1872 by the work of the Italian anthropologist Cesare Lombroso. Influenced by the modern development of the biological sciences and particularly by Darwin's writings on evolution, Lombroso contended that: (1) there is *a distinct born-criminal type*; (2) this type can be identified by certain stigmata or anomalies, such as protruding jaws, asymmetrical skull, and so on; (3) the stigmata are symptoms of atavism or degeneracy, especially that characterized by epileptic tendencies; and (4) the born-criminal type will commit crimes unless he lives under exceptionally favorable circumstances.[9] Lombroso never contended that all criminals belonged to the born-criminal type, and he gradually modified his theory to the point where he conceded that most criminals should not be so classified. Even so, he exaggerated the biological factors in human life and underestimated the social and cultural influences; and the positive school failed to prove the existence of a born-criminal type.

Another biological interpretation of crime appeared with the development of the science of endocrinology, which devotes itself to the study of the glands of internal secretion. The tendency in some works on endocrinology is to make *the offender the product of endocrine defi-*

---

[8] Cesare Beccaria, *Essay on Crimes and Punishments*, trans. Henry Paolucci (Indianapolis: The Bobbs-Merrill Co., Inc., 1963); Caldwell, pp. 172–174.

[9] Cesare Lombroso, *Crime, Its Causes and Remedies* (Boston: Little, Brown and Co., 1911).

*ciencies, excesses, and disturbances,*[10] but it is highly unlikely that any theory about glands can ever completely explain the existence of crime. Personality is something more than glands, and many persons with defective glands never become criminals.

By the publication of his book *Crime and the Man* in 1939, Earnest A. Hooton, an anthropologist of Harvard University, founded what has been called the neo-Lombrosian school of criminology. The offender, he claimed, is not a born type but rather *a person with an inherited predisposition.* Biological inferiority is the primary cause of crime, but it is not a direct one. Instead, crime is the resultant of a complex process of biological and social forces by which mentally and physically inferior individuals are selected for criminality.[11] Hooton's research has been severely criticized, and it does not appear that he has made any significant contribution to our understanding of the causes of crime. This judgment does not imply, however, that we can afford to disregard the biological factors in our study of the causation of crime and delinquency.

## Other Views

After intelligence tests became available, many investigators began to use them to measure the mentality of prisoners. Henry H. Goddard, director of the research laboratory of the New Jersey Training School for the Feeble-Minded at Vineland, was a leader among those who argued that *low-grade mentality was the greatest single cause of delinquency and crime.*[12] Eventually, however, Goddard admitted that everyone is a potential delinquent. Moreover, modern research indicates that there is a wide range of intelligence among criminals and that low-grade mentality is no more prevalent among the inmates of correctional institutions than among free persons in the United States.

With the development of psychiatry, the mental health of offenders has come increasingly under examination, and many psychiatrists believe that mental illness is an important cause of crime. In fact, some, like Benjamin Karpman, hold that crime and delinquency, without exception, are *symptomatic of abnormal mental states and an expression of them.*[13] On the basis of the existing evidence, however, the sound view appears to be that mental disease does not inevitably cause crime and delinquency and that, although some mentally disordered persons do violate the law,

[10] See, for example, Max G. Schlapp and Edward H. Smith, *The New Criminology* (New York: Boni and Liveright, 1928).
[11] See Earnest A. Hooton, *Crime and the Man* (Cambridge: Harvard University Press, 1939).
[12] See Henry H. Goddard, *Human Efficiency and Levels of Intelligence* (Princeton, N.J.: Princeton University Press, 1920).
[13] See Benjamin Karpman, "Criminality, Insanity, and the Law," *Journal of Criminal Law and Criminology,* XXXIX (January–February, 1949), 584–605.

the great majority of delinquents and criminals, like the great majority of law-abiding persons, have normal mentalities.

Some students of the problem, like William Healy,[14] John Dollard, and Leonard Doob,[15] have argued that *personality conflict* is the central element in the causation of conduct problems. Suffering from the emotional discomfort that personality conflict and the ensuing frustration cause, the individual seeks to remove this pain by such substitute behavior as crime and delinquency. The difficulty here, as many writers have explained, is that everyone suffers from frustrations, that so highly emotional an experience as frustration may not even produce aggressiveness but may be reduced through mirth and jocularity, and that emotional disturbances may actually result from, rather than cause, criminal or delinquent behavior. Still, of course, personality conflict may be a factor in the causation of crime or delinquency in the individual case.

Another point of view has been presented by some sociologists. They have taken the position that only the social and cultural factors need to be considered in the causation of crime and delinquency, and thus, for them, *the offender is an environmental product*.[16] Critics of this view, however, have pointed out that both law-abiding persons and criminals and delinquents have come from about the same environment, and that the environmental factors must be seen in their interaction with the biological and psychological factors in a complex process of causation.

Some other sociologists have preferred to use the symbolic interaction theory to explain crime and delinquency.[17] According to this theory, a person develops the conception that he has of himself in a process of interaction with others. Through the use of gestures and language, he engages in symbolic interaction, and seeing himself as others see him, he learns what is expected of him and acts to strengthen and defend his self image. Thus his *self conception*, based on his perceptions of the way others view him and react to his behavior, becomes the important

---

[14] See William Healy, *The Individual Delinquent* (Boston: Little, Brown and Co., 1915); William Healy and Augusta F. Bronner, *Delinquents and Criminals* (New York: The Macmillan Co., 1926); William Healy and Augusta F. Bronner, *New Light on Delinquency and Its Treatment* (New Haven: Yale University Press, 1936).

[15] John Dollard, Leonard Doob, *et al.*, *Frustration and Aggression* (New Haven: Yale University Press, 1939).

[16] See, for example, Edwin H. Sutherland and Donald R. Cressey, *Principles of Criminology* (Philadelphia: J. B. Lippincott Co., 1966).

[17] See, for example, Marshall B. Clinard, *Sociology of Deviant Behavior* (New York: Holt, Rinehart, and Winston, Inc., 1963), pp. 45–59; Richard R. Korn and Lloyd W. McCorkle, *Criminology and Penology* (New York: Holt, Rinehart, and Winston, Inc., 1959), pp. 327–39.

factor in the causation of his behavior, whether it be criminal or law-abiding. Many critics, however, have severely criticized this theory, insisting that it grossly oversimplifies human behavior, deprives man of his creative powers, and reduces him to a mere reflection of the group's specifications.

In this discussion, we have seen the delinquent as a willful offender, a born offender, a person with defective glands, a person with an inherited predisposition, a mentally deficient person, a mentally ill person, a frustrated person, a person who is the product of his environment, and a person with a delinquent self concept. Each of the points of view presented has given us some insight into human behavior, but even a combination of all of them provides us with only a partial picture. This is not to argue that theories are of no value (for they help us to accumulate knowledge), but rather that the area of the unknown is so great that conclusions based on any one theory must be considered as only tentative, and the possible validity of other theories, clearly recognized.[18]

## DEFINITION OF JUVENILE DELINQUENCY

Thus far we have indicated various points of view regarding juvenile delinquency, but as yet we have not defined it; and this must be done, for, obviously, more than a point of view is necessary. A decision must be made as to what kind of children committing what kind of acts under what kind of conditions are to be subject to official action. To do this we need a standard by which we can judge. When such a standard is officially created by legislative action, it is called a law.

The loose usage of the term "juvenile delinquency" has caused considerable confusion. Some psychiatrists, psychologists, sociologists, and social workers have used the term in various ways, without regard to the legal definition, in order to express their points of view. And other writers, using the legal definition, have labeled juveniles as delinquents at various stages in the process of official action. Thus children have been called delinquents when they have been detected, when they have been held for court, and when they have been found delinquent by the court. In order to avoid this confusion, we shall use the legal definition and apply it strictly. And certainly this is a realistic approach, for the term "juvenile delinquency" is a legal one, and all official action and records regarding juvenile delinquency are based on legal principles. Therefore, in this textbook, a juvenile who violates a social norm will

[18] For further discussion of the theories presented above, see Caldwell, pp. 171–219.

be called a *social deviant*; and his act, a social deviation. If a juvenile is accused of violating the law which defines delinquency—one of the social norms—he will be referred to as an *alleged delinquent*; and his act, as an alleged act of delinquency. However, not until a person is adjudged a delinquent in a juvenile court, will he be termed a *delinquent*; and his act, delinquency.[19]

[19] To avoid encumbering the language of the text, the terms "crime," "delinquency," "criminal," and "delinquent" will be used instead of "alleged crime," "alleged delinquency," "alleged criminal," and "alleged delinquent," although in the strict sense of the words, an act is not a crime or delinquency and a person is not a criminal or delinquent until they have been properly adjudicated as such in the criminal or juvenile court.

# 2

# Delinquency as a
# Social Problem

When you read that a boy has been adjudged guilty of car theft and committed to a training school, what thoughts come to your mind? You probably wonder what the boy looks like, what kind of car was stolen, how the boy felt when he entered the training school, and so on—in other words, the individual aspects of the case. These aspects, of course, are important, for the individual has a reality apart from the group, an independent identity that cannot be ignored, and the action of the police and the court in the handling of the case should be carefully considered. But there is more to the case than this. There are all the social relationships involved in the development of the boy and in the reaction of the community to his behavior.

Take Bill, for example. He is the oldest of four brothers. When he was five years old, his father deserted the family, and the mother was forced to go to work to support the children. Left unsupervised by a tired and despairing mother, who drifted into bad company, wild parties, and drunken brawls, the children became quite a problem for the school and the welfare agencies in the community. Bill was twelve when, as a result of persistent truancy, he was first brought to the juvenile court. During the next five years, acts of theft, vandalism, and breaking and entering sent Bill into foster homes, probation, and training schools. Meanwhile, the other children were traveling the same road. Although school authorities and many welfare agencies tried to help the mother and her children, little success was achieved, and Bill's brother eventually followed him into the state reformatory.

Again, consider the case of Mike. When Mike was a small child, his family was comfortably fixed, but the prolonged illness of the father compelled them to sell their home and move into a poor neighborhood of a large city. In his despondency, the father turned to drink and became an alcoholic, while a worn and tired mother sought relief in the company of other men. Mike, an only child, found entertainment and excitement in the streets, where he ran with a gang of older boys, who ransacked and plundered empty houses and stole food and clothing from neighborhood stories. Caught in the act of shoplifting, Mike, at the age of fourteen, was taken to the juvenile court, which placed him in a foster home. Meanwhile, several churches and welfare agencies tried to help the parents, but despite good medical care, the father died, and the mother ran off with another man. Mike stayed with his foster parents for about two years and then left and joined his old gang. For several years he was able to support himself by thievery and odd jobs, but he grew tired of this and, with several other young men, began to hijack trucks and rob supermarkets. Arrested, he was convicted on several charges and committed to the state reformatory.

Here, then, we have more than just Bill and Mike, two young men who were sent to prison. We have, in fact, a whole fabric of social relationships, into which are woven husbands, wives, children, neighbors, victims of crimes and delinquencies, doctors, teachers, clergymen, social workers, lawyers, policemen, judges, foster parents, correctional workers, and probation and parole officers. It is to such relationships that we now turn our attention for additional understanding of crime and delinquency.

## CULTURE, GROUPS, AND PROCESSES

Men in their struggle with the forces of nature and in their interaction with one another have created an artificial environment composed not only of material objects, such as houses, factories, vehicles, machinery, and tools, but also of supporting, defining, and instrumental ideas, customs, and traditions. Social scientists have applied the term *culture*[1] to this crystallization of man's experience which not only enables him to promote his interests and to satisfy his wishes, but also restricts, regulates, and controls his activities and enterprises.

The nonmaterial culture consists of patterns of behavior, or social norms, ranging on an ascending scale of rationality, complexity, and compulsiveness from *folkways* through *mores* to *social institutions*, which are considered so important to the group welfare that they are enforced not merely by public opinion, as the mores are, but by authority. *Folkways* are spontaneous, unpremeditated, common ways of behaving.

[1] Culture may be defined as all of the transmittible results of living together. For a critical review of the concepts and definitions of culture, see A. L. Kroeber and Clyde Kluckhohn, *Culture* (New York: Random House, Inc., 1963).

*Mores* are patterns of behavior which are related to group welfare and vested with definite ideas of right and wrong. Although violation of the folkways elicits only mild disapproval, a breach of the mores, which strongly affect our attitudes toward such important matters as sex, property, and the persons of others, provokes moral indignation. A *social institution* is a complex, integrated organization of group behavior, established in the culture, meeting some persistent need or want, and enforced by authority.

Domestic, economic, political, religious, educational, and all other social institutions are interdependent and functionally related to one another and to the folkways and mores, without whose support they tend to lose their meaning and influence, and each acts and reacts upon all others, helping to produce the organic whole called society. Thus, although the law, one of the political institutions, depends upon the mores for much of its effectiveness, it can initiate and foster changes in the mores themselves, and has in fact done so in our rapidly changing society.

Social interaction expresses itself in terms of culture, but these expressions vary in mode and level. Sometimes, in such *primary groups* [2] as the family, the old-fashioned neighborhood, and the spontaneous play-group, it appears in very intimate, face-to-face association and cooperation.[3] Here social interaction is the nursery of human nature, the soil which nourishes the roots of social institutions. In it, basic and enduring ideals, attitudes, and habits are formed, and individuals are fused into cohesive units where loyalties are strong, affections deep, and controls spontaneous. At other times, in such *secondary groups* as corporations, unions, and political parties, social interaction is only partial and indirect association—association limited by special purpose, geographical distance, complex rules, social status, and similar barriers.

The *social processes* are the fundamental ways in which men interact. The most basic of these processes are *opposition* (including competition and conflict) and *cooperation*, and from these develop other social processes, such as differentiation, stratification, accommodation, and assimilation. All of these processes are to be found in every area of human behavior, whether it be lawful or unlawful. Through *differentiation*, roles (or sets of socially expected and approved behavior patterns associated with statuses or positions in a social structures) are ascribed or achieved in a society, each role bestowing certain rights and privileges

[2] A group may be defined as two or more people in a state of social interaction. Kimball Young, *Sociology* (New York: American Book Co., 1949), p. 617. See also George C. Homans, *The Human Group* (New York: Harcourt, Brace, Jovanovich, Inc., 1950).

[3] Cooley called such groups primary because they are first both in time and importance. Charles Horton Cooley, *Social Organization* (New York: Charles Scribner's Sons, 1929), p. 23.

and imposing certain duties and responsibilities, as defined by the pre-
vailing culture. Thus in every society the child's role is different from
that of the adult, the boy's from that of the girl; and the group's judgment
of both lawful and unlawful behavior is affected accordingly. Castes,
classes, and other status-giving groups in society are formed by the
process of *stratification*; and, to the extent that this affects the standards
of behavior and the opportunities for development, it must be considered
in the analysis of the problem of delinquency. *Accommodation* is the
process by which arrangements are worked out so that opposing individuals and groups can get along. *Assimilation*, on the other hand, is
the process by which divergent habits, attitudes, and ideas of two or
more individuals or groups are fused into a common set of habits, attitudes, and ideas. Accommodation is at work in the juvenile court when
arbitration and compromise dispose of quarrels that have upset families
and neighborhoods, and assimilation functions when a boy joins a delinquent gang and afterward when a probation officer effects his rehabilitation in the community.

All of the social processes coexist in every society, where they interact
and interweave in infinite ways. Thus we may visualize society as a
moving equilibrium in which cooperation and its related processes,
which tend to unify and increase conformity to the established rules of
behavior, interact with opposition and its related processes, which tend
to divide and reduce the conformity to the established rules of behavior.
Furthermore, the social processes interact with the social groups and the
culture of every society, and so all three must be recognized and understood if we are to have an adequate picture of social problems.[4]

## SOCIAL CHANGE, SOCIAL PROBLEMS, AND DISORGANIZATION

Every society has *social controls* for bringing human behavior into
conformity with its rules and standards, or social norms, which tend to
reflect the dominant values of the group. Some of these controls are
informal, like public opinion, scolding, gossip, the praise and condemnation of the community, and the respect and ridicule of friends and acquaintances. Others, however, like those exerted by the domestic, religious, economic, and political institutions, are highly formalized and
carry the weight of authority. The law, a political institution, must be
seen as only one element in this system of social control; but even so,
because of its definition of crime and delinquency and of its prescrip-
tion of penalties, its general applicability to all members of a society,

[4] Robert G. Caldwell, *Criminology* (New York: The Ronald Press Co., 1965),
Chapter 3.

and its enforcement by political agencies with the full support of the authority of the state, the law has a specificity, universality, officiality, and compulsiveness not possessed by the other elements.

However, no society or community, regardless of how simple or isolated it may be, is ever without *social change*. Inventions, migrations, diffusion of new ideas, floods, earthquakes, wars, and the like tend to foster change everywhere, and in a complex industrial society such as ours, change may become great and rapid. And—what is more significant—the different, but interrelated and interdependent, parts of culture change at different rates of speed, and thus some parts tend to diverge from others, placing a strain on the social structure, making it difficult for the existing social institutions to meet human needs, and causing social values to collide, as culture conflicts, in situations which sociologists have called *social problems*. Although the term "social problem" has been defined in various ways, it seems to be generally agreed that this type of problem exists when there is a situation which involves a considerable number of persons, which some persons deem to be a threat to certain values, and which can be dealt with only through collective action. Since juvenile delinquency involves all elements of this definition, it may be called a social problem. Thus, for example, the theft or destruction of property by children presents a situation threatening to the interests of many persons, who seek to deal with it through the courts and law-enforcement agencies.

Social change has been particularly swift and far-reaching in the United States and many of the countries of Western Europe, where such developments as industrialization, urbanization, and the amazing growth of new methods of communication and transportation have caused an erosion of the neighborhood and the family and increased the influence of corporations, labor unions, political pressure groups, professional societies, welfare agencies, and many other rapidly expanding forms of secondary association. As a result, the individual has emerged from the close bonds of primary-group life—from the intimate association with friends, neighbors, and relatives, all of whom have about the same set of values—and is now interacting in much more impersonal relationships with many other persons, who often have different and conflicting sets of values. Since the number of choices for the satisfaction of needs is thus increased, the compulsiveness of custom and tradition is reduced and new situations must be handled by the adoption of new sets of values. In the face of this decline of the primary groups as important agencies of social control, society has had to turn more and more to the less efficient methods provided by laws and governmental rules and regulations.

Unless a society can cope with its social change[5] by making the necessary counteracting adjustments, its social organization will no longer adequately regulate human behavior so that human needs can be satisfied in terms of a generally accepted set of values. Moreover, if this condition persists, the influence of existing social rules of behavior declines and there appears that phase of social change called *social disorganization*,[6] whose onset is marked by the increase of social problems, including juvenile delinquency. More recently, Merton defined social disorganization in terms of status and role and stated that it "refers to inadequacies or failures in a social system of interrelated statuses and roles such that the collective purposes and individual objectives of its members are less fully realized than they could be in an alternative workable system."[7] The greater the amount of social disorganization that a society has, the larger the number of social problems it will have, but a society may have many social problems without necessarily having social disorganization.

As Caldwell explained: "The amount of social disorganization is the resultant of the interaction between the divisive and cohesive forces at work in society. Some parts of society are always more organized or disorganized than others, and some may be organized while others are disorganized. Regardless of these variations, however, the resultant is measured in terms of the dominant values of society, although the very maintenance of these values, which are always opposed by some individuals and groups, may be a factor in the increase of social problems. Moreover, whereas society as a whole is organized or disorganized in terms of the dominant values, groups within it may be organized or disorganized in terms of their own values, and these subcultures in turn may be contributing to social disorganization."[8]

## SOCIETY AND THE INDIVIDUAL

But how does the individual—for example, Bill or Mike, whose cases were mentioned above—fit into all this? The individual acquires his culture and becomes a member of society by a process of learning. At

[5] For an analysis of industrialization as a major contributing factor in the causation of social problems, see Russell R. Dynes, Alfred C. Clarke, Simon Dinitz, and Iwao Ishino, *Social Problems: Dissensus and Deviation in an Industrial Society* (New York: Oxford University Press, 1964), Chapters 1, 2.

[6] W. I. Thomas and Florian Znaniecki, *The Polish Peasant* (New York: Alfred A. Knopf, Inc., 1927), II, p. 1128.

[7] R. K. Merton and R. A. Nisbet, *Contemporary Social Problems* (New York: Harcourt, Brace, Jovanovich, Inc., 1966), p. 800.

[8] Caldwell, p. 56.

first innate drives and impulses largely control his behavior; but his original nature readily lends itself to environmental influences, and he expresses himself more and more in terms of the values he receives from others, who previously have acquired them from their life's experiences. Thus the individual obtains not only the social rules and standards of society but also much of the basis of his attitudes and personal controls. Although he begins his learning in the intimate and informal association of the home, other and often conflicting forces soon impinge upon him; and he meets with increasingly rigid and formal controls as he moves first into other primary groups, such as the neighborhood and the play-group, and then into such secondary groups as the church, the school, the corporation, and the union.

In every society the individual plays many and often conflicting roles. At the same time, he seeks status in terms of the values of his culture. In modern society rapid social change has greatly complicated the processes by which he behaves in these ways. In America, for example, he lives in a "mass society" where the clamps of an unstable, external, and segmental interdependence have fastened him to a large number of other culturally uprooted individuals in a relationship which provides little nourishment for his emotional needs. As a result, he must constantly shift from one in-group to another in an ever-changing and frequently confusing pattern of cooperation and opposition; and in his uncertainty and emotional insecurity, he appears to respond more and more to the influences of reference groups [9] and the mass media of communication.

No one entirely conforms to all the social rules and standards in even the most simple, stable, and homogeneous community or society. Many factors, such as differences in heredity, the uniqueness of the individual, his creativeness and artistry, the variations in the learning and teaching processes, and divergence in social change, oppose this everywhere; and in modern, complex, rapidly changing communities and societies, where the individual encounters diverse and conflicting values in a stream of impersonal relationships, the amount of nonconformity, including crime and delinquency, becomes especially great. When social disorganization appears, individuals who have already become nonconformists find new opportunities for violating the social norms, and others who have usually conformed become violators on a large scale for the first time. If social

---

[9] A reference group is one the values of which influence a person's attitudes and behavior regardless of whether or not he is recognized by others as a member. Thus a boy may idolize "big league" baseball players as he prepares himself for a career in athletics. A membership group, for example, the family, is one in which a person is recognized by others as belonging.

disorganization persists, crime and delinquency tend to become institutionalized in certain areas and neighborhoods, which attract, produce
and protect law violators and contribute to the growth of professiona.
and organized crime.[10]

We can now appreciate the importance of the social relationships ir
the causation of juvenile delinquency, but we must also understand the
mechanics of these relationships in the reaction of the community to the
behavior of the delinquent.  Here is a case that should help us to do this.

## A Case History

The Jones [11] family first came to the attention of the county probation
office in October, 1960.  At that time, the family consisted of a thirty-
five-year-old father, a thirty-three-year-old mother, and eight children,
ranging in age from three to fifteen, but shortly thereafter, the father,
who had a police record extending back over a period of eighteen years,
deserted and eluded efforts to find him.  Referrals regarding the family
had come from both the police and the school authorities, because of
the vandalism, thievery, and persistent truancy of the children.  An investigation by the probation department revealed that the family had
been on relief for over fourteen years, and that the ramshackle, dirty
house where they lived had only two bedrooms and no basement, toilet
facilities, or running water.

After a hearing, the juvenile court adjudged all eight children to be
dependent and neglected and placed them in the custody of the probation department.  The three oldest children, John, James, and William,
were placed in foster homes, and the other children were returned to
the mother but kept under the supervision of the welfare and probation
departments.  A few weeks later, John, the oldest child, died in a farm
accident, and James and William ran away from their foster homes.  Both
of these boys were then sent to the state training school, and after their
release from that institution, they were eventually convicted of armed
robbery and committed to the state reformatory.

A year after the younger children had been returned to their mother,
the court found that this arrangement was unsatisfactory and placed all
of the children in foster homes.  The mother had become an alcoholic,
and the court sent her to a state hospital, where she died within a few
months.  The initial foster home placements were unsuccessful for all of
these children; and, after a number of other placement failures, three
of the children were sent to the state home for dependent and neglected
children and two were committed to the state training school for boys.

[10] Caldwell, pp. 197, 198.
[11] All names used in this case are fictitious.

During all of this time, the children, each of whom was of average intelligence, were being treated in mental health clinics, child development clinics, pediatric departments, university hospitals, and speech and hearing clinics. In fact, in the work that was done to help the Jones family during a period of six years, twenty-five agencies were called upon for services of various kinds, numerous foster home placements were made, one probation officer alone was involved in 165 contacts, and thousands of dollars were spent in welfare and correctional services by the county and the state. Yet, despite all this, we now find that the mother is dead and the father is missing, and, of the eight children, one is dead, two are in the state reformatory, two are in the state training school for boys, and three are in the state home for dependent and neglected children.

Thus we can see how complex the reaction of the community to juvenile delinquency can become and appreciate that, even in the average case, it probably involves far more than most people realize. Indeed, it is in this reaction that we may find additional causes of delinquency. Clumsy, thoughtless, inadequate, incompetent, or cruel handling of children may send those who are dependent or neglected into delinquency and those who are already delinquent into additional and perhaps more serious violations of the law. Lemert uses the concept "secondary deviation" in referring to this type of delinquency. Social reactions to delinquency, he says, may actually promote it by creating a deviant self conception in the delinquent, who then finds more satisfactory solutions to his problems through deviance than through non-deviance.[12]

## The Role of the Individual

The analysis of juvenile delinquency as a social problem which we have just made helps us to have a better understanding of its nature. We should now appreciate why the individual must be seen—not apart from others—but in his lawful and unlawful relationships with many other individuals. Furthermore, from this view, we can see that juvenile delinquency, having many of its roots in social relationships, is interrelated with all other social problems, that it is relative to time and place, being subject to the changes that occur in the social rules and standards, and that it is produced by a multiple causation, and so programs for its control and prevention must be many–sided.

But we cannot forget the individual. Although he must be seen in his relations with others, he has a reality apart from the group. He is a unique combination of heredity and environment, and his personality organization is never the same as the social organization in which he

[12] See Edwin M. Lemert, *Human Deviance, Social Problems, and Social Control* (Englewood Cliffs, N.J.: Prentice-Hall, Inc., 1967), pp. 17, 18, 40–60.

functions.  Not to appreciate this is to underestimate, or even to ignore the creativeness of man, the fertility of his imagination, and the contro that he can exercise over his own behavior, and thus to invite the con clusion that the problem of juvenile delinquency can be reduced only by manipulations of the environment.  In the political arena, this mini mizing of the individual may lend itself to the support of a collectivist usually a socialist, philosophy, and thus to the advocacy of a planned society and its management by a centralized bureaucracy.

# 3

# Juvenile Drinking and Drug Abuse

## JUVENILE DRINKING

Some passing motorists noticed lights in an abandoned farmhouse and notified the police. A squad car was dispatched to the farm, and the police found twenty high school boys and girls having a beer party and gaily celebrating that afternoon's football victory. On questioning the students, the police learned that a local tavern owner had sold them ten cases of beer and some whisky after they had promised not to tell anybody about the transaction. The students were taken to headquarters and then released pending action by the juvenile court. The tavern owner was picked up the next day and charged with selling alcoholic beverages to minors.

Does this story seem familiar to you? It should, for we hear and read about incidents like this almost every day. According to most estimates, the drinking of alcoholic beverages by juveniles has considerably increased during the past decade—increased to such an extent, in fact, that the police have become greatly concerned about it. This, however, should not come as a surprise to those who have kept themselves informed about the "drinking problem" in the United States.

In 1967, it was estimated that 68 per cent of all American adults had had at least one drink during the preceding year, and that the number of alcoholics, or compulsive drinkers, in the country probably ranged somewhere between 4,500,000 and 6,800,000.[1] As the task force report states, the actual number of alcoholics is not known and may be more

[1] The President's Commission on Law Enforcement and Administration of Justice, *Task Force Report: Drunkenness*, Appendix B (Washington, D.C.: Government Printing Office, 1967), pp. 29, 30.

or less than the range indicated above, depending on the definition of alcoholism that is used. In a bill for the control of drunkenness that was introduced into the United States Senate in May, 1967, the term "chronic alcoholic" was defined as "any person who chronically and habitually uses alcoholic beverages (a) to the extent that it injures his health or interferes with his social or economic functioning, or (b) to the extent that he has lost the power of self-control with respect to the use of such beverages." [2]

Although there are no national studies on the amount of drinking among juveniles, estimates regarding its extent have been made. One estimate states that between 2 and 6 per cent of the nation's juveniles have one drink or more a day; another, that fewer than half of the college students drink more than once a month. [3] Furthermore, an examination of surveys made in many different places in the United States indicates that an average of about 60 per cent of teenagers use alcoholic beverages before they leave high school. [4] Even so, alcoholism does not ordinarily occur among young persons, and one must also keep in mind that drinking habits change. A century ago most Americans were either heavy drinkers or abstainers, distilled spirits being the favorite drink. Today drinking is more extensive but also more moderate, the use of beer and wine now accounting for more than half of the per capita consumption. [5]

## Drunkenness and Delinquency

Drunkenness in itself is not a crime. It becomes one only when the drunken person exhibits his condition publicly, or disturbs, endangers, or injures others. Many laws have been enacted in the United States to control the antisocial effects of drinking. Thus, public drunkenness is a crime in almost all jurisdictions. In addition, every state has at least one statute dealing with drunken drivers, and most states make it unlawful for minors to purchase alcoholic beverages. Drinking, therefore, may bring the juvenile directly into conflict with the law. But it may do more than this, for it may contribute to his involvement in many kinds of unlawful behavior, ranging all the way from the destruction of property to homicide. For example, Eldefonso expressed the opinion that a search of probation records throughout the United States would probably show that between 50 and 60 per cent of all juvenile offenses are

[2] *Ibid.*, Appendix A, pp. 23, 24.

[3] *Ibid.*, Appendix B, p. 30; Mark Keller, "The Definition of Alcoholism and the Estimation of Its Prevalence," *Society, Culture, and Drinking Patterns*, eds. David J. Pittman and Charles R. Snyder (New York: John Wiley and Sons, Inc., 1962), p. 326.

[4] U.S. Children's Bureau and National Institute of Mental Health, *Thinking About Drinking* (Washington, D.C.: Government Printing Office, 1968), p. 5.

[5] The President's Commission on Law Enforcement and Administration of Justice, Appendix B, p. 30.

involved with alcoholic beverages, and that many petty larcenies, burglaries, auto thefts, gang fights, and acts of vandalism and violence are committed after the offenders have been drinking.[6]

David Pittman, while not referring specifically to juveniles, stated: "There are certain criminal categories that are intimately related to the use of alcoholic beverages. Most clearly involved are violations of public intoxication statutes and closely related charges of disorderly conduct, vagrancy, trespassing, and peace disturbance." Then, after an examination of several studies, he concluded: "Thus, the closest relationship between intoxication and criminal behavior (except for public intoxication) has been established for criminal categories involving assaultive behavior."[7] Furthermore, Richard Blum, with specific reference to juveniles, has written, "Studies of delinquent youths suggest a strong likelihood of heavy and illicit drinking as part of their pattern of asocial or antisocial conduct."[8] It must be emphasized, however, that the mere fact that drinking preceded the commission of an offense does not necessarily mean that drinking caused that offense. Often both drinking and delinquency are produced by more basic forces operating in the personality of the juvenile. Nevertheless, in a particular case, drinking may be the major factor in the causation of unlawful behavior.

One view of the magnitude of the drinking problem in this country is provided by the *Uniform Crime Reports*, which show that year after year more persons are arrested for drunkenness than for any other offense except violation of traffic and motor vehicle laws. For 1969, a total of 5,862,246 arrests were reported in the United States. Of these, 1,420,161 were for drunkenness, 349,326, for driving while intoxicated, and 212,660, for violations of liquor laws. Thus, about 35 per cent of all arrests were for offenses that were connected in some way with the consumption of alcoholic beverages. In addition, for the same year, there were 573,502 arrests for disorderly conduct and 106,269 arrests for vagrancy, and some of these, also, involved the use of alcohol. In fact, in many states, disorderly conduct is virtually synonymous with drunkenness.

Now let us take a look at the number of arrests of persons under eighteen. During 1969, these arrests totaled 1,500,215, and of this total, 42,903 were for drunkenness, 3,891 were for driving while intoxicated, and 71,159 were for violations of liquor laws. Thus only about 7 per cent of the arrests that involved persons under eighteen were for violations of

[6] Edward Eldefonso, *Law Enforcement and the Youthful Offender: Juvenile Procedures* (New York: John Wiley and Sons, Inc., 1967), p. 285.
[7] The President's Commission on Law Enforcement and Administration of Justice, Appendix A, pp. 13, 14.
[8] *Ibid.*, Appendix B, p. 44.

laws dealing directly with the consumption of alcohol. In fact, only approximately 5 per cent of all arrests for these violations concerned persons under the age of eighteen. Furthermore, few juveniles under fifteen were arrested for violations of liquor laws; few under sixteen, for drunkenness; and few under seventeen, for driving while intoxicated.[9] It must be added, however, that some of the 139,727 juveniles who were arrested for disorderly conduct and vagrancy were undoubtedly also drunk, and that many of the drunken juveniles who committed felonies and serious misdemeanors were charged with these and that no record was kept of their alcoholic condition. Also, many juveniles who violated laws regulating the use of alcohol were not arrested at all, either because they were not detected or because their cases were handled in some other way. A study of teen-age drinking and the law in St. Louis found that juvenile arrests for alcohol-related offenses rose 28 per cent in St. Louis from 1950 to 1960. According to the analysis, the increase suggested the need for effective and intensive alcohol education in the secondary schools and cooperation between police and social work authorities for selective referral for treatment and re-education of those whose offenses warn of later serious behavior disorders and criminality.[10] Clearly, then, the statistics that we have quoted understate the law-enforcement problem caused by juveniles who use alcohol.

## Causes of Drinking

Why do juveniles drink alcoholic beverages? Why does anybody do this? No single theory can help us very much, although certain conditions do seem to contribute significantly to the use of alcohol. Naturally, among these is the nature of alcohol itself. When alcohol is taken into the body, it is immediately absorbed into the blood, which carries it quickly to the brain. Alcohol is a drug, which acts on the nervous system after it reaches the brain. Although alcohol contains calories, it is not a proper substitute for the usual foods in a balanced diet. The body burns up alcohol through the process of oxidation, most of which occurs in the liver, and in this way disposes of one-half ounce of alcohol in about one hour. This is approximately the amount contained in one average highball, one glass of wine, or one can of beer. The unoxidized alcohol, of course, remains in the blood, and until it is eliminated, it continues to affect the brain and the nervous system.

What many people do not know is that alcohol is not a stimulant

[9] Federal Bureau of Investigation, *Uniform Crime Reports, 1969*, Table 27. The figures quoted here are based on reports received from 4,759 agencies serving an estimated total population of 143,815,000.

[10] See Muriel W. Sterne, David J. Pittman, and Thomas Coe, "Teen-agers, Drinking, and the Law," *Crime and Delinquency*, XI (January, 1965), 78–85.

(although with the first few sips it may seem to have stimulating effects) but a depressant in the sense that it retards assimilation, reduces circulation, and decreases respiration. It is for these effects that it is prescribed as a drug and used as a beverage. At first, alcohol releases inhibitions and makes the drinker feel relaxed, and it is this which gives him the impression that he is being stimulated; but as the action of the drug continues, his body functions are more and more depressed. As a result, reason, judgment, and muscular coordination become more and more uncertain, and if the person continues to drink, he loses consciousness. In fact, if he quickly gulps down an unusually large amount of alcohol (more than a pint), he may die.

Reactions to alcohol, however, vary widely, depending on many complex physical and psychological factors, such as the rate of drinking, the presence of food in the stomach, the type of beverage, the drinker's weight, his body chemistry, his mood, his attitude toward drinking, his drinking experience, and so on. Moderate amounts of alcohol usually do not harm the well-nourished person, but large amounts and high concentrations of it may irritate and inflame the digestive system, and prolonged and heavy drinking may seriously affect the heart, liver, stomach, and other organs. Continued drinking may also lead to alcoholism, or compulsive drinking. The alcoholic loses control of his drinking, and it becomes his only source of satisfaction.[11]

The first "tasting" experience with alcohol usually occurs before the boy or girl reaches the age of thirteeen. If parents drink, this often involves having a few sips from the father's or mother's glass at home. Ordinarily, curiosity and the urge to experiment prompt the child to take his first taste. Afterward he may not drink again, for he may not like drinking, his parents may oppose it, his religious principles may forbid it, his friends may not approve of it, or his athletic training rules may prohibit it. On the other hand, he may continue to use alcohol, because he enjoys it, his family's habits and customs encourage it, his status with his "crowd" is enhanced by it, his rebellion against parental authority is expressed through it, or his deep hurts and confusions and the nagging pains of failures, inferiorities, and frustrations may be eased, and his battered ego given support, by it. And in our society, the possibility of a juvenile's using alcohol is heightened by the fact that drinking is not

[11] Haven Emerson, *Alcohol and Man* (New York: The Macmillan Co., 1932), pp. 1–22, 266–70; E. M. Jellinek, "Phases in the Drinking History of Alcoholics," *Quarterly Journal of Studies on Alcohol*, VII (June, 1946), 1–88; U.S. Children's Bureau and National Institute of Mental Health, *Thinking About Drinking*, pp. 22–31. Some of the material about the nature of alcohol which is presented above is adapted from the pamphlet, *Thinking About Drinking*. For a summary of some theories on causes of drinking, see Robert G. Caldwell, *Criminology* (New York: The Ronald Press Co., 1965), pp. 106–8.

only widely accepted but also even considered a symbol of success in some circles.

Studies of delinquency lend support to the contention that, of all the influences that play upon the juvenile and affect his attitude toward alcohol, the most important is that exerted by his family. What they say and do about drinking strongly affect his feelings about its use. The Gluecks, for example, found that 62.8 per cent of the fathers and 23.0 per cent of the mothers of the 500 delinquents included in their study drank to the point of intoxication. On the other hand, only 39.0 per cent of the fathers and 7.0 per cent of the mothers of the 500 nondelinquents who were studied used alcohol excessively. In addition, 37.0 per cent of the fathers and 46.8 per cent of the mothers of the delinquents came from homes in which one or more members repeatedly drank to the point of intoxication. This contrasted with 31.4 per cent of the fathers and 35.4 per cent of the mothers of the nondelinquents who came from such homes. Finally, 21.4 per cent of the delinquents, as compared with only 6.4 per cent of the nondelinquents, had one or more siblings who drank to the point of intoxication.[12]

In many homes where alcohol is used, the parents come from ethnic groups or social classes whose habits and customs have long favored its consumption, and they teach their children to drink and enjoy it. Often in these homes—and, as a matter of fact, in many other homes—the parents do not know about the laws which forbid the giving or selling of alcohol to minors or they deliberately flout the laws. Thus, these parents not only encourage drinking among their children but also foster disrespect for the law.

## Control of Juvenile Drinking

The question of how to handle the increased drinking among juveniles has evoked a confusing variety of suggestions. Apparently, there is only one point upon which all educators, physicians, psychologists, psychiatrists, and sociologists agree: uncontrolled drinking is dangerous. Certainly, both parents and children should be educated to understand the nature of alcohol, its effects on those who drink it, and the provisions of the laws regulating its use as a beverage. Moreover, these laws, realistically adjusted to meet the complex problems of modern living, should be courageously, impartially, and strictly enforced. In addition —and this is very important—children should be trained to exercise self-control and to assume the moral obligations which they owe to their parents, relatives, friends, and other members of the community. Finally,

[12] Sheldon and Eleanor T. Glueck, *Unraveling Juvenile Delinquency* (New York: The Commonwealth Fund, 1950), pp. 98, 101–3.

in the enforcement of liquor laws, the police should solicit the help and cooperation of all dispensers of alcoholic beverages and encourage them to adopt their own codes of self-regulation.[13]

## JUVENILE DRUG ABUSE

A crowd stared in horror at the shattered body of a youth, sprawled grotesquely at their feet. He had just leaped from the tenth floor of an apartment building. One woman said: "I saw the whole thing. It was awful." And a man remarked, "It looked like he was trying to fly."

Apparently, that is exactly what the youth thought he was doing. A police investigation revealed that he and two other high school boys had been experimenting with drugs. The one who leaped had taken LSD, and before the others could interfere, he "flew" from the window of his parents' apartment.

No one knows how many young people, like these boys, are taking drugs today in the United States. Many observers are convinced that the number is large, and that it is getting larger. Some even say that several million American college students have at least experimented with marihuana, hashish, LSD, amphetamines, or barbiturates. This may or may not be true; the available statistical evidence on drug usage among young people is not conclusive. The Bureau of Narcotics estimated that there were 62,045 active narcotic addicts in this country at the end of 1967, which represented an increase of 2,325 addicts since the end of 1966. Of the 62,045 active narcotic addicts, more than 79 per cent were in the four states of New York (52.1 per cent), California (12.0 per cent), Illinois (10.6 per cent), and New Jersey (4.6 per cent). Of the total, 75 per cent were distributed among ten cities; about 50 per cent were white and about 50 per cent were black; almost 46 per cent were between the ages of 21 and 30; and less than 4 per cent were under the age of 21.[14]

---

[13] Selden D. Bacon, "Alcohol and Complex Society," *Society, Culture, and Drinking Patterns*, eds. David J. Pittman and Charles R. Snyder (New York: John Wiley and Sons, Inc., 1962), pp. 78–93; Morris E. Chafitz and Harold W. Demone, Jr., *Alcoholism and Society* (New York: Oxford University Press, 1962), pp. 39–56; John J. Conger, "Perception, Learning, and Emotions: The Role of Alcohol," *The Annals of the American Academy of Political and Social Science*, CCCXV (January, 1958), 31–39 (this issue of *The Annals* contains a series of articles on alcoholism); John D. Armstrong, "The Search for the Alcoholic Personality," *ibid.*, 40–47.

[14] *Traffic in Opium and Other Dangerous Drugs*, Report of the Bureau of Narcotics for the year ended December 31, 1967, U.S. Treasury Department (Washington, D.C.: Government Printing Office, 1968), pp. 23–52. For some estimates that differ from that of the Bureau of Narcotics, see The President's Commission on Law Enforcement and Administration of Justice, *Task Force Report: Narcotics and Drug Abuse*, Appendix A-2 (Washington, D.C.: Government Printing Office, 1967), pp. 2, 3, 47, 48.

According to this report, 92 per cent of the active narcotic addicts were in the District of Columbia and the nine states of New York, California, Illinois, New Jersey, Michigan, Pennsylvania, Maryland, Texas, and New Mexico. The ten cities that had 75 per cent of the active narcotic addicts were New York, Chicago, Los Angeles, Detroit, Baltimore, Philadelphia, Washington, D.C., Newark (New Jersey), San Diego, and Buffalo.

Thus, according to the Bureau of Narcotics, the narcotic problem in the United States is neither big nor widespread, being largely limited to a few cities and states. Many informed persons, however, believe that the reports of the Bureau of Narcotics understate the actual size of the narcotic problem. As they explain, the Bureau's reports cover only those who are arrested for the use of opiates and cocaine. Obviously, there are many users who are either unknown or, if known, not arrested. Furthermore, of course, the statistics do not include the users of marihuana, the barbiturates, and the amphetamines. In expressing their opinion that the estimate of the Bureau of Narcotics was low, Maurer and Vogel said that they had difficulty in understanding how some 50,000 addicts could support a contraband market of the proportions then assumed to exist. Even so, they believed that there were fewer than 100,000 opiate addicts in the United States in 1967.[15]

The *Uniform Crime Reports* show that 182,909 arrests were made for the violation of narcotic drug laws (federal laws excluded) in the United States during 1969, which meant that these arrests were nearly five times greater in number than they had been in 1960. In this total of arrests for 1969, there were 42,434 persons who were under 18 years of age, and, therefore, the arrests for this age group had increased by 40,772, or 2,453.2 per cent, since 1960.[16] However, these statistics cannot be regarded as a reliable index of the drug addiction problem in this country. For example, as pointed out above, many drug addicts are not discovered, or, if they are, they are not arrested. Furthermore, arrests do not measure the specific number of individuals taken into custody, since one person may be arrested several times for the same or different offenses, and besides, an arrest does not necessarily result in a conviction. In fact, arrests are primarily a measure of police activity. The number of arrests, therefore, may vary considerably even though the habits and activities of the people may not change in any significant way. All this, then, points to one conclusion: No one really knows how many drug addicts— juvenile or adult—there are in the United States.

---

[15] David W. Maurer and Victor H. Vogel, *Narcotics and Narcotic Addiction* (Springfield, Ill.: Charles C. Thomas, 1967), p. 9.

[16] Federal Bureau of Investigation, *Uniform Crime Reports, 1969*, Table 24. The figures quoted above are based on comparable reports from 1,832 cities, representing a total population of 78,027,000, and 642 counties, representing a total population of 16,826,000.

## Nature of Drug Addiction

But what do we mean by drug addiction?   One definition views it as "a state in which a person has lost the power of self-control with reference to a drug and abuses the drug to such an extent that the person or society is harmed." [17]   According to another, "drug addiction is a state of periodic or chronic intoxication, detrimental to the individual and to society, produced by the repeated consumption of a drug (natural or synthetic).   Its characteristics include: (1) an overpowering desire or need (compulsion) to continue taking the drug and to obtain it by any means; (2) a tendency to increase the dose; (3) a psychic (psychological) and sometimes a physical dependence on the effects of the drug." [18]

In drug addiction, say many authorities, one or more of the following related but distinct conditions are always present:

1. *Tolerance*, which means that there is a gradual decrease in the effect produced by the repeated administration of the drug, and the user must take progressively larger amounts to secure the initial euphoric or analgesic effect.
2. *Physical dependence*, with resulting abstinence illness when the drug is withheld.
3. *Habituation* or psychological dependence. [19]

Viewed in this way, a person might become addicted to alcohol, tobacco, or even coffee.   In criminology, however, the term "drug addiction" usually has reference to opium, cocaine, marihuana, and peyote (or mescal) and their various derivatives, compounds, and preparations, although there is some uncertainty as to whether peyote is an addicting drug. [20]   Of these, cocaine and peyote are stimulants, while opium and marihuana are depressants.   Federal legislation is directed primarily against these four drugs and their synthetic equivalents, such as the synthetic opiates Demerol, Methadone, Numorphan, and Prinadol.   However, congressional action is not necessary to put a drug under federal control.   At present, this can be done quickly and easily by presidential proclamation upon the recommendation of the commissioner of narcotics if tests made under the auspices of the U.S. Public Health Service show

[17] V. H. Vogel, H. Isbell, K. W. Chapman, "Present Status of Narcotic Addiction, with Particular Reference to Medical Indications and Comparative Addiction Liability of the Newer and Older Analgesic Drugs," *Journal of the American Medical Association*, CXXXVIII (December 4, 1948), 1019.
[18] "Expert Committee on Drugs Liable To Produce Addiction," *World Health Organization Technical Report Series*, No. 21 (March, 1950), 6, 7.
[19] Maurer and Vogel, *op. cit.*, pp. 37, 38.
[20] See, for example, *ibid.*, pp. 155–57; Edwin M. Schur, *Narcotic Addiction in Britain and America* (Bloomington: Indiana University Press, 1962), p. 34.

that a new drug is addicting. According to the federal law, an addict is a person who habitually uses any drug (which it defines as habit-forming) so as to endanger public morals, health, safety, or welfare, or who has become so addicted that he has lost the power of self-control with reference to his addiction. In addition to the four drugs named above, federal laws regulate other drugs which are usually classified as "dangerous," including the barbiturates (which are sedatives), amphetamines and similar drugs (which are stimulants), and lysergic acid diethylamide (LSD) and other hallucinogenic drugs. The stimulants increase physical and mental perception and thus bring the addict into more intimate contact with the environment and give him an increased sense of power. The depressants, on the other hand, decrease physical perception or the acuity of certain mental processes and thus enable the addict to escape innate difficulties and disagreeable features or situations of the environment.[21] The term "narcotic drugs" is sometimes used to refer to both depressants and stimulants, but in the strict sense of the word, narcotics are only those drugs which, like opium, are sleep-inducing. In the federal law, the controls on so-called "narcotic drugs" do not cover all true narcotics and include some drugs which are not really narcotic in nature.

It should be explained that there is a difference of opinion regarding the definition of addiction. Some writers, for example, use this term only in reference to persons who have a physical dependence on a drug, whereas others employ it in connection with those who have only a psychological dependence. Taking note of this variation in usage, the World Health Organization Expert Committee on Addiction-Producing Drugs has recommended that the term "drug dependence," with a modifying phrase linking it to a particular drug, be used instead of the term "addiction." However, "addiction" seems too deeply rooted in the popular vocabulary to be so easily discarded, and, therefore, it is important to make certain in each instance what meaning is being given to this term.

## Types of Drugs

Those who use opium or any of its derivatives develop a tolerance, and likewise, perhaps, users of cocaine, marihuana, or peyote.[22] Further-

---

[21] Lawrence Kolb, "Drug Addiction as a Public Health Problem," *The Scientific Monthly*, XLVIII (May, 1939), 391.

[22] A question exists as to whether cocaine, marihuana, and peyote users develop a tolerance. See, for example, Maurer and Vogel, pp. 125, 132, 147; Schur, 32, 33; Donald D. Pet and John C. Ball, "Marihuana Smoking in the United States," *Federal Probation* XXXII (September, 1968), 8–15; *Drug Abuse: Escape to Nowhere* (Philadelphia: Smith Kline and French Laboratories, 1968), "Drug Abuse Products Reference Chart," p. 105.

more, all forms of opium, cocaine, marihuana, and peyote cause habituation or psychological dependence, but of these four drugs, only opium
and its derivatives produce a physical dependence in the user.   When
a person becomes physically dependent, the drug becomes as necessary
as food in maintaining the physiological balance of his body, and abrupt
withdrawal results in distressing symptoms.[23]   Among the drugs which
are usually classified as "dangerous," the barbiturates, amphetamines, and
similar drugs and LSD cause tolerance and habituation, and, in addition,
the barbiturates produce physical dependence.[24]

Although all these drugs have come under public scrutiny in the
United States, marihuana, LSD, and the solvent fumes from glue, gasoline, paint thinner, and lighter fluid especially have attracted attention,
for apparently an increasing number of young people are using them.
No one knows, however, to what extent this has happened, and, of course,
a person may use these drugs once or twice and never use them again.

Marihuana is derived from the Indian hemp plant, and its use causes
hallucinations, a peculiar distortion of the sense of time, and a releasing
of inhibitions.   Hashish is a powdered and sifted form of the resin
derived from this plant.   Some investigators tend to minimize the effects
of marihuana and regard its use as a relatively innocuous vice.   Others,
however, are convinced that it is dangerous to both the individual and
society.   For example, the Federal Bureau of Narcotics has called marihuana a "harmful and dangerous drug" and conducts a vigorous campaign to educate the public against its use.   Furthermore, the New York
State Narcotic Addiction Control Commission stated that the smoking
of a single marihuana cigarette has been known to precipitate a psychotic
episode, and that heavy use of it can cause visual distortions, false beliefs,
and hallucinations and thus lead to accidents and aggressive and antisocial acts.[25]   And in reply to the contention that marihuana can be less
dangerous than alcohol, Dr. Lawrence Kolb, former Assistant Surgeon
General of the United States Public Health Service, said: "Alcohol, during the past 2,500 years, has apparently become an irreplaceable part of
our social structure.   We know that it does much harm, but the fact that
we tolerate this harm is no reason for permitting the indiscriminate use
of another intoxicant." [26]

[23] Maurer and Vogel, pp. 60–158; National Research Council, Committee on Drug
Addiction, "Studies on Drug Addiction," *Public Health Reports,* Supp. No. 138
(Washington, D.C., 1938), pp. 115, 116; Abraham Wikler, *Opiate Addiction* (Springfield, Ill.: Charles C. Thomas, 1953).
[24] Maurer and Vogel, pp. 122–27, 147–57; Pet and Ball, 11; *Drug Abuse: Escape
to Nowhere,* p. 105.
[25] *Federal Probation* (September, 1968), p. 17.
[26] *Drug Abuse: Escape to Nowhere,* p. 62.

Despite this difference of opinion regarding marihuana, many authorities seem to be in agreement on these points:

1. The widespread use of marihuana in the United States constitutes a significant mental-health problem.
2. A conservative estimate indicates that about 5 million young people and adults in the United States have used marihuana at least once, although the large majority of them are "triers" rather than habitual "potheads."
3. The use of marihuana in American high schools and colleges is increasing.
4. Significant danger is involved in using the drug consistently or in taking strong doses of it.
5. The persistent use of this drug can have a psychological effect in reducing the incentive and motivation of an individual to plan and achieve goals for himself, which could be more serious than the physical effects, and possibly causes some physical damage—perhaps even genetic damage.
6. The drug adversely affects one's ability to drive an automobile, because it causes a lessening of muscular coordination and the distortion of space and time perception.
7. Marihuana leads some of its users (exactly how many is not known) into more serious forms of addiction.

Although there may be some disagreement about the dangers of marihuana, this is certainly not true in the case of LSD. All authorities agree that this is a powerful and highly dangerous drug that should be kept under strict control. In fact, stringent federal legislation was enacted in 1968 for this purpose.

LSD, a hallucinogenic drug, is a tasteless, odorless, white powder which may be prepared either synthetically or from ergot, a fungus growth on rye grain. It is usually taken orally but may be injected. When a person uses it, his mental functioning is profoundly altered. What he sees, hears, and smells is distorted, and sometimes he sees things that do not exist. The total experience can be pleasant and interesting, or it can be most unpleasant and even terrifying. Dominated by false beliefs, the user may commit aggressive acts, become involved in accidents, or try to kill himself. In some cases, the user may suffer an acute psychotic episode for which he must be hospitalized and from which he may never fully recover. Furthermore, recent studies show that repeated use may cause chromosomal abnormalities which may produce undesirable changes in the user's future children. Moreover, at present, there is no approved general medical use for LSD, and, despite the claim of users, tests show that it does not increase the quality of creative activity. Thus, all the evidence proves how utterly foolish it is to experiment with this drug.

The inhalation of solvent fumes from glue, gasoline, paint thinner, and lighter and cleaning fluids has become a major problem in the larger cities and has caused increasing concern among medical and law-enforcement authorities. Apparently the inhalation of these fumes is practiced most often by juveniles between the ages of ten and fifteen and sometimes up to the age of eighteen. For the purpose of inhalation, glue is usually squeezed into a handkerchief or bag, which is then placed over the nose and mouth. The thinner fumes from gasoline and paint, however, may be inhaled directly from tanks and cans. Although these substances are central-nervous-system depressants, the intoxicating effect releases inhibitions and thus may produce hyperactivity.

After the individual has taken a number of "drags," he experiences excitation, exhilaration, and excitement resembling the initial effects of alcoholic intoxication. Often, too, he staggers and has blurred vision, ringing ears, slurred speech, and hallucinations. Following this phase of intoxication, which lasts for thirty to forty-five minutes after the inhalation, drowsiness, stupor, and even unconsciousness of about an hour's duration occur. However, after the individual recovers, he usually does not recall what happened during the period of intoxication.

Our present knowledge about solvent inhalation indicates that it does not cause physical dependence, but a tendency to increase the amount inhaled and the repeated use and relapse to usage suggest the development of both tolerance and habituation, or psychic dependence. In addition, solvent inhalation may endanger the health and even the life of the individual. Death by suffocation and the development of psychotic behavior are possibilities, and a severe type of anemia has been observed in glue-sniffers who have an inherited defect of the blood cells (sickle-cell disease). Furthermore, many solvents can damage kidneys, liver, heart, and blood-forming organs of the body; and, although it has not yet been established that the inhalation of solvents has caused such damage, this remains a distinct possibility.[27]

## Drugs and Delinquency

Any person who illegally imports, manufactures, purchases, sells, or possesses drugs may be guilty of a crime. The federal regulation of drugs is administered in accordance with the provisions of the Harrison Narcotic Law and the Federal Food, Drug, and Cosmetic Act and other such

[27] Maurer and Vogel, pp. 116–30, 142–44, 147–55, 310–12; *Drug Abuse: Escape to Nowhere*, pp. 38–43; *Federal Probation* (September, 1968), 16, 17.

acts and amendments.   The federal statutes are supplemented by state and municipal laws and regulations.

As in the case of drunkenness, the use of drugs is related to the commission of other crimes, although considerable disagreement exists as to the nature of this relationship.   There is no question, however, that occasionally an addict, while under the influence of a drug, commits a violent offense and that many others resort to offenses against property in order to secure money for the purchase of drugs.   Nevertheless, the fact that a drug user commits a crime does not necessarily mean that his addiction produced his criminality.   Other, more basic factors may have been operating in the process of causation of the crime, just as, perhaps, they were in the development of his addiction.   In fact, some authorities even go so far as to claim that, in the great majority of cases, criminal addicts were criminals before they began to use drugs.   This may be an extreme view, but all authorities agree that the relationship between crime and drugs is a very complex one.

## Causes and Treatment

Various theories have been advanced to explain drug addiction, but they have been of little help to us in our efforts to understand this problem.   Many factors interact in the causation of drug addiction, and since these vary from patient to patient, their influence can be analyzed only by an intensive study of the individual case.   In fact, our knowledge of drug addiction appears to be more incomplete than that of alcoholism. Nevertheless, studies have emphasized such causative factors as pain, illness, fatigue, mental abnormalities, escapism, medical habituation, association with drug addicts, curiosity about the effects of drugs, and "proselytizing" by confirmed addicts.[28]   Although some progress has been made in the treatment of drug addiction, most addicts return to the use of drugs after their treatment has been completed.   Studies on the subject indicate that, unfortunately, more than 75 per cent of the treated narcotic addicts do this.[29]

Of course, the juvenile drug addict should be given the best available medical and psychiatric treatment, but in view of the poor record that

[28] For some of these studies, see Lawrence Kolb, "Drug Addictions: A Study of Some Medical Cases," *Archives of Neurology and Psychiatry*, XX (July, 1928), 171–83; M. J. Pescor, "The Kolb Classification of Drug Addicts," *Public Health Reports*, Supp. No. 155 (Washington, D.C., 1939); Alfred R. Lindesmith, "A Sociological Theory of Drug Addiction," *American Journal of Sociology*, XLIII (January, 1938), 593–609; and J. D. Reichard, "Narcotic Drug Addiction, a Symptom of Human Maladjustment," *Diseases of the Nervous System*, IV (September, 1943), 275–81.

[29] See, for example, Victor H. Vogel, "Treatment of the Narcotic Addict by the U.S. Public Health Service," *Federal Probation*, XII (June, 1948), 45–60.

we have had in our efforts to cure drug addiction, we must emphasize prevention. Every possible means should be used to educate the public —especially juveniles—about the dangers of drug abuse and the moral responsibility that each citizen has in the attack on this problem. Programs for this purpose should be conducted through churches, schools, colleges, universities, clubs, lodges, labor unions, business organizations, the press, the radio, and television. All school areas, parks, and places of public recreation and entertainment should be regularly patrolled and inspected so that children and young people will be protected from those who peddle drugs and seek to enslave the unwary in the deadly drug habit. Periodic meetings for public officials and community leaders should be arranged to promote greater cooperation and coordination among all those who are engaged in the struggle against drug abuse. And in support of all these moves, laws designed to control and regulate the manufacture, distribution, sale, purchase, and possession of drugs should be strictly enforced, and persons who violate these laws should be vigorously prosecuted and punished.

# 4

# Measurements of the Problem

## VOLUME AND TRENDS

Data compiled by both the Federal Bureau of Investigation's *Uniform Crime Reports* and the United States Children's Bureau Statistical Series publication, *Juvenile Court Statistics*, support the observation that, with minor exceptions, delinquency has been rising at a more rapid rate than the number of persons in the 10-to-17-year-old age group since 1949. For the period between 1960 and 1969 the number of arrests made for allegedly delinquent conduct increased 105 per cent (see Table 1). In 1969 alone, while it is estimated that approximately 16 per cent of the total population was between the ages of 10 and 17, persons in these age groups accounted for 26 per cent of the arrests made in connection with the entire crime problem. (See Table 2.)

Do these data suggest that there is more delinquency now than there used to be in the United States, especially prior to World War II? Although this may seem to be true, it is not necessarily so, say some authorities. For example, they explain, the previous time period used for comparison may affect the answer to this question. Teeters and Matza, after carefully reconstructing the data available on delinquency in such a way that there could be some basis for comparison, observed that delinquency rates are no higher now than in the years following World War I. In fact, they add, the current rates may not be so high. In general, their position falls, as they put it, somewhere between that of the "alarmists," who feel that the present generation of adolescents is the most unlawful and irresponsible ever, and that of the "skeptics," mostly academicians, who contend that increasing rates of delinquency reflect more and better police contacts with juveniles, more laws to break, and more adolescents to break them to a greater extent than they reflect an increasing amount of lawlessness and irresponsibility. As Teeters and

Matza see it, "For the years between 1940 and 1957, our belief is that although the official statistics perhaps overrate the increase in the delinquency rates, there has, nevertheless, been some real increase. However, we do not believe that one may assume lower and lower rates for years previous to 1940." [1]

Of course, almost all investigators are aware of the dangers associated with comparisons of delinquency rates from year to year, even in the same country and on the basis of the same sources of satistical information. Virtually no one, for example, feels that meaningful year-to-year comparisons of crime and delinquency rates can be made on the basis of *Uniform Crime Reports* data, especially for the years prior to 1958. Too many changes in the format of the reports, in the methods used to obtain information, in the kinds of data presented, and in the extent to which records are voluntarily submitted to the Federal Bureau of Investigation by local police departments occur to make accurate comparisons possible. Still, it is all too easy to speculate about whether or not increasing delinquency rates represent a trend toward lawlessness. No complete answer exists at the present time and it is doubtful that a scientifically acceptable one will ever be available. In the long run, what matters more than any scientifically verifiable conclusions concerning whether there is actually more delinquency now than in some previous time is how the citizens of a country tend to interpret such rates to support their own preconceived views.

But our pessimism about being able to determine the relative lawlessness of our adolescent population should not keep us from finding answers to other important questions about the incidence of delinquency or from recognizing other trends within that segment of our adolescent population apprehended for delinquency. There are some interesting and provocative variations in rates within the delinquent population in terms of age, sex, race, and career patterns.

## CHARACTERISTICS OF DELINQUENTS

### Age

Although patterns of delinquency which result in an arrest can and do appear prior to the age of ten, most officially registered delinquency occurs from the age of thirteen on. The highest rates appear for the fifteen-, sixteen-, and seventeen-year-old age groups. It would appear from

[1] Negley K. Teeters and David Matza, "The Extent of Delinquency in the United States," reprinted from *The Journal of Negro Education* in Rose Giallombardo (ed.), *Juvenile Delinquency: A Book of Readings* (New York: John Wiley and Sons, Inc., 1966), pp. 33–44.

## TABLE 1 Total Arrest Trends ᵃ

| Offense Charged | Number of Persons Arrested | | | | | | | | |
|---|---|---|---|---|---|---|---|---|---|
| | Total All Ages | | | Under 18 Years of Age | | | 18 Years of Age and Over | | |
| | 1960 | 1969 | Percent Change | 1960 | 1969 | Percent Change | 1960 | 1969 | Percent Change |
| Total | 3,323,741 | 4,126,216 | + 24.1 | 477,262 | 980,453 | +105.4 | 2,846,479 | 3,145,763 | + 10.5 |
| Criminal homicide: | | | | | | | | | |
| (a) Murder and nonnegligent manslaughter | 4,809 | 8,827 | + 83.6 | 364 | 914 | +151.1 | 4,445 | 7,913 | + 78.0 |
| (b) Manslaughter by negligence | 1,931 | 2,016 | + 4.4 | 139 | 152 | + 9.4 | 1,792 | 1,864 | + 4.0 |
| Forcible rape | 6,862 | 10,747 | + 56.6 | 1,191 | 2,214 | + 85.9 | 5,671 | 8,533 | + 50.5 |
| Robbery | 32,538 | 63,534 | + 95.3 | 7,837 | 21,713 | +177.1 | 24,701 | 41,821 | + 69.3 |
| Aggravated assault | 54,893 | 84,573 | + 54.1 | 6,383 | 14,209 | +122.6 | 48,510 | 70,364 | + 45.1 |
| Burglary—breaking or entering | 117,359 | 178,334 | + 52.0 | 54,392 | 93,728 | + 72.3 | 62,967 | 84,606 | + 34.4 |
| Larceny—theft | 192,450 | 353,897 | + 83.9 | 91,844 | 184,091 | +100.4 | 100,606 | 169,806 | + 68.8 |
| Auto theft | 54,369 | 94,329 | + 73.5 | 32,781 | 53,557 | + 63.4 | 21,588 | 40,772 | + 88.9 |
| Violent crime | 99,102 | 167,681 | + 69.2 | 15,775 | 39,050 | +147.5 | 83,327 | 128,631 | + 54.4 |
| Property crime | 364,178 | 626,560 | + 72.0 | 179,017 | 331,376 | + 85.1 | 185,161 | 295,184 | + 59.4 |
| Subtotal for above offenses | 465,211 | 796,257 | + 71.2 | 194,931 | 370,578 | + 90.1 | 270,280 | 425,679 | + 57.5 |
| Other assaults | 121,179 | 187,381 | + 54.6 | 12,558 | 31,627 | +151.8 | 108,621 | 155,754 | + 43.4 |
| Forgery and counterfeiting | 20,529 | 26,911 | + 31.1 | 1,509 | 2,937 | + 94.6 | 19,020 | 23,974 | + 26.0 |
| Embezzlement and fraud | 33,114 | 49,540 | + 49.6 | 787 | 2,505 | +218.3 | 32,327 | 47,035 | + 45.5 |
| Stolen property; buying, receiving, possessing | 9,476 | 34,405 | +263.1 | 2,503 | 10,343 | +313.2 | 6,973 | 24,602 | +245.1 |

| | | | | | | | | |
|---|---|---|---|---|---|---|---|---|
| Weapons; carrying, possessing, etc. | 30,736 | 66,750 | +117.2 | 6,413 | 10,969 | + 71.0 | 24,323 | 55,781 | +129.3 |
| Prostitution and commercialized vice | 25,633 | 41,265 | + 61.0 | 393 | 860 | +118.8 | 25,240 | 40,405 | + 60.1 |
| Sex offenses (except forcible rape and prostitution) | 45,246 | 37,452 | − 17.2 | 9,297 | 7,321 | − 21.3 | 35,949 | 30,131 | − 16.2 |
| Narcotic drug laws | 30,904 | 182,909 | +491.9 | 1,662 | 42,434 | +2,453.2 | 29,242 | 140,475 | +380.4 |
| Gambling | 118,299 | 67,590 | − 42.9 | 1,441 | 1,333 | − 7.5 | 116,858 | 66,257 | − 43.3 |
| Offenses against family and children | 37,010 | 35,690 | − 3.6 | 488 | 465 | − 4.7 | 36,522 | 35,225 | − 3.6 |
| Driving under the influence | 138,390 | 239,776 | + 73.3 | 1,080 | 2,503 | +131.8 | 137,310 | 237,273 | + 72.8 |
| Liquor laws | 81,029 | 130,945 | + 61.6 | 16,564 | 40,256 | +143.0 | 64,465 | 90,689 | + 40.7 |
| Drunkenness | 1,204,668 | 1,040,493 | − 13.6 | 12,500 | 30,221 | +141.8 | 1,192,168 | 1,010,272 | − 15.3 |
| Disorderly conduct | 396,155 | 426,588 | + 7.7 | 44,506 | 78,374 | + 76.1 | 351,649 | 348,214 | − 1.0 |
| Vagrancy | 127,319 | 83,980 | − 34.0 | 6,540 | 7,752 | + 18.5 | 120,779 | 76,228 | − 36.9 |
| All other offenses (except traffic) | 438,843 | 678,284 | + 54.6 | 164,090 | 339,975 | +107.2 | 274,753 | 338,309 | + 23.1 |
| Suspicion (not included in totals) | 89,449 | 72,391 | − 19.1 | 19,416 | 14,525 | − 25.2 | 70,033 | 57,866 | − 17.4 |

SOURCE: *Uniform Crime Reports*, 1969, Table 24, p. 110. Based on comparable reports from 1,832 cities representing 78,027,000 population ᵃ 2,474 agencies; 1969 estimated population 94,853,000. tion and 642 counties representing 16,826,000 population. Violent crime is offenses of murder, forcible rape, robbery and aggravated assault. Property crime is offenses of burglary, larceny $50 and over, and auto theft.

**TABLE 2** Total Arrests of Persons Under 15, Under 18, Under 21, and Under 25 Years of Age [a]

| Offense Charged | Grand Total All Ages | Percentage | | | |
|---|---|---|---|---|---|
| | | Under 15 | Under 18 | Under 21 | Under 25 |
| Total | 5,862,246 | 9.7 | 25.6 | 38.9 | 51.4 |
| Criminal homicide: | | | | | |
| (a) Murder and nonnegligent manslaughter | 11,509 | 1.4 | 9.4 | 23.9 | 42.1 |
| (b) Manslaughter by negligence | 3,197 | .9 | 7.5 | 24.8 | 44.7 |
| Forcible rape | 14,428 | 3.7 | 20.1 | 42.1 | 65.1 |
| Robbery | 76,533 | 11.8 | 33.4 | 56.2 | 76.8 |
| Aggravated assault | 113,724 | 5.3 | 16.4 | 29.8 | 47.0 |
| Burglary—breaking or entering | 255,937 | 25.3 | 53.7 | 71.2 | 83.5 |
| Larceny—theft | 510,660 | 27.7 | 53.1 | 67.8 | 77.9 |
| Auto theft | 125,686 | 15.9 | 58.0 | 76.7 | 87.7 |
| Violent crime | 216,194 | 7.3 | 22.3 | 39.7 | 58.5 |
| Property crime | 892,283 | 25.3 | 54.0 | 70.1 | 80.9 |
| Subtotal for above offenses | 1,111,674 | 21.8 | 47.7 | 64.0 | 76.4 |
| Other assaults | 259,825 | 7.0 | 17.6 | 29.9 | 46.2 |
| Arson | 8,691 | 43.4 | 62.1 | 71.4 | 79.1 |
| Forgery and counterfeiting | 36,727 | 2.3 | 11.3 | 29.2 | 52.5 |
| Fraud | 63,445 | 1.5 | 4.7 | 14.7 | 34.2 |
| Embezzlement | 6,309 | .7 | 3.9 | 13.9 | 35.1 |
| Stolen property; buying, receiving, possessing | 46,176 | 10.4 | 31.6 | 51.8 | 68.5 |
| Vandalism | 106,892 | 48.1 | 73.5 | 82.4 | 88.2 |
| Weapons; carrying, possessing, etc. | 88,973 | 4.5 | 17.1 | 32.5 | 59.9 |
| Prostitution and commercialized vice | 46,410 | .2 | 2.0 | 17.7 | 58.5 |
| Sex offenses (except forcible rape and prostitution) | 50,143 | 8.6 | 21.8 | 34.0 | 51.0 |
| Narcotic drug laws | 232,690 | 3.5 | 24.7 | 54.8 | 77.2 |
| Gambling | 78,020 | .3 | 2.2 | 6.4 | 14.7 |
| Offenses against family and children | 50,312 | .3 | 1.6 | 12.5 | 30.8 |
| Driving under the influence | 349,326 | a | 1.1 | 7.0 | 19.7 |
| Liquor laws | 212,660 | 2.9 | 33.5 | 74.4 | 81.7 |
| Drunkenness | 1,420,161 | .4 | 3.0 | 8.6 | 17.2 |
| Disorderly conduct | 573,502 | 7.2 | 20.4 | 36.6 | 52.4 |
| Vagrancy | 106,269 | 1.8 | 10.4 | 27.6 | 43.8 |
| All other offenses (except traffic) | 664,634 | 11.9 | 30.6 | 47.3 | 62.0 |
| Suspicion | 88,265 | 6.0 | 23.6 | 47.6 | 66.5 |
| Curfew and loitering law violations | 101,674 | 25.7 | 100.0 | 100.0 | 100.0 |
| Runaways | 159,468 | 39.6 | 100.0 | 100.0 | 100.0 |

SOURCE: *Uniform Crime Reports*, 1969, Table 28, p. 115.

[a] 4,759 agencies; 1969 estimated population 143,815,000. Less than one-tenth of 1 percent. Violent crime is offenses of murder, forcible rape, robbery and aggravated assault. Property crime is offenses of burglary, larceny $50 and over and auto theft.

## TABLE 3 Age Variations of Delinquent Youths

| | Age | | | | | |
| --- | --- | --- | --- | --- | --- | --- |
| | 10 and Under | 11–12 | 13–14 | 15 | 16 | 17 |
| Percentage of total police arrests ........ | 1% | 2% | 6% | 5% | 6% | 5% |
| Percentage of arrests for Index crimes .... | 3 | 7 | 16 | 11 | 10 | 8 |

SOURCE: *Uniform Crime Reports,* 1969, Table 27, p. 113. These figures are based upon information obtained from 4,759 agencies representing an estimated 1969 population of 143,815,000. The percentages are rounded for convenience.

the data summarized in Table 3 that, the younger the person, the more serious the offense must be to have official recognition of it. Arrests for Crime Index offenses, which include felonious homicide, forcible rape, aggravated assault, robbery, burglary, larceny of 50 dollars or more, and auto theft, are consistently higher than the total arrest rates. In fact, those under eighteen years of age, while comprising approximately one-fourth of the total arrest pattern, account for nearly one-half of the Crime Index offenses.

## Sex

It has long been recognized that delinquency is predominantly a problem with males (Table 4). In 1969, for example, there were 1,075,-101 arrests of males in contrast to 274,675 arrests of females under the age of eighteen, a ratio of about 4:1.[2] Males under eighteen are most frequently apprehended for burglary, larceny of 50 dollars or more, auto theft, vandalism, disorderly conduct, curfew and loitering violations, and running away from home.

Females under eighteen are generally arrested for larceny of 50 dollars or more, disorderly conduct, curfew and loitering violations, and running away from home. The larceny engaged in by young girls generally takes the form of shoplifting merchandise from department stores. The other offenses for which a relatively large number of arrests are made are usually felt to be closely related to aberrant sex behavior. Evidence to support arrests for sex offenses is much more difficult to obtain than is that for a charge of disorderly conduct or running away from home and, as a consequence, it is for these latter offenses that females are specifi-

[2] *Uniform Crime Reports*, 1969, Table 30, p. 117. These figures are based upon information obtained from 3,999 agencies representing an estimated population of 128,095,000.

**TABLE 4  Total Arrest Trends by Sex** [a]

| Offense Charged | Males | | | | | | Females | | | | | |
|---|---|---|---|---|---|---|---|---|---|---|---|---|
| | Total | | | Under 18 | | | Total | | | Under 18 | | |
| | 1960 | 1969 | Percent Change | 1960 | 1969 | Percent Change | 1960 | 1969 | Percent Change | 1960 | 1969 | Percent Change |
| Total | 2,963,564 | 3,564,368 | + 20.3 | 406,473 | 785,188 | + 93.2 | 360,177 | 561,848 | + 56.0 | 70,789 | 195,265 | +175.8 |
| Criminal homicide: | | | | | | | | | | | | |
| (a) Murder and nonnegligent manslaughter | 3,986 | 7,466 | + 87.3 | 340 | 838 | +146.5 | 823 | 1,361 | + 65.4 | 24 | 76 | +216.7 |
| (b) Manslaughter by negligence | 1,736 | 1,794 | + 3.3 | 132 | 135 | + 2.3 | 195 | 222 | + 13.8 | 7 | 17 | +142.9 |
| Forcible rape | 6,862 | 10,747 | + 56.6 | 1,191 | 2,214 | + 85.9 | | | | | | |
| Robbery | 30,953 | 59,479 | + 92.2 | 7,471 | 20,179 | +170.1 | 1,585 | 4,055 | +155.8 | 366 | 1,534 | +319.1 |
| Aggravated assault | 46,698 | 73,318 | + 57.0 | 5,722 | 12,341 | +115.7 | 8,195 | 11,255 | + 37.3 | 661 | 1,868 | +182.6 |
| Burglary—breaking or entering | 113,559 | 170,557 | + 50.2 | 52,752 | 89,830 | + 70.3 | 3,800 | 7,777 | +104.7 | 1,640 | 3,898 | +137.7 |
| Larceny—theft | 160,696 | 259,802 | + 61.7 | 78,483 | 140,414 | + 78.9 | 31,754 | 94,095 | +196.3 | 13,361 | 43,677 | +226.9 |
| Auto theft | 52,381 | 89,261 | + 70.4 | 31,521 | 50,632 | + 60.6 | 1,988 | 5,068 | +154.9 | 1,260 | 2,925 | +132.1 |
| Violent crime | 88,499 | 151,010 | + 70.6 | 14,724 | 35,572 | +141.6 | 10,603 | 16,671 | + 57.2 | 1,051 | 3,478 | +230.9 |
| Property crime | 326,636 | 519,620 | + 59.1 | 162,756 | 280,876 | + 72.6 | 37,542 | 106,940 | +184.9 | 16,261 | 50,500 | +210.6 |

| | | | | | | | | |
|---|---|---|---|---|---|---|---|---|
| Forgery and counterfeiting | 17,187 | 20,766 +20.8 | 1,161 | 2,235 +92.5 | 3,342 | 6,145 +83.9 | 348 | 702 +101.7 |
| Embezzlement and fraud | 28,088 | 36,662 +30.5 | 642 | 2,001 +211.7 | 5,026 | 12,878 +156.2 | 145 | 504 +247.6 |
| Stolen property; buying, receiving, possessing | 8,664 | 31,460 +263.1 | 2,335 | 9,638 +312.8 | 812 | 2,945 +262.7 | 168 | 705 +319.6 |
| Weapons; carrying, possessing, etc. | 29,033 | 62,326 +114.7 | 6,225 | 10,460 +68.0 | 1,703 | 4,424 +159.8 | 188 | 509 +170.7 |
| Prostitution and commercialized vice | 7,452 | 8,512 +14.2 | 121 | 261 +115.7 | 18,181 | 32,753 +80.1 | 272 | 599 +120.2 |
| Sex offenses (except forcible rape and prostitution) | 36,904 | 32,400 −12.2 | 6,659 | 5,747 −13.7 | 8,342 | 5,052 −39.4 | 2,638 | 1,574 −40.3 |
| Narcotic drug laws | 26,384 | 155,035 +487.6 | 1,421 | 33,835 +2,281.1 | 4,520 | 27,874 +516.7 | 241 | 8,599 +3,468.0 |
| Gambling | 107,640 | 62,116 −42.3 | 1,399 | 1,288 −7.9 | 10,659 | 5,474 −48.6 | 42 | 45 +7.1 |
| Offenses against family and children | 33,963 | 32,237 −5.1 | 328 | 351 +7.0 | 3,047 | 3,453 +13.3 | 160 | 114 −28.8 |
| Driving under the influence | 130,288 | 224,663 +72.4 | 1,025 | 2,401 +134.2 | 8,102 | 15,113 +86.5 | 55 | 102 +85.5 |
| Liquor laws | 68,967 | 113,927 +65.2 | 14,195 | 33,664 +137.2 | 12,062 | 17,018 +41.1 | 2,369 | 6,592 +178.3 |
| Drunkenness | 1,110,400 | 968,746 −12.8 | 11,210 | 26,267 +134.3 | 94,268 | 71,747 −23.9 | 1,290 | 3,954 +206.5 |
| Disorderly conduct | 343,189 | 364,211 +6.1 | 38,374 | 65,612 +71.0 | 52,966 | 62,377 +17.8 | 6,132 | 12,762 +108.1 |
| Vagrancy | 117,840 | 74,351 −36.9 | 5,885 | 6,636 +12.8 | 9,479 | 9,629 +1.6 | 655 | 1,116 +70.4 |
| All other offenses (except traffic) | 371,358 | 540,194 +45.5 | 127,180 | 242,798 +90.9 | 67,485 | 138,090 +104.6 | 36,910 | 97,177 +163.3 |
| Suspicion (not included in totals) | 79,693 | 61,352 −23.0 | 16,830 | 12,500 −25.7 | 9,756 | 11,039 +13.2 | 2,586 | 2,025 −21.7 |

SOURCE: *Uniform Crime Reports*, 1969, Table 25, p. 111. [a] 2,474 agencies; 1969 estimated population 94,853,000. Based on comparable reports from 1,832 cities representing 78,027,000 population and 642 counties representing 16,826,000 population. Violent crime is offenses of murder, forcible rape, robbery and aggravated assault. Property crime is offenses of burglary, larceny $50 and over and auto theft.

cally arrested. Therefore, while the number of arrests of female runaways under eighteen in 1969 closely approximated the number of arrests of male runaways under eighteen, the patterns of misconduct associated with that offense are quite different.

## Race

During 1969 in the United States, 72 per cent of the arrests of persons under eighteen years of age involved whites; 26 per cent of the arrests of persons under eighteen years of age, Negroes; and 2 per cent of the arrests of persons under the age of eighteen, Indians, Chinese, Japanese, and persons of other racial groups. For the offenses included in the Crime Index, 63 per cent of the arrests were of white persons under eighteen years of age; 35 per cent of the arrests were of Negroes under the age of eighteen, and 2 per cent of the arrests of those under the age of eighteen were of persons of other racial groups.[3] In view of the fact that Negroes comprise approximately one-tenth of the total population in the United States, the disproportionate concentration of Negro arrests in delinquency and adult criminality over a long period of time has sparked a considerable amount of controversy. Regardless of how one chooses to interpret the data, the over-representation of Negroes in the delinquency problem is as persistently evident as the under-representation of females.

## Careers in Delinquency

Just as variation can be detected in the extent to which there is participation in delinquency on the basis of age, sex, and race, so differences are observable concerning the degree to which some adolescents are more heavily committed to a delinquent way of life than others. By comparing fingerprint data obtained from local, state, and federal law enforcement agencies, the Federal Bureau of Investigation has, since 1963, been able to document in a modest but interesting way the "career" development of criminal offenders. Because law enforcement agencies do not, as a rule, submit fingerprint data on juvenile offenders to the Federal Bureau of Investigation, the information compiled to this point on "careers" is only suggestive of the patterns which might be found to exist among delinquents. In a five-year follow-up study of 18,333 offenders released from federal judicial control in 1963, it has been determined that, of the

[3] *Uniform Crime Reports*, 1969, Table 31, p. 119. Figures based on information from 4,627 agencies representing an estimated population of 133,028,000.

offenders under the age of twenty, 22 per cent were re-arrested on a new charge before the end of the first year. During subsequent years, the accumulative re-arrest rates increased as follows for the group of offenders under twenty years of age: [4]

| 1964 | 52% |
|------|-----|
| 1965 | 63 |
| 1966 | 68 |
| 1967 | 71 |
| 1968 | 73 |
| 1969 | 74 |

By the end of 1969, then, close to three-fourths of those who had entered the five-year study prior to their twentieth birthday had been re-arrested at least once. More important, perhaps, is the fact that the bulk of these offenders had been re-arrested before the end of the third year. The fourth, fifth, and sixth years were characterized by a marked reduction in the number of re-arrests.

These data, of course, tell us nothing of the nature and types of delinquent activities that might have characterized the background of these youthful criminal offenders. But the evidence that patterns of re-arrest follow relatively soon after release from custody for offenders in young age groups hints that similar findings might obtain within delinquent age groups. Similarly, it might be expected that, the more extensive the participation in officially recognized delinquency, the greater would be the likelihood of becoming a criminal offender as an adult.

Tentative support for these conclusions is available from an early study by McKay. After studying the rates of re-arrest as adults of 412 delinquent offenders, 58 per cent of whom had acquired adult arrest records, McKay concluded that careers in crime frequently arise out of a "gradual process of habituation to forms of illegal behavior." [5]

There are, then, interesting parallels between the information collected by the Federal Bureau of Investigation on youthful criminal offenders and that obtained by McKay in his study of delinquents. Needless to say, a considerable amount of costly and time-consuming research needs to be conducted before any substantial conclusions can be reached. Data linking delinquency with adult criminality will be very difficult to obtain. Perhaps, as technological innovations and the impact of automation make the collection and storage of comparable data on delin-

---

[4] *Uniform Crime Reports, 1969*, Table D, p. 39.
[5] President's Commission on Law Enforcement and Administration of Justice, *Task Force Report: Juvenile Delinquency and Youth Crime* (Washington, D.C.: Government Printing Office, 1967), Appendix E, pp. 107–13.

quency and crime more feasible, such studies will be forthcoming.[6] At the present time the desire to insure the confidentiality of delinquent records and to guard against treating them as criminals precludes the use of such information.

Even if a spirit of cooperation were to prevail among the various law-enforcement agencies which might enable them to pool information and still protect youngsters from a "criminal" status, questions persist about the feasibility of examining the problem of delinquency too un-critically from a "career" perspective. Adolescence, after all, is a period calling for numerous adjustments as a youngster goes through the process of emerging into adulthood. A degree of experimentation and of challenge to established codes of conduct has always characterized those in these age groups. As a result, a few acts of delinquency need not be interpreted as a commitment to a "career" in delinquency. Besides, as studies by scholars, such as Lyle Shannon, have indicated, the arrest records of delinquents and youthful offenders display a considerable amount of variation in terms of both the types of acts engaged in and the frequency of delinquent activities.[7] Furthermore, it should not be forgotten that even delinquents spend most of their time interacting with others in normal, accepted ways.

Still, there is mounting evidence that certain youths are arrested more persistently than others, that these re-arrests follow each other rather quickly in time, that they involve activities related to property offense more often than to offenses against the person, and that they tend to be highly correlated with acts of truancy. The consistency with which these findings are reported certainly suggests an area deserving more systematic and searching inquiry. Additional knowledge will provide insights into the developmental processes which promote habitual delinquent conduct and, furthermore, offer clues to the effectiveness with which juvenile correctional facilities and procedures operate. On this latter point, as evidence continually suggests that the risk of re-arrest after correctional attention is actually enhanced, criticism of existing facilities has mounted. Caution must be exercised in overdramatizing the alleged failure of police departments, courts, and correctional institutions, however. A variety of factors which intervene between release from custody and re-arrest has not yet been examined. The unwillingness of the community to accept uncritically those who have run afoul of the law is one such factor. The inability to change the local environment to which the delinquents, more

[6] One example of how data collection and retrieval is effectively used is to be found in the Federal Bureau of Investigation's National Crime Information Center (NCIC), which has a computerized index of known facts about crimes and criminals.

[7] Lyle W. Shannon, "Scaling Juvenile Delinquency," *Journal of Research in Crime and Delinquency*, V (January, 1968), 52–65.

ɔften than not, return, is a second. Until the part played by these and ɔther factors in the development of "careers" in delinquency has been determined, it is premature to engage in wholesale condemnation of ɔfficial efforts at delinquency control.

## SOURCES OF STATISTICS

The data presented in the foregoing pages clearly document the argument that there is no precise way to measure the extent to which children are involved in delinquency. Neither is there a way to establish accurately which factors are critical in causing delinquent behavior. Those who are the best informed are painfully aware that most of the questions raised about the nature and extent of delinquency must, for the present, either go unanswered or be couched in the most tentative and restrictive terms. Nevertheless, the questions persist: How much delinquency is there? How is it distributed throughout the adolescent population? Is there more delinquency now than there used to be? Are our adolescents more "lawless" and less "responsible" than those of previous generations? Are delinquents "different" from others?

How to answer these and many similar inquiries continually taxes the minds and energies of those dedicated to the systematic exploration, eventual understanding, and, hopefully, control of delinquency. Several approaches to the general problem of the measurement of delinquency have been utilized, and anything approaching a comprehensive understanding of the subject will depend on data obtained in many ways from numerous sources. It is very important, then, that the major similarities and differences in the types of data available to us through different sources be understood. Otherwise, there would be no way for us to determine whether the information at our disposal is really that which is most relevant to answering the questions we have concerning delinquency in the United States today. Whether we personally like them or not, statistics are among our most important tools as we search for more knowledge about our subject. There is no possible way for us to avoid their use, nor should we want to find a way. Statistics are convenient because they enable us, in a sense, to feel more comfortable about reaching conclusions and making observations that are not just descriptive in nature. And to interpret data accurately, it is necessary to know something about the specific source of the information.

### Uniform Crime Reports

Although a variety of reports are available from local, state, and federal agencies, the most systematically compiled and frequently cited data on delinquency are found in the *Uniform Crime Reports* and *Juve-*

*nile Court Statistics.* Now published annually, the *Uniform Crime Reports* were initiated in 1930 as part of a program stressing uniformity in police practices, sponsored by the International Association of Police Chiefs. At the present time, police departments throughout the country are asked to voluntarily submit uniformly developed summary reports of their law-enforcement activities to the Federal Bureau of Investigation. These summaries contain two basic types of data on police contacts with offenders: (1) offenses known to the police, which are used as the basis for a yearly Crime Index; and (2) arrests made by the police.

Offenses can become known to the police in various ways. Private citizens may register complaints, welfare agencies, schools, churches, or similar community institutions may refer cases to the police, the district attorney's office may initiate legal proceedings, or the police themselves may detect delinquent acts during their routine patrolling duties. Virtually no systematic research exists to indicate which of these, if any, is more frequently the source of official information than the others, or to reveal the conditions under which official knowledge of delinquency is more or less likely to exist regardless of its source.[8] But, regardless of how they are brought to the attention of the police, offenses need not culminate in arrests. Auto theft, for example, an offense committed predominantly by youths under 18 years of age, is usually reported to the police immediately upon discovery by the distraught victim. Yet nearly 80 per cent of these offenses, while known to the police, are not cleared by arrests. Frequently, for example, the car is found abandoned but unharmed, having been "borrowed" for a short time by a group of male teen-agers for a "joyride."

Even when offenses known to the police do result in arrest, there is seldom a 1:1 correlation between the two. Several arrests can be and, in fact, frequently are made during the course of investigating a single offense. Especially when a serious offense has been committed, a number of arrests may be made just to obtain additional information. More often than not in typical cases of delinquency, such as vandalism or auto theft, a single arrest may clear several offenses known to the police.

Whether data regarding offenses known to the police or those of arrests more accurately indicate the extensiveness of delinquency is a matter of some concern. For a long time, criminologists have accepted Thorsten Sellin's conclusion that the further away from the actual offense an administrative source of statistics is, the less it reflects the actual extent of the misconduct being measured. Thus, offenses known to the police are more valuable than arrests, arrests more valuable than convictions, and convictions more valuable than incarcerations as statistics por-

---

[8] For an indication of the complexity of this problem, see Jerome Skolnick, *Justice Without Trial* (New York: John Wiley and Sons, 1967).

traying the incidence of possible delinquency.[9] As usual, the matter is not so simple as that. Stinchcombe has shown, for example, that variations occur among offenses in terms of being known to the police, cleared by arrest, and resulting in conviction. These variations, he contends, are related to different rates of "apprehendability" based on differing degrees of privacy accorded citizens by the law.[10] Thus, variations in the extent to which privacy is legitimately provided to citizens affect their opportunities to disregard or conceal certain offenses and therefore account for at least some of the discrepancies in these types of data.

Still, complex as the relationships among them are, the data furnished in the *Uniform Crime Reports* provide the most comprehensive official information available on the delinquency problem. When it is understood that in any given year a very large number of the delinquency cases handled by the police are not officially handled by the courts, that is, do not involve the filing of a petition to take judicial action, the relative importance of the police data is underscored.

## Juvenile Court Statistics

Three years before the *Uniform Crime Reports* were begun, in 1927, the United States Children's Bureau began receiving summary reports from various state and local juvenile courts. Until 1956, this information was not systematically accumulated. Since then, however, the data in their *Juvenile Court Statistics*, which appear annually, have been obtained from a national sample of juvenile courts. Currently, there is information in them on the number, manner of handling, the rate per 1,000 population (calculated on the basis of the 1960 child population at risk, i.e., from age 10 to the limit of the juvenile court's jurisdiction), and percentage of change in juvenile court cases from year to year. Traffic cases are separated from all other delinquencies; such data appear in a specific section. There is, in addition, information on dependency and neglect cases as to number and rate, percentage of change, and trends.

By and large, *Juvenile Court Statistics* have escaped the searching criticisms which have accompanied the *Uniform Crime Reports*. Because they are usually felt to be a potentially more accurate barometer of the actual amount of delinquency in the United States, the data contained

[9] Thorsten Sellin, "The Significance of Records of Crime," *The Law Quarterly Review*, LXVII (October, 1951), 496–98. See also Thorsten Sellin, "The Basis of a Crime Index," *Journal of Criminal Law and Criminology*, XXII (September, 1931), 335–56, and *Research Memorandum on Crime in the Depression* (New York: Social Science Research Council, Bull. 27, 1937), Chap. 4.

[10] Arthur L. Stinchcombe, "Institutions of Privacy in the Determination of Police Administrative Practice," *American Journal of Sociology*, LXIX (September, 1963), 150–60.

in the *Uniform Crime Reports* have been subject to the most exacting scrutiny in an effort to improve their sensitivity to the extensiveness of the problem. Whether police data are actually any more accurate than court data in the long run is open to some speculation. As has been repeatedly pointed out in *Juvenile Court Statistics*, "both series of data —police arrests of juveniles reported by the Federal Bureau of Investigation, and juvenile court delinquency cases reported here—show a remarkable similarity in their trends over a long period of time despite their differences in definitions, units of count, extent of coverage, and the like. Both figures surged forward during World War II, fell off sharply in the immediate postwar years, and then began to climb again." [11] (See Fig. 1.) Keeping these broad similarities in mind, let us turn to a review of the criticisms of the police data on the delinquency problem.

## Criticism of *Uniform Crime Reports*

From their inception, the *Uniform Crime Reports* have had the primary objective of establishing uniform reporting of police arrest activities. They exist to provide some measure of the effectiveness and efficiency of police departments in combating crime and delinquency. As Peter Lejins aptly observed, "The reports are intended to be a statistical house organ of the police" regardless of any other uses found for them.[12]

Placed in sharp relief against this quest for uniformity is the high degree of independence and autonomy accorded individual police departments in this country. Although it has resulted in a tremendous amount of inefficiency due to overlapping jurisdictions, duplication of effort, and a lack of cooperation, this independence is carefully guarded by law-enforcement officials.

As you can see, these potentially conflicting conditions can lead to certain difficulties. A failure to elicit the full-fledged support and cooperation of local law-enforcement officials in *voluntarily* agreeing to uniform reporting procedures has resulted in a number of shortcomings in the *Uniform Crime Reports*. First, there has been imbalance in the participation of urban and rural areas. More than 90 per cent of the urban areas have submitted reports, while only approximately 75 per cent of the rural jurisdictions have done so. This disparity has led to a more general geographical imbalance in that the highly urbanized northeast section of the country is more fully represented in national statistics on crime and delinquency than are some predominantly rural areas of the South and West. Second, inconsistencies persist in the ways in which

[11] *Juvenile Court Statistics, 1966*, p. 3.
[12] Peter Lejins, "Uniform Crime Reports," *Michigan Law Review*, LXIV (April, 1966), 1011–30.

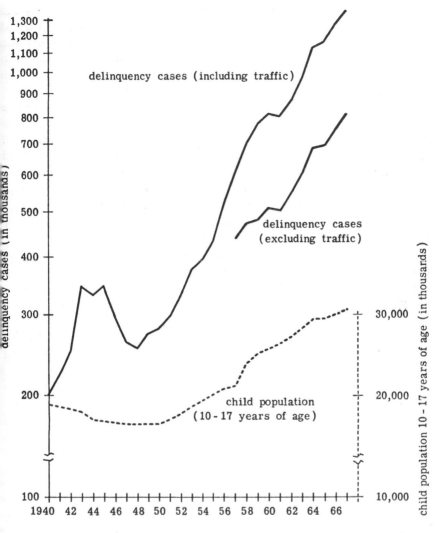

**Figure 1.** Trend in juvenile court delinquency cases and child population en to seventeen years of age, 1940–67 (semilogarithmic scale). (Source: Jnited States Children's Bureau, *Statistical Series, Juvenile Court Statistics,* 1967, p. 8.)

:eported offenses are classified. What constitutes auto theft in one police department may not be so considered in another; aggravated assault in one place is interpreted as disorderly conduct in another; and so on through the range of offenses. Finally, variations exist in the emphasis given to certain offenses at different times. Sudden community interest and concern for a particular type of offense can lead to increased police activity for a time in connection with it. Then, too, the administrative concern of the police departments themselves with such matters as maintaining reasonable quotas of arrests in various offense categories can exert some influence over the compilation of statistical data. Despite precautionary measures to allow for them, each of these factors has an undetermined effect on the information that eventually reaches the Federal Bureau of Investigation. Just how much is irretrievably lost between the alleged act of delinquency and the eventual reporting of it in *Uniform Crime Reports* is anybody's guess. One thing is certain—there is a complex set of factors which influences both decisions to arrest and to submit data on that activity to the Federal Bureau of Investigation.[13] Until more is known about the impact of such factors, caution will have to be exercised in accepting the accuracy of delinquency rates.

For the most part, little can be done to alter those weaknesses arising from inherent features of the reports. But not all of the inadequacies encountered in them present such intractable problems. Thus, several criticisms have to do with aspects of the reporting and examination of offense data that can be changed to provide more accurate and meaningful information about the extent and seriousness of crime and delinquency. One such criticism concerns the manner in which information is presented in the reports. Robison, for example, charged that features of the reports such as "crime clocks" tend to dramatize the crime problem in a way designed to scare the public into a state of alarm and concern.[14] A second criticism is directed at the occasional practice of reaching conclusions about certain issues in the crime problem rather than adhering strictly to the presentation of data. Several years ago, for example, a furor was raised when, in one of the annual reports, a definite stand was taken on the question of capital punishment.[15] A third criticism has dealt with the population base used in the compilation of delinquency rates. Until recently, the population base was determined by the previous decennial census. Thus, the rates of delinquency for each year of a decade were not sensitive to population changes during that period of time. Currently, rates of delinquency and crime are calculated from the most recent annual population estimates as determined by the U.S. Census Bureau. Numerous critics, however, have argued that this refine-

[13] Egon Bittner, "The Police on Skid-Row: A Study of Peace Keeping," *American Sociological Review*, XXXII (October, 1967), 699–715.

[14] Sophia Robison, "A Critical View of the *Uniform Crime Reports*," *Michigan Law Review*, LXIV (April, 1966), 1031–54.

[15] *Uniform Crime Reports, 1959*, p. 14.

ment, important as it is, does not go far enough in making reported rates more sensitive to population changes. Eisner, among others, has made a compelling point for calculating rates on the basis of the "population at risk," [16] that is, of the segment of the population potentially involved. This practice is partially adhered to in the compilation of delinquency rates in the *Juvenile Court Statistics*. However, they are still based on the latest decennial census data rather than the revised annual estimates of the U.S. Census Bureau. Only when such age-specific data are available on an annual basis can much reliance be placed in delinquency rates.

A fourth criticism has focused on the lumping together of widely disparate offenses within the same category. Auto theft is perhaps the most vulnerable to attack in this regard. No distinction is made between "joy-riding," when an auto is "borrowed" simply for the purpose of having some fun with it, and auto theft for profit. In terms of the probability that the police will be informed of the offense, auto theft, unlike other property offenses, ranks very high. One reason for this is the matter of insurance. To receive compensation from an insurance company, a report must have been filed with the police.[17] The likelihood that an arrest will be made to "clear" the case is, on the contrary, very low. Only 18 per cent of these offenses were cleared by arrests in 1969. However, although knowledge of the failure of the police to distinguish clearly between types of auto theft tells us something about police activity in connection with the problem, it tells us almost nothing about the delinquent's activities.

This brings us to the fifth shortcoming, namely, the selection of offenses for use in the Crime Index and the use of this index as a measure of the seriousness of delinquency and crime. In essence, the Crime Index figures are constructed from data on offenses known to the police instead of from arrests actually made. In the light of our earlier discussion of the differences between these two types of data, it is clearly hazardous to draw meaningful comparisons between data based on these counting procedures, even within the same annual report.

There is also the problem of weighting the offenses in the index. As it now stands, stealing $50 or more is as "serious" as homicide; and auto theft, even for a brief "joyride," is given the same weight as forcible rape. Except in a most arbitrary and general way, there have traditionally been few procedures of sufficient refinement to measure a community's views on what it regards as serious and what it does not in the

[16] Victor Eisner, *The Delinquency Label: The Epidemiology of Juvenile Delinquency* (New York: Random House, Inc., 1969).

[17] See Daniel Glaser, "National Goals and Indicators for the Reduction of Crime and Delinquency," *American Academy of Political and Social Sciences*, CCCLXXI (May, 1967), 104–26.

way of delinquency and crime. Therefore, perhaps no other problem poses more difficulties than that concerning the relative seriousness of offenses.

Unhappy with the present practice of including in the Crime Index those offenses which command the bulk of police departments' activities, Sellin and Wolfgang carefully studied one possible solution to the dilemma. They began by examining some 1,300 cases in the files of the Philadelphia police department and separating offenses into Class I and Class II on the basis of whether there was injury, theft, or damage (or a combination of them) or whether there was not. Next they obtained detailed descriptions of approximately 140 Class I offenses, which, incidentally, they found to be much less susceptible to variations in police administrative practices than Class II offenses, and asked groups of policemen, judges, and students to assess their seriousness by assigning a "score" to each of them. A high degree of consensus was found to exist in these groups regarding the level of seriousness attached to the various offenses. It is a finding made all the more impressive by the fact that the procedure used to assign scores was designed to allow each respondent to evaluate the offense *subjectively*.[18]

In sum, these criticisms expose serious inadequacies in the official data available on the delinquency problem. To be content with the reports as they now exist, especially when several changes can be made which would greatly enhance their utility, is unacceptable. Hence, certain recommendations can be made for improving them.

## Recommendations for Improvement

From among the many suggestions for upgrading the *Uniform Crime Reports*, the following seem most realistic in terms of the possibility of their being incorporated:

1. The population base figures from which delinquency rates are calculated need to be refined to provide information on rates for the "population at risk." This can be done by calculating delinquency rates on the basis of the population in the 10-through-17-year-old age group in any given year. Of course, it would be desirable to provide even more refined age-specific data on the incidence of delinquency, but this change would help.
2. A concerted effort should be made to distinguish auto theft for "joyrides" from auto theft for financial gain. In view of the large number of arrests made of those under 18 for this offense, it is particularly crucial in obtaining useful information on the delinquency problem.

[18] Thorsten Sellin and Marvin Wolfgang, *The Measurement of Delinquency* (New York: John Wiley and Sons, Inc., 1964).

3. If the Crime Index is to contain information on the extent to which serious crimes are committed in this country, then special attention must be given to both the selection of offenses to be included in it and the measures used to determine seriousness. As it is, the distinct *impression* is left that the offenses comprising it are indeed the most socially damaging ones, even though this might not be so when criteria other than those reflecting legitimate administrative policies are employed in the assessment. Whether the Sellin-Wolfgang proposal is the most appropriate solution is open to debate. It certainly has the greatest merit of any proposal made thus far.

4. Additional information should be provided about the victims of offenses. This is being done in murder cases and should be expanded to include other offenses, at least the serious ones. Such data would serve to underscore the interactive nature of offender-victim relations, a dimension of the crime problem almost totally ignored in official sources of statistical information.

5. All pressures to present statistics in a way designed to over-dramatize the problems of crime and delinquency should be resisted, and interpretive statements by the compilers of the reports should be kept to a minimum.

Of course, it is assumed that a concerted effort to obtain *uniform* data on crime and delinquency will continue, and that the battle to acquire reports from all law enforcement agencies in rural, suburban, and urban areas will go on unabated. But when all of these changes have been made, shall we be able to say much more about the nature of delinquency? Or shall we simply have a more accurate count? In all candor, we must concede that it is exceedingly doubtful that the reports will ever be refashioned in such a way that their usefulness to others, such as those in the scientific community, will outweigh their utility to law-enforcement officials. Lejins correctly argued that certain types of information are more appropriately gathered by other agencies. No matter how refined they become, the *Uniform Crime Reports* will not be able to provide some of the data essential to an understanding of the delinquency problem.

## Scientific Measures of Delinquency

Measuring any form of social behavior is never a simple matter of "getting the facts." Delinquency is certainly no less difficult to investigate than any other type of conduct. Even gathering data on something as fundamental as the incidence of the problem as it is officially handled poses perplexing questions, as we have just seen. Yet, compared with the dilemmas encountered in the development of scientific measures of delinquency, these issues appear small. Confronting the scientific investigator are several rigorous and exacting criteria which are not imposed on those who gather data on the delinquency problem for other purposes.

Three important demands are made of data in order to enhance their utility from a scientific standpoint, although they by no means exhaust the conditions of acceptability applied to data and are seldom attained in contemporary social research except in the most minimal way. First, are they *reliable?* That is, do essentially the same findings emerge after repeated replications of a study? If consistently similar results are obtained, it is likely that our measures are reliable. Second, are the data *valid?* In other words, are we measuring what we actually purport to measure? Only when we can be assured that the behavior under consideration is delinquent behavior can we have much confidence in the results of our investigations. Third, are the data *representative?* Do they, to put it differently, enable us to generalize our findings with respect to populations that we have not directly studied but that have characteristics essentially similar to the populations about which we do have data? When it is possible to say that our measurements are sensitive to the variations which exist in the total population and do not tend to be biased by over-representation or under-representation in regard to selected characteristics such as age, sex, and social class, it can be assumed that the data obtained are representative.

Research in delinquency, not unlike that in nearly every other area of the behavioral sciences, has been slow to conform to these demands. Except for a few notable "continuity" studies in selected areas, only the most modest claims of reliability can be made regarding findings about delinquency. Likewise, the rather facetious claim that our knowledge of delinquency must be restricted to selected adolescent populations in a few large cities such as Chicago, New York, and Detroit at least serves to emphasize the fact that allegations about the representativeness of our samples are not infrequently dictated by circumstances of time, money, and location. Perhaps more illustrative of the lopsidedness of our data than anything else is the paucity of information regarding the delinquent activities of middle-class youths.[19]

## Official vs. Self-Reporting Measures

An especially relevant controversy has been emerging in connection with the problems of validity in delinquency research. It highlights both the concern for establishing a valid body of data and the exceedingly short distance that has been covered in an effort to do so. In its most

---

[19] For a summary of some of this literature, see Edmund W. Vas (ed.), *Middle Class Juvenile Delinquency* (New York: Harper and Row, 1967).

essential form, the controversy centers about the question of whether self-reporting techniques, consisting of responses to questionnaire items, or contact with law enforcement officials, as revealed through an examination of official records, is the more valid measure of delinquent behavior.[20] Proponents of the "self-reporting" technique argue that a considerable amount of unlawful behavior goes undetected by the police. Furthermore, the findings obtained from such measures challenge some more or less "established" relationships between social class and delinquency.

One of the most direct ways to obtain data on the extent to which such conduct occurs is to ask youngsters whether they have ever engaged in certain types of behavior which, technically, are violations of the law even though there has been no official knowledge of the behavior. Nye, for example, devised a scale based on the following items: (1) ever driven a car without a driver's license or permit, (2) skipped school without a legitimate excuse, (3) defied parents' authority (to their face), (4) taken little things (worth less than $2) that did not belong to you, (5) bought or drank beer, wine, or liquor, (6) purposely damaged or destroyed public or private property that did not belong to you, (7) had sex relations with a person of the opposite sex. If a respondent admitted to having done five or more of these things, he was classified as "most delinquent." If he claimed to have done from none to five, he was classified as "least delinquent." It was on the basis of these self-reports that an assessment of the relations between delinquency and various facets of family life was made.[21]

To the proponents of the alternative view, any act which does not come to the attention of law enforcement officials cannot be regarded as a delinquent act. Supported by a considerable body of theory which contends that the *reactions to* behavior are an essential part of the defining process, these scholars argue that any measure which is not sensitive to official reactions to behavior, as well as to the behavior itself, is not a valid measure of delinquency. In an important study specifically de-

---

[20] For various approaches to this problem, see the following literature: William R. Arnold, "Continuities in Research: Scaling Delinquent Behavior," *Social Problems,* XIII (Summer, 1965), 59–66; Robert A. Dentler and Lawrence J. Monroe, "Social Correlates of Early Adolescent Theft," *American Sociological Review,* XXVI (October, 1961), 733–43; F. Ivan Nye, *Family Relationships and Delinquent Behavior* (New York: John Wiley and Sons, 1958), Chapter 2, "Measuring Delinquent Behavior," pp. 10–22; James F. Short and F. Ivan Nye, "Reported Behavior as a Criterion of Deviant Behavior," *Social Problems,* V (Winter, 1957), 207–21; Stanton Wheeler, "Criminal Statistics: A Reformulation of the Problem," *Journal of Criminal Law, Criminology, and Police Science,* LVIII (September, 1967), 17–24; Marvin E. Wolfgang, "International Criminal Statistics: A Proposal," *Journal of Criminal Law, Criminology, and Police Science,* LVIII (March, 1967), 65–69.

[21] Nye, *op. cit.*, pp. 10–22.

signed to test the validity of self-reporting techniques of delinquency, Clark and Tifft concluded that the validity of such measures is, indeed, doubtful.[22]   In general, while intensive research regarding all facets of the issue is needed, it seems reasonable to contend that an important distinction must be made between measures of *behavior* which, in the judgment of the investigator, has at least the technical potential of being officially reacted to as delinquent and measures of the actual *delinquency* of behavior.   Self-reporting devices, important as they are as measures of behavior, do not appear to have much utility as measures of the delinquency of behavior.

Constantly mindful of these and many more specific conditions which must prevail to insure the acceptability of his data, the scientific investigator, interested in finding out what causes delinquency, employs a variety of methodological procedures and statistical techniques to formulate and test theoretically relevant hypotheses about delinquency.   Whether through individual case studies, participant observation, interviews, or questionnaires, the major objective in delinquency research is to find out as much as possible about which factors contribute most frequently to such conduct and to integrate these findings into a logically consistent, interrelated set of propositions about the conditions under which it can be expected to occur.

As noble and as lofty as these efforts are, measuring the extent to which certain variables are related to delinquency and, from among these, determining which ones are more significant than others and under what conditions present considerable difficulty.   Whether an investigator chooses, as the Gluecks did in their monumental work *Unraveling Juvenile Delinquency*,[23] to compare a group of delinquents with a matched sample of nondelinquents, or to determine which variables in a selected group tend to be significantly related to delinquency in a sample population of delinquents, numerous pitfalls await him at every turn in his effort to establish relationships between particular variables and delinquency.   Three types of errors are frequently encountered in delinquency research: (1) the *post hoc, ergo propter hoc* error; (2) tautological findings; and (3) imposing false criteria of causality.

**Post hoc, ergo propter hoc Errors.**   Basically, this kind of error arises when it is assumed that that which comes after something has neces-

---

[22] John P. Clark and Larry L. Tifft, "Polygraph and Interview Validation of Self-Reported Deviant Behavior," *American Sociological Review*, XXXI (August, 1966), 516–23.

[23] Sheldon and Eleanor Glueck, *Unraveling Juvenile Delinquency* (Cambridge: Harvard University Press, 1950). Some of the difficulties of such procedures are discussed in Albert J. Reiss, Jr., "Unraveling Juvenile Delinquency, II: An Appraisal of the Research Methods," *American Journal of Sociology*, LVII (September, 1951), 115–20.

sarily been caused by that which comes before it. Because broken homes, for example, precede delinquency, it is asserted that such conditions "cause" delinquency when, in fact, such a relationship is very difficult to establish. Not only is it difficult to determine a *causal* connection when the time order is known, it is frequently not possible to accurately place the variables being studied in a proven time-order sequence. Premature and undocumented assertions about what causes delinquency consistently reveal this type of error.

**Tautological Findings.** In effect, this fallacy develops when, instead of actually finding a causal connection, all an investigator is really doing is saying the same thing in different ways. It occurs in even the most sophisticated kinds of research. Lander, for example, in *Toward an Understanding of Juvenile Delinquency*,[24] uses high delinquency rates as an indication of "anomie" and claims that "anomie" is, in turn, responsible for high delinquency rates. Although additional indicators were used, the net effect of his claim is to use high delinquency rates to "explain" high delinquency rates! He also falls victim to the *post hoc* error by assuming that his other indicators (percentage of nonwhites in the area and percentage of owner-occupied dwellings in the area), because they occur prior to delinquency, contribute to its causation. It must be pointed out that Lander's study is, for numerous other reasons, a very important one in delinquency, and our use of it as an example of tautological comments is merely intended to illustrate the extreme difficulty of avoiding such errors.

**False Criteria of Causality.** Hirschi and Selvin have pointed out that scientists occasionally impose criteria on their findings which cannot be defended and which, in effect, serve to hamper rather than enhance the search for causes of delinquency.[25] An easy understanding of some of their observations requires a certain amount of training in sociological methods and so these will not be discussed here. However, because two of the "false criteria" are so frequently included in the thinking brought to the subject of delinquency causation by beginning students, these criteria need to be specifically exposed. First, to contend that, unless a perfect relation is found between some variable and delinquency, that variable cannot be considered a cause of delinquency is incorrect. As Hirschi and Selvin suggest, "perfect association implies single causation, and less-than-perfect association implies multiple causation." [26] On no other point can more agreement be found among serious students of the

[24] Bernard Lander, *Toward an Understanding of Juvenile Delinquency* (New York: Columbia University Press, 1954).

[25] Travis Hirschi and Hanan Selvin, *Delinquency Research: An Appraisal of Analytic Methods* (New York: Free Press, 1967), Chapter 8.

[26] *Ibid.*, p. 118.

problem of delinquency than that one which insists that the factors which contribute to delinquency are many and varied. Perfect associations are, from a multiple-causation standpoint, not to be found.

Secondly, to argue that unless a factor is outstanding in cases of delinquents it cannot be a cause of delinquency is false. If, for example, it is found that, in a comparative study of 100 delinquents and 100 nondelinquents, 10 per cent of the nondelinquents and 30 per cent of the delinquents came from broken homes, the findings *could* have causal significance even though "broken homes" was not an outstanding feature of either population. Furthermore, this argument is also inconsistent with a multiple-causation approach to delinquency causation. For, as Hirschi and Selvin are quick to note, if delinquency is really traceable to a plurality of causes, then some of the apparently unimportant factors may actually operate in the causation of a minority of delinquents.[27]

## Conclusions About Measures of Delinquency

It has not been our purpose in this chapter to merely present the latest statistical information on delinquency so that one can sit around and impress his uninformed but interested friends with "the facts." Rather, we have tried to stress the hazards of doing this. It is far better to approach all data regarding the delinquency problem with a critical frame of mind. By revealing some of the weaknesses of existing data, we have tried to encourage the development of this frame of mind. Objectivity, vigilance, and sympathy are seen by Hirschi and Selvin as most crucial to this sort of healthy skepticism.[28] They combine to keep us from dismissing out of hand data which do not conform to some rigid, dogmatic formula, from ignoring important data which have known errors in it, and from turning our backs on the problem of measurement simply because it is so difficult.

It is certainly true that "the only way to avoid making mistakes altogether is not to do any research."[29] By the same token, the only way to avoid errors in measuring delinquency is not to compile any data on its incidence. But if we were to do this, we should be greatly handicapped in our study of the problem. Of necessity, then, there must be a continuing effort to devise new and more accurate measures of the problem and some appreciation of the fact that any measuring device will be less than perfect.

[27] *Ibid.*, p. 274.
[28] *Ibid.*, pp. 273–274.
[29] *Ibid.*, p. 274.

# 5

# Delinquent Conduct: Types and Typologies

A great variety of children are adjudged delinquent every year by the juvenile courts of the United States. Here, for example, are a few of these cases.

Ed was a seventeen-year-old high-school dropout with an intelligence quotient of 131 but with no apparent goals in life. His parents explained that he began "to act strangely at home" and "started running the streets with the wrong crowd." When Ed left home with some of the family's savings, they became alarmed and contacted the juvenile court. The police initiated a search for the boy, and after tracking him across the southwestern states and through Mexico, they finally located him in California. He was returned to his parents, and an investigation revealed that he had been using a variety of drugs, including LSD and marihuana. After a court hearing, Ed was placed in a mental hospital for a thorough examination, which established that he had become addicted to drugs, that he had serious personality problems, and that he had no desire to change his behavior. In fact, during a weekend leave from the hospital, he obtained drugs and smuggled them into his room. As a result, Ed was committed to an institution where he could receive treatment for his problems under maximum-security conditions, but his future remains uncertain.

Chuck was a fourteen-year-old boy from an extremely unstable home. His parents had been divorced and remarried three times, and Chuck and his three sisters were tossed about in a turbulent stream of domestic bickerings and conflict. The father was an alcoholic and a bad-check writer, who had served two prison sentences for forgery. The mother was passive and overprotective of her children, and Chuck, the only son, was completely out of control in the home. Unrestrained by parental supervision, Chuck dropped out of school, left his mother's home, and joined his father in a nearby town, where he was permitted "to do anything that he pleased." As a result of several law violations, including car theft, he was brought to the juvenile court and then placed on probation, with the stipulation that he return to his mother's home, go back to school, and remain under the supervision and guidance of a probation officer. Chuck has now been on probation for several months and appears to be doing quite well.

Rick, a fifteen-year-old boy, was referred to the juvenile court for making telephone threats to bomb his high school. An investigation showed that he was unhappy with his parents and was convinced that he had been unfairly treated at school. Both his sister and brother, who were older than Rick, were doing very well in school and excelled in sports. Although Rick was a good student and an average athlete, he was not the equal of his brother in any activity, and continual urgings by his parents "to try harder" had produced only confusion, frustration, and unnecessary failures. In desperation, and struggling to relieve his pent-up feelings, he had threatened "to blow up everybody." Sessions with Rick and his parents created a better understanding of the situation and more realistic expectations regarding his behavior. After a short period under supervision, he was once again happy at home and enjoying himself in school, where he made the honor roll and became a substitute on both the football and basketball teams. Apparently the problems that brought him so much unhappiness have now disappeared.

Fred was a junior high school student who refused to attend classes, remained at home all day, and appeared "to have lost interest in everything." Continued truancy brought him to the juvenile court, which placed him on probation after he had agreed to return to school. However, Fred again became a truant, and only the persistence of the probation officer revealed the reasons for his behavior. Through the efforts of this officer, it was learned that Fred had had a homosexual relationship with a male cousin during the previous summer, that he had intense feelings of guilt about this, that he had the false notion that he had contracted a venereal disease and that other students knew of his condition and would make fun of him, and that he was so afraid of his puritanical mother that he would not tell her of his problem. The court obtained psychiatric help for Fred, and he now seems to have overcome his difficulties.

Debbie was bright, attractive, and sixteen. The only child of a father who was a lawyer and of a mother who was a physician, life had been serene for Debbie until the father joined a prominent influential law firm in a big city and the mother became associated with the municipal health department. Denied nothing and indulged in every way by her now wealthy parents, she felt miserable and alone in her large new home as her mother and father became more and more absorbed in community and professional affairs. One day when she felt especially depressed and neglected, Debbie and a boy friend broke into a neighbor's home, took some money and jewelry, stole a car, and drove off to California. After several weeks, they were found, returned to their homes, and placed on probation. The parents, who deeply love Debbie, now seem sufficiently alerted and aware of her emotional needs, and the court expects no further difficulties in her case.

Mike was born in a slum area of a large city. He was the sixth and last child of a family in which the father was a laborer and the mother a factory worker. The father died when Mike was only six months old, leaving the mother with six small children, the oldest of whom was only ten. At first the mother left the children in the nursery of a settlement house, but as they grew older, they had little supervision and roamed the streets. Mike, who was large for his age, ran with a gang of older boys, who admired him for his daring and strength. With them, he became involved in vandalism, house-breaking, and shoplifting. At the age of sixteen he appeared in juvenile court on a charge of robbery and was placed on probation, but within a few weeks he stole several cars and held up a filling station and is now serving a prison term in the state reformatory.

## THE NATURE OF TYPES AND TYPOLOGIES

These examples give some idea of the wide range of delinquency cases appearing before our juvenile courts. The fact is that all kinds of children—the rich and the poor, the strong and the weak, the bright and the dull, the well and the sick, the white and the colored, the native-born and the foreign-born, the male and the female; alleged truants, runaways, incorrigibles, vandals, thieves, robbers, rapists, and killers—all come to the court and are adjudged delinquent. And the only thing that they all have in common is that they have violated the law which defines delinquency. It should be clear, then, that no simple theory will help us to understand either crime or juvenile delinquency. Indeed, nothing less than an explanation of all human behavior will give us the complete answer to these problems, and, of course, this is far from our reach. In view of the great complexity of these problems and the paucity of our knowledge regarding them, many criminologists now recommend that we give up our search for a general theory of causation and seek instead separate theories of the various types of crime and delinquency.[1]  There is really nothing new or startling about this recommendation.  Whenever man has found a problem too complex for his comprehension, he has always tried to facilitate a solution of the problem by a study of its component parts, the hope being that greater knowledge of the parts will bring a deeper understanding of the whole.  In effect, this procedure reduces the complex to the simple and thus increases the possibility that an utterly incomprehensible problem will be more accessible to our limited understanding.

The construction of types is a basic part of the methodology of science, which seeks to discover what is uniform and recurrent and to express its findings in terms of what is probable.  Like all concepts, a type is an abstraction.  It is part of what is larger and is separated in terms of certain criteria for the purpose of comparison and a better understanding.  Since it is a simplification of the concrete, all individual concrete occurrences will differ from the type in some respect.  Thus a type is a selective, purposive simplification, constructed in terms of certain criteria and constituting a bridge between a theoretical approach on one side and empirical observations on the other.  A typology is a collection of types having certain characteristics in common but also sufficiently different to be distinguishable from one another.

Although the function of types has been implicit in what has been said, it may be helpful to be more explicit regarding this.  The primary function of types is to identify, simplify, and order concrete data so that they may be more easily described, compared, measured, and understood.  Thus the type is not only a tool for the simplification of data but also a heuristic device.  It assists in the discovery of inconsistencies between the empirical data and the theories used to explain them, stimulates further research for better theories regarding such data, and, by increasing our knowledge along specific lines, contributes to the development of general theory.[2]

---

[1] See, for example, Harry Elmer Barnes and Negley K. Teeters, *New Horizons in Criminology* (Englewood Cliffs, N.J.: Prentice-Hall, Inc., 1959), pp. 206–10; Sheldon Glueck, "Theory and Fact in Criminology," *British Journal of Delinquency*, VII (October, 1956), 108; George B. Vold, *Theoretical Criminology* (New York: Oxford University Press, 1958), pp. 313–15; John M. Martin and Joseph P. Fitzpatrick, *Delinquent Behavior*, pp. 152, 153; Julian B. Roebuck, *Criminal Typology* (Springfield, Ill.: Charles C. Thomas, 1967), pp. 3–27; Theodore N. Ferdinand, *Typologies of Delinquency: A Critical Analysis* (New York: Random House, Inc., 1966), pp. 3–17.

[2] John C. McKinney, *Constructive Typology and Social Theory* (New York: Appleton-Century-Crofts, 1966), pp. 1–19, 83, 201–3, 216; Roebuck, 15, 18; Ferdinand, 43–45; Don C. Gibbons, *Changing the Lawbreaker: The Treatment of Delinquents and Criminals* (Englewood Cliffs, N.J.: Prentice-Hall, Inc., 1965), pp. 39–40.

## TYPOLOGIES IN CRIMINOLOGY

For a long time criminologists have made many attempts to classify offenders into various types and have used different criteria for this purpose. An obvious way to do this is in terms of the offense committed. For example, offenders may be classified into larcenists, robbers, embezzlers, rapists, murderers, and so on, but this is not very helpful, since different kinds of persons commit the same kind of offense. For this reason scholars have tended to look beyond the offense and center their attention on the offender. In doing this, sometimes they have emphasized biological factors in the construction of typologies; sometimes, psychological-psychiatric factors; sometimes, sociological factors. Our examination will follow these lines of emphasis.[3]

### Biological Typologies

Cesare Lombroso (1835–1909), the founder of the Italian or positive school of criminology, was especially influenced by the writings of Darwin. He divided offenders into the born, the insane, the occasional, and the passionate.[4] Enrico Ferri, another member of the positive school, classified offenders into the insane, the born, the habitual, the occasional, and the passionate.[5] Raffaele Garofalo, a third member of the same school, divided offenders into murderers, violent offenders, offenders deficient in probity, and lascivious offenders.[6]

Within recent years, William Sheldon, following the lines laid down by the earliest work of the German Ernst Kretschmer,[7] has advanced the thesis that behavior is a function of anatomical structure and can be predicted on the basis of careful physical measurements.[8] He has proposed this threefold classification of body-build types (somatotypes):

[3] Some of the typologies presented here do not refer specifically to juvenile delinquency but do include it to some extent by implication, since the same general factors operate in the process of causation of both crime and delinquency.

[4] Cesare Lombroso, *Crime, Its Causes and Remedies* (Boston: Little, Brown, and Co., 1911).

[5] Enrico Ferri, *Criminal Sociology*, trans. J. Kelly and J. Lisle (Boston: Little, Brown, and Co., 1917), pp. 138, 139.

[6] Raffaele Garofalo, *Criminology*, trans. Robert W. Miller (Boston: Little, Brown, and Co., 1914), pp. 111–32.

[7] Ernst Kretschmer, *Physique and Character*, trans. W. J. H. Sprott (New York: Harcourt, Brace, Jovanovich, Inc., 1925).

[8] See William H. Sheldon, S. S. Stevens, and W. B. Tucker, *Varieties of Human Physique* (New York: Harper and Row, 1940); William H. Sheldon and S. S. Stevens, *Varieties of Temperament* (New York: Harper and Row, 1942); and William H. Sheldon, Emil M. Hartl, and Eugene McDermott, *Varieties of Delinquent Youth* (New York: Harper and Row, 1949).

endomorphs, ectomorphs, and mesomorphs. Endomorphs are convivial and gluttonous and tend to be fat. Ectomorphs are thin, linear, fragile, and extremely sensitive. Mesomorphs are assertive, muscular, athletic, and vigorous. As a result of his research, Sheldon concluded that delinquent boys are significantly more mesomorphic than nondelinquent boys.

## Psychological-Psychiatric Typologies

Several decades ago Alexander and Staub presented a typology of criminals which was greatly influenced by the teachings of Freud. In the latest edition of their book, they divided offenders into the acute and the chronic, and subdivided the chronic into the normal, the neurotic, and the pathological. The acute criminal is one who commits a single crime, or only a few crimes, because of unusual or extreme circumstances. The normal criminal is largely a product of his environment. As a result of his association with criminals, he has become a criminal. The neurotic criminal is one who violates the law because of his anxieties, guilt feelings, and personality conflicts. The pathological criminal is one who engages in criminal behavior because of an organic condition. This category includes the mentally deficient and the organically psychotic.[9]

Abrahamsen formulated another typology in terms of psychoanalytic theory and divided offenders into six types, each type depending upon a particular interrelationship of the offender's ego, superego, and id impulses.[10] The first, the momentary types, also called the situational, the accidental, or the associational, commits an offense once or infrequently and then only when the situation provides an opportunity for the expression of his antisocial traits. After the offense, he experiences great remorse and does not want to know what he has done. Usually he has been raised in a home full of emotional tension, and, in committing antisocial acts, he unconsciously punishes his parents.

The second type, the neurotic offender, develops out of a neurotic condition. He suffers from manias, phobias, compulsions, and obsessions, often because he was emotionally starved or overprotected during childhood. In many cases, he is a kleptomaniac or a pyromaniac, and his offense is a symbolic or substitute expression of a suppressed desire, usually of a sexual nature.

Offenders who suffer from unconscious guilt feelings constitute the third type. They unconsciously want to be punished, a desire they satisfy by committing a crime for which they can be punished. Thus their guilt feelings are the prime mover in instigating the antisocial act.

[9] Franz Alexander and Hugo Staub, *The Criminal, the Judge, and the Public* (New York: The Free Press, 1956), pp. 42–46.

[10] David Abrahamsen, *Who Are The Guilty?* (New York: Grove Press, Inc., 1952), pp. 148–71.

The fourth type includes those offenders who suffer from character disorder. They show their neurotic taint in irrational behavior and can commit almost any kind of crime. Usually such persons come from families where there has been little or no supervision, little or no development of a superego structure, and little love or understanding.

The fifth type is the psychopath. He is neither psychotic nor mentally defective. He is asocial, amoral, narcissistic, impulsive, and infantile, and lacking in ability to form real relationships with others. Since he has developed no superego structure, he differs from the person with a character disorder, who has some conscience. His home life has been filled with frustrations, bitterness, and quarreling. He is unreliable, unstable, and egocentric, and having no conscience, he feels no remorse.

Individuals suffering from a psychosis belong to the sixth type. Usually they are not criminally responsible and are declared insane. Schizophrenics are perhaps the most common of all psychotic offenders. Unlike the neurotics, the psychotics lose touch with the world, and so the criminal law holds little meaning for them.

Hewitt and Jenkins constructed another typology which utilizes the psychiatric approach, although some sociocultural factors are included.[11] This typology, which applies exclusively to juvenile delinquents, includes three major types: the unsocialized aggressive delinquent; the socialized delinquent; and the over-inhibited neurotic. The unsocialized aggressive delinquent is cruel, defiant, remorseless, quarrelsome, mischievous, boastful, selfish, rude, evasive, and hostile. He is defiant toward those in authority, destroys property, and physically attacks others. Since he has little superego, he experiences little remorse. He comes from the lower class, a deteriorated neighborhood, a discordant or broken home, and a family torn by internal conflict and disliked by the neighbors. Subjected to selfish and inconsiderate treatment in the home, suffering from lack of love and affection, full of bitterness and hate, he strikes out blindly against all authority figures.

The socialized delinquent is usually a member of a gang, in which he is accepted and adjusted. The product of a delinquent subculture, he commits acts against the larger society, defies authority, avoids responsibility for his acts, and experiences little remorse, even though he has deep feelings of guilt when he violates the code of his peer group. His home is overcrowded and in a deteriorated neighborhood, and although he is not rejected by his parents, he is not well supervised. He is social-

---

[11] Lester E. Hewitt and Richard L. Jenkins, *Fundamental Patterns of Maladjustment: The Dynamics of Their Origin* (Springfield: Illinois State Printer, 1947), pp. 25–36; Richard L. Jenkins, "Diagnoses, Dynamics, and Treatment in Child Psychiatry," *Psychiatric Research Report*, XVIII, American Psychiatric Association (October, 1964), 91–120.

ized within a delinquent group rather than within his family, and his behavior is motivated more by acquisitiveness than by a desire for revenge.

The over-inhibited neurotic suffers from a conflict between impulses and repressive forces. Shy, seclusive, fearful, and jealous, he has tics, sleep disturbances, and bites his nails. His parents, who belong to the middle or upper class, are repressive, cold, and unsocial. The mother compensates for some rejection by being overprotective, but the father tends to be an intolerant perfectionist. The child, who lacks close emotional contact with his parents, fears that he may lose their love and feels secure only by being excessively good, but the pressure of primitive impulses produces an acute internal conflict, which may be relieved by neurotic disorders.

## Sociological Typologies

Since World War II, a number of sociologists, following in the footsteps of Shaw, McKay, and Thrasher,[12] have studied the delinquency subculture, especially the relationship between social class and the delinquent gang. Among these have been Cloward and Ohlin, who claim that the gap between financial success, which American culture emphasizes, and the limited access to it causes frustration and alienation among lower-class youths who aspire to economic advancement. This, in turn, produces three types of subcultures (and thus three types of juvenile delinquents): namely, the criminal, the conflict, which features acts of violence, and the retreatist, or drug-use, among lower-class boys who blame the system rather than themselves for their impending or actual failure. The criminal subculture develops in stable neighborhoods that provide illegitimate opportunities for financial success; the conflict subculture, in very disorganized neighborhoods that do not offer even illegitimate opportunities; and the retreatist, among youth who fail to find either legitimate or illegitimate opportunities for financial success and whose inhibitions restrain them from violence and theft.[13]

A few years ago, Gibbons constructed another typology of juvenile delinquents,[14] which some writers have called the most inclusive one that has ever been presented by a sociologist.[15] In this typology, Gibbons

---

[12] Frederic M. Thrasher, *The Gang* (Chicago: University of Chicago Press, 1936).

[13] Richard A. Cloward and Lloyd E. Ohlin, *Delinquency and Opportunity: A Theory of Delinquent Gangs* (New York: The Free Press, 1960). See also Richard A. Cloward, "Illegitimate Means, Anomie, and Deviant Behavior," *American Sociological Review*, XXIV (April, 1959), 164–76.

[14] Gibbons, pp. 74–97.

[15] See, for example, Roebuck, p. 67.

described offender patterns as role-careers within the definitional dimensions of offense behavior, interactional setting, self-image, attitudes, and background data related to social class, family, peer group, and such "defining agencies" [16] as the police and the courts. Using these dimensions, he divided delinquents into the following nine types:

**1. The Predatory Gang Delinquent.** This offender is involved in a variety of property offenses, including repetitive and serious thefts and burglaries, and is usually labeled a "gang delinquent," for he frequently associates with delinquent peers. He exhibits a delinquent self-image, thinking of himself as "cool" and "tough," has antisocial attitudes, usually enters into delinquent activities when he is about eight or nine, comes from a lower-class background, suffers from parental neglect and exposure to delinquency patterns, receives psychological support from his delinquent associates, and has frequent contacts with the police and other defining agencies.

**2. The Conflict Gang Delinquent.** This type is a male who is closely identified with a gang that engages in "rumbles," "bopping," and street fights. He begins his delinquency in his adolescent years, tends to think of himself as "tough" rather than criminalistic, has cynical rather than hostile attitudes toward society, comes from a lower-class family, usually one that recently arrived in an urban slum area, and has a variety of contacts with defining agencies that label him as "bad."

**3. The Casual Gang Delinquent.** This offender participates in a variety of delinquent activities with peers who may be loosely or firmly organized into a gang. He regards his activities as "fun," and himself as nondelinquent, exhibits some hostility toward police, begins his delinquent activities at an early age, comes from a working-class, urban neighborhood, has parents who tend to be law-abiding and interested in his welfare, and has infrequent contacts with the police and other defining agencies.

**4. The Casual Delinquent, Nongang Member.** This type, the so-called "hidden delinquent," engages in relatively few minor acts of misbehavior. He thinks of himself as nondelinquent, associates with peers who view themselves as nondelinquent (and are similarly regarded by adults), has no strong feelings of hostility toward society, frequently begins his delin-

---

[16] According to Gibbons, "defining agencies" refer to those official and semi-official agencies that are given the responsibility for the detection, apprehension, punishment, and treatment of offenders. Contact with these agencies may result in defining the boy or girl in a certain way, for example, as a "delinquent" or as a "bad child," and so, argues Gibbons, may be an important causal experience (Gibbons, p. 57).

quency during the teen-age period, usually comes from a middle-class family, and has few contacts with the police and other defining agencies.

**5. The Auto Thief—"Joyrider."** He steals cars for joyriding, not for profit, in association with several companions, begins his delinquency during adolescence, does not think of himself as a delinquent, usually comes from a middle-class family that provides him with close supervision and consistent discipline, has adequate peer-group adjustments, and has contacts with the police and other defining agencies that seem to confirm his opinion that he is "tough."

**6. The Heroin User.** Usually this delinquent is a boy and a member of a drug-user subculture. He thinks of himself as a drug addict rather than as a delinquent, believes that he is being harassed by a society that provides him with few satisfying experiences, and often continues his use of drugs into adulthood. He usually comes from an urban slum area, a lower-class background, and a relatively conventional family, usually associates with other addicts, and has numerous contacts with defining agencies.

**7. The Overly Aggressive Delinquent.** He is a "lone wolf" offender who engages in seemingly meaningless assaults upon peers and sometimes upon adults. He does not think of himself as a delinquent but as a victim of a hostile environment, often begins his delinquency before adolescence, may come from any of the social classes, almost always suffers from severe parental rejection, seldom associates intimately with his peers, and has numerous contacts with the police and other defining agencies.

**8. The Female Delinquent.** Usually a sex delinquent, she is not a member of a gang, does not consider herself a delinquent, feels hostile toward her parents and correctional agents, begins her delinquency during postpuberty, may belong to any of the social classes, usually comes from a home where there are family tensions, is on poor terms with one or both parents, and has numerous contacts with the police and other defining agencies.

**9. The "Behavior Poblem" Delinquent.** This type commits individualistic, "bizarre" offenses which are often quite serious. He is a "lone wolf" who does not see himself as a delinquent, has conventional attitudes toward the police, the school, and other such agencies, commits few offenses, may belong to any of the social classes, and comes from a family situation that is atypical in a variety of ways. The contacts that he has with defining agencies seem to have little influence on his behavior.

## SOME CONCLUSIONS ABOUT TYPOLOGIES

Typologies are almost always rooted in a single theoretical approach and so share in the weaknesses of that approach and tend to be one-sided. This is as true in criminology as it is elsewhere. Thus in each of the typologies included above, we are asked to view offenders from a certain theoretical position (e.g., the biological, the psychological-psychiatric, or the sociological) to the exclusion of other possible theoretical positions.

Criminologists have been aware of this problem, and, from time to time, some have urged that more than one theoretical approach should be used in the construction of a typology. For example, in 1941, Lindesmith and Dunham explained that sociology was concerned with the "social criminal" and psychiatry with the "individualized criminal," that each discipline was attempting to extend to all types the theories evolved with respect to one, and that such a procedure ignored the possibility that the term "criminal" referred to many different kinds of individuals whose behavior might have developed in totally different ways.[17] More recently, Roebuck has said that we must use a multidisciplinary approach in the construction of criminal typologies. Cooperative research by various disciplines, he has explained, would not only lead to the pooling of findings but also to the development of new frames of reference.[18] Ferdinand, recognizing the importance of using more than one theoretical approach in the construction of a typology, has presented what he calls a "synthetic typology" of delinquency. Beginning with the assumption that delinquency is influenced by both psychological and social forces, he explains that a synthetic typology attempts to describe the behavior of individuals with typical personality styles in typical social situations.[19] Despite such efforts as this, however, no typology of offenders constructed on an interdisciplinary basis has as yet been anywhere near successful in blending the biological, psychological, social, and cultural factors into a single causal process or even in bringing separate causal processes into interaction.

Although we must recognize the one-sided nature of typologies, we must also remember that a type is an abstraction. It represents something lifted out of the total situation for the purpose of simplification and study. Like all concepts, it is merely a tool to be used for gaining

---

[17] Alfred R. Lindesmith and H. Warren Dunham, "Some Principles of Criminal Typology," *Social Forces*, XIX (March, 1941), 307–14.
[18] Roebuck, p. 21.
[19] Ferdinand, pp. 55–77.

greater knowledge and is never an exact copy of anything that is real. For example, we will never find a delinquent who is just like the "predatory gang delinquent" of Gibbons or the "unsocialized aggressive delinquent" of Hewitt and Jenkins. Therefore, we should not consider any type as having a concrete existence apart from the total situation out of which it has been taken. To do so is to convert a simplification into a reality and to invite a superficial appraisal of what may be a most complex situation.

Only a few typologies have been presented here,[20] but they have been enough to reveal the difficulties involved in their construction. We do not know much about the causes of human behavior, in general, or criminal behavior, in particular, or how and why offenders differ from one another, and typologies cannot escape from this ignorance. Therefore, the categories in a classification of offenders cannot be precise, stable, and mutually exclusive, and different criteria have to be combined in various ways to construct them. And here another problem confronts the criminologist. If a typology is to be very effective in opening the door to greater knowledge, it must go beyond a few simple types to a wide range of detailed types. However, in criminology the more refined the typology strives to be, the more it must resort to fitting criteria loosely together in various combinations by the use of such qualifying terms as "chiefly," "usually," "frequently," "as a rule," "for the most part," "to some extent," "in general," "likely," and so on, thus clearly revealing not only the complexity of the problem but also the meagerness of the knowledge regarding it.

Nevertheless, the futility of formulating general theories of crime and delinquency is causing more and more criminologists to turn their attention to separate theories of various types of offenders. The fact remains, however, that all kinds of people violate the law. A complete classification of offenders, therefore, would amount to nothing less than a complete classification of all human beings. Obviously, this is impossible. Still, we can continue to classify offenders into more homogeneous subgroups by means of different criteria, and although this is always more or less arbitrary, it should provide us with deeper insights into delinquent and criminal behavior, better programs for treatment and rehabilitation, and a more systematic basis for further research.[21]

[20] For additional typologies of criminals, see Gibbons, pp. 97–125; Ruth Shonle Cavan, *Criminology* (New York: Thomas Y. Crowell Co., 1962), pp. 44–67; Marshall B. Clinard and Richard Quinney, *Criminal Behavior Systems: A Typology* (New York: Holt, Rinehart, and Winston, Inc., 1967), pp. 1–19.

[21] Robert G. Caldwell, *Criminology* (New York: The Ronald Press Co., 1965), pp. 101, 102.

# II

# CAUSATION

# 6

# Personal Factors

## HEREDITY

Heredity is the stream of life that flows from one generation to the next, carrying with it what is usually called the original nature of man and thus bringing to each generation all the anatomical and physiological materials out of which the entire human body is made. Although it does not completely determine the destiny of man in this way, since original nature is greatly modified by social experience, heredity furnishes potentialities and imposes limits and so affects man's development. Furthermore, heredity varies among men and therefore contributes to individual differences. When this variation is great, heredity tends to stand out, seriously handicapping in some instances and extraordinarily facilitating in others. And from the interaction of heredity with all the other factors in man's life, both personal and environmental, emerges the human personality. However, the characteristics that man acquires during his life do not change the germ plasm and are not inherited, and so each generation must begin anew and try to preserve its cultural gains through the process of education and learning.

How much of the human being comes from heredity and how much from the environment? Unfortunately, this question cannot be fully answered even by an intensive study in the individual case—and for a number of reasons. The human genetic system is very complex, and the threads of heredity are already inextricably interwoven with those of the environment during the prenatal period. Furthermore, much of man's heredity remains latent in recessive genes, and we have no way of knowing what this is at any particular time. Besides, since recessive genes can be defective, a normal person may carry undetectable hereditary defects, and these, if not counteracted by normal genes, may become manifest in his children.

Consequently, even if we could prevent those who have manifest hereditary defects from reproducing, the next generation would still have a whole new set of such defects. And the problem is made even more complex by the fact that a defect of a certain kind, for example, feeble-mindedness, may be caused by heredity in one person and by the environment in another. Moreover, some hereditary characteristics appear only gradually through the process of maturation, and their nature is thus obscured by environmental influences. Thus, it can be seen how difficult the problem is and why we can not disentangle hereditary and environmental influences. In fact, we must conclude that all the other personal factors, except race, which is hereditary, contain elements of both heredity and environment, and that the individual has both in indeterminable proportions.

## The Positive School

Man has always speculated on the importance of heredity in the causation of crime. His thoughts regarding this were greatly stimulated by the advances of the biological sciences during the nineteenth century and especially by Darwin's writings on evolution. Cesare Lombroso, in founding the positive school of criminology, claimed that there was a born-criminal type who could be identified by certain anomalies (such as protruding jaws, receding forehead, and so on), which were symptoms of atavism (reversion to a more primitive type) or degeneracy, especially that characterized by epileptic tendencies, and who could not refrain from criminal activity unless the circumstances of his life were exceptionally favorable. Garofalo, Ferri, and others made modifications in this theory, and the school gradually lost its earlier, clearly defined characteristics. Lombroso never contended that all criminals belonged to the born-criminal type and eventually admitted that most of them should not be so designated.[1] Finally, however, the writings of Charles Goring, an Englishman, and Gabriel Tarde, a Frenchman, convinced most scholars

---

[1] Gina Lombroso Ferrero, *Criminal Man, According to the Classification of Cesare Lombroso* (New York: G. P. Putnam's Sons, 1911), pp. XI–XX; Cesare Lombroso, *Crime, Its Causes and Remedies* (Boston: Little, Brown and Co., 1911); George B. Vold, *Theoretical Criminology* (New York: Oxford University Press, 1958), pp. 27–32; Marvin E. Wolfgang, "Cesare Lombroso," *Pioneers in Criminology*, ed. Hermann Mannheim (Chicago: Quadrangle Books, Inc., 1960), pp. 168–227; Enrico Ferri, *Criminal Sociology*, trans. Joseph I. Kelly and John Lisle (Boston: Little, Brown and Co., 1917); Thorsten Sellin "Pioneers in Criminology: Enrico Ferri (1856–1929)," *Journal of Criminal Law, Criminology, and Police Science*, XLVIII (January–February, 1958), 481–92; Raffaele Garofalo, *Criminology*, trans. Robert W. Millar (Boston: Little, Brown and Co., 1914); Francis A. Allen, "Pioneers in Criminology: Raffaele Garofalo (1852–1934)," *Journal of Criminal Law, Criminology, and Police Science*, XLV (November–December, 1954), 373–90.

that a born-criminal type, which can be identified by certain stigmata, did not exist.[2] Even so, despite its exaggeration of the role of the biological factors, the positive school did call attention to the study of the criminal and thus helped to offset the influence of the classical school,[3] which had placed its emphasis on the crime.

## Other Approaches

The belief in the importance of heredity, however, persisted, and in 1939, after a long period of research, Earnest A. Hooton, published *Crime and the Man*, in which he claimed that inherited inferiority is the primary cause of crime. Although, according to Hooton, this does not directly cause crime, it does predispose the individual to it, and he commits crime when his weakness is acted upon by environmental forces. Crime, therefore, can be prevented only by the elimination of those with inherited inferiority or by their complete segregation. Severely criticized on the grounds that its methodology was faulty and that it failed to disentangle heredity from environment, Hooton's study does not appear to have helped us very much in our efforts to understand the causes of crime.[4]

Two other noteworthy approaches have been used to show the importance of heredity in the causation of crime. One of these involves the study of family trees; the other, the study of twins. The results obtained by the first show that there is a pronounced tendency for criminality to run in the families studied, and so it is claimed that this proves that criminality is inherited. As the critics have contended, however, the studies of family trees have not been successful in separating heredity from environmental influences. In general, such studies have been criticized on the grounds that they have used neither precise measurements nor comparative statistical analyses of other families, which might have been considered "normal," as controls. One may just as easily conclude,

[2] Charles Goring, *The English Convict* (abridged ed.; London: His Majesty's Stationery Office, 1919), pp. iii–xvi, 9–33, 269–75. See also Edwin D. Driver, "Pioneers in Criminology: Charles Buckman Goring (1870–1919)," *Journal of Criminal Law, Criminology, and Police Science*, XLVII (January–February, 1957), 515–25; Margaret S. Wilson, "Pioneers in Criminology—Gabriel Tarde," *Journal of Criminal Law, Criminology, and Police Science*, XLV (May–June, 1954), 3–11.

[3] Alfred Lindesmith and Yale Levin, "The Lombrosian Myth in Criminology," *American Journal of Sociology*, XLII (March, 1937), 653–71; Thorsten Sellin, "The Lombrosian Myth in Criminology," *American Journal of Sociology*, XLII (May, 1937), 897–99.

[4] Earnest A. Hooton, *Crime and the Man* (Cambridge: Harvard University Press, 1939). For appraisals of Hooton's work, see T. C. McCormick in *American Sociological Review*, V (April, 1940), 252–54; F. A. Ross, in *American Journal of Sociology*, XLV (November, 1939), 477–80; and E. H. Sutherland in *Journal of Criminal Law and Criminology*, XXIX (March–April, 1939), 911–14.

therefore, that members of the families persisted in committing crimes not because they had a common heredity, but because they were all subject to environmental conditions conducive to crime.[5]

The second of these approaches, the study of twins, clearly shows that, when one of a set of identical twins (those with identical heredities) violated the law, the other twin was more likely to do so than was true in the case of fraternal twins (those with heredities no more alike than those of ordinary brothers or sisters). Therefore, it is argued, these studies demonstrate the influence of heredity in the causation of crime. Critics, however, have insisted that the number of cases studied is too small to be conclusive, that not enough care was exercised to make certain that twins were identical instead of fraternal, and that the factor of environment was largely neglected.[6] Although the studies of twins and family trees have not been conclusive, improved studies like them in the future may well give us valuable information about the role of heredity in human behavior.

## Heredity and Criminal Behavior

Must we, then, conclude that, because we cannot precisely measure the influence of heredity in criminal behavior, it is not a factor in such behavior? No, of course not, any more than we should conclude that environmental influences are not factors in the causation of crime, because we cannot precisely measure them. Nevertheless, sociologists, who emphasize "the group" and culture in their studies, tend to minimize or entirely disregard the influence of heredity; and in their determination to articulate an environmental theory of human behavior, they have been reluctant to compromise. However, this reluctance is no longer justified, not only because the evidence from genetics, anthropology, and psychometrics with respect to mental growth can no longer be refuted, but also because heredity and culture can be shown to interact in the evolution of human sociteies. Furthermore, sociologists should not permit the

[5] Arthur H. Estabrook, *The Jukes in 1915* (Washington, D.C.: The Carnegie Institution of Washington, Publication No. 240, 1916); Henry H. Goddard, *The Kallikak Family* (New York: The Macmillan Co., 1912); Charles Goring, *The English Convict* (London: His Majesty's Stationery Office, 1919).

[6] Horatio Hackett Newman, *Multiple Human Births* (New York: Doubleday and Co., 1940); Robert S. Woodworth, *Heredity and Environment: A Critical Survey of Recently Published Material on Twins and Foster Children* (New York: Social Science Research Council, Bull. 47, 1941); Walter C. Reckless, *The Etiology of Delinquent and Criminal Behavior* (New York: Social Science Research Council, Bull. 50, 1943), pp. 5, 6; Ernest R. Mowrer, "Some Factors in the Affectional Adjustment of Twins," *American Sociological Review*, XIX (August, 1954), 468–71; George B. Vold, *Theoretical Criminology* (New York: Oxford University Press, 1958), pp. 96–98.

equalitarian ideology, which is popular among them, to interfere in any way with the scientific approach to their subject matter.[7]

We must, therefore, see heredity for what it really is: an important factor in criminal behavior, just as it is in all human behavior. Indeed, in a particular case heredity may be the major influence in the development of any career, whether it be criminal or not. On the other hand, we must remember that even though heredity may cause a person's social adjustment to be exceedingly difficult, this does not mean that heredity, regardless of other factors, will cause him to be a criminal. As Caldwell explained:

The problem is far too complex for so simple an answer. Crime is what the law defines it to be, and the law varies with the time and the place during a person's life, while his heredity remains constant. A law which defines a particular type of behavior as criminal may greatly increase the possibility that a person with certain hereditary traits will become a criminal, but whether he does so will still depend upon the interaction of these traits with many other factors, such as family life, medical care, education, economic opportunity, programs of law enforcement and crime prevention, and so on.[8]

## RACE

A race may be defined as a group of individuals who have in common certain hereditary characteristics. On the basis of certain physical characteristics, races have been classified into three main divisions: (1) the Caucasoid, (2) the Mongoloid, and (3) the Negroid. Does the fact that races differ in their physical characteristics mean that they differ also in their innate capacities and abilities? This question has generated a great controversy and continues to agitate the deep feelings of men everywhere.

Those who have taken the negative side of this question argue that human races are subspecies of the species *Homo sapiens*, and that, therefore, they share in a common pool of genes, differing only because environmental influences have evoked the necessary characteristics for racial adaptation and survival. Thus, apparently different, races tend to remain equal, and given what approximates equality of opportunity, they will demonstrate what tends to be equality in their abilities and capacities.

[7] Bruce K. Eckland, "Genetics and Sociology: A Reconsideration," *American Sociological Review*, XXXII (April, 1967), 173–94. For criticism of this article and a reply by Eckland, see *American Sociological Review*, XXXII (December, 1967), 996–1001.

[8] Robert G. Caldwell, *Criminology* (New York: The Ronald Press Co., 1965), p. 223.

Furthermore, contends this school, existing tests, however devised and for whatever purposes, cannot separate nature from nurture and so the results obtained by testing, wherever they show racial differences, cannot be used to prove differences in innate qualities.[9]

However, evidence from zoology, anatomy, anthropology, and psychology has been advanced in support of the view that the races do differ in their innate capacities and abilities. Authorities in these fields contend:

1. The various races appeared at different times in the evolutionary process.
2. The white race appeared first and, therefore, had the advantage of evolving as a race for 200,000 years before the Negro came upon the scene.[10]
3. Each race thus has its own pool of genes, which is like those of other races in some respects, different in other respects, and distinctive in many ways related to innate capacities and abilities.
4. The available biological evidence indicates the superiority of the white race in the creation and development of culture.[11]
5. The intelligence quotients of American Negroes average from 15 to 20 points below those of American whites, the overlap of intelligence in the two races ranging from 10 to 25 per cent.
6. Large and significant differences in favor of whites appear in the testing of intelligence even when socioeconomic factors have been equated.[12]
7. The Negro race is the only one among the primary races that has

[9] For the views of some of those who believe that the races do not differ in their innate capacities and abilities, see Franz Boas, *The Mind of Primitive Man* (New York: The Macmillan Co., 1938); Theodosius Dobzhansky, *Mankind Evolving* (New Haven: Yale University Press, 1962); Otto Klineberg, *Race Differences* (New York: Harper and Row, 1935); M. F. Ashley Montagu, *Man's Most Dangerous Myth: The Fallacy of Race* (New York: Columbia University Press, 1942); Ashley Montagu (ed.), *The Concept of Race* (New York: The Free Press, 1964); Gunnar Myrdal, *An American Dilemma* (New York: Harper and Row, 1944). For adverse comment on the work of Boas, see Henry Pratt Fairchild, *Race and Nationality* (New York: The Ronald Press Co., 1947), pp. 96–106.

[10] Carleton S. Coon, *The Origin of Races* (New York: Alfred A. Knopf, 1962), pp. 27–37, 59–62; *The Story of Man* (New York: Alfred A. Knopf, 1962), pp. 31–35.

[11] See, for example, Wesley C. George, *The Biology of the Race Problem* (New York: National Putnam Letters Committee Reprint, 1962).

[12] Audrey M. Shuey, *The Testing of Negro Intelligence* (New York: Social Science Press, 1958, 1966); Henry E. Garrett, *How Classroom Desegregation Will Work* (Richmond, Va.: The Patrick Henry Press, 1966). For additional reading on the subject, see Ernest Van den Haag, "Intelligence or Prejudice?," *National Review* (December 1, 1964), reprinted with special permission by the International Association for the Advancement of Ethnology and Eugenics, Inc.; Nathaniel Weyl and Stefan T. Possony, *The Geography of Intellect* (Chicago: Henry Regnery Co., 1963); Carleton Putnam, *Race and Reason* (Washington, D.C.: Public Affairs Press, 1961); *ibid., Race and Reality* (Washington, D.C.: Public Affairs Press, 1967).

failed to make a creative contribution to the world's civilizations and that this failure cannot be entirely explained in terms of climate, isolation, and other environmental factors.

The complexity of our social problems is challenging the outstanding minds of the nation. To meet this challenge, we need the best that both nature and nurture can give. If one race is innately superior to another and so has more to give than another, then, say those who argue in this way, we must frankly recognize this superiority, openly enlist its services, and courageously protect it from the dangers of miscegenation. Above all, scientists should not let political and religious pressures interfere with the study of race and the possible discovery of innate racial differences.

In this connection, Weyl and Possony wrote:

When scientists themselves engage in a revolting scramble to impose orthodox ideologies (which are popular with the government and hence the key to sinecures and good salaries), when they attack those who have the courage to dissent and when they refuse to subject the evidence offered by the dissenters to calm and objective examination, then they simply prove themselves unworthy of a free society and unfit to be members of it.[13]

And in referring to the activities of "academic debunkers" and "soft-peddlers" in the field of anthropology, Carleton S. Coon said that "certain writers, who are mostly social anthropologists, consider it immoral to study race, and produce book after book exposing it as a 'myth.' Their argument is that because the study of race once gave ammunition to racial fascists, who misused it, we should pretend that races do not exist."[14]

Thus, it is urged, science must try to learn the facts about races and clearly state them, so that its findings can be used in dealing with social problems, and where racial inequalities exist, they must be taken into consideration in the analysis of the causation of crime and delinquency. However, even where racial inequality does exist, it must be seen in its interaction with other factors. Like any other single factor, it cannot inevitably cause crime or delinquency, but it may be a very important cause in a particular case. So if one were limited by racial inequalities and forced into competition with persons of another race, he might, in the bitterness and desperation of failure, strike out against them by committing vandalism, theft, or even murder. Furthermore, entirely apart from the question of innate racial differences, the physical characteristics of a race, as measured by cultural values, affect what it is and what it can be in any society, and thus indirectly the nature and extent

[13] Weyl and Possony, pp. 274, 275.
[14] Coon, The Story of Man, pp. 187, 188.

of its law violations. In any event, regardless of how the factor of race is interacting with other factors in the process of causation, all of the evidence indicates that the amount of crime and delinquency of the Negro in the United States is clearly out of proportion to his numbers in the population.

## PHYSICAL CHARACTERISTICS

### Age and Sex

In the United States during 1969, persons under fifteen years of age constituted 10 per cent of the total police arrests; persons under eighteen years of age, 26 per cent; and persons under twenty-one years of age, 39 per cent.[15]  Furthermore, persons who were under eighteen made up 58 per cent of the auto theft cases, 54 per cent of the burglary cases, 53 per cent of the larceny cases, 43 per cent of the robbery cases, 32 per cent of the forcible rape cases, 18 per cent of the aggravated assault cases, and 13 per cent of the criminal homicide cases.[16]

About seven times as many males as females were arrested during 1969, although female arrests increased more than male arrests during the year.  In fact, the arrests for young females under eighteen years of age increased 176 per cent from 1960 to 1969, inclusive, whereas the arrests for males under eighteen rose only 93 per cent during the same period.[17]

In the delinquency cases handled by the juvenile courts of the United States, the boys outnumber the girls by about four to one.  Apparently, boys tend to commit offenses against property, whereas most girls are referred to the court for being ungovernable, running away, truancy, and sex offenses.[18]  However, for as long as statistics on crime have been compiled, "they have shown that males between the ages of 15 and 24 are the most crime-prone group in the population." [19]

Thus, it can be seen that both age and sex are important factors in the causation of juvenile delinquency, but in this process the nature of

[15] *Uniform Crime Reports*, 1969, Table 27, p. 113.

[16] *Ibid.*, pp. 5–28.

[17] Federal Bureau of Investigation, *Uniform Crime Reports, 1969*, p. 111.

[18] U.S. Children's Bureau, *Juvenile Court Statistics, 1965*, Statistical Series, No. 85, pp. 3, 4; *ibid., Juvenile Court Statistics, 1966*, Statistical Series, No. 90, p. 4; *ibid., Juvenile Court Statistics, 1967*, Statistical Series, No. 93, pp. 2, 3.

[19] The President's Commission on Law Enforcement and Administration of Justice, *The Challenge of Crime in a Free Society* (Washington, D.C.: Government Printing Office, 1967), p. 5.

their relationship with other factors is not a simple one.  It is true that profound and disturbing physiological and psychological changes occur during the growth and maturation of every person, and that the upsetting thrust of puberty, the ill-defined strivings, persistent restlessness, clumsy gropings, and awkward ambitions of adolescence, and the failure of inner controls to keep pace with the onrush of biological development tend to generate problems of adjustment for young people in every culture.  This much is quite clear.  And obvious, also, is the fact that the nimbleness, agility, daring, and adventurous spirit of youth facilitate the committing of some unlawful acts, while other offenses must wait for the skill, education, and judgment of later years.  But what is sometimes overlooked is the relationship of all this to the cultural influences that play upon the individual in every society.  Different cultures ascribe different meanings to childhood, adolescence, adulthood, and old age; the duties, responsibilities, rights, and privileges carried by each of these periods vary from society to society; and finally, of course, the law, which tends to reflect the dominant values of a society, decides what acts are criminal and delinquent.

And, so, too, it is with sex.  The biological differences between the sexes are important.  Boys, in general, are physically stronger, and girls, with the onset of puberty, receive the promise of motherhood.  But neither sex is good or bad simply because of its biology.  This can be decided only by the culture in which the person is seeking adjustment— and cultures vary.  In the United States, the female, even though she now has more freedom than ever before, is still more closely supervised and carefully protected than the male.  Shielded from much of the harsh conflict and bitter competition of the business world and expected to assume the duties of wife and mother in the home, she receives preferential treatment in many social relationships, including those in law enforcement and corrections.  Thus, each sex tends to receive different training, opportunities, challenges, and temptations, and all this is reflected in both the lawful and unlawful acts that each commits.  Here, then, as in the case of age, we see an intricate interweaving of the biological, psychological, and cultural factors.

## Anatomical and Physiological Factors

As we have seen, the decline of the views of Lombroso did not stop the efforts to prove the importance of heredity in the causation of crime. Some of these efforts were more specifically directed toward showing the relationship between certain types of body build and certain types of personality.  The Germans W. Jaensch, E. Jaensch, and Kretschmer were

especially active in this work,[20] and a few years later they were followed
by the American William H. Sheldon and his associates at Harvard
University, who began their extensive studies shortly before the United
States entered World War II. Sheldon sought to demonstrate that
behavior is a function of structure and can be predicted on the basis of
careful physical measurements. Applying his theoretical formulation to
delinquents, he concluded that they are chiefly mesomorphic; that is, they
are significantly more vigorous, muscular, athletic, and assertive than
nondelinquents.[21] Studies by the Gluecks point to about the same conclusion; although they do not state that body build causes delinquency,
their findings do indicate a close relation between physique and delinquency and a differential response of body types to the influences of the
environment.[22] Sheldon [23] and the Gleucks [24] deserve credit for calling
attention to the possible importance of biological factors, but their views
remain largely unsubstantiated. In fact, it does not appear that body
build bears a direct relationship to personality and thus to delinquency
and crime.

Rather, it seems that the individual reacts to body build in terms of
the meaning that it has in his life. Thus even when an individual has
a body build which is considered unattractive by his culture, he does not
necessarily become embittered and seek relief from his tortured feelings
by committing crime or delinquency. He has, perhaps, been trained to
accept his lot and find happiness in it, or if he does not have such training, he may be driven by a deep sense of insecurity, not to crime or
delinquency, but to great heights of ambition and success in some lawful
business or profession. Body build may well be an important factor in
the individual case, yet it does not seem to operate alone but always in
interaction with many other factors, such as parental love and under-

[20] For the work of some of the Germans, see Ernest Kretschmer, *Physique and
Character*, trans. W. J. H. Sprott (New York: Harcourt, Brace, Jovanovich, Inc.,
1925); Adolf Lenz, *Grundriss der Kriminalbiologie* (Vienna: Springer, 1927).

[21] William H. Sheldon, S. S. Stevens, and W. B. Tucker, *Varieties of Human
Physique* (New York: Harper and Row, 1940); William H. Sheldon and S. S.
Stevens, *Varieties of Temperament* (New York: Harper and Row, 1942); and Wil-
liam H. Sheldon, Emil M. Hartl, and Eugene McDermott, *Varieties of Delinquent
Youth* (New York: Harper and Row, 1949).

[22] Sheldon and Eleanor T. Glueck, *Unraveling Juvenile Delinquency* (New York:
The Commonwealth Fund, 1950); *ibid.*, *Physique and Delinquency* (New York:
Harper and Row, 1956).

[23] For a review of Sheldon's *Varieties of Delinquent Youth*, see E. H. Sutherland
in *American Sociological Review*, XVI (February, 1951), 10–13. See also George
B. Vold, *Theoretical Criminology* (New York: Oxford University Press, 1958), pp.
50–74.

[24] For an analysis of the Glueck's *Physique and Delinquency*, see the critique
by Albert Morris in the *Harvard Law Review*, LXX (February, 1957), 753–58.

standing, economic status, education, opportunity for legitimate activity, medical care, and so on. *

Physical defects, abnormalities, and disorders, as in the case of body build, may produce troublesome behavioral problems,[25] but even when this happens, the result is not necessarily crime or delinquency. Malnutrition may gravely impede mental and physical development, glandular deficiencies may bring obesity, stunted growth, delayed puberty, and mental retardation; excessive glandular activity may produce restlessness, excitability, impulsiveness, and aggressive behavior; and blindness, deafness, lameness, speech impediment, and facial disfigurement may cause frustration, despondency, and bitterness. But even if these conditions generate critical behavioral problems, they do not inevitably plunge the individual into crime or delinquency. Parental love and guidance, medical care, education, and counseling may successfully intervene. In fact, such serious disorders as hypoglycemia (abnormally low blood-sugar content), encephalitis lethargica (sleeping sickness), and epilepsy, which so deeply disturb the individual, can often be brought under control. Furthermore, in some cases, when the condition does not completely overwhelm the afflicted, he may see his handicap as a challenge and, reacting strongly against it, fight his way to success and prominence.

Now, then, what can we conclude regarding the importance of physical defects, abnormalities, and disorders in the causation of crime and delinquency? Obviously, many persons who have these conditions violate the law, but so do many normal, healthy persons; and many others who suffer from them make satisfactory adjustments without engaging in serious misconduct. Moreover, we do not know how many of the afflicted persons are either law-abiding or law-violating. Thus, although a physical defect, abnormality, or disorder may be a contributing or even a

[25] See, for example, Laurance F. Shaffer, *The Psychology of Adjustment* (Boston: Houghton Mifflin Co., 1936); Allan W. Rowe, "A Possible Endocrine Factor in the Behavior Problems of the Young," *American Journal of Orthopsychiatry*, I (October, 1931), 451–75; Cyril Burt, *The Young Delinquent* (New York: Appleton-Century-Crofts, Inc., 1925); William Healy and Augusta F. Bronner, *New Light on Delinquency and Its Treatment* (New Haven: Yale University Press, 1936); Sheldon and Eleanor T. Glueck, *One Thousand Juvenile Delinquents* (Cambridge: Harvard University Press, 1934); *ibid., Juvenile Delinquents Grown Up* (New York: The Commonwealth Fund, 1940); Ralph S. Banay, "Physical Disfigurement as a Factor in Delinquency and Crime," *Federal Probation*, VII (January–March, 1943), 20–24; *ibid., Youth in Despair* (New York: Coward-McCann, 1948). See also Max G. Shlapp and Edward H. Smith, *The New Criminology* (New York: Boni and Liveright, 1928); Louis Berman, *The Glands Regulating Personality* (New York: The Macmillan Co., 1921); I. G. Cobb, *The Glands of Destiny* (London: William Heinemann, Ltd., 1936). For an interdisciplinary approach to the problems of human behavior, see Harry F. Harlow and Clinton N. Woolsey (eds.) *Biological and Biochemical Bases of Behavior* (Madison: University of Wisconsin Press, 1958).

major factor in the individual case of law violation, we do not have enough knowledge to generalize about the importance of these conditions and their interaction with other factors in the causation of crime and delinquency.

## PERSONALITY

### The Nature of the Personality

In still another approach to the causation of crime and delinquency, many studies have sought to learn the relationship between these problems and the personality. Although the term "personality" has been defined in various ways, here we shall use it to refer to the totality of the characteristics of an individual. Thus it is the unique combination of heredity and environment brought to a focus in the individual. Functioning in terms of the satisfaction of its needs, the personality is developed, nourished, and organized or frustrated, dwarfed, distorted, and disorganized as its needs are satisfied or not.

These needs are predominantly organic at birth, but they grow increasingly social as the individual passes through childhood and adolescence into adulthood and becomes more and more involved in relationships with others. Among the important needs of every individual are those which W. I. Thomas called the wish for response, the wish for recognition, the wish for new experience, and the wish for security.[26] However, obstacles, both personal and environmental, interfere with the satisfaction of the personality's needs, thus causing personality conflicts and pain. Wisdom counsels that the individual face his conflicts realistically and resolve them on a factual basis, either by himself or with the help of others, but even if he fails to do this, changes in the situation may remove conflicts, as, for example, when surgery corrects a physical defect or an inheritance eliminates poverty.

Yet, many conflicts persist, and the individual strives to adjust to them by using such mechanisms as repression, daydreaming, regression, sublimation, rationalization, compensation, and projection. All of these are normal devices employed every day by normal people to reduce tensions and relieve anxiety, although often the individual is completely, or partially, unaware that this is happening. Used to excess, however, such mechanisms may twist the personality and sicken the mind, and even though they usually do not lead the individual into crime or delinquency, sometimes they do. Thus, through the fantasies of daydreaming the individual may drift from reality into the delusions of a psychosis, or a

[26] William I. Thomas, *The Unadjusted Girl* (Boston: Little, Brown and Co., 1923), pp. 1–40.

frustrated youth may compensate for his feelings of inferiority by committing armed robberies; but—and this is important—even though the mechanisms of adjustment send the individual into crime or delinquency, this does not necessarily mean that he has become mentally ill. In fact, usually the mental health of the individual is not affected at all.

## Personality Conflicts and Delinquency

For many years psychologists and psychiatrists have sought the answer to the problem of crime and delinquency in the conflicts of the personality. For example, in 1915, William Healy, a psychiatrist, after an analysis of the cases of 1,000 juvenile delinquents, concluded that personality conflict is the central element in the causation of conduct problems, including juvenile delinquency. According to Healy, the frustrations accompanying personality conflicts cause emotional distress. Delinquency, a form of substitute behavior, provides an escape from the conflict, removes the pain of frustration, and restores the equilibrium of the personality.[27] But why do some frustrated individuals commit crimes and acts of delinquency while others do not? In his book *New Light on Delinquency and Its Treatment*, published in 1936, Healy attempted to answer this question by explaining that nondelinquents are better able to find substitute satisfactions for their wishes in acceptable channels and so suffer from fewer emotional disturbances than delinquents, who, in order to relieve the cumulative pains of their frustrations, are driven into the channels of delinquency provided by the community.[28] John Dollard and his associates argued that the urge to aggression varies directly with the amount of frustration, provided that the anticipation or threat of punishment remains constant.[29] Many students of the problem, however, have not been satisfied with this explanation. They have insisted not only that Healy's bias misled him into finding what his theory of criminality prepared him to find, but also that such explanations as Healy's are at best only superficial and partial, providing little insight into how and why those who violate the law differ from those who do not.

"But what about personality traits?" you may ask. Does the mere possession of certain of the traits, for example, anxiety, aggressiveness, shyness, frankness, disagreeableness, and irritability, necessarily cause crime or delinquency? In an effort to throw some light on this question,

[27] William Healy, *The Individual Delinquent* (Boston: Little, Brown and Co., 1915).

[28] William Healy and Augusta F. Bronner, *New Light on Delinquency and Its Treatment* (New Haven: Yale University Press, 1936), pp. 1–13, 121, 122.

[29] John Dollard, Leonard Doob, *et al.*, *Frustration and Aggression* (New Haven: Yale University Press, 1939), p. 38. For another view of frustration, see Ellsworth Faris, "Some Results of Frustration," *Sociology and Social Research*, XXXI (November–December, 1946), 87–92.

Schuessler and Cressey made a survey of 113 studies in which personality tests had been used. Publishing the results of this survey in 1950, they concluded that "as often as not the evidence favored the view that personality traits are distributed in the criminal population in about the same way as in the general population." [30] Vold, however, said that this conclusion would have been more impressive if the survey had not thrown together indiscriminatively "a jumble of well, badly, and indifferently controlled studies, so that percentages computed on the total are of quite uncertain meaning." [31] Furthermore, the Gluecks took a somewhat different view of personality traits in their book *Unraveling Juvenile Delinquency*. What seems to be the chief conclusion that may be drawn from this study is that offenders differ from nonoffenders more in the interrelatedness of characteristics in their personalities than in the presence or absence of characteristics. [32]

Even so, in Vold's opinion, published in 1958, tests and scales had not yet provided a basis for "significant theoretical formulations about personality deviation and delinquency." [33] And in 1965, after a review of some recent studies that attempted to demonstrate differences in personality between delinquents and controls, Quay concluded that while some studies of heterogeneous groups of delinquents had produced "interesting and conceptually meaningful results," it appeared that greater rewards would come from "the detailed study of more homogeneous subgroups" as these might be isolated by statistical means. "Certainly," he added, "it is time to stop considering delinquents as anything like psychologically homogeneous." [34] More recently (1967), Waldo and Dinitz analyzed ninety-four research studies, made between 1950 and 1965, and came to this conclusion:

Although the results appear more positive than they did a few years ago, in terms of the number of studies showing differences between criminals and

[30] Karl F. Schuessler and Donald R. Cressey, "Personality Characteristics of Criminals," *American Journal of Sociology*, LV (March, 1950), 476–84.

[31] George B. Vold, *Theoretical Criminology* (New York: Oxford University Press, 1958), p. 127.

[32] Sheldon Glueck and Eleanor T. Glueck, *Unraveling Juvenile Delinquency* (New York: The Commonwealth Fund, 1950).

[33] Vold, pp. 127–38. See Starke R. Hathaway and Elio D. Monachesi, *Analyzing and Predicting Juvenile Delinquency with the MMPI* (Minneapolis: University of Minnesota Press, 1953); E. D. Monachesi "Some Personality Characteristics of Delinquents and Nondelinquents," *Journal of Criminal Law and Criminology*, XXXVIII (January–February, 1948), 487–500; *ibid.*, "Personality Characteristics of Institutionalized and Non-Institutionalized Male Delinquents," *Journal of Criminal Law and Criminology*, XLI (July–August, 1950), 167–79; Starke R. Hathaway and Elio D. Monachesi, "The Personalities of Pre-delinquent Boys," *Journal of Criminal Law, Criminology, and Police Science*, XLVIII (July–August, 1957), 149–63.

[34] Herbert C. Quay, *Juvenile Delinquency: Research and Theory* (New York: Van Nostrand Reinhold Co., Inc., 1965), pp. 139–66.

noncriminals, the findings are far from conclusive. The conflict over the role of personality in criminality has not been resolved. The results of this review indicate that "personality" cannot be dismissed readily, as it is by many sociologists, and its etiologic role cannot be assumed casually, as it is by many psychiatrists and psychologists.[35]

Cressey, basing his belief on the study which he and Schuessler published in 1950, and to which we have referred above, stated that "the explanation of criminal behavior must be sought in something else than personality traits." [36] What seems to be the sounder view, however, is that personality traits alone do not cause crime or delinquency—although they cannot be disregarded—that in the analysis of causation, they must be seen in their functional relationship with one another and with many other factors, and that emotional disturbances and personality traits may largely result from criminal or delinquent behavior as well as contribute to its causation. In any event, as the individual's personality develops, he assimilates the values of the culture in which he functions; and although he inevitably suffers from personality conflicts, he tends to become law-abiding. Nevertheless, the personality, like the society in which it functions, is never completely organized, containing, as it always does, inconsistent and inharmonious elements.[37]

## THE SELF

The term "personality needs" has been severely criticized, especially by sociologists. Critics dislike it, because they believe that it puts too much stress on the biological factors, that most needs spring entirely from social relationships, and that since a need cannot be directly perceived, any explanation of it readily lends itself to circular reasoning—the need being inferred from the act and then used to explain the act. Many social scientists who object to the term "personality needs" prefer the concept "self," because it emphasizes the social and cultural factors and the rationality and purposiveness of human behavior. How, then, should we define this concept? Although different meanings have been given to it, "self" is often defined as that organization of qualities which the person attributes to himself.

The theory regarding the nature and development of the self has

[35] Gordon P. Waldo and Simon Dinitz, "Personality Attributes of the Criminal: An Analysis of Research Studies, 1950–65," *Journal of Research in Crime and Delinquency*, IV (July, 1967), 185–202.

[36] Edwin H. Sutherland and Donald R. Cressey, *Principles of Criminology* (Philadelphia: J. B. Lippincott Co., 1955), p. 128.

[37] For a discussion of recent development in psychological theory, see Melvin H. Marx (ed.), *Theories in Contemporary Psychology* (New York: The Macmillan Co., 1963).

appeared in various forms. One of the most important of these, symbolic interaction theory,[38] has been mentioned already. To a great extent, it has grown out of the writings of such scholars as James, Baldwin, Cooley, Mead, Thomas, Faris, Dewey, Blumer, and Young. According to this theory, the self originates and develops in the process of socialization. Through the use of language and gestures, the person engages in symbolic interaction, and coming to see himself as others see him, he learns what is expected of him in various situations. Thus, since he tends to fashion his behavior in accordance with the group's expectations, the character of the group and its culture largely determine the development of the self, and what a person thinks of himself—his self conception—becomes the important factor in the causation of his behavior, whether it be law-abiding or law-violating.

However, the self never becomes completely organized, and, like the personality, always contains inconsistent and inharmonious elements. Nevertheless, the individual tends to become the kind of person he conceives himself to be, and seeking to defend his self image against the personal and environmental conflicts that threaten it, he resorts to various mechanisms of adjustment, similar to those already described above in the section on the personality. Symbolic interaction theorists explain that these mechanisms are more rational and conscious than those used in the functioning of the personality, but, even so, the possible results with respect to law violation and mental health are about the same.

The symbolic interaction theory has found support among many sociologists and social psychologists, but, despite this, critics have vigorously attacked it with strong arguments. Human behavior, these critics contend, is not entirely conscious. In fact, the unconscious exercises considerable influence, and this influence the theory largely ignores. Furthermore, we have no way of measuring anything so subtle, changing, and elusive as the self appears to be. Mechanisms of adjustment and the passage of time tend to blur and distort man's memory, perception, and understanding, and even if the person knows a great deal about himself, he may be unable or unwilling to relate this to others.

Moreover, this theory tells us very little about the learning process, apparently being satisfied with saying that the person plays roles and internalizes the expectations of the group—not a very profound observation. And, say the critics, the flimsiness of the theory becomes even more obvious when the question of motivation is raised. To argue that roles

[38] Another important form of the self theory has been developed by Carl Rogers, who puts more stress on the individual and his psychology than do the symbolic interaction theorists. See Carl Rogers, *Client-Centered Therapy: Its Current Practice, Implications, and Theory* (Boston: Houghton Mifflin Co., 1951).

are motives, as the theory does, without being able to explain how and why this is so, is to take refuge in this kind of circular reasoning: a person acts the way he does, because he has learned to play certain roles, and this we know, because of the way he acts. Besides, we should not neglect the study of the value structure of society, in terms of which the self must function. But this may well happen if we become preoccupied with the concept "self"—and this seems to be the tendency among many sociologists.

What is even more serious, however, is that the theory overlooks the fact that the individual has a reality apart from the group. Indeed, it strips man of his creative powers and reduces him to a mere shadowy reflection of the group's specifications. Thus, conclude the critics, the symbolic interaction theory, like all forms of self theory, in its search for clearcut simplicity, slips into the error of reductionism. By reducing the explanation to the concept "self," it extends this concept too far and neglects or excludes other important considerations.[39]

## CHARACTER

The concept "character" can provide us with a more complete view of human behavior than either personality or self. Even so, like them, character has been given various meanings, some writers making it almost synonymous with personality. Here, however, it is defined as the aggregate of the individual's distinctive qualities expressed and measured in terms of the values of his culture.

But more specifically, how does it differ from personality and self? Heredity, social experience, and culture—all interweave in the making of character; but, in addition, we must see it as a unique combination of values—what is objective in culture becoming subjective in character. Indeed, morality is of the essence of character, which, accordingly, is

[39] For further reading on the subject, see Charles Horton Cooley, *Human Nature and the Social Order* (New York: Charles Scribner's Sons, 1902); George H. Mead, *Mind, Self and Society* (Chicago: University of Chicago Press, 1934); C. Addison Hickman and Manford H. Kuhn, *Individuals, Groups and Economic Behavior* (New York: The Dryden Press, 1956), pp. 3–48, 80–100; Tamotsu Shibutani, *Society and Personality: An Interactional Approach to Social Psychology* (Englewood Cliffs, N.J.: Prentice Hall, Inc., 1961), pp. 247, 248, 532, 533; *Psychology: A Study of a Science*, "Sensory, Perceptual and Physiological Formulations," ed. Sigmund Koch (New York: McGraw-Hill Book Co., Inc., 1959), Vol. I; Calvin S. Hall and Gardner Lindzey, *Theories of Personality* (New York: John Wiley and Sons, Inc., 1957), pp. 370–75; Theodore R. Sarbin, "Role Theory," *Handbook of Social Psychology*, ed. Gardner Lindzey (Cambridge, Mass.: Addison-Wesley Publishing Co., Inc., 1954), Vol. I, pp. 223–58; Dennis H. Wrong, "The Oversocialized Conception of Man in Modern Sociology," *American Sociological Review*, XXVI (April, 1961), 183–93; *Society and Self*, ed. Bartlett H. Stoodley (New York: The Free Press, 1962); *Current Perspectives in Social Psychology*, eds. E. P. Hollander and Raymond G. Hunt (New York: Oxford University Press, 1963).

described as good or bad. More important than this, however, is what character tells us about the nature of man. Personality and self readily lend themselves to an interpretation that turns the individual into a mechanical man, the first activating him by psychological forces, the second, by social ones. Character, on the other hand, fully recognizes the creative and self-directing powers of man. In its view, he has a reality apart from the group.

Never just a creature of his environment, he is able to formulate his own standards and rules and to use them to initiate, plan, and control; his adaptation is always creative. Character thus pictures man as having the power to weave the environmental and personal influences in his life into a choice and holds him responsible for his choice. He need not transfer his conscience to an "expert" to find relief from his problems, for he has the capacity to carry his griefs and sorrows and to handle the stigmas and the penalties from which he may suffer and to use them as a factual basis for building a better life.

Character development begins at an early age, the influence of the home being crucial during the formative years. Gradually, through his social relationships, the individual learns the values and norms of his culture and acquires a range of favorable and unfavorable attitudes toward them. In this way, each individual develops not only his own distinctive system of values but also a conscience, that is, a consciousness of the moral goodness or badness of his thoughts, character, and conduct, together with a sense of duty to be good and to do right. Nevertheless, in dealing with his moral problems, everyone must struggle with the conflicts and inconsistencies in his character and with other personal and environmental obstacles that interfere with his being a moral person as defined by the standards of his culture. Victory in this struggle strengthens the character; yielding to temptation, on the other hand, may cause regret, remorse, personal disorganization, and sometimes even crime or delinquency. Obviously, therefore, every society must concern itself with the character development of its members and endeavor to direct it to the support of law and order.

## MENTAL ABNORMALITIES

Mental deficiency, sometimes called feeblemindedness or *amentia*, may be defined as a state of mental retardation or incomplete development, existing from birth or early infancy, as a result of which the person is unable to meet the social expectation of his society.[40] On the

---

[40] See A. F. Tredgold, *Mental Deficiency* (New York: William Wood and Co., 1915), p. 8; *Dictionary of Sociology* (New York: The Philosophical Library, 1944), p. 191.

basis of mental age and intelligence quotient, mental deficiency has been divided into idiocy, imbecility, and moronity. Mental age is a person's level of performance as measured by that expected of persons at various chronological ages. The intelligence quotient of a person is derived by dividing his mental age by his chronological age and multiplying by 100 (to remove decimal places). However, the maximum chronological age used in obtaining the intelligence quotient is set at about 14 to 16, since the evidence indicates that general intelligence tends to reach maturity at about these ages. Usually, persons with an intelligence quotient of less than 70 have been classified as mentally deficient, but the intelligence quotients for the three levels of mental deficiency have varied somewhat in different classifications. Within recent years, however, there has been a tendency to classify mental deficiency as severe (I.Q. below 50), moderate (I.Q. 50–70), and mild (I.Q. 70–85), and the use of the term "mental age" has been declining.

Since the idiot and the imbecile are easily recognizable and usually under such care and supervision as to prevent them from getting into any trouble, the interest of the criminologist is focused chiefly on the moron, who often has a normal appearance and blends imperceptibly into the borderline groups. But apparently even he does not offer a major threat to society, for the available evidence—although admittedly inadequate—indicates that his offenses tend to be of a minor nature. Often they are the result of his being exploited by more intelligent companions.

Although early studies, for example, those by Henry H. Goddard,[41] led to the conclusion that feeblemindedness was the major cause of crime and delinquency, the work of Murchison, Tulchin, Zeleny, and others has helped to change this point of view.[42] The evidence, which is still far from complete, now seems to support the belief that only a small proportion of the feebleminded are delinquent or criminal, and that offenders and the general population have about the same distribution of intelligence levels.[43] And the relative impact of other conditions on the delinquent conduct of the mentally deficient has not been systematically explored. Kennedy, for example, found that a group of morons had

[41] Henry H. Goddard, *Human Efficiency and Levels of Intelligence* (Princeton, N.J.: Princeton University Press, 1920).

[42] Carl Murchison, *Criminal Intelligence* (Worcester, Mass.: Clark University, 1926); L. D. Zeleny, "Feeble-mindedness and Criminal Conduct," *American Journal of Sociology*, XXXVIII (January, 1933), 564–76; Simon H. Tulchin, *Intelligence and Crime: A Study of Penitentiary and Reformatory Offenders* (Chicago: University of Chicago Press, 1939).

[43] E. O. Lewis, "Mental Deficiency and Criminal Behavior," in *Mental Abnormality and Crime*, eds. L. Radzinowicz and J. W. C. Turner (English Studies in Criminal Science [London: Macmillan and Co., Ltd., 1949]), Vol. II, pp. 93–104; Richard L. Masland, Seymour B. Sarason, Thomas Gladwin, *Mental Subnormality* (New York: Basic Books, Inc., 1958).

higher arrest and recidivism rates than a group of nonmorons. However, the family members of the morons, also, had a higher arrest rate than that of the nonmorons, and consequently, the family associations of the morons may have been more influential than their low-grade intelligence in giving them the higher arrest rate.[44]

However, the problem of mental deficiency is a complex one, and this must be kept in mind in any analysis of the relationship between it and crime and delinquency. In the first place, the various levels of mental deficiency blend into one another, and no sharp line divides mental deficiency from normal intelligence. Furthermore, mentally deficient persons may suffer also from some mental disease or disorder; intelligence tests cannot separate hereditary influences from those of the environment; and intelligence quotients may vary under the influence of certain environmental changes, for example, the improvement of the nutrition of the individual. Thus, at present any conclusion regarding mental deficiency must be highly tentative.

Similar difficulties confront the investigator in the field of mental disease. In fact, there is considerable disagreement among psychiatrists regarding the nature of the mental diseases, their causes and classification, and the methods of diagnosis. Besides, the terminology in psychiatry is not consistent, the mental disorders are not clearly defined entities, and much of the content of psychiatry cannot be scientifically substantiated.

Nevertheless, mental disease, or mental disorder, may be defined as a state of mental unbalance or derangement which prevents a person from assuming responsibility for his own support or causes him to be a positive menace to the health and safety of the community.[45] Unlike mental deficiency, it does not imply a lack, retardation, or incompleteness of mental development, but rather refers to a mind that has developed normally, almost always to maturity, but has become disordered or deranged. It is possible, however, for a mentally deficient person to become mentally diseased, and for mentally diseased persons to deteriorate from normal intelligence to moronity.

## Psychoses

The two major types of mental disease are the psychoses and the psychoneuroses or neuroses. The psychoses, the most severe disturbances of the personality, cause the person to lose contact, completely or partially, with the world of reality and require medical or even special insti-

---

[44] See Ruby Jo Reeves Kennedy, *The Social Adjustment of Morons in a Connecticut City* (Hartford: Governor's Commission to Study the Human Resources of the State of Connecticut, 1948).

[45] *Dictionary of Sociology*, p. 191.

tutional care. They may be divided into those caused, or associated with, an impairment of the brain and those without clearly defined structural change in the brain, which are often called "functional psychoses." Among the most common psychoses of the former type are psychosis with epilepsy, psychosis with syphilis, psychoses with cerebral arteriosclerosis, and toxic psychoses. Important among those of the latter type are schizophrenia, manic-depressive psychosis, and paranoia. Schizophrenia, often called dementia praecox, because it usually makes its appearance during youth or early adulthood, is characterized chiefly by a gradual withdrawal into a world of fantasy and a growing incoherence of thought and speech, ending in the disintegration of the personality. The manic-depressive psychosis produces alternating periods of depression or melancholia and periods of mental exaltation or mania. On the other hand, paranoia, a rare type of psychosis, brings delusions of grandeur and persecution.

## Neuroses

The psychoneuroses, or neuroses, tend to make the person less efficient socially and personally but usually do not necessitate special care or institutionalization. Until recent years, the most widely recognized classification of psychoneuroses consisted of the three categories of neurasthenia, psychasthenia, and hysteria, but these are now usually broken down into a number of subdivisions. Generally believed to be functional, that is, caused by emotional and mental conflicts, rather than organic, in origin, these diseases produce various symptoms, such as exaggerated feelings of fatigue, pronounced sensitiveness to noises, anxieties, morbid fears, obsessions, compulsions, the loss of some faculty, and the paralysis of some muscles. The neurotic symptom is a compromise of some sort between unexpressed thoughts and the repressive forces of the personality, especially the conscience. Since the symptom does not fully satisfy the unexpressed thoughts, the conflict persists, tending to manifest itself over and over again in about the same way.

In general, mental diseases are disorders of maturity, although sometimes early manifestations of these conditions can be detected during childhood and adolescence. This often happens, for example, in the hebephrenic form of schizophrenia, which is marked especially by silliness and incongruity of actions. But how many children do suffer from mental disease? Unfortunately, we cannot answer this question. In fact, we do not know how many persons are mentally diseased or how many mentally diseased persons are delinquent or criminal.

Nevertheless, we do know this: Neither mental deficiency nor mental disease inevitably causes crime or delinquency. Some persons who suffer from mental abnormalities do violate the law, but many others do not; and the great majority of delinquents and criminals, like the great majority of law-abiding persons, can be classified as normal. This is not to say that a mental abnormality may not be a factor in criminal or delinquent behavior—even the major one in a particular case. But, like all the other personal factors, mental abnormalities must be seen in their interaction with all other factors in the causation of human behavior, whether it be law-abiding or law-violating.[46]

[46] Angus Macniven, "Psychoses and Criminal Responsibility," *Mental Abnormality and Crime*, pp. 8, 9, 40–49; Kimball Young, *Personality and Problems of Adjustment* (New York: Appleton-Century-Crofts, Inc., 1940), pp. 708–10; American Psychiatric Association, *Diagnostic and Statistical Manual of Mental Disorders* (Washington, D.C.: American Psychiatric Association, 1968); Ruth L. Munroe, *Schools of Psychiatric Thought* (New York: The Dryden Press, 1955), pp. 82–84; Arthur Burton and Robert E. Harris (eds.) *Case Histories in Clinical and Abnormal Psychology* (New York: Harper and Row, 1947), pp. 307–80; Edward A. Strecker, *Fundamentals of Psychiatry* (Philadelphia: J. B. Lippincott Co., 1943), pp. 91–165; Hulsey Cason, "The Psychopath and the Psychopathic," *Journal of Criminal Psychopathology*, IV (January, 1943), 522–27; Harrison G. Gough, "A Sociological Theory of Psychopathy," *American Journal of Sociology*, LIII (March, 1948), 359–66; Seymour L. Halleck, *Psychiatry and the Dilemmas of Crime* (New York: Harper and Row, 1967).

# 7

# The Home and the Family

## THE FUNCTIONS OF THE FAMILY

How would you define anything so complex, so enduring, so intimate, and yet so pervasive as the family? Many definitions have been offered, but this short one, which was used over thirty years ago by MacIver, is quite suitable for our purposes: "The family is a group defined by a sex relationship sufficiently precise and enduring to provide for the procreation and upbringing of children." [1]

As such a group, the family functions to serve the interests of society, the husband and wife, and the children. For society, it supplies the only certified agency of propagation and an effective source for the transmission and preservation of culture. For the husband and wife, it regulates sex, provides companionship, enlarges experience, and gives social and economic security. For the children, it furnishes protection, teaches survival and social techniques, inculcates social values, and supplies a haven for relief from the conflict and competition of the community. Thus the family has biological, affectional, economic, recreational, religious, educational, and protective functions. [2] These functions, however, are greatly affected by the culture in which they operate. In other words, we must see the family not only as a group but also as a social institution.

## THE FAMILY AS A SOCIAL INSTITUTION

All social institutions have the same essential features. As Sumner explained many years ago, each social institution has a concept and a

[1] Robert M. MacIver, *Society: Its Structure and Changes* (New York: Ray Long and Richard R. Smith, Inc., 1932), p. 112.

[2] M. F. Nimkoff, *The Family* (New York: Houghton Mifflin Co., 1934), pp. 47–77; Ernest R. Groves, *The American Family* (Philadelphia: J. B. Lippincott Co., 1934), pp. 3–5; Ray E. Baber, *Marriage and the Family* (New York: McGraw-Hill Book Co., Inc., 1939), pp. 3–6.

structure.[3]  Here "concept" refers to the purposes and functions of the institution; "structure," to the personnel, equipment, and organization by which the purposes are achieved.  Like other social institutions, the family originated to meet a persistent human need—in its case, the procreation and rearing of children—and with other institutions, and the folkways and mores, it functions in an interdependent relationship in the process of social change.  Again like other institutions, the family carries with it the force of authority and has a structure in order to achieve its purposes.  Thus it has its own distinctive personnel composed of the parents, usually one of each sex, children, and sometimes other related persons; its equipment, or property, sometimes held in common with other families, and its organization, which may be patriarchal, matriarchal, or equalitarian.

However, no society or community is ever without social change, and its influence is felt in all parts of culture, including the family.  It is to the effects of social change on the American family that we shall now direct our attention.

## THE EARLY AMERICAN FAMILY

The form of the American family which prevailed during the colonial period changed only gradually until almost the twentieth century.  Essentially patriarchal, it rested, as Bossard has said, upon three bases.[4]  The first of these was the economic and social importance of the home, which produced much of the food and clothing of the members of the family and tended to be the center of their religious, educational, and recreational activities.  The second basis was the dominance of the male.  The husband and father was the only person recognized by the law, and in him were vested almost all rights over other members of the family and its property.  Moreover, the customs and traditions of the people and the conditions of the country strongly supported his position of authority. The third basis was the dependence of the individual upon the family. In fact, the individual had virtually no status except as a member of a family group.  This was especially true of the woman, since there were few opportunities for her outside of the home.  She was expected to marry at an early age and devote herself to domestic duties.  As one would expect in a society having this form of the family, the birth rate was high, the supervision and discipline of children were strict, and

[3] William Graham Sumner, *Folkways* (New York: Dover Publications, Inc., 1959), pp. 53–55.

[4] James H. S. Bossard, *Social Change and Social Problems* (New York: Harper and Row, 1938), pp. 595–98. See also Willystine Goodsell, *A History of Marriage and the Family* (New York: The Macmillan Co., 1939), 355–425; Groves, pp. 78–96.

separation, desertion, and divorce were generally disapproved. All this added up to one result: The family was an important agency of social control.

## CHANGES IN THE AMERICAN FAMILY

Rapid and widespread social changes, however, have almost completely transformed the American family. Under the impact of industrial development, economic production has been largely transferred from the home to the factory and the workshop, and mechanization has greatly reduced the labor involved in what remains. In fact, as Bossard has explained, for the first time in many centuries, we are experimenting with a form of the family that is not held together by the coercive bonds of a common economic enterprise.[5]

Along with our great industrial development, and interrelated with it, have come many other changes, such as extensive urbanization, unprecedented migrations and mobility of populations, decline of rural life, acceleration of transportation and communication, tremendous exploitation of natural resources, stupendous accumulation of inventions and discoveries, amazing growth of economic specialization and interdependence, and great expansion of public education, recreation, welfare, and health programs. All of these, also, have left a deep mark upon the American family. The large family unit, composed of various relatives living close together, sometimes in a single house, and providing mutual aid, comfort, and protection, has almost entirely disappeared in most sections of the country. In fact, many families have only tenuous ties with relatives, and the grown child often lives far from his parents and conducts his affairs independently of them. Furthermore, specialized organizations and agencies now exert great influence in the education, training, care, guidance, and protection of children; and, although this may create new opportunities for children, it often brings them into sharp conflict with parents who have different views and standards. And the family situation is further complicated by the fact that the father's employment keeps him away from the home for many hours during the week and forces the mother to assume most of the responsibilities in the management of the home at the very time when the family sorely needs the balanced leadership which only two parents can provide. Indeed, in an increasing number of homes, the mother, also, is employed and the care and training of children are often entrusted to babysitters and nurseries. Thus, although the American family has more material wealth than ever before,

---

[5] Bossard, p. 599. See also J. P. Lichtenberger, *Divorce* (New York: McGraw-Hill Book Co., Inc., 1931), p. 278.

parents are finding it increasingly difficult to give constructive guidance and protection to their children.

Clearly, then, the home is no longer the sole economic and social center of community life, the male has been deprived of much of his power and authority, and the individual has been freed from many of his family bonds and obligations.[6] The trend in the American family, therefore, has been from patriarchy to equalitarianism, from "familism" to individualism, from authoritarianism to democracy. Although, of course, procreation remains a primary function of the family, affection and companionship now play a much greater role than ever before.

In fact, in a society that has become more and more competitive, impersonal, and industrialized, the home offers one of the few remaining places where the need for intimate and emotionally comforting experiences can be satisfied. Similar demands are being made on other functions of the family. While economic production has largely passed from the home, its importance as a consumption unit has greatly increased. Household management and domestic science, therefore, are now firmly fixed in the scheme of family affairs. Furthermore, for the protection of the family, keen judgment, wise counsel, and intelligent leadership, rather than physical strength and brute force, are required, so that the members may be directed to the opportunities and specialized services open to them in the community. And so it is also with the educational, religious, and recreational functions of the family, where, to an increasing extent, the importance of the home rests, not on its performance of the ultimate services, but instead on its ability to counsel, guide, manage, select, and bring its members into touch with the best that the community has to offer.[7]

Thus the family has not lost its functions, it is just changing the way in which they are used; and although it has declined as an agency of social control, it remains society's best defense against the generation of lawless tendencies. This does not mean, of course, that the family can exert its influence independently of other institutions. On the contrary, it is functionally related to them and is affected by, and contributes to, their organization or disorganization. Nevertheless, the family system still constitutes the very foundation of our society. In fact, if it should

[6] Nimkoff, pp. 191–220; Groves, pp. 97–163; Bossard, pp. 598–613.

[7] Meyer F. Nimkoff, *Marriage and the Family* (Boston: Houghton Mifflin Co., 1947), pp. 78–82; James H. S. Bossard and Eleanor Stoker Boll, *The Sociology of Child Development* (New York: Harper and Row, 1966), pp. 57–102, 192–231, 289–361; Clifford Kirkpatrick, *The Family as Process and Institution* (New York: The Ronald Press Co., 1963), pp. 101–107; William M. Kephart, *The Family, Society, and the Individual* (Boston: Houghton Mifflin Co., 1961), pp. 232–64; William F. Ogburn and Meyer F. Nimkoff, *Technology and the Changing Family* (Boston: Houghton Mifflin Co., 1955), pp. 53–57, 167–213.

disintegrate, all the public funds that might be spent and all the social and welfare services that might be offered would be to no avail. We should, therefore, recognize that forces both within and without the American family have produced serious strains and tensions in it, breaking down relationships and pushing it toward disorganization.

Every society, if it is to survive, must establish and preserve rules and standards (social norms) for the guidance and regulation of its members. According to the norms of family life in the United States, the normal home in our country appears to have these characteristics:

1. Structural completeness (presence of both parents in the home).
2. Functional adequacy (interaction of members with a minimum of friction and frustration).
3. Physical and psychological normality (no chronic invalid or mentally deficient person in the home).
4. Racial homogeneity (father, mother, and children of the same race).
5. Cultural and moral conformity (the same language, customs and morality in the home as in the surrounding social world).
6. Economic security (income adequate to maintain physical and mental health).[8]

## DEVIANT HOMES

To the extent that a home departs from what is considered normal, it is a deviant home and a center of deviation pressures and thus may contribute to crime and delinquency. In other words, although it does not make crime and delinquency inevitable, it does increase the possibility of such behavior. For the purposes of discussion, deviant homes may be classified into these four major types:

1. The broken home.
2. The functionally inadequate home.
3. The socially, morally, or culturally abnormal home.
4. The economically insecure home.

### The Broken Home

In the monogamous family, the relatively permanent union of a father and a mother enables both to play important parts in the rearing of children. To this process, the father brings a male, the mother a female, point of view, and thus each supplements and complements the other

---

[8] Lowell Juilliard Carr, *Delinquency Control* (New York: Harper and Row, 1950), pp. 166–68.

in the functioning of the family. Consequently, when the home is broken —by the loss of one parent, because of death, divorce, separation, desertion, or commitment to an institution—there is a serious interference with the normal processes of family life. Usually the children suffer the most as a result of this. Often their bonds of loyalty and affection are cruelly torn apart, and they are forced into new psychological and social adjustments. Since it is assumed that the presence of both parents is essential to the development of well-balanced and socially adjusted children, broken homes are generally believed to contribute disproportionately to crime and delinquency.

In fact, many children from broken homes find their way into the juvenile court and thus seem to lend support to this belief. Take the case of Jerry, for example. Jerry, a tall, blonde, athletic youth of sixteen, was brought to court on a charge of car theft. He was an only child and lived with his mother in a large brick home in an upper-class neighborhood, where the family was liked and respected by many friends and acquaintances. The father had deserted the family shortly after Jerry was born, and the mother soon obtained a divorce. She never remarried, and they lived well on the income of a large estate, which the mother had inherited from her father. The pride and joy of his mother, pampered and indulged, he became wild and irresponsible, continually seeking new excitement and adventure. When asked what he was trying to prove, he would always say, "A man has to prove that he is a man."

Do we have any statistics on the number of juveniles who, like Jerry, come from broken homes? Yes, we do, although the figures are neither complete nor conclusive. However, many juvenile court reports and investigations based on them show that from about 30 to 60 per cent of delinquents come from broken homes, and that such homes, therefore, seem to constitute a serious handicap for children.[9]

But, one must ask, what about children who do not become delinquent? Do many of them come from broken homes? And should we not know this before we can properly interpret these reports and studies? Obviously, this line of questioning must be answered, but the efforts to do this have not brought uniform results. Some studies have found that about twice as many delinquents as nondelinquents come from broken homes and thus indicated that it should be considered an important factor

[9] See, for example, Robert G. Caldwell, *Criminology* (New York: The Ronald Press Co., 1965), pp. 257–61; Donald R. Peterson and Wesley C. Becker, "Family Interaction and Delinquency," *Juvenile Delinquency: Research and Theory*, ed. Herbert C. Quay (Princeton, N.J.: Van Nostrand Reinhold Co., Inc., 1965), pp. 68–70; Charles J. Browning, "Differential Impact of Family Disorganization on Male Adolescents," *Social Problems*, VIII (Summer, 1960), 37–44; Walter L. Slocum and Carol L. Stone, "Family Culture Patterns and Delinquent-Type Behavior," *Marriage and Family Living*, XXV (May, 1963), 202–08.

in the causation of delinquency.[10]   Other studies, however, have found that this type of home of itself is relatively unimportant in causing delinquency.[11]

Nevertheless, the majority of court reports and studies show that more delinquents than nondelinquents come from broken homes, and that this is true even when such factors as age and ethnic background are taken into account.   Shulman, in referring to this, says that although it does not necessarily prove that the broken home causes delinquency, it does suggest this.[12]   However, the relationship between the broken home and delinquency now appears to be much more complex than it was formerly assumed to be.   Other factors, such as age, sex, social class, offense, and race, also, must be taken into consideration.

In a study of male and female broken home rates, Weeks, while finding a positive relationship between delinquency and the broken home, showed that the incidence of such homes varied by sex and offense. Broken homes were more frequent among girls and cases involving ungovernability, running away, and truancy than among boys and cases involving property offenses, traffic violations, and misdemeanors.[13]   And Nye found less delinquent behavior in happy broken homes than in unhappy ones.[14]

Caldwell, in calling attention to this, said:

What appears to be far more important as a cause of delinquency, regardless of whether the home is broken or not, is the relationship existing among the members of the family—the meaning of the home to them and their reactions to what the community thinks of it, to what happens in it, and to the behavior of one another.   In other words, here as elsewhere, causation must be seen as a functional relationship in which many factors interact in a changing situation. The concept "broken home" is too broad to enable us to

---

[10] See, for example, E. H. Shideler, "Family Disintegration and the Delinquent Boy in the United States," *Journal of Criminal Law and Criminology*, VIII (January, 1918), 709–32; Cyril Burt, *The Young Delinquent* (New York: Appleton-Century-Crofts, Inc., 1925), pp. 60–98; Maud A. Merrill, *Problems of Child Delinquency* (New York: Houghton Mifflin Co., 1947), pp. 66, 67.

[11] See, for example, Clifford R. Shaw and Henry D. McKay, *Social Factors in Juvenile Delinquency*, Report No. 13, Vol. II, of the reports of the National Commission on Law Observance and Enforcement (Washington, D.C.: Government Printing Office, 1931), pp. 261–84; Baruch Silverman, "The Behavior of Children from Broken Homes," *American Journal of Orthopsychiatry*, V (January, 1935), 11–18; N. D. M. Hirsch, *Dynamic Causes of Juvenile Crime* (Cambridge, Mass.: Sci-art Publishers, 1937); Marian Campbell, "The Effect of the Broken Home upon the Child in School," *Journal of Educational Sociology*, V (January, 1932), 274–81.

[12] Harry Manuel Shulman, "The Family and Juvenile Delinquency," *The Annals of the American Academy of Political and Social Science*, CCLXI (January, 1949), 26.

[13] H. Ashley Weeks, "Male and Female Broken Home Rates by Type of Delinquency," *American Sociological Review*, V (August, 1940), 601–9.

[14] See F. Ivan Nye, *Family Relationships and Delinquent Behavior* (New York: John Wiley and Sons, Inc., 1958), p. 51.

do this. The way that the home is broken and the reaction of the members of the family to the break must be considered. The death of a father may consolidate the remaining members of a family as nothing else could, while a divorce might have shattered their relationship forever; and a separation of parents may eliminate tensions that are contributing to crime and delinquency.[15]

## The Functionally Inadequate Home

Dennis was referred to the juvenile court by the police on a charge of breaking and entering. At the time of his appearance in court he was sixteen years old and lived with his parents and three brothers in a middle-class neighborhood. The youngest of the children and definitely inferior to his brothers in mental and athletic ability, Dennis was subjected to much joking and teasing in the home, which made him angry and sometimes caused him to cry. The father had lost interest in the mother and paid little attention to what went on in the home, letting the mother assume the entire responsibility for handling the family's affairs.

However, he was proud of the athletic prowess of his three older sons but ashamed of Denny's failures, often goading his youngest son into furious outbursts of temper and provoking violent exchanges of accusations and abuse. On such occasions the brothers did not hesitate to enter the fight, apparently with little concern over the outcome. The mother, however, always rushed to Dennis's defense and protected him from his father and brothers. In fact, she was overprotective, and her pampering and indulgence of Denny aroused jealousy and resentment in his brothers and disgust and anger in the father. But for Dennis his mother's actions were disastrous, interfering with his emotional development and keeping him dependent upon her.

It is evident that there was a great deal of friction and frustration in Dennis's home, and so it can be said to have been functionally inadequate. This type of home is filled with discord and dissension between the parents, favoritism, parental rejection of children, sibling rivalry, emotional insecurity, self-pity, jealousy, domination, pampering, neglect, or any of the other conditions that distort, impoverish, or disorganize the personalities of children. Many studies and clinical experience have shown that the functionally inadequate home contributes to delin-

[15] Caldwell, *op. cit.*, p. 261. See, also, Charles W. Coulter, "Family Disorganization as a Causal Factor in Delinquency and Crime," *Federal Probation*, XII (September, 1948), 14, 15; Sheldon and Eleanor Glueck, *Family Environment and Delinquency* (Boston: Houghton Mifflin Co., 1962), pp. 122–29; Theodore N. Ferdinand, "The Offense Patterns and Family Structures of Urban, Village, and Rural Delinquents," *Journal of Criminal Law, Criminology, and Police Science*, LV (March, 1964), 86–93; William W. Wattenberg and Frank Saunders, "Sex Differences Among Juvenile Offenders," *Sociology and Social Research*, XXXIX (September-October, 1954), 24–31.

quency.[16]  Suffering from conflict and frustration, the child may find relief in acts of delinquency, or fleeing from a home taut with friction, he may seek comfort in the companionship of a delinquent gang. Lack of love and affection and faulty discipline, especially when it is highly permissive, excessively severe or grossly inconsistent, appear to be particularly detrimental to the sound development of the child, leaving him sometimes cruel and aggressive, sometimes insecure, confused, and anxious, and always unprepared to cope with life's problems and disappointments.

In referring to the effects of the functionally inadequate home, Wood and Waite state that the subtler influences of personality conflicts in families are probably more destructive of the social adjustment of children than the broken home.[17]  Peterson and Becker, after an analysis of numerous studies, conclude that "the importance of parental affection, and the serious consequences of its lack, cannot be denied."  They then add:

The development of stable behavior tendencies depends on the intensity and consistency with which emotionally effective rewards and punishments are administered.  Excessively harsh treatment, especially if unaccompanied by generally affectionate acceptance, ordinarily arouses resentment, and this reduces the effectiveness of discipline.  Excessive leniency is tantamount to neglect.[18]

[16] See, for example, Carl R. Rogers, *The Clinical Treatment of the Problem Child* (Boston: Houghton Mifflin Co., 1939), pp. 179–81; Helen Witmer and Students, "The Outcome of Treatment in a Child Guidance Clinic," *Smith College Studies in Social Work*, III (June, 1933), 365–71; William Healy and Augusta F. Bronner, *New Light on Delinquency and Its Treatment* (New Haven: Yale University Press, 1936), pp. 47–52, 128–30; E. M. Bushong, "Family Astrangement and Juvenile Delinquency," *Social Forces*, V (September, 1926), 79–83; Austin L. Porterfield, "Delinquency and Its Outcome in Court and College," *American Journal of Sociology*, XLIX (November, 1943), 199–208; August Aichhorn, *Wayward Youth* (New York: The Viking Press, 1951); Raymond A. Mulligan, "Family Relationships and Juvenile Delinquency," *Pacific Sociological Review*, I (Spring, 1958), 40.

[17] Arthur Evans Wood and John Barker Waite, *Crime and Its Treatment* (New York: American Book Co., 1941), p. 183.  See also William Healy, "The Psychiatrist Looks at Delinquency and Crime," *The Annals of the American Academy of Political and Social Science*, CCXVII (September, 1941), 70.

[18] Peterson and Becker, pp. 93, 94.  See also Joan and William McCord, "The Effects of Parental Role Model on Criminality," *Journal of Social Issues*, XIV (1958), No. 3, 66–75; Robert Everett Stanfield, "The Interaction of Family Variable and Gang Variables in the Aetiology of Delinquency," *Social Problems*, XIII (Spring, 1966), 411–17; R. G. Andry, "Faulty Paternal and Maternal-Child Relationships, Affection, and Delinquency," *British Journal of Delinquency*, VIII (July, 1957), 34–48; *ibid.*, "Parental Affection, and Delinquency," *The Sociology of Crime and Delinquency*, eds. Marvin E. Wolfgang, Leonard Savitz, and Norman Johnston (New York: John Wiley and Sons, 1962), pp. 342–52; John Bowlby, Mary Ainsworth, Mary Boston, and Dina Rosenbluth, "The Effects of Mother-Child Separation: A Follow-Up Study," *British Journal of Medical Psychology*, XXIX (1956), 211–47; Michael Hakeem, "A Critique of the Psychiatric Approach," *Juvenile Delinquency*, ed. Joseph S. Roucek (New York: Philosophical Library, Inc., 1958), pp. 79–112; Siri Naess, "Mother-Child Separation and Delinquency," *British Journal of Delinquency*, X (July, 1959), 22–35.

Since many studies have shown that usually both delinquents and nondelinquents come from the same family, efforts have been made to determine whether certain relationships within the family are more productive of delinquency than others. So studies have been made of the only child, the youngest, the oldest, the "in-between" child, the foster child, the child in the large and in the small family, and so on, but these studies, although numerous, have been conflicting and inconclusive.[19] It seems, then, that none of these relationships, of itself, necessarily causes delinquency. The pattern of causation is entirely too complex for so simple an answer, for it is obvious that many other factors are involved.

Some writers, for example, have stated that the factor of social class must be considered in estimating the possible effects of frustration in children.[20] The middle-class child, they argue, tends to endure the denial of his immediate wishes, because he can expect adequate rewards for his patience, whereas children of the poor, who can expect little in their lives, are far less inclined to bear their frustrations. Thus one must recognize the complexity of family relationships, but he must also understand that no two children have the same experiences in a home and that, therefore, if for no other reason, their reactions to it can never be exactly the same.

## The Socially, Morally, or Culturally Abnormal Home

In this type of home, racial differences, a physically or psychologically abnormal parent, immorality, criminality, or diverse cultural standards make it difficult for children to receive a system of values generally accepted in the community and so interfere with adequate training for successful living. In the United States interracial marriages are not generally favored, and children born of them, comfortable in neither race and often bitter, resentful, and emotionally insecure, face serious obstacles in their search for success and happiness. In much the same way, children with a parent suffering from a serious disability, like blindness, deafness, paralysis, or mental illness, also have some difficult problems of adjustment. These children may feel ashamed or apologetic

---

[19] For a summary of the findings of some of these studies, see Stephan Hurwitz, *Criminology* (London: George Allen and Unwin, Ltd., 1952), pp. 324–27; Emanuel Miller, "The Problem of Birth-Order and Delinquency," in *Mental Abnormality and Crime*, ed. L. Radzinowicz and J. W. C. Turner (English Studies in Criminal Science [London: Macmillan and Co., Ltd., 1949]), Vol. II, pp. 227–37. See also J. A. Shield and A. E. Grigg, "Extreme Ordinal Position and Criminal Behavior," *Journal of Criminal Law and Criminology*, XXXV (September–October, 1944), 169–73; William W. Wattenberg, "Delinquency and Only Children: Study of a 'Category,'" *Journal of Abnormal and Social Psychology*, XLIV (July, 1949), 356–66; Nye, p. 37; J. P. Lees and L. J. Newson, "Family or Sibship Position and Some Aspects of Juvenile Delinquency," *British Journal of Delinquency*, V (July, 1954), 46–65.

[20] See, for example, Shulman, p. 30.

about the condition of their parent, weary in their efforts to soothe his feelings and care for his needs, or resentful under the burden he imposes. In any event, seeking relief from their tensions, frustrations, feelings of guilt, and conflicts, they may find comfort in undesirable or even delinquent or criminal associations.[21]

Children exposed to lewdness, vulgarity, drunkenness, brutality, immorality, vice, and crime in the home tend to accept these conditions as normal and desirable, fashion themselves after the models so seductively exhibited, and, hardened and debased at an early age, easily slide into delinquency and crime. The road to law violation, of course, is even more accessible if parents deliberately teach the child to engage in criminal practices.[22]   Burt, in his classical study of vice and crime in England, concluded that these types of conditions existed five times as often in the homes from which delinquents came as in the homes of nondelinquents; and the Gluecks, in a series of three studies, found that over four-fifths of the juvenile delinquents, women delinquents, and male felons came from homes in which there were other offenders.[23]

This is what happened to Jack, who was sixteen years old when he was referred to the juvenile court on a charge of car theft. Through investigation by the police, it was learned that two other cars had been stolen by the boy within a twenty-four hour period. Jack consistently denied his guilt and stated that he knew nothing about the cars. In his denial, Jack was supported by his parents, who at first insisted that their boy could not possibly be involved in the alleged thefts. Later, however, they said that if he was involved, the blame should be place on others who had influenced him. But when they also argued that "anything Jack did was all right as long as he was not caught," the police became suspicious and continued their investigation. As a result, they discovered that the father had taught Jack to steal cars, and that they had worked together on various "jobs." The court adjudged Jack a delinquent and committed him to a training school. The father was convicted and sent to prison.

The findings of many studies and investigations seem to support the

---

[21] Coulter, p. 16.
[22] William Healy and Augusta F. Bronner, *Delinquents and Criminals: Their Making and Unmaking* (New York: The Macmillan Co., 1926), pp. 126–29; Mabel A. Elliott, *Correctional Education and the Delinquent Girls* (Harrisburg, Pa.: 1928), pp. 26–28; Sheldon and Eleanor T. Glueck, *Unraveling Juvenile Delinquency* (New York: The Commonwealth Fund, 1950), pp. 278–81; John Lewis Gillin, *Criminology and Penology* (New York: Appleton-Century-Crofts, Inc., 1945), p. 173.
[23] See Burt, *op. cit.*, pp. 60–98; Sheldon and Eleanor T. Glueck, *One Thousand Juvenile Delinquents* (Cambridge: Harvard University Press, 1934), pp. 79, 80; *ibid., 500 Criminal Careers* (New York: Alfred A. Knopf, Inc., 1930), pp. 111–13; *ibid., Five Hundred Delinquent Women* (New York: Alfred A. Knopf, Inc., 1934), pp. 72, 73.

belief that culture conflict is an important cause of crime and delinquency, but these findings should be carefully examined, for the delinquency and crime rates of American-born children of immigrants are affected not only by this factor but also by the poverty, minority status, and conditions of delinquency areas in which many foreign-born families live. Still, the children in the homes of immigrants are often torn by culture conflicts that eventually may contribute to the violation of the law. Divided in their loyalties between parents, who tend to resist the upsetting forces of their strange surroundings, and friends, teachers, and neighbors, they are steadily pressed into assimilation in the new culture by the teachings and influences of the neighborhood, school, church, motion pictures, radio, and television. Often confused, rebellious, reckless, and even ashamed of their parents as they seek acceptance and respect by playmates and companions, these children may sever the ties of parental restraint and seek satisfaction for their wishes in delinquency and crime.[24]

However, as we have seen, generalizations about the home must be guarded, for many subtle influences operate in it. A tragedy may unify the members of a family and thus enable them to solve the most serious problems, and such deleterious conditions in the home as vice and vulgarity may be more than counterbalanced by the love, affection, and emotional security which the child receives there.[25]

## The Economically Insecure Home

The economic conditions found in this type of home may directly contribute to crime and delinquency, as, for example, when a child steals so that he will not suffer from hunger or cold, but far more often its influence is exerted through a complex set of relationships. Thus, poverty may cause the absence from home of working parents and the loss of their restraint and guidance, the early employment of children

---

[24] For a general summary of the criminal record of immigrants, see Donald R. Taft, *Criminology* (New York: The Macmillan Co., 1950), pp. 110–12.

Limitations of space preclude a discussion of the subject of immigration and crime, but the student is referred to the following: National Commission on Law Observance and Enforcement, *Report on Crime and the Foreign Born*, Report No. 10 (Washington, D.C.: Government Printing Office, 1931); C. C. Van Vechten, "The Criminality of the Foreign Born," *Journal of Criminal Law and Criminology*, XXXII (July–August, 1941), 139–47; Hans von Hentig, "The First Generation and a Half; Notes on the Delinquency of the Native White of Mixed Parentage," *American Sociological Review*, X (December, 1945), 792–98. For a summary of the studies on the crime rates of various immigrant groups, see Arthur Lewis Wood, "Minority-Group Criminality and Cultural Integration," *Journal of Criminal Law and Criminology*, XXXVII (March–April, 1947), 398–510.

[25] Paul W. Tappan, *Juvenile Delinquency* (New York: McGraw-Hill Book Co., Inc., 1949), p. 141.

and their subjection to great temptations, the association of children with delinquent gangs in slum areas, the overcrowding of the home and its attendant sacrifice of privacy, the flight of children from the home to escape its unpleasant conditions, and the bitter reaction of children to their lot. Any one of these results may in turn involve the child in delinquency or crime, but this does not necessarily happen. In fact, many law-abiding adults and children come from poor homes, and, on the other hand, many of the rich, also, violate the law. Nevertheless, the great majority of criminals and delinquents do come from economically insecure homes, and although this type of home usually operates indirectly to produce law violations, it still constitutes a criminal or delinquency risk.[26]

## THE IMPORTANCE OF THE FAMILY

The cohesion of the modern American family depends far more on its internal forces than on its external pressures. No longer bound together by the dominance of one will, its existence requires the harmony of two—the continuous balancing of a dual set of complex relationships. Consequently, to a greater extent than ever before, internal conflicts tend to tear the family apart, causing divorce, desertion, or separation.

Nevertheless, the family remains the basic social institution and the most primary of the primary groups. In the intimacy of the family life, the child receives basic physical and emotional satisfactions, as well as protection, guidance, and moral instruction, during his most impressionable years. In it he first learns about himself and his physical, social, and cultural surroundings; and there, too, he acquires attitudes, habits, character traits, and a sense of right and wrong that tend to endure throughout his entire lifetime. Furthermore, since the family is so important in the transmission and preservation of culture, it is not only the cradle of personality but also the nursery of all other social institutions, and being functionally related to them, it tends to reflect and augment their organization and disorganization.

Research and investigation have clearly revealed the great importance of the family, and have indicated that whatever in its structure, its internal functioning, or its external relationships reduces its authority and

---

[26] Carr, p. 166; Hurwitz, pp. 319–24; Ernest W. Burgess, "The Economic Factor in Juvenile Delinquency," *Journal of Criminal Law, Criminology, and Police Science,* XLIII (May–June, 1952), 29–42; A. J. Reiss, Jr., "Delinquency as the Failure of Personal and Social Controls," *American Sociological Review,* XVI (April, 1951), 196–208; Lee N. Robins, Harry Gyman, and Patricia O'Neal, "The Interaction of Social Class and Deviant Behavior," *American Sociological Review,* XXVII (August, 1962), 480–92.

influence in the rearing of children also increases the possibility of delinquency. Indeed, even when the family suffers from serious handicaps, it can still exert a powerful influence in the lives of children. That this is true is reflected in the fact that most of the children of the lower class do not become chronic delinquents. This is why all students of crime and delinquency believe that the family is very important and why a strong, effective, and viable family system continues to be our strongest bulwark against these problems.

# 8

# Neighborhoods and Gangs

## NEIGHBORHOODS AND DELINQUENCY

The neighborhood, or what McKay has referred to as "the area of participation," is the area beyond the family but not inclusive of the community at large where many particularly meaningful experiences occur in a youngster's life.[1] Where stable and enduring patterns of social conduct exist in an area, the impact of indigenous institutions and activities on the behavior of those living there is clearly felt. The young people, the church, school, and recreational activities assume special significance when the influence is exerted through the informality of the play group. Within the spatial context of the neighborhood, conduct supportive of conventional institutional arrangements can be effectively regulated by the playgroup through a variety of spontaneous, more or less natural forms of communication. Strong pressures to conform to certain standards of conduct acceptable to the group and to resist or ignore other modes of behavior, while not always organized and consistent, are prevalent in nearly all playgroup activities. When there is fundamental accord between the patterns of conduct supported by adults and those accepted by juveniles in their informal activities, neighborhood controls can serve to diminish the risks of delinquency's developing as positively valued behavior. Under conditions contributing to a forceful and dramatic blending of the basic patterns of social life into an integrated, relatively autonomous unit, the neighborhood can assume the qualities of a ghetto. Whether ghettos promote delinquency depends, in part, on whether their value systems are contrary to those of the law. Differences in the use of the term "ghetto" threaten, however, to confuse our efforts to shed light on the problem.

[1] Henry D. McKay, "The Neighborhood and Child Conduct," *The Annals of the American Academy of Political and Social Science*, CCLXI (January, 1949), 32–41.

## Ghettos and Delinquency

Historically, the term "ghetto" was applied to those sections of a community in which Jews resided. There the tightly knit fusion of religious, family, economic, political, social, and recreational activities reached perhaps its most notable dimensions. Practically all patterns of daily living, including the sorts of activities engaged in by youngsters as play, were integrally bound together. Under such conditions, control over young people's behavior was far-reaching. There tended to be very little flagrant violations of established standards in the form of delinquency. Even today, although the strictly physical ghetto-like features of their neighborhoods have been rapidly disappearing, the consistently low rates of delinquency in such groups as the Jews and Chinese can be attributed partially to the strong controls exerted by the continuing emphasis on institutionalized forms of conduct dominant in the areas where they live.

Contemporary usage of the concept "ghetto" has, oddly enough, come to have a meaning which is the antithesis of its historical one. Now the term is used to refer to the most disorganized and deteriorated areas where there is little evidence of effective social controls. It has, unfortunately, begun to serve as a shorthand term for high delinquency rates, substandard housing, economic instability, racial and ethnic discrimination, urban blight, and practically every other manifestation of undesirable social relations in our increasingly urbanized society. Rather than drawing our attention toward certain underlying conditions which have contributed greatly to these problems, namely, those which operate to weaken the development of integrated institutional controls in neighborhoods, the current distortion of the meaning of ghetto is perhaps unwittingly leading to a deemphasis of these factors. Little constructive benefit can be derived from its continued use in this manner. Only by pin-pointing as directly and precisely as possible the factors associated with the disorganized living conditions in the most deteriorated and poverty-stricken areas of our cities can we hope to see any progress in their eradication. Lumping all of the existing social ills in an area together, and attributing them to "ghetto conditions" not only grossly oversimplifies the complex explanations for these problems but also serves to detract from a more rigorous investigation into their causation.

Sociologists have devoted a considerable amount of time to ferreting out those particular factors which appear to have a consistently high correlation with delinquency and crime. There is, in fact, a rich and growing body of empirical literature in sociology which bears on the relationship between a selected group of variables in neighborhoods and delinquency.  The findings have been especially useful in explaining inter-city variations in delinquency rates.

## Intra-City Variations in Delinquency Rates

In addition to our knowledge of variations in delinquency rates from rural to urban areas, most of us have long been aware of the variations in delinquency rates from area to area within a given city.  Although this commonplace observation had captured the imagination of a few early investigators, it was not until the 1930's and early 1940's that systematic empirical documentation was forthcoming.  Clifford Shaw and Henry McKay, along with others at the University of Chicago, conducted a series of investigations into the ecological distribution of delinquency throughout the city of Chicago.[2]  Judith Wilk has summarized their major findings as follows:

1. Rates of delinquency and crime vary widely in different neighborhoods within a city, town, or SMSA [standard metropolitan statistical area].
2. The highest crime and delinquency rates generally occur in the low-rent areas located near the center of the city, and the rates decrease with increasing distance from the city center.  (This finding is often referred to as the gradient hypothesis, and is most frequently illustrated by computing offender rates for concentric residence zones radiating out from the city center.)
3. High delinquency rate areas tend to maintain their high rates over time, although the population composition of the area may change radically within the same time period.
4. Areas which have high rates of truancy also have high rates of juvenile court cases and high rates of adult offenders.  In addition, if an area has a high rate of male delinquency, it usually has a high rate of female delinquency.
5. The differences in area rates reflect differences in community background. High rate areas are characterized by such things as physical deterioration and declining population.
6. The delinquency rates for particular nationality and ethnic groups show the same general tendency as the entire population; namely, to be high in the central area of the city and low as these groups move toward the outskirts of the city.
7. Delinquents living in areas of high delinquency rates are the most likely to become recidivists, and among all recidivists, they are likely to appear in court several times more often than those from areas with low delinquency rates.

[2] Clifford R. Shaw and Henry D. McKay, *Social Factors in Juvenile Delinquency*, Report No. 13, Vol. II of the reports of the National Commission on Law Observance and Enforcement (Washington, D.C.: Government Printing Office, 1931); Clifford R. Shaw, *Delinquency Areas* (Chicago: University of Chicago Press, 1929); Clifford R. Shaw and Henry D. McKay, *Juvenile Delinquency and Urban Areas* (Chicago: University of Chicago Press, 1969).

8. In summary, delinquency and crime follow the pattern of the social and physical structure of the city with concentration occurring in disorganized, deteriorated areas.[3]

These findings and other similar to them based on investigations in other cities in the United States have led sociologists to the development of the "gradient hypothesis." Put in quintessential form, this hypothesis asserts that "urban crime and delinquency rates in the United States tend to be highest near the central business district and heavily industrialized areas and to decrease from the center of the city outward." [4]

Although widely heralded for a time, it was not long before careful reflection began to chip away at the explanatory value of the "delinquency area" concept. Numerous cogent criticisms have been made of the Shaw-McKay studies over the years. Among those which bear most fundamentally on their observations are the following: [5]

1. The effects of selective migration on delinquency rates in the areas examined were not sufficiently considered. Persons who already have persistent delinquent and criminal inclinations tend to be drawn more readily to areas of high delinquency and crime than do those whose lives have been considerably more law-abiding. Whether the high rates of delinquency are due to conditions peculiar to the area, as Shaw and McKay maintained, or to certain predilections of the people who moved into the area is open to some debate.

2. The statistics used in the compilation of area delinquency rates were not very reliable. As our own discussion of the problems of measurement made clear, it is hazardous to base interpretations of delinquent conduct on official sources of statistics, which is what Shaw and McKay did. It is difficult to know whether the delinquency rates of an area were high or low because of the nature of the area or because of high or low police patrolling and surveillance. There is no question but that law-enforcement officers concentrate much more on certain areas than others. These, most often, happen to be the "high delinquency areas" of a city.

3. Shaw and McKay's contention that the ethnic composition of the population in an area has no appreciable effect upon delinquency rates

[3] Judith A. Wilks, "Ecological Correlates of Crime and Delinquency," in President's Commission on Law Enforcement and Administration of Justice, *Task Force Report: Crime and Its Impact—An Assessment* (Washington, D.C.: Government Printing Office, 1967), Appendix A, pp. 138–56.

[4] Robert G. Caldwell, *Criminology* (New York: The Ronald Press Co., 1965), p. 249.

[5] *Ibid.*, pp. 250–53. For a critique of the delinquency-area studies, see Terence Morris, *The Criminal Area: A Study in Social Ecology* (London: Routledge and Kegan Paul, 1958), esp. pp. 85–106.

is open to question. Various racial and ethnic minorities have, as Taft explains,[6] faced somewhat different obstacles in their adjustment to new social demands. For some of these groups, conflict with the law can become more frequent simply because of the uniqueness of their own cultural heritage and life style. That, as much as the area, could account for high delinquency rates for given ethnic groups.

4. An insufficient amount of attention is given to the presence of negative cases. Seldom does an area or neighborhood have a totally delinquent adolescent population. By not adequately accounting for the presence in high delinquency areas of nondelinquents and in low-delinquency areas of delinquents, the delinquency area approach is an oversimplification of the causal problem. This criticism is not intended so much to detract from whatever causal significance the gradient hypothesis may have as it is to caution against placing too much emphasis on environmental conditions. Personal differences, especially those stressing the uniqueness and creativity of an individual, must not be overlooked in our assessment of factors contributing to delinquent behavior.

## Recent Ecological Studies

For some time after the initial criticism of gradient hypothesis, interest in the ecological dimensions of delinquency waned. In 1954, however, Bernard Lander rekindled the spark of intellectual inquiry into the relationships between selected ecological variables and delinquency rates. Reporting on the findings of a study of variations in delinquency rates by census tracts in the city of Baltimore,[7] he found general support for the gradient hypothesis. Two factors, percentage of nonwhites in a tract and percentage of owner-occupied homes, were found to be independently correlated with the delinquency rate for a tract. By conducting a factor analysis of his variables, Lander was able to conclude that delinquency is due to a lack of normative control in an area, as reflected by the relationships between the nonwhite and owner-occupied variables and delinquency. Economic status, he concluded, was not of fundamental importance.

Lander's research, in addition to having been criticized, has been replicated in several cities.[8] For the most part, these studies duplicate Lander's findings in some ways but not in all. Bordua and Polk, for example, tend to agree that economic status is less important than dis-

---

[6] Donald R. Taft, *Criminology* (New York: The Macmillan Co., 1950), p. 166.
[7] Bernard Lander, *Toward an Understanding of Juvenile Delinquency* (New York: Columbia University Press, 1954).
[8] David J. Bordua, "Juvenile Delinquency and 'Anomie': An Attempt at Replication," *Social Problems*, VI (Winter, 1958–1959), 230–38.

organization or anomie. Chilton, on the other hand, was unable to support such a conclusion in a replication carried out in Indianapolis.[9]

Serious questions have been raised by Rosen and Turner about the research techniques employed in these studies.[10] They contend that the procedures used are not appropriate for assessing the ways that variables combine to interact with each other in different ways under varying circumstances. Their criticism points to one of the most disturbing features of the renewed interest in ecological correlates of delinquency, and that is the extent to which highly refined and sophisticated statistical procedures accurately approximate the social reality of the delinquent world. This growing methodological issue is perhaps the most important one to be faced if the ecological dimensions of delinquency are to be accorded an important place in causal analyses of the problem.

Until such time as we can be assured that our methodological procedures are appropriate to the social behavior we are measuring, no final evaluation of the gradient hypothesis can be made. On the basis of a careful and critical evaluation of the evidence marshalled so far, however, Judith Wilk concluded:

> In general, the gradient hypothesis has been supported by empirical evidence. This is the case for both offender rates and offense rates. What discrepancies occur can usually be accounted for by geographical anomalies, the location of industrial and commercial complexes away from the center of the city, the existence of cultural enclaves, and the irregular distribution of opportunities to participate in crime. The major irregularity found is the increasing concentration of offenses and offenders in peripheral urban areas, especially as these areas take on the characteristics of the city center—industrial and commercial concentrations, low economic and family status, and high population mobility.[11]

## GANGS AND DELINQUENCY

It is estimated that anywhere from 60 to 90 per cent of all delinquent activity occurs in the company of others. This suggests that there is support and encouragement from others to participate in delinquency. Just how extensive and highly structured these peer-group-oriented patterns of conduct are is of great interest to sociologists. For the past

[9] Roland J. Chilton, "Continuity in Delinquency Area Research: A Comparison of Studies for Baltimore, Detroit, and Indianapolis," *American Sociological Review*, XXIX (February, 1964), 71–83.

[10] Lawrence Rosen and Stanley H. Turner, "An Evaluation of the Lander Approach to Ecology of Delinquency," *Social Problems*, XV (Fall, 1967), 189–200.

[11] Judith Wilk, *op. cit.*, p. 146. For additional views, see Kenneth Polk, "Juvenile Delinquency and Social Areas," *Social Problems*, V (Winter, 1957–1958), 214–17, and Robert A. Gordon, "Issues in the Ecological Study of Delinquency," *American Sociological Review*, XXXII (December, 1967), 927–44.

ifteen years in particular, more attention has been devoted to the study of delinquent gangs than to any other single facet of the delinquency problem. Still, for all the theoretical and empirical observations made n the voluminous literature related to gangs, very little is known about he most fundamental dimensions of gang life. Most of what we have earned about delinquent gangs can be organized around the answers o three related questions. First, what are the characteristics of a delinquent gang? Second, how many different types of gangs can be distinguished? Third, what are the characteristics of the members of delinquent gangs?

## Characteristics of Delinquent Gangs

It is not so easy as might at first appear to differentiate delinquent gangs from other types of adolescent groups. Frequently, patterns of conduct which emerge as supportive of delinquency during adolescence have their genesis in the give-and-take of informal play activity in the neighborhood setting. Gangs develop as a natural by-product of associations established earlier and for other purposes. They are formed rather spontaneously and may be short-lived and without much direction or organization or may grow into stable groups of adolescents joined together for the purpose of engaging in highly specialized types of delinquency. Regardless of variations in their duration and organization, however, all delinquent gangs share certain common characteristics. Frederic M. Thrasher, in *The Gang*, offered the following definition:

The gang is an interstitial group originally formed spontaneously, and then integrated through conflict. It is characterized by the following types of behavior: meeting face to face, milling, movement through space as a unit, conflict, and planning. The result of their collective behavior is the development of tradition, unreflective internal structure, *esprit de corps*, solidarity, morale, group awareness, and attachment to a local territory.[12]

More recently, William Arnold, after a study of these characteristics, has suggested that there are five which enable us to define the concept gang more explicitly:[13]

1. Gangs are integrated. There is evidence that the members identify with the group.
2. Gangs experience conflict. It may be in the form of conflict with parents, teachers, police, and other gangs.
3. Gangs have a structure. There are certain rules that must be

[12] Frederic M. Thrasher, *The Gang* (abridged ed.; Chicago: University of Chicago Press, 1963), p. 46.
[13] William R. Arnold, "The Concept Gang," *Sociological Quarterly,* VII (Winter, 1966), 59–75.

adhered to, and at least the position of leader must be differen
tiated.

4. Gangs must be large enough to permit milling and the exercise
of group pressure. At least five or six boys are needed to be
certain that group pressure develops.

5. Gangs do not try to change social standards. While the conflic
engaged in is definitely "antisocial," it is not aimed at changing
the social structure.

While the characteristics felt to be important by Arnold do not diffe
sharply from those posited by Thrasher, it is of some interest that Arnold
chose not to stress either the interstitial aspects of gang life or the attach
ment to a local territory.

Richard Cloward and Lloyd Ohlin have taken a step toward delimit
ing delinquent gangs even more precisely.[14] As they see it, illegal activi
ties such as truancy, vandalism, theft, illicit sexual experiences, and
drunkenness are all types of behavior which can and often do receive
official reaction. But, even though these are types of behavior which
occur in a group context and are tolerated when they happen, the group
is not considered a delinquent gang (or subculture) unless this behavior is
basic to the organization of the group. *"A delinquent subculture is one
in which certain forms of delinquent activity are essential requirements
for the performance of the dominant roles supported by the subculture."* [1]

At what point in time a group is transformed from one where a variety
of delinquent activities are acceptable sorts of behavior to one where
these illegal actions become *prerequisites* for membership is not easily
determined. We would agree with the effort of Ohlin and Cloward to
restrict the meaning of the term "delinquent gang" in this manner. How
ever, it is questionable that any empirical evidence can be obtained to
document directly the distinction, except on an *ex post facto* basis. In
all probability, it is perhaps best to reason that no two gangs will re
flect all of the characteristics spoken of here in the same way. We should
tend to look on them as characteristics of "ideal types" which are imper
fectly mirrored in social reality.

## Types of Delinquent Gangs

To the extent that there are observable differences in neighborhood
and in so far as the delinquent gangs which emerge out of interaction
in the neighborhood setting reflect these differences, we should expect
to find various types of gangs distributed throughout our social structure

[14] Richard A. Cloward and Lloyd E. Ohlin, *Delinquency and Opportunity: A
Theory of Delinquent Gangs* (New York: The Free Press, 1960).
[15] *Ibid.*, p. 7. (Emphasis in original.)

We have already considered the general problem of typologies of delinquent behavior, and the reader should, by this time, be thoroughly familiar with the limitations inherent in any constructed typology. One typology of delinquent gangs, that is, Cloward and Ohlin's distinction on the basis of conflict, criminal, and retreatist orientations, was mentioned in that earlier chapter. Another, somewhat more detailed one has been outlined by Albert Cohen and James F. Short.[16] Limiting their observations to male gangs, which accounts for practically all such groups, they distinguish five general types of subcultures.

First among them is the parent-male subculture. Essentially, it is the one Cohen had portrayed in *Delinquent Boys*.[17] It is characterized by maliciousness, negativism, nonutilitarianism, versatility, short-run hedonism, and group autonomy. Cohen and Short call it the "garden variety" subculture because it is considered the type most commonly found in American society. Furthermore, it is felt by them to be a working-class phenomenon.

The second type, the conflict-oriented subculture, generally receives the most publicity. In its ideal form, the conflict-oriented subculture is depicted as a large, highly organized group with numerous roles differentiated largely around fighting and demonstrations of toughness. "These gangs have names, a strong sense of corporate identity, a public personality or 'rep' in the gang world. The gang is identified with a territory or 'turf' which it tries to defend or to extend."[18] As a rule, the full-blown organization characteristic of certain large conflict-oriented gangs in New York is not duplicated elsewhere. More often than not, what is found is "a loosely organized and amorphorus coalition of cliques with only a vague sense of corporate identity, coalescing sporadically and frequently for displays of open violence."[19]

The third subculture identified by Cohen and Short is the drug-addict subculture. Different from the parent and conflict orientations by having a definitely utilitarian characteristic related to the addict's way of life, the drug-addict subculture is still to be seen as being closely related to these other types. Research conducted in New York by Chein and his associates [20] points out that heroin addicts frequently have been members of highly organized delinquent gangs. Their participation in gang activities diminishes as their interest in drugs picks up. Those

[16] Albert K. Cohen and James F. Short, Jr., "Research in Delinquent Subculture," *Journal of Social Issues*, XIV (July, 1958), 20–37.
[17] Albert K. Cohen, *Delinquent Boys: The Culture of the Gang* (New York: The Free Press, 1955).
[18] Cohen and Short, *op. cit.*, 25.
[19] *Ibid.*, 25.
[20] Isidor Chein, Donald L. Gerhard, Robert S. Lee, and Eva Rosenfeld, *The Road to H: Narcotics, Delinquency, and Social Policy* (New York: Basic Books, 1964).

members of a gang who become addicted generally break away from the main core of the gang and replace "general hell-raising" kinds of behavior with activities specifically designed to support their habit.

Finestone's study [21] of Chicago heroin addicts, or "cats," does not see the addict as a peripheral participant in more organized gangs (but, instead, as one who identifies with the central themes of the cat culture. There are two such themes, the "kick" and the "hustle." Kicks are acts which place an emphasis on intensifying immediate experiences to make them as different from routine living as possible, and the hustle is a nonviolent way of obtaining money without working. These two themes, of course, run counter to the central values of planning ahead and work in the larger culture. Both Chein's and Finestone's studies are in agreement, however, that the heroin addiction problem is largely restricted to Negro and Puerto Rican males of the age sixteen or older in the most deteriorated sections of our large cities.

The fourth subculture distinguished by Cohen and Short is oriented around semiprofessional theft. Like the drug addict orientation, this one has marked utilitarian qualities. About the age of sixteen or seventeen, when most participants in the parent subculture cease their delinquent activities for more constructive modes of conduct, some acquire a more highly specialized interest in theft as a regular way of life. Those who participate in semiprofessional theft are characterized as using strong-arm tactics to obtain money, selling stolen goods rather than keeping them for their own use, and as continuing to steal because of the profit involved and not for the excitement or thrill involved.

The fifth and final type is the middle-class delinquent subculture. With an admitted paucity of empirical research to document the characteristics dominant in this type, these authors distinguish middle-class delinquent gangs on essentially theoretical grounds. They reason that middle-class delinquency will be patterned differently from lower- or working-class delinquency because of the relatively different problems of adjustment faced by adolescents in these different social strata. Subtle but crucial differences make it "probable that the qualities of malice, bellicosity, and violence will be underplayed in the middle-class subcultures and that these subcultures will emphasize more the deliberate courting of danger (suggested by the epithet 'chicken') and a sophisticated, irresponsible 'playboy' approach to activities symbolic, in our culture, of adult roles and centering largely around sex, liquor, and automobiles." [22]

Perhaps the most significant point underscored by this typology is

[21] Harold Finestone, "Cats, Kicks, and Color," *Social Problems*, V (July, 1957), 3–13.
[22] Cohen and Short, *op. cit.*, 28.

the rich and dynamic complexity of delinquent gang activity. A variety of possible explanations will have to be carefully sorted through to unravel the intricate and frequently shifting patterns of delinquency supported by group standards. At this point in time, we must be prepared to move cautiously and be ready to abandon assumptions which, while held in order to initiate or expand research, cannot stand the weight of empirical data. Whether the various types of gangs discussed here are variants of a common subculture, each to be explained differently, or extremes of the same subculture and thereby all explainable with the same variables is a major problem in the study of delinquent gangs.[23]

## Characteristics of Gang Members

From fragments of information scattered throughout the literature on delinquent gangs, certain observations can be made about the social attributes of gang members. Since there has been surprisingly little large scale, systematic research on the subject, however, only the most general and tentative kinds of statements can be made. Any composite picture will have to be sketched in a very rough and unfinished manner.

**Sex.** It is generally agreed that "ganging" is an almost exclusively male phenomenon. There are occasional reports of a highly organized girls' gang operating in certain sections of our largest cities, but solid empirical documentation for the persistence of girls' gangs is notably absent. Usually, the closest approximation to female gangs is found in the auxiliary groups formed around an organized male gang. Even in these instances, it is highly questionable whether the central purposes of the girls' groups are oriented around delinquent activities. It seems more appropriate to view them as being organized because of their interest in males, even though they may engage frequently in delinquent activities.

**Age.** Beyond this point, there tends to be less and less knowledge of even the most basic characteristics of gang members. We have known, at least since Thrasher's classic study, that gangs are not so clearly differentiated on the basis of age as they are in terms of sex. He found that in 38 per cent of 1,213 gangs in Chicago, the ages of gang members ranged from eleven to seventeen years of age, and in 25 per cent of the gangs, the range of ages was from sixteen to twenty-five years of age.[24] These observations tend to be consistent with the view that what is significant is not so much the age similarity as it is activities and the enjoyment derived from participation in them on a group basis, where one gets the feeling of counting for something. As we have noted earlier,

23 *Ibid.*, 30.
24 Frederic Thrasher, *The Gang*, pp. 60, 61.

however, there seems to be a rather sharp reorientation of interests some-where between sixteen and seventeen years of age which causes some boys to form more highly specialized gangs. This is most clearly evident in the case of those boys who turn to heroin addiction.

**Minority Group Status.** Delinquent gang members frequently come from those racial and ethnic groups which rank at or near the bottom of the American social order. The majority of the gangs studied by Thrasher were, for example, of Polish extraction. Through the process of competition, conflict, invasion, and succession, the Polish immigrants were eventually replaced at the bottom of the social ladder by the Negroes and Puerto Ricans. Today, while some qualifications must be made for types of gangs, there is a disproportionate number of Negro and Puerto Rican youngsters in delinquent gangs. But minority group status, it must be remembered, is intimately bound up with social class position. Thus, while the majority of gang members are of one or an-other minority group, they are also a part of the lower-class segment of American society.

**Lower-Class Status.** The differential distribution of delinquency in the American social class structure has been observed and debated for a considerable period of time by sociologists. It has, until recently, been widely held that delinquency, generally, and delinquent gang behavior, in particular, were confined to the lower-class segments of our social order. Increasing concern with middle-class delinquency by social in-vestigators, coupled with sharp, persistent criticism of the lower-class bias of official sources of information on the distribution of the problem, has forced on sociologists the realization that the lower-class focus of most theory and research is in need of balancing.[25] We can no longer be content to assume that all delinquent gang members are "lower-class," even though low-income position is highly correlated with official delin-quency. As Don Gibbons has suggested, "Generalization about urban social structure and delinquency must be stated in detailed and sophisti-cated terms. Delinquency rates are correlated with economic status levels, but that statement does not do full justice to the complexity of the relationship it summarizes." [26]

---

[25] For an overview of the literature on middle-class delinquency, see Ralph W. England, Jr., "A Theory of Middle Class Juvenile Delinquency," *Journal of Criminal Law, Criminology, and Police Science,* L (March–April, 1960), 535–40; Edmund W. Vas (ed.), *Middle-Class Juvenile Delinquency* (New York: Harper and Row, 1967).

[26] Don C. Gibbons, *Delinquent Behavior* (Englewood Cliffs, N.J.: Prentice-Hall, Inc., 1970), p. 111. See also Albert J. Reiss, Jr., and Albert Lewis Rhodes, "The Distribution of Juvenile Delinquency in the Social Class Structure," *American Sociological Review,* XXV (October, 1961), 720–32.

In sum, we know that delinquent gang members are male, typically between the ages of eleven and twenty-five (depending on the types of delinquent activities extensively engaged in), more likely than not members of minority groups and, at least in so far as there is official recognition of their delinquency, from the lower class.  Boys who associate with delinquent gangs are, from evidence compiled by Hewitt and Jenkins [27] and Albert J. Reiss,[28] relatively well-adjusted, normal youths. What, then, accounts for the emergence and persistence of delinquent gangs in our social order?  As we shall see, there are several competing explanations, all of which have some merit, none of which is without serious limitations.

## Theories of Delinquent Gangs

Sociologists have never lost their interest in delinquent gangs, even though there was little of theoretical or empirical consequence produced between the publication of Thrasher's *The Gang* in 1927 and Cohen's *Delinquent Boys* in 1955.  The years since 1955 have seen a flourish of provocative but essentially untested theoretical developments.  At the present time, four theoretical orientations can be singled out as dominating much of our thinking about the etiology of delinquent gang life:

1. The status-deprivation approach.
2. The opportunity-structure approach.
3. The lower-class culture approach.
4. The drift approach.[29]

**Status Deprivation.**  The first, and usually regarded as the most influential of the approaches from the standpoint of the subsequent theoretical and empirical interest generated, was set forth by Cohen.[30]  Essentially, he reasoned as follows: Achievements of lower-class youths are, like those of their middle-class counterparts, assessed in terms of a "middle-class measuring rod."  Unlike middle-class youths, however, lower-class adolescents are unable to command the resources needed to compete successfully and on an equal footing with other youths for the recognition sought by anyone.  Thwarted in their desires, particularly in the atmosphere of the school where middle-class standards of evaluation are especially prevalent, lower-class boys undergo a "reaction formation" and

[27] Richard L. Jenkins and Lester Hewitt, "Types of Personality Structure Encountered in Child Guidance Clinics," *American Journal of Orthopsychiatry*, XIV (January, 1944), 84–94.

[28] Albert J. Reiss, Jr., "Social Correlates of Psychological Types of Delinquency," *American Sociological Review*, XVII (December, 1952), 710–18.

[29] David J. Bordua, "Sociological Perspectives," *Social Deviancy Among Youth* (Chicago: National Society for the Study of Education, 1966), Chapter 4.

[30] Albert K. Cohen, *op. cit.*

establish standards in the delinquent gangs for which they can more realistically compete. It is in this setting and because of the "status frustration" that the characteristics of negativism, maliciousness, versatility, short-run hedonism, group autonomy, and, most significantly, non-utilitarianism assume special significance.

Cohen's approach, as he originally outlined it, was admittedly restricted to an explanation of gang delinquency as it occurs among lower-class boys. In part, because it was the first serious attempt to chart a new direction in the study of delinquent subculture and, in part, because Cohen's portrayal of the origin of delinquent subculture was quite general, the status-deprivation approach has received a sizable amount of critical comment. From among the various critical essays, the following points appear to have been those most persistently aired: [31]

1. The explanation does not adequately account for middle-class delinquency. On both theoretical and empirical grounds, Cohen's claim that middle-class delinquency results from problems related to masculine identity can be questioned. Miller [32] and Wilensky and Lebeaux,[33] for example, are more inclined to see masculine identification problems as more characteristic of lower-class than middle-class males.

2. There is little evidence to document the assumption that lower-class boys more or less unequivocally accept middle class standards as those most worth striving for. Boys in the lower-class frequently prefer to emulate their own lower-class parents and accept their parents' standards as legitimate.

3. Although it might help in explaining the mechanisms brought into play in the origin of the gang, Cohen's approach does not enable us to explain how it persists as an organized set of responses to status problems over time.

4. While education and the family have a dominant place in Cohen's scheme, ethnic factors are glossed over. As has been pointed out earlier, one recurring characteristic of gang members is their minority status.

---

[31] David J. Bordua, *Sociological Theories and Their Implications for Juvenile Delinquency*, Children's Bureau, Juvenile Delinquency, Facts and Facets, No. 2 (Washington, D.C.: Government Printing Office, 1960); "Delinquent Subcultures: Sociological Interpretations of Gang Delinquency," *Annals of the American Academy of Political and Social Science*, CCCXXXVIII (November, 1961), 119–136; "Some Comments on Theories of Group Delinquency," *Sociological Inquiry*, XXXII (Spring, 1962), 245–60; John I. Kitsuse and David L. Dietrick, "Delinquent Boys: A Critique," *American Sociological Review*, XXIV (April, 1959), 208–15; Harold L. Wilensky and Charles N. Lebeaux, *Industrial Society and Welfare* (New York: Russell Sage Foundation, 1958); Walter B. Miller, "Lower Class Culture as a Generating Milieu of Gang Delinquency," *Journal of Social Issues*, XIV (July, 1958), 5–19.

[32] Miller, *op. cit.*

[33] Wilensky and Lebeaux, *op. cit.*, pp. 187–207.

5. The approach overplays the nonutilitarian aspects of delinquency. There are innumerable instances of a certain amount of activity being engaged in for gain, even though utilitarian motives might not always be of primary concern to delinquents.

Perhaps the most significant contribution made by the status-deprivation approach has been that it served as a powerful stimulant to those who have gone on to examine delinquent gangs more closely. It is also generally credited, aside from Cohen's emphasis on the psychological mechanism of reaction-formation, with placing the problem of gangs in a distinctly sociological context again.

**Opportunity Structure.**  The status-deprivation approach did not enjoy the limelight as a solo act for long.  Soon after it had been introduced, Ohlin and Cloward proposed an alternative explanation for the existence of delinquent gangs.[34]  Extending and refining the position of Merton,[35] they posited the following explanation: Lower-class adolescents share, along with others, a desire to be "successful" in American society.  Legitimately recognized avenues for becoming successful are differentially allocated throughout our social structure in such a way that lower-class youth are systematically denied access to the more acceptable methods for bettering one's position socially.  Thus, "adolescents who form delinquent subcultures, we suggest, have internalized an emphasis on conventional goals.  Faced with limitations on legitimate avenues of access to these goals, and unable to revise their aspirations downward, they experience intense frustrations; the exploration of nonconformist alternatives may be the result." [36]

Ohlin and Cloward stress the fact that not only are there pressures creating a differential access to legitimate means of achieving aspirations but there are also pressures which create differential access to illegitimate or deviant means as well.  It is on this basis that they account for three different types of delinquent subcultures, the conflict, criminal, and retreatist.  Conflict subcultures are most prevalent in areas marked by an absence of social constraints.  Criminal subcultures, dependent as they are on adult criminal role models to emulate and requiring as they do some integration with the adult underworld in order to get rid of "hot" goods, are generally found in stable lower-class areas where the underworld flourishes.  Retreatist subcultures develop when there is an inability or unwillingness to participate in the tough life of the conflict gang or in the cunning, well-organized activities of the criminal gang.

[34] Ohlin and Cloward, *op. cit.*
[35] Robert K. Merton, *Social Theory and Social Structure* (rev. ed.; New York: The Free Press, 1957), Chapter 4.
[36] Ohlin and Cloward, *op. cit.*, p. 86.

Falling as it does within a well-established theoretical perspective in deviance, the opportunity-structure approach has received widespread acclaim. However, research increasingly questions the threefold classification of subcultures. Not only do they not exist in reality in any "pure" form, but at least one of them, the retreatist subculture, seems to be nonexistent.[37]

**Lower-Class Concerns.** In ways sharply at odds with Cohen, Walter B. Miller has championed an approach which stresses delinquency as a normal response to well-established lower-class focal concerns.[38] Rather than depicting gang life as a reaction against middle-class values, Miller views it as normal responses to the central core interests of the lower-class community. Having frequently come from a "female-centered" household, that is, one in which the father is notably lacking as a consistent model, lower-class males are attracted to these "focal concerns" to prove themselves men and thereby be accepted as members of the group. Miller identifies the major focal concerns as "trouble," "toughness," "smartness," "fate," "excitement," and "autonomy." The net result of behaving in ways which support these interests is delinquency and criminality.

Miller's approach can be seen as having made us much more aware than we previously were of the distinctiveness of lower-class behavior patterns. On the other hand, he tends to draw the line between lower-class and middle-class interests too sharply. By emphasizing the unique features of lower-class focal concerns, he neglected to pay sufficient attention to the similarities in the behavioral orientations of the two classes.

**Drift.** Of the four approaches being briefly reviewed, the drift hypothesis developed by David Matza is the one most recently advanced.[39] According to Matza "There is a subculture of delinquency but it is not a delinquent subculture."[40] His explanation is as follows: Running through the American value system and cutting across social-class lines are several widely held but contradictory values. Some we accept but do not discuss much; they are kept fairly well in the background while

---

[37] James F. Short, Jr. and Fred L. Strodtbeck, *Group Process and Gang Delinquency* (Chicago: University of Chicago Press, 1965), pp. 1–26. See also Irving Spergel, *Racketville, Slumtown, Haulburg: An Exploratory Study of Delinquent Subcultures* (Chicago: University of Chicago Press, 1964).

[38] Walter B. Miller, *op. cit.*

[39] David Matza, *Delinquency and Drift* (New York: John Wiley and Sons, Inc., 1964); David Matza and Gresham M. Sykes, "Juvenile Delinquency and Subterranean Values," *American Sociological Review,* XXVI (October, 1961), pp. 712–19; Gresham M. Sykes and David Matza, "Techniques of Neutralization: A Theory of Delinquency," *American Sociological Review,* XXII (December, 1957), pp. 664–70. For a similar view see David M. Downes, *The Delinquent Solution: A Study in Subcultural Theory* (New York: The Free Press, 1966).

[40] Matza, *Delinquency and Drift,* p. 33.

our acceptance of others is openly voiced.   Adolescents are aware of, and to some extent identify with, the "subterranean values."   At a general level, these basic cultural inconsistencies serve to neutralize the moral impact of the law.   Several specific "techniques of neutralization" are available to expose the inconsistencies and enable adolescents to capitalize on the resultant neutrality.   Five such techniques are: [41]

1. The denial of responsibility, in which case the delinquent assumes a "billiard ball" posture and sees himself more acted upon than acting, more as being pushed around by the forces of contemporary society than as shaping his own conduct.
2. The denial of injury, where, if the behavior does not directly harm some person—as in instances where an auto is "borrowed" with little more than inconvenience to the owner—illegal conduct is acceptable.
3. Denial of the victim, which involves turning him into someone who deserves to be injured.   In that capacity, the offended party "gets what he has coming to him" and is not viewed as a victim.
4. Condemnation of the condemners, which consists of concentrating on the shortcomings and weaknesses of those who challenge the delinquents' illegal conduct.
5. The appeal to higher loyalties, or a falling back on the importance of going along with one's friends, even when it includes violating the law.   By insisting that the pressures of friendship are more demanding and have a higher claim to one's value priorities, the delinquent can resolve a major and frequently encountered dilemma in his social relations.

The overall effect of their neutralizing influence is to place the adolescent in a condition of drift.   In such a state, one may drift toward or away from persistent involvement in delinquent patterns of conduct without personally encountering any seriously damaging moral conflicts.

One of the merits of the drift approach is the way in which it exposes the complex nature of the American value system and addresses itself directly to observable inconsistencies and their relation to delinquency. A major difficulty is in directly testing certain central tenets in the approach.   Whether the techniques of neutralization, for example, are motivating factors prior to delinquent acts or constitute after-the-act rationalizations poses an especially difficult methodological problem.

## Delinquent Gangs: An Overview

These approaches regarding gangs are not, of course, the only ones being presented today.   Other views can be found.   Lewis Yablonsky,

[41] Gresham Sykes and David Matza, *op. cit.*, 667–70.

for example, holds the view that delinquent gangs ought to be viewed as "near-groups" rather than as highly structured responses to social strains and pressures.[42] Bloch and Niederhoffer argue for another approach, one which would place delinquent gang behavior in the context of the general crisis encountered by youngsters in nearly every culture as they move from adolescence to adulthood.[43] No matter which approach one tends to favor, it must be agreed that the various contemporary views, when taken together, offer some fresh and stimulating insights about gang life not carefully examined before. In this regard, the most impressive thrust has been in the direction of recognizing that delinquency, especially that generally found to exist in the conflict gang, "cannot be assumed to be a potentially of human nature which automatically erupts when the lid is off."[44] The types of conduct characteristic in the lives of delinquent gang members derive as much from social sources as from anything else and reflect conformity standards supporting violence.[45]

Still, given the particular significance of this thrust, one cannot help but be disturbed about certain recurrent weaknesses in the literature designed to support it. It is, or certainly should be, somewhat perplexing to find that Thrasher's *The Gang* continues to be the best single source of information on delinquent gangs. With occasional notable exceptions,[46] most contemporary reflections about, and inquiry into, gang life suffer on two main counts.

First, there has been little done to refine conceptually, at least in a manner acceptable to those studying the problem, the term "delinquent gang." For the most part, it continues to be a term used in a variety of ways to cover a broad range of collective delinquent activities. Until rigorous conceptual differentiation is obtained, little substantial progress can be made toward examining persistent relations between gang life and other variables.

Secondly, gangs are continually viewed in a highly oversimplified manner and in ways which fail to account for the rich but very complex social milieu in which they develop and persist over time. Two examples

[42] Lewis Yablonsky, *The Violent Gang* (New York: The Macmillan Co., 1962); "The Delinquent Gang as a Near-Group," *Social Problems*, VII (Fall, 1959), 108–17.

[43] Herbert A. Bloch and Arthur Niederhoffer, *The Gang* (New York: Philosophical Library, 1958).

[44] Albert Cohen and James F. Short, Jr., *op. cit.*, 30.

[45] Solomon Kobrin, "The Conflict of Values in Delinquency Areas," *American Sociological Review*, XVI (October, 1951), 653–61.

[46] For summaries of this research, see Malcolm W. Klein (ed.), *Juvenile Gangs in Context: Theory, Research, and Action* (Englewood Cliffs, N.J.: Prentice-Hall, Inc., 1967) and James F. Short, Jr. (ed.), *Gang Delinquency and Delinquent Subcultures* (New York: Harper and Row, 1968).

of this tendency toward undue oversimplification are the views of gang life as predominantly negative behavior from which the participants presumably obtain no enjoyment and the neglect of basic related aspects of the social structure, such as minority-group status and family life. While delinquents might be frustrated, it would seem reasonable to balance this portrayal with a picture which also sees them as enjoying their delinquency to a considerable extent.[47] And while the gang does assume an independence that demands and obtains strong allegiance, it is an independence which blends into, and derives from, other basic patterns of conduct in the total social environment of the delinquent.

[47] Bordua has been especially cognizant of this point in his writings.

# 9

# Other Environmental Factors

## RELIGION

The traditional teachings of both Christianity and Judaism stress reverence for God, the highest spiritual values of man, the worth and dignity of the individual, and respect for his person and property. Accepted as the expression of the will of God, these teachings thus have the support of His judgment, and those who violate them become subject to Divine punishment. Religion in the United States, therefore, should exert a powerful influence for social control and law observance, and you might naturally expect Christians and Jews to have low crime and delinquency rates.

"But," you may ask, "have any efforts been made to obtain definite evidence regarding the effect of religion on law observance?" Yes, such studies have been made, and here are some of the findings that have been widely cited. In an early study, Dunn analyzed the populations of twenty-seven state penitentiaries and nineteen reform and industrial schools and learned that 71.8 per cent of the inmates claimed membership in some denomination of Christianity.[1] A few years later Hartshorne and May found no essential difference between the moral behavior of children who attended Sunday school regularly and that of children who did not.[2] Kvaraceus studied 761 delinquents in Passaic, New Jersey, and discovered that almost all of them were affiliated with some church and that about three-fourths attended church regularly or occasionally.[3] Wattenberg interviewed over 2,000 male delinquents in Detroit and found

[1] C. V. Dunn, "The Church and Crime in the United States," *The Annals of the American Academy of Political and Social Science,* CXXV (May, 1926), pp. 200–28.

[2] Hugh Hartshorne and Mark A. May, *Studies in the Nature of Character* (New York: The Macmillan Co., 1928–30), Vol. I, *Studies in Deceit,* Book I, pp. 339–67, 410, Vol. III, *Studies in the Organization of Character,* pp. 128–32.

[3] William C. Kvaraceus, "Delinquent Behavior and Church Attendance," *Sociology and Social Research,* XXVIII (March–April, 1944), 284–89.

that about 69 per cent attended church regularly or occasionally. Recidivists among the boys had only a slightly poorer church attendance record than the nonrecidivists.[4]

The Gluecks found that 39 per cent of the delinquents in their study attended church regularly, 54 per cent attended occasionally, and only 7 per cent never attended. Among the nondelinquents (the control group), 67 per cent attended regularly, 29 per cent occasionally, and only 4 per cent never attended.[5] In a study made by Nye, 75 per cent of the boys and 78 per cent of the girls who regularly attended religious services were in the least delinquent group. On the other hand, of those who never attended religious services, 62 per cent of both girls and boys were in the least delinquent group. The attendance of parents at religious services was at about the same level as that of their children.[6]

These findings do not seem to throw a very favorable light on the role of religion, but actually they tell us very little. In fact, the results of other studies, similar to the ones already quoted, might be included here, but they would not alter the fact that we have no conclusive statistical evidence regarding the effects of religion on crime and delinquency. Essentially this conclusion was reached by Dunn in the early study cited above, and since then authorities, in general, have held the same view.[7]

The reasons for this are not difficult to find. The studies have not extricated the factor of religion from the web of relationships into which it is woven along with such other factors as the home, the neighborhood, nativity, education, economic status, and race. Because of this, the investigators have given us information not about religion but about the effects of the interaction of many factors, religion included. Moreover, they have not gone beyond such externals as church membership, attendance at religious meetings, avowals of faith, and so on, and thus, if

[4] William W. Wattenberg, "Church Attendance and Juvenile Misconduct," *Sociology and Social Research*, XXXIV (January–February, 1950), 195–202.

[5] Sheldon and Eleanor T. Glueck, *Unraveling Juvenile Delinquency* (New York: The Commonwealth Fund, 1950), p. 166.

[6] F. Ivan Nye, *Family Relationships and Delinquent Behavior* (New York: John Wiley and Sons, Inc., 1958), pp. 35, 36.

[7] See, for example, Martin H. Neumeyer, *Juvenile Delinquency in Modern Society* (New York: Van Nostrand Reinhold Co., Inc., 1961), pp. 236, 237; Ruth Shonle Cavan, *Juvenile Delinquency* (Philadelphia: J. B. Lippincott Co., 1962), pp. 200–02; Sophia M. Robison, *Juvenile Delinquency: Its Nature and Control* (New York: Holt, Rinehart, and Winston, Inc., 1960), pp. 163–69; Herbert A. Bloch and Frank T. Flynn, *Delinquency: The Juvenile Offender in America Today* (New York: Random House, Inc., 1956), pp. 228–33; Edwin H. Sutherland and Donald R. Cressey, *Principles of Criminology* (Philadelphia: J. B. Lippincott Co., 1966), pp. 248–50; Robert G. Caldwell, *Criminology* (New York: The Ronald Press Co., 1965), pp. 273–74; David Dressler, *Practice and Theory of Probation and Parole* (New York: Columbia University Press, 1959), pp. 97–99.

for no other reason, they have told us very little about the real meaning and influence of religion in the lives of those who were examined.

In commenting on this, Caldwell said: "Since all kinds of people from all kinds of social and economic backgrounds belong to the various religious denominations, religious doctrines and teachings exert varying influences in the lives of people regardless of their religious affiliations. Furthermore, moral precepts and ethical considerations of a nonreligious nature are so interwoven with religious principles that they cannot be separated for the purpose of evaluation even in the individual case." [8]

However, despite the absence of any conclusive statistical evidence regarding the effects of religion on crime and delinquency, it seems reasonable to assume that social norms, including the law, are greatly strengthened when they are given the support of religion and associated with the regular inculcation of religious principles. When this is done, violations of the law are not just crimes; they become also abhorrent acts that are condemned by deep religious convictions. Religion can thus create a strong resistance to criminal impulses and desires.[9]

## EDUCATION

America has great faith in education. Indeed, many of her major national policies are based on the assumption that, the more education her people have, the more they will respect and obey the law, the greater happiness and prosperity they will experience, and the stronger and better their government will become. And there appears to be evidence that this faith is not entirely misplaced. At least, there seems to be some support for it in the fields of law enforcement and corrections. For example, many studies and investigations have revealed that a large percentage of offenders have had low grades in their studies, serious school behavior difficulties, truancy problems, and inadequate education.

Thus in 1931, MacCormick estimated that about 17 per cent of all prisoners could not read a newspaper or write a letter,[10] and several decades later, Chenault expressed the opinion that from 10 to 30 per cent of the persons admitted to correctional institutions in the United States were functionally illiterate.[11] Healy and Bronner found a much

[8] Caldwell, p. 274.

[9] See, for example, Alfred C. Kinsey et al., Sexual Behavior in the Human Female (Philadelphia: W. B. Saunders Co., 1953), pp. 304–7, 686, 687; Edwin M. Schur, Crimes Without Victims (Englewood Cliffs, N.J.: Prentice-Hall, Inc., 1965), p. 54; Erwin Stengel, Suicide and Attempted Suicide (Baltimore: Penguin Books, 1964), pp. 22, 23; Herbert Hendin, Suicide and Scandinavia (New York: Grune and Stratton, Inc., 1964), p. 6.

[10] Austin H. MacCormick, "Education in the Prisons of Tomorrow," Annals of the American Academy of Political and Social Science, CLVII (September, 1931), 72, 73.

[11] Price Chenault, "Education," Contemporary Correction, ed. Paul W. Tappan (New York: McGraw-Hill Book Co., Inc., 1951), pp. 224–37.

greater dislike of school among delinquents than among nondelinquent siblings,[12] and a study by Merrill showed that more delinquents than matched nondelinquents disliked school.[13]

In a study of 761 delinquent children referred to the Passaic Children's Bureau, Kvaraceus found that 34 per cent of them were truants, whereas only 6.8 per cent of the entire school population could be so classified; [14] Healy and Bronner reported that 60 per cent of the delinquents in their study had a record of repeated—often excessive—truancy; [15] and a study by the Gluecks published in 1950 showed that 94.8 per cent of the delinquents had truanted at one time or another during their school careers, whereas only 10.8 per cent of the nondelinquents had done so—and then only occasionally.[16] ¬Gold, Short, Polk, Cooper, Kvaraceus, and many others have reported on the low academic grades and school failures of delinquents; [17] and in their important investigations, the Gluecks found that delinquents had lower grades, more academic failures, poorer conduct records, higher truancy rates, and more school dropouts than nondelinquents.[18]

Many other studies similar to those cited above might be quoted here, but their findings would not change the general picture that we have presented.[19]   In fact, the cumulative thrust of all the studies and investigations pushes us to the conclusion that delinquents tend to have poorer

[12] William Healy and Augusta F. Bronner, *New Light on Delinquency and Its Treatment* (New Haven: Yale University Press, 1936), p. 62.

[13] Maud A. Merrill, *Problems of Child Delinquency* (New York: Houghton Mifflin Co., 1947), pp. 105, 106.

[14] William C. Kvaraceus, *Juvenile Delinquency and the School* (New York: World Book Co., 1945), pp. 144, 145.

[15] Healy and Bronner, p. 76.

[16] Sheldon and Eleanor T. Glueck, *Unraveling Juvenile Delinquency*, p. 148.

[17] For a discussion of these studies, see Walter E. Schafer and Kenneth Polk, "Delinquency and the Schools," *Task Force Report: Juvenile Delinquency and Youth Crime, Appendix M,* The President's Commission on Law Enforcement and Administration of Justice (Washington, D.C.: Government Printing Office, 1967), pp. 228–34.  See also James F. Short, Jr., "Gang Delinquency and Anomie," *Anomie and Deviant Behavior,* ed. Marshall B. Clinard (New York: The Free Press, 1964), p. 107; Kvaraceus, *Juvenile Delinquency and the School,* p. 141.

[18] See Sheldon and Eleanor T. Glueck, *One Thousand Juvenile Delinquents* (Cambridge: Harvard University Press, 1934), pp. 87, 88; *ibid., Unraveling Juvenile Delinquency,* Chapter 12.   See also Sheldon Glueck, The Problem of Delinquency (Boston: Houghton Mifflin Co., 1959).

[19] See, for example, Harrison E. Salisbury, *The Shook-Up Generation* (New York: Harper and Row, 1958), pp. 132–65; R. J. Havighurst, P. H. Bowman, G. P. Liddle, C. V. Matthews, and J. V. Pierce, *Growing Up in River City* (New York: John Wiley and Sons, Inc., 1962), pp. 49–88; A. B. Hollingshead, *Elmtown's Youth* (New York: John Wiley and Sons, Inc., 1949), pp. 172, 173.   For a review of some of the studies on the education of delinquents, see John R. Eichorn, "Delinquency and the Educational System," *Juvenile Delinquency: Research and Theory,* ed. Herbert C. Quay (New York: Van Nostrand Reinhold Co., Inc., 1965), pp. 298–332.

See Nelson S. Burke and Alfred E. Simons, "Factors Which Precipitate Dropouts and Delinquency," *Federal Probation,* XXIX (March, 1965), pp. 28–32.

academic and conduct records while they are in school, drop out of school sooner, and so receive less education than nondelinquents.[20]

Does this mean, then, that formal education, of itself, bears an important causal relationship to delinquency and crime? No, this is not necessarily true and cannot be shown to be true in general, although it may be so in the individual case. Of course, education is important, and it can do much to prepare the individual for a happy and successful life; but the influence of education must be seen in its interaction with many other factors, such as heredity, the home, the child's personality, the playgroup, the neighborhood, and so on. But does the school in its education of the child contribute to delinquency? Obviously, the school may do this in the individual case, but the extent to which it contributes to delinquency in general and what should be done to reduce any such influence are subjects of considerable controversy,[21] which will be discussed later in the chapters on the prevention of delinquency.

## RECREATION

Most delinquencies are committed by children during their leisure time. This has led many writers to conclude that the misuse of leisure time is the major cause of delinquency, and that the solution of this serious social problem is to be found in the establishment of wholesome recreation programs. The child, they argue, must be taught how to use his leisure time most effectively and given an opportunity to direct his play activities along lines that are beneficial to both himself and society.

Furthermore, some studies seem to support this contention. Thurston, for example, in an early Cleveland survey, concluded that 75 per cent of the delinquents included in the investigation had behavioral difficulties because of the habitual misuse of leisure time.[22]

Thrasher, in his classic study of the gang, published many years ago, wrote:

The fourth negative factor which contributes to a situation favorable to ganging is the lack of proper guidance for spare-time activities. The recreation of boys who become "wholesome citizens" is guided by parents, friends, teachers, and recreational leaders, but this guidance is largely absent in gangland areas. The point is not that children do not play in gangland. They

[20] See Robert M. MacIver, *The Prevention and Control of Delinquency* (New York: Atherton Press, 1966), pp. 78, 105.

[21] For an attempt to determine the extent to which this occurs, see Delbert S. Elliott, "Delinquency, School Attendance, and Dropout," *Social Problems*, XIII (Winter, 1966), 307–14.

[22] Henry W. Thurston, *Delinquency and Spare Time*, The Cleveland Recreation Survey (New York: The Cleveland Foundation, 1918), pp. 105–20.

do. . . . The common assumption that the problem of boy delinquency will be solved by the multiplication of playgrounds and social centers in gang areas is entirely erroneous. The physical layout of gangland provides a realm of adventure with which no playground can compete. The lack is not of this sort. The real problem is one of developing in these areas or introducing into them leaders who can organize the play of the boys, direct it into wholesome channels, and give it social significance.[23]

In New York City, Shulman traced the number of dropouts among problem children referred by city-wide family welfare and child guidance agencies to social group work agencies in East Harlem and discovered that only 5 per cent were members of supervised recreation agencies.[24] In a study of a group of delinquents handled by a county juvenile court in California, Merrill found that 45 per cent of them had never belonged to a club as compared with 23 per cent of the nondelinquent children in the control group, and that 78 per cent of the nondelinquents, as contrasted with 46 per cent of the delinquents, made good or excellent use of their leisure time.[25]

The Gluecks in a study of 510 reformatory youths learned that only 81 (15.8 per cent) had ever belonged to any social club or organization for the constructive use of leisure.[26] In their study of 1,000 delinquents, the Gluecks found that only 3 (.3 per cent) had used their leisure time constructively, 61 (6.3 per cent) had used this time negatively, and 912 (93.4 per cent) had used it harmfully, and that at the time of arrest, only 104 (10.6 per cent) belonged to organized leisure-time programs (such as those provided by the YMCA and the Boy Scouts), whereas 75.2 per cent had never participated in any such program.[27]

All these studies—and others like them—tend to show that more delinquents than nondelinquents misuse their leisure time. Do these studies prove that the misuse of leisure time is an important cause of juvenile delinquency? Actually, they do not help us at all in our efforts to understand the causes of this problem. To say that delinquents do not use their leisure time constructively is quite different from saying that their failure to do this causes their delinquency. Even if these studies tend to show the former, they in no way prove the latter. Other studies, however, have gone beyond this and sought to determine whether there is a causal relationship between participation in organized recrea-

[23] Frederic M. Thrasher, The Gang (Chicago: The University of Chicago Press, 1936), pp. 493, 494.

[24] Harry Manuel Shulman, Juvenile Delinquency in American Society (New York: Harper and Row, 1961), p. 658.

[25] Merrill, pp. 92, 93.

[26] Sheldon and Eleanor T. Glueck, 500 Criminal Careers (New York: Alfred A. Knopf, Inc., 1930), pp. 128, 129.

[27] Sheldon and Eleanor T. Glueck, One Thousand Juvenile Delinquents, pp. 93, 94.

tion and juvenile behavior, but a discussion of these studies will be postponed until we take up the question of the prevention of delinquency.

Here we need only to point out that children may engage in unguided play without becoming delinquent, that many persons who never become delinquent prefer and need such recreation, that many delinquents take part in organized recreation and remain delinquent, and that no one has proved that organized recreation, of itself, prevents juvenile delinquency or that its absence alone causes it. Even so, none of these facts can be used as an argument against organized recreation. Every child should have access to wholesome leisure-time activity, and some children need and enjoy supervised recreation, both delinquents and nondelinquents often benefiting by their participation in it. Indeed, organized recreation, when it is wisely planned and competently administered, can be an important element in a program for the prevention of crime and delinquency.

## MASS MEDIA

The term "mass media" is now used to refer to such impersonal means of communication as newspapers, magazines, comic books, radio, television, and motion pictures. These media have grown to such proportions that there can be no denying that they now greatly affect the lives of the people of the United States. If you have any doubt about this, take a look at these statistics: In 1958, English-language newspapers in the United States had a daily circulation of nearly 58 million; at the beginning of 1960, this country had close to 160 million radio receivers and about 50 million television sets; each month we now buy about 70 to 100 million comic books, and estimates of the sales of pornographic material have placed the total at $500 million a year.[28] Clearly, then, these media exert a tremendous influence—far more, in fact, than all forms of organized leisure-time activities combined.

Since these media do affect the lives of so many people, reaching irresistibly into the privacy of millions of homes, their increasing power has engendered widespread fears about what they are doing to the morality of the nation and especially to the minds of children. As a result, the mass media have been charged with causing crime and delinquency by peddling lurid tales of immorality and the licentious affairs of notorious persons, by making crime seem attractive, exciting, glamorous, and profitable, by featuring violence, brutality, and lawlessness, by giving publicity and prestige to crooks, gangsters, gamblers, confidence men, racketeers, and hoodlums, by converting leaders of the

[28] Martin H. Neumeyer, *Juvenile Delinquency in Modern Society* (New York: Van Nostrand Reinhold Co., Inc., 1961), pp. 218–28.

underworld into heroes and generating sympathy for them after their apprehension, by teaching the techniques of crime and delinquency, by denigrating and ridiculing the courts and law-enforcement agencies, by creating the impression that punishment is futile and outmoded and escape from justice is easy if you know the "right people," and by conducting "trials by newspapers" and thus undermining the administration of justice.

The mass media tend to deny these charges or claim that they are grossly exaggerated, and, in addition, maintain that their influence can be beneficial. This is true, they contend, for they can provide vicarious experience, draining off tensions and directing antisocial tendencies into imaginary adventures, keep young people away from mischief, hooliganism, and vice, educate the public regarding scientific advances in the detection, apprehension, and correction of offenders and the prevention of crime and delinquency, arouse public opinion against undesirable social conditions, stimulate public demand for civic reform, and marshal public support for vigorous law enforcement and effective judicial action.

Undoubtedly, then, the mass media, especially the motion picture and television programs with their visual imagery, in one way or another, affect the ideas, attitudes, and behavior of adults and children and change the morality and habits of the nature. Nevertheless, we do not know how or to what extent they do this; and our knowledge regarding their relationship to crime and delinquency is so uncertain that generalizations on the subject are extremely hazardous. This uncertainty obtains despite some strenuous efforts that have been made to learn the nature of this relationship. Indeed, more than a decade ago, a subcommittee of the United States Senate held extensive hearings over a period of many weeks to determine the effects of the mass media on juvenile delinquency. Although the reports of this subcommittee contain the opinions and speculations of many expert witnesses, they supply us with very little substantial evidence.[29]

## Motion Pictures

Over the years, however, various studies have given us some information about the relationship between the mass media and juvenile delinquency. In 1925, Burt reported that over 7 per cent of his delin-

[29] See U.S. Senate Subcommittee to Investigate Juvenile Delinquency, *Comic Books and Juvenile Delinquency* (Washington, D.C.: Government Printing Office, 1955); *ibid., Obscene and Pornographic Literature and Juvenile Delinquency* (Washington, D.C.: Government Printing Office, 1956); *ibid., Motion Pictures and Juvenile Delinquency* (Washington, D.C.: Government Printing Office, 1956); *ibid., Television and Juvenile Delinquency* (Washington, D.C.: Government Printing Office, 1956).

quent boys had an "excessive passion" for motion pictures, and he expressed the opinion that films advertise crime as a form of behavior and show criminal techniques.[30]   Healy and Bronner wrote in 1936 that a larger number of the delinquents than the nondelinquents in their study attended motion pictures regularly, but that only a few of the delinquents had definitely imitated the criminal techniques which they had seen on the screen.[31]   Blumer and Hauser, in a study which is still our principal source of information about the effects of motion pictures on crime and delinquency, concluded that films were a factor of importance in the delinquent or criminal careers of about 10 per cent of the male and 25 per cent of the female offenders included in their study.   Although these investigators concluded that a motion picture affects individuals in different ways, depending upon their backgrounds and personalities, yet, according to them, a child from a high-rate delinquency area is more likely to engage in delinquency because of the influence of motion pictures than a child from an area of low delinquency rates.[32]

However, Paul Cressey, in a study published a few years later, while admitting that some boys, when suitably disposed, might use certain techniques of crime that they had seen on the screen, concluded that motion pictures did not have any significant effect on the causation of juvenile delinquency.[33]   Furthermore, the study by Blumer and Hauser has been criticized on the grounds that it relied too much on the statements of the children examined and failed to use a control group of nondelinquent children for the purpose of comparison.[34]   Although the United States Senate Subcommittee, to which we have already referred, was unable to secure any conclusive evidence about the effects of motion pictures on delinquency, it did report that, in its opinion, films could provide the triggering mechanisms in the delinquencies of emotionally disturbed children, and that the continual viewing of sadistic and crime movies would have a negative impact on the normal nondelinquent child.[35]   The fact is that we still do not have any conclusive information about the relationship between motion pictures and juvenile delinquency, either in the case of normal or emotionally disturbed children.

[30] Cyril Burt, *The Young Delinquent* (New York: Appleton-Century-Crofts, Inc., 1925), pp. 137–43.

[31] Healy and Bronner, p. 72.

[32] Herbert Blumer and Philip M. Hauser, *Movies, Delinquency, and Crime* (New York: The Macmillan Co., 1933), pp. 35, 38–72, 81, 198, 199, 201, 202.

[33] Paul G. Cressey, "The Motion Picture Experience as Modified by Social Background and Personality," *American Sociological Review*, III (August, 1938), 516–25.

[34] See Mortimer J. Adler, *Art and Prudence* (New York: Longmans, Green and Co., 1937), pp. 279–83.

[35] U.S. Senate Subcommittee to Investigate Juvenile Delinquency, *Motion Pictures and Juvenile Delinquency*, pp. 18, 19, 61, 62.

## Comic Books

Moreover, our knowledge about the effects of comic books on the behavior of boys and girls is even more fragmentary and uncertain. The great majority of sociologists and psychologists take the position that there is no empirical study which shows any positive relationship between comic books and juvenile delinquency, but even so, this form of mass media has been severely criticized by a large group of lay and professional people. Among the leaders of this group is Dr. Frederic Wertham, a psychiatrist, who maintains that comic books that give prominence to horror and crime are a significant contributing factor in the causation of delinquency.[36] In replay to this charge, the opponents of Wertham have insisted that his case rests on an inadequate sample, that he presents no statistical summary to support his views, and that he has used no comparative control groups.[37]

## Television

The criticism of the influence of the mass media on juvenile delinquency is now focused on television. Wertham is again a leader in this attack. Denouncing television as a school for violence that most of our children attend regularly, he argues that it is an important cause of crime. However, not all of his colleagues in psychiatry agree with him. In a recent survey of 313 psychiatrists, for example, 30 per cent believed that fictional violence portrayed in comic books, television shows, and movies teaches actual violence, 24 per cent felt that it helped to dissipate aggression, and 46 per cent were undecided.[38]

These percentages, of course, represent only opinions, but we do have two comprehensive studies, one in this country and one in England, that tried to secure more definite information about the effects of television on the lives of children. In the American study, Schramm, Lyle, and Parker state that very little delinquency can be traced directly to television. In their opinion, delinquency is complex behavior that usually has a number of roots—"often a broken home, or a feeling of rejection by parents or peer group." They conclude that "television is at best a

---

[36] Frederic Wertham, *Seduction of the Innocent* (New York: Holt, Rinehart, and Winston, Inc., 1954).

[37] For a critique of the earlier research of Wertham, see Frederic M. Thrasher, "The Comics and Delinquency: Cause or Scapegoat," *Journal of Educational Sociology*, XXIII (December, 1949), 195–205.

[38] Joyce Brothers, "Are the Seeds of Violence Nurtured Through the Public's Airwaves?" *T.V .Guide*, XVI (August 24, 1968), 5–9, 12.

contributory cause." [39]   In the English study, published several years earlier, Himmelweit and associates, finding no more aggressive, maladjusted, or delinquent behavior among the children who looked at television than among those in the control group, arrived independently at similar conclusions.[40]

All that we have said about television and the other mass media forces us to admit that we know little about their effects on human behavior. Even so, we can draw some tentative conclusions from the evidence that we do have.   Persons who have already acquired delinquent or criminal tendencies or who have abnormal psychogenic traits may have these tendencies aggravated by motion pictures, comic books, or radio or television programs.   It is doubtful, however, whether persons who do not have such tendencies or traits become criminals or delinquents solely because of the effects of the mass media.   Yet, we should add that children are more susceptible to the influence of the mass media than adults, that there are many highly suggestible, restless, and unstable persons with criminal and delinquent tendencies who can be influenced by the mass media, and that the number of these persons is probably growing. Finally, we must understand that the mass media are exerting an increasing influence in our complex society and profoundly affecting its culture. To the extent that these media are creating a cynical indifference to questions of morality and an irresponsible permissiveness, they are producing changes that, in turn, will ultimately contribute to crime and delinquency.

## ECONOMIC FACTORS

Many studies and public investigations have indicated that the poor contribute disproportionately to crime and delinquency in the United States.   Does this mean, then, that poverty, *per se*, is a cause of crime and delinquency?   The economic determinists would like us to think so. In fact, Marxian Communists argue that all of our social problems, including crime and delinquency, are rooted in the capitalist system,[41] and that they can be eliminated only through the creation of a communist society.   However, economic determinism, like all the other forms of

---

[39] Wilbur Schramm, Jack Lyle, Edwin B. Parker, *Television in the Lives of Our Children* (Stanford, Calif.: Stanford University Press, 1961), pp. 163–66, 173–75.

[40] Hilde T. Himmelweit, A. N. Oppenheim, and Pamela Vince, *Television and the Child: An Empirical Study of the Effects of Television on the Young* (New York: Oxford University Press, 1958).

[41] W. A. Bonger, *Criminality and Economic Condition* (Boston: Little, Brown and Co., 1916).

particularist explanations, is a gross oversimplification of the causal process. The economic factors must be seen as functionally related to many other factors, such as the biological, geographical, psychological, domestic, religious, political, and educational factors, and a social problem, like crime or delinquency, is produced by the interaction of all of them, and not by the action of only one. Of course, crime and delinquency in the United States are related to the operation of our capitalist system, but all kinds of societies, including the communist ones, have these problems, and it is impossible to predict whether ours would increase or decrease if we changed our economic system.

In an effort to determine the relationship between the economic factors and delinquency, two important methods have been used:

1. Comparative analysis of the economic status of offenders and nonoffenders.
2. Study of the relation of delinquency rates and the business cycle.

Burt, using the first method in his definitive study, *The Young Delinquent*, found that over half of the total number of the delinquents of London came from poor and very poor families.[42]  Caldwell discovered that 33.4 per cent of the parents of boy delinquents and 52.7 per cent of those of girl delinquents in the correctional institutions of Wisconsin were unskilled in comparison with 11.8 per cent of the entire employed population of that state.[43]  Merrill found marked differences in the economic status between a group of delinquents and a control group of nondelinquents, even though the members of both groups came from the same neighborhoods.[44]  Kvaraceus, in his study of delinquency in Passaic, New Jersey, reported that the fathers of delinquents had occupational ratings that were much lower than that of the city's general population.[45]  Reinemann, in a study of 220 truants in Philadelphia, learned that the family income was so low in 30 per cent of the cases that the mothers were compelled to secure part-time or full-time employment.[46]  The Gluecks, in their study, *Unraveling Juvenile Delinquency*, showed that the usual economic status of the families of delinquents was much lower than that of the control group of nondelinquents.[47]  Many other studies such as

[42] Burt, pp. 64–67.
[43] Morris G. Caldwell, "The Economic Status of Families of Delinquent Boys in Wisconsin," *American Journal of Sociology*, XXXVII (September, 1931), 231–39.
[44] Merrill, pp. 76–88
[45] William C. Kvaraceus, "Juvenile Delinquency and Social Class," *Journal of Educational Sociology*, XVIII (September, 1944), 51–54.
[46] John Otto Reinemann, "The Truant Before the Court," *Federal Probation*, XII (September, 1948), 8–12.
[47] Sheldon and Eleanor T. Glueck, *Unraveling Juvenile Delinquency*, pp. 84–88, 104, 106, 280.

these might be quoted here—each one indicating that the poverty-stricken contribute more than their share to the ranks of delinquents; but all of the studies of this kind (that is, those dealing with the economic status of offenders and nonoffenders) are inconclusive.

Where they have used official delinquency statistics, they are exposed, in general, to the criticism that they are incomplete, inaccurate, and non-representative, and, in particular, to the charge that they are unfair to the poor, since, it is contended, the children of the poor are more likely to be detected, arrested, and adjudicated delinquents than are those of the rich. Furthermore, the causal relationship between poverty and delinquency is not so simple and direct as it may seem to be. Carpenter, for example, in a study of English juvenile delinquents made over one hundred years ago, recognized the complexity of the causal process and rejected the idea that poverty is the cause of most delinquency, although she admitted that it might be an important factor in certain cases.[48] Both Burt and Merrill, whose works are cited above, concluded that poverty alone does not produce delinquency, and Healy and Bronner, in their 1936 study, *New Light on Delinquency and Its Treatment*, stressed the unsatisfactory human relationships usually associated with poverty, rather than poverty *per se*, as a cause of delinquency.[49] Additional studies, such as those by Nye, Akers, Clark and Wenninger, and Wattenberg and Balistrieri,[50] might be mentioned here, but the general conclusion would remain the same: the relationship between economic conditions and delinquency is very complex.

This conclusion has been reinforced by studies that have sought to relate delinquency rates to the business cycle. One of these studies, made by Bogen, indicated that, during the years 1925 to 1941, juvenile delinquency in Los Angeles decreased in the Depression and increased during prosperity.[51] Another, by Reinemann, for the years 1923 to 1945, found that delinquency in Philadelphia was high during a depression period,

[48] Mary Carpenter, *Juvenile Delinquents, Their Condition and Treatment* (London: W. and F. G. Cash, 1853), pp. 23–43.

[49] William Healy and Augusta F. Bronner, *New Light on Delinquency and Its Treatment* (New Haven: Yale University Press, 1936), pp. 1–13, 200–05.

[50] See F. Ivan Nye, *Family Relationships and Delinquent Behavior*, pp. 25–31; Ronald L. Akers, "Socio-Economic Status and Delinquent Behavior: A Retest," *Journal of Research in Crime and Delinquency*, I (January, 1964), 38–46; John P. Clark and Eugene P. Wenninger, "Socio-Economic Class and Area as Correlates of Illegal Behavior Among Juveniles," *American Sociological Review*, XXVII (December, 1962), 826–34; William W. Wattenberg and James Balistrieri, Automobile Theft: A 'Favored-Group' Delinquency," *American Journal of Sociology*, LVII (May, 1952), 575–79.

[51] David Bogen, "Juvenile Delinquency and Economic Trend," *American Sociological Review*, IX (April, 1944), 178–84.

low in a period of fairly normal economic development which can be classified as neither prosperity nor depression, but highest during a period of extreme prosperity.[52] However, such studies as those that have attempted to relate delinquency to economic status cannot be considered conclusive, if for no other reason than they have failed to separate the economic factors from other factors.

But let us pursue this matter further. Why, according to such studies as those of Bogen and Reinemann, does juvenile delinquency increase during prosperity and decrease during periods of depression, which is the opposite of what would happen if poverty, *per se*, were the cause of delinquency? Neumeyer cited various reasons that have been given to explain this. For example, it has been suggested that when income declines during a depression, families tend to spend more time at home, supervise their children more closely, and discipline them more strictly. And while a shortage of public funds is causing a reduction in police personnel and a relaxation of law enforcement, citizens and officials are developing a more lenient view of petty thievery by poor children and a greater reluctance to press charges against them. All of which, it is explained, tends to reduce the number of delinquency cases.

On the other hand, during prosperity, jobs are plentiful, money flows freely, more women and children work, parents and children spend more time away from home and apart from one another, supervision of children declines, patronage of commercialized recreation increases, the consumption of liquor rises, family ties weaken, and all these tendencies contribute to the growth of delinquency. Whether such speculation actually elucidates the rise and fall of delinquency is relatively unimportant. What is important is that studies of the business cycle seem to indicate that much more than poverty is involved in the causation of delinquency.[53]

Although our efforts to determine the relationship between economic conditions and delinquency have not been very fruitful, they have shown that it is not a simple and direct one. Poverty, it appears, is related to delinquency chiefly through such conditions as bad housing, inadequate education and recreation, domestic discord, neglect and improper discipline, early employment of children, immoral neighborhood influences, and so on. Furthermore, we are persistently reminded of the complexity of this relationship by the fact that many poverty-stricken children never

[52] John Otto Reinemann, "Juvenile Delinquency in Philadelphia and Economic Trends," *Temple University Law Quarterly,* XX (April, 1947), 576–83.

[53] Martin H. Neumeyer, *Juvenile Delinquency in Modern Society* (New York: Van Nostrand Reinhold Co., Inc., 1961), pp. 56–58. See also Jerome Hall, "Theft, Law, and Society—1968," *American Bar Association Journal,* LIV (October, 1968), 960–67.

become delinquent, that some wealthy children do, that both delinquent and nondelinquent children come from the same poor family and from the same blighted neighborhood, and that many children in slum areas do not become chronically delinquent at all. Even so, the lower economic classes do have higher rates of delinquency than the upper economic classes in the United States, and certainly poverty does constitute a delinquency risk, that is, its presence increases the possibility of delinquency.

# 10

# Summary View of Causation

## THE MEANING OF "CAUSE"

The word "cause" has been used a number of times thus far in our discussion of delinquency. Perhaps the reader has concluded that it has more than one meaning; and that, indeed, is the case. For example, in science, "cause" means the sufficient antecedent conditions necessary for the evocation of a given phenomenon, and in this sense it refers to the conditions, or factors, which science can isolate and identify in the immediate situation. Thus science does not deal with the ultimates in reality, although it constantly endeavors to extend the area in which it can function. Philosophy, on the other hand, looks beyond the immediate situation. When the philosopher uses the term "cause," he may have in mind the ultimates in reality, referring, for example, to the origin and destiny of man.

The lawyer employs the word "cause" in still another sense. He explains his usage in this way. The law cannot take into consideration all the possible causes of an act, for to do so would stir up boundless conflicts in every community, fill the courts with endless litigation, and eventually destroy the judicial structure. In the law, therefore, the meaning of "cause" is limited by a social policy called "justice," which tends to be an expression of the dominant values of the group. Accordingly, within the limits imposed by justice, a person's act may be said to be the *legally recognized* cause of the consequences, and if these are defined as a crime or delinquency, the adult may be held to be criminally responsible or the juvenile may be adjudged a delinquent. Thus we can see how in any particular case, the law, guided by the tenets of justice, may regard certain factors as too trivial or too remote to be called causes, even though science would include them in its analysis of causation, and philosophy would ponder them in its speculations.

But let us return to the work of the scientist. Restricted by his limited knowledge, the scientist cannot work with reality in its entirety; to simplify his problem, he abstracts from various aspects of reality and concentrates his attention on these. Through this process of abstraction, he hopes to gain deeper insight into all of reality. There is nothing inherently wrong in this, and it has borne fruit through the efforts of the geologist, the geographer, the biologist, the psychiatrist, the psychologist, the sociologist, and other specialists, as each has labored with his own tools in his own vineyard, but there are dangers involved.[1] For example, each of these specialists tends to overemphasize the importance of those aspects of reality that he has studied and to insist that the truth can be found only in his vineyard, and that work in the others can contribute little or nothing. Indeed, the danger here is even greater, for a particular specialist—for instance, a sociologist or a psychologist—may be misled into believing that his favorite theory provides the only valid approach to an understanding of life's problems.

To guard against this danger, we must remember that when a part of reality—this or that factor or condition—is abstracted for a more complete study of it in its separation from the other parts, we must not reify it, that is, we must not give it an independent and concrete existence. Instead, we must see it not merely in its abstracted form, but also in its interaction with—not just in its addition to—the other parts or factors in the total situation. Furthermore, we must understand that some of the parts exert more influence than others, and that the functioning of all is necessary to produce what we observe, which would be different if there were the least modification in the total situation. So, as we shall see, in our attempt to understand the causation of delinquency, we must take into consideration the interaction of many influences of varying strengths, both personal and environmental.


## APPROACHES TO THE CAUSATION OF DELINQUENCY

As we have indicated in the earlier chapters of this book, various approaches have been made to an understanding of the causes of juvenile delinquency. Here we shall briefly review the progress that has been made in these approaches, which, for our purposes, will be divided into the biological, psychiatric, psychological, and sociological. It should be kept in mind, however, that these approaches are not mutually exclu-

---

[1] Robert G. Caldwell, *Criminology* (New York: The Ronald Press Co., 1965), pp. 13, 14, 35–37.

sive, and that each of the theories mentioned is classified according to the approach that it emphasizes.

## Biological Approach

This approach was given considerable impetus by the work of Cesare Lombroso, who founded the positive school of criminology during the 1870's. Although he contended that there was a distinct, born-criminal type that could be recognized by certain physical characteristics, he never asserted that all offenders belonged to this type. Subsequent study and research, however, especially that of Charles Goring and Gabriel Tarde, discredited Lombroso's concept of a born-criminal type, but belief in the importance of heredity persisted. In fact, Goring, like Lombroso, strongly stressed the role of the biological factors. Hooton argued that inherited inferiority, acted upon by environmental forces, was the primary cause of crime. Sheldon sought to demonstrate that body build bore a direct relationship to personality and thus to crime and delinquency, and the Gluecks explained that they had found some evidence to support Sheldon's hypothesis. Other writers have used the studies of family trees, twins, and the malfunctioning endocrine glands and other mental and physical abnormalities and defects to show the importance of biological conditions in the causation of criminal and delinquent behavior. Thus far, however, the biological approach has failed to prove that the biological factors cause crime and delinquency or even that they are a major cause. However, this does not mean that they are unimportant or can be disregarded, but only that there is not sufficient knowledge for us to generalize about their influence in human behavior.

## Psychiatric Approach

Psychiatry is that branch of medicine which deals with mental disorders. Although it is primarily a product of the nineteenth and twentieth centuries, it remained for Sigmund Freud (1856–1939) to originate psychoanalysis, which has exerted far more influence in the field of criminology than any other approach to psychiatry.[2]

[2] For a study of the psychoanalytic theory, see *The Basic Writings of Sigmund Freud*, trans. and ed. A. A. Brill (New York: The Modern Library, 1938); Sigmund Freud, *A General Introduction to Psychoanalysis* (New York: Boni and Liveright, 1920); A. A. Brill, *Freud's Contribution to Psychiatry* (New York: W. W. Norton and Co., 1944); William Healy, A. F. Bronner, and A. M. Bowers, *The Structure and Meaning of Psychoanalysis* (New York: Alfred A. Knopf, Inc., 1930); *The Complete Psychological Works of Sigmund Freud*, ed. James Strachey (New York: The Free Press, 1962); Ruth L. Munroe, *Schools of Psychoanalytic Thought* (New York: The Dryden Press, Inc., 1955).

The psychoanalytic theory analyzes the psychic life of man in terms of the three concepts, the id, the ego, and the superego. The id is vast and powerful. Composed largely of the instinctive sexual urges, it constitutes the driving power behind human actions. The ego, developing out of the id through the contact of the self with external reality, curbs the id but also makes possible whatever satisfactions the id receives. The superego corresponds roughly to the conscience; it incorporates the ideals and moral standards which the child receives, principally those he learns from his parents.

Man's psychic struggle begins in infancy, as the unsocial and instinctive impulses of the id come into contact with social pressures and training procedures, and continues throughout the life of the individual. These impulses, although frustrated and held down by the ego, live on and persistently strive to circumvent their prohibitions, covertly influencing behavior and finding expression in dreams, which, according to Freud, are disguised satisfactions for desires that have been repressed during waking hours.

When the id, ego, and superego are not well balanced, the unsocial and instinctive impulses break through, and the individual, seeking relief from his inner conflict, engages in abnormal behavior. According to some psychiatrists, this abnormal behavior takes the form of delinquency or criminality when the suffering of the ego, caused by submission to the person's inhibitions, becomes greater than the expected punishment. In such a case, the ego casts off the inhibitions and joins its forces with those of the id. Thus, according to the psychoanalyst, both crime and delinquency are symptoms of internal maladjustment and alternate forms of adjustment, giving expression to needs and appetites, providing release for accumulated tensions and frustrations, and designed to restore the integrity of the personality. Many proponents of the psychoanalytic theory, however, concede that it cannot explain all criminality and delinquency, and that environmental influences are largely responsible for some offenders.

Healy used the psychiatric method in analyzing all the factors in the individual case instead of seeking to find some trait that might be employed to identify persons as criminals or delinquents. In his work, he tried to integrate the personal and environmental factors in his explanation of causation. According to him, the environment contains patterns of delinquency, but the individual is driven into delinquency because he fails to find socially approved ways of satisfying his impelling desires, of reducing personality conflicts, and of relieving emotional distress. Aichhorn, a leading exponent of the Freudian theory, found the cause of delinquency in disturbed or faulty ego development, and Friedlander and Redl, two disciples of Aichhorn, further developed his theory of delinquency.[3]   Hewitt and Jenkins, however, used both personality maladjustments and environmental situations, in their construction of a typlogy of delinquents.

Critics have severely attacked the psychoanalytic theory, some denouncing it as pseudoscientific drivel.[4]   They assert, for example, that it greatly overemphasizes the biological factors, the abnormalities of man, and the role of sex, that it fails to give enough recognition to the influence of culture, and that it is largely a speculative concept whose meaning is obscured by a vague and confusing terminology.   Furthermore, the critics argue, its method of free association is merely a device by which the preconceived ideas of the analyst are read into the statements of the patient.   By this method, the patient is encouraged to relax, express himself freely, conceal nothing because it seems embarrassing, objectionable, or trivial, and thus bring back to consciousness the repressed or disagreeable thoughts or experiences that have caused his difficulties.   This, it is argued, will give him insight into the nature of his situation, release him from his painful conflicts and frustrations, and enable him to overcome his problems.   With all its faults, however, the psychoanalytic theory has called attention to the importance of seeing the personality as a dynamic whole and of understanding the influence of childhood, the nonrational, and sex in human behavior.

## Psychological Approach

For many years, the psychological approach was especially interested in the possible relationship between mental deficiency and crime, and some psychologists, for example, Goddard, took the extreme position that mental defects were the most important cause of criminality and delinquency.   Further research, however, by Murchison, Zeleny, Tulchin, and others has shown that this position is untenable, and the available evidence, although far from conclusive, seems to indicate that in general, the intelligence of offenders does not greatly differ from that of nonoffenders.

During the past few decades, many psychologists have devoted much of their time to a study of the personality traits of offenders, but thus far they have not been able to prove that the possession of certain traits necessarily causes crime or delinquency.   Nevertheless, it is true that

[3] August Aichhorn, *Wayward Youth* (New York: The Viking Press, Inc., 1936); Kate Friedlander, *The Psycho-analytical Approach to Juvenile Delinquency* (New York: International Universities Press, Inc., 1947); *ibid.*, "Latent Delinquency and Ego Development," *Searchlights on Delinquency*, ed. Kurt R. Eissler (New York: International Universities Press, Inc., 1949), pp. 205–15; Fritz Redl and David Wineman, *Children Who Hate* (New York: The Free Press, 1951).

[4] See, for example, Dale G. Hardman, "The Case for Eclecticism," *Crime and Delinquency*, X (July, 1964), 201–16.

these traits, like mental deficiency and other personal factors, may contribute in an important way to crime or delinquency in the individual case.

## Sociological Approach

The sociological approach emphasizes the importance of the social environment. Since World War I, this approach has had its greatest development in the United States, where it received much strength and support from the work of Shaw and McKay and their associates, who used the ecological method [5] in the study of delinquency in Chicago and other cities. Although this method has contributed valuable information regarding the distribution of crime and delinquency, it has thrown little light on the internalization of environmental influences in the causation of these problems. In their attempts to explain causation, some American sociologists, while stressing the social factors, see crime and delinquency as the products of the interaction of all factors, including the biological, the psychological, and the social, in the total situation. However, many others, like Edwin H. Sutherland, regard all factors except the social as of little or no importance.

**Differential-Association Theory.** Sutherland has probably exerted more influence than any other American sociologist in the field of criminology. He presented his differential-association theory in its original form in the 1939 edition of his textbook *Principles of Criminology.*[6] Admitting that existing knowledge was not sufficient to explain why a particular person committed a certain crime, he concentrated his attention on systematic criminal behavior, either in the form of criminal careers or organized criminal practices. In his theory, he stated that systematic criminal behavior is caused in a process of association with those who commit crimes, and that the individual's characteristics are involved only to the extent that they affect this association. The term "differential association" was used because the process of association that produces systematic criminal behavior contains values that are different from those in the process that produces systematic lawful behavior. The basic cause of systematic criminal behavior, however, is social disorganization,

---

[5] Human ecology is that branch of science which treats of the reciprocal relations between man and environment. See the *Dictionary of Sociology* (New York: The Philosophical Library, 1944), p. 101. Shaw utilized the life-history method to supplement the ecological method. In his books *The Natural History of a Delinquent Career* (1931) and *The Jack Roller* (1930), the individual tells his own story and thus provides insights into the causes of his behavior.

[6] Edwin H. Sutherland, *Principles of Criminology* (Philadelphia: J. B. Lippincott Co., 1939), pp. 4–9.

that is, a decline in the influence of existing social rules, for without this, persons are generally law-abiding, and so association with those who commit crimes is not likely.

Sutherland presented the last statement of his differential-association theory in the 1947 edition of his text *Principles of Criminology*.[7] This time, however, he did not confine his theory to systematic criminal behavior but offered it as an explanation of all criminal behavior. In this version of the theory, he states that criminal behavior is learned in interaction with other persons in a process of communication, especially in the intimacy of personal association, and that a person becomes delinquent because in his association with others the net results of his learning are favorable to violation of law. It is important to note that, as the theory now stands, the term "differential association" appears to mean association with patterns of behavior—not with criminals—regardless of the character of the person presenting them. According to this interpretation of the theory, a person may become delinquent or criminal even if he has never met a criminal or delinquent or has never been aware of coming into contact with delinquent or criminal patterns of behavior.

Although this theory has been stoutly defended by many sociologists, it has been persistently criticized by others. Thus critics have said: (1) that its scope has been variously defined, causing confusion about its real meaning; (2) that it erects a completely determinist and closed system of thought on the shaky foundation of our meager knowledge of human behavior; (3) that it does not attach sufficient importance to the biological and psychological factors; (4) that it oversimplifies the process of learning; and (5) that, as many of its exponents concede, it is not susceptible of empirical testing and cannot be proved.[8] In concluding his critical analysis of the differential-association theory, Caldwell observed that if the claim is now made that this theory explains all criminal behavior, then the claim is made with the admission by Cressey, its chief exponent, that it is doubtful whether the theory can be proved. "But," Caldwell continues, "if the theory merely means that many persons learn to be criminals because most of the environmental influences in their lives do not produce a proper respect for the law, then it has been reduced to a polysyllabic elaboration of the obvious—a fate that has befallen many oversimplifications of human behavior."[9] Nevertheless, despite its serious—perhaps fatal—weaknesses, the differential-association theory

---

[7] Edwin H. Sutherland, *Principles of Criminology* (Philadelphia: J. B. Lippincott Co., 1947), pp. 5–9.

[8] For a critical analysis of the differential-association theory, see Robert G. Caldwell, *Criminology* (New York: The Ronald Press Co., 1965), pp. 211–19.

[9] *Ibid.*, pp. 217, 218.

has called attention to the importance of the social factors and to the fact that criminality cannot be explained entirely in terms of personality maladjustments.

**Other Theories.** Various features of the social structure have been stressed in determining the sociological sources of delinquency and crime. Vold, for example, called attention to the role that antagonism and conflicts between groups play in the causation of such crime and delinquencies as those perpetrated by gang warfare, political turmoil, labor-management disputes, and syndicate activities.[10]

Parson, Merton, and others have used the concept of anomie to refer to the breakdown in the cultural structure, that is, to a condition of relative normlessness in society. Merton claims that a source of anomie exists when goals that are deemed appropriate for all are accessible through legitimate means for only a few, for this leads to social deviation (one form of which is crime and delinquency) by many of those who face this deprivation, and thus to a breakdown in the social norms. Since World War II, a number of sociologists, following the path marked out by Shaw, McKay, and Thrasher, have examined the relationship between social class and the delinquent gang. Among these have been Whyte, Cohen, Miller, Cloward, and Ohlin, the latter two combining Merton's theory of social structure and anomie with Sutherland's theory of differential association. Approaching the problem of delinquent gangs from a different point of view, Bloch and Niederhoffer have sought its causes in the difficulties adolescents may experience in achieving adult status.

Other sociologists in the field of criminology, endeavoring to bridge the gap between psychology and sociology, have embraced self theory in its symbolic interaction form, which they prefer to theories about personality needs, since it emphasizes the social and cultural factors. Reckless, however, believing that the search for a general theory of causation is probably unrealistic, urges that containment theory be substituted for causal theory. According to his view, a containing external social structure (principally the family and other supportive groups) and a containing internal buffer (components of the self) hold individuals in line and protect them against deviation from the social and legal norms. Thus, he explains, if there are "causes" which produce deviant behavior, the two containing buffers parry and neutralize them.[11]

The sociological approach to the causation of crime and delinquency has stimulated considerable research and has demonstrated the impor-

---

[10] George B. Vold, *Theoretical Criminology* (New York: Oxford University Press, 1958), pp. 203–19.

[11] Walter C. Reckless, *The Crime Problem* (New York: Appleton-Century-Crofts, Inc., 1961), pp. 335–59.

tance of social and cultural factors. Nevertheless, although it has proved that these factors cannot be disregarded, sociology cannot provide all the answers to the question of why we have crime and delinquency.

## SOME CONCLUSIONS

During the past several centuries, our knowledge of human behavior has increased, and we have acquired some effective techniques for its regulation, but so much of it remains unknown that we cannot claim that we have a science of human behavior. Certainly, no one discipline, be it biology, psychiatry, psychology, or sociology, can aver that it alone can show the way to a greater understanding of delinquency and criminality or of any other form of human behavior. Under the circumstances, each discipline should press forward along its own lines, and at the same time foster cooperation with all others in the hope that the pooling of resources will eventually bring a broader and deeper understanding of man's problems.[12]

Human behavior, whether law-abiding or law-violating, is the resultant of the interaction of personal and environmental factors. As Caldwell explains, "In any given case, some of these conditions exert more influence than others, but the functioning of all in their interaction is necessary to produce the observed phenomenon, which would be different if there were the least modification in the total situation." [13] Thus in some cases of crime or delinquency the causal factors may be more personal than environmental, whereas in other cases, the reverse may be true; but never, for example, is a person a criminal or a delinquent only because of personality maladjustments or only because of the learning of anti-social values. Always there is a mixture of both personal and environmental influences in varying proportions.[14]

The fact is that the paucity of our knowledge is such that the frame of reference in criminology must be rather wide, and the conclusions loosely drawn. "This is not to say that a certain theory should not be employed as a guide in a specific research project—indeed, this must be done—but it does mean that the conclusions of such research must be primarily related to the area explored and the level of abstraction used. Thus within a broad frame of reference, a closely reasoned theoretical

---

[12] See, for example, Harry Elmer Barnes and Negley K. Teeters, *New Horizons in Criminology* (Englewood Cliffs, N.J.: Prentice-Hall, Inc., 1959), pp. 206–10; Sheldon Glueck, "Theory and Fact in Criminology," *British Journal of Delinquency,* VII (October, 1956), 108; Vold, pp. 313–15; Reckless, pp. 335–59.

[13] Caldwell, p. 277.

[14] *Ibid.,* pp. 277, 278.

system can be created on this or that level of abstraction, but the possibility of other theories on the same or other levels of abstraction should be clearly recognized by such a system." [15]

In fact, the area of the unknown is so great that there may well be an element of free will in every human act. However, there has been some relenting on both sides of the freedom-of-will controversy. For example, those who believe in the doctrine of freedom of the will (known as "libertarians") now speak of freedom of choice rather than freedom of will, thus conceding that the will is affected by previous experience and attendant circumstances and so not completely free. On the other side of the question, some determinists, who reject the doctrine of freedom of the will for a belief that man is completely controlled by the forces of heredity and environment, now use the term "soft determinism," thus indicating their admission that there may be elements of indeterminism in human behavior. [16] Although these two views had their beginnings on opposite sides of the freedom-of-will controversy, each sees man as endowed with creative ability and capable of making choices.

Character more than any other term incorporates this conception of man. Certainly, it does this more than "personality" or "self," both of which lend themselves to a hard-determinist view of man, the former filling man with psychological forces, the latter, with social forces. In sharp contrast to this, character pictures man as having a reality apart from the group and of having the ability to weave the environmental and personal influences in his life into a choice. Furthermore, it holds him responsible for his choices and thus emphasizes his creative and self-directing powers.

We have now completed our summary view of causation, and it points to the following conclusions regarding juvenile delinquency:

1. Heredity is an important factor in human behavior, and in any particular case it may be the major influence in the development of delinquency.

2. The significance of racial differences remains a controversial question. Nevertheless, ideological considerations should not deter us from continuing our scientific examination of these differences to the end that we may learn more about them and the extent to which they affect human behavior.

3. Age and sex are important factors in the causation of juvenile delinquency, but they must be seen in their interaction with the social and cultural influences that play upon the individual in every society.

---

[15] *Ibid.*, pp. 278, 279.
[16] See, for example, David Matza, *Delinquency and Drift* (New York: John Wiley and Sons, Inc., 1964), pp. 5–10, 13, 27.

4. Although we do not know enough to generalize about the importance of physical and mental defects, abnormalities, and disorders in the causation of delinquency, it is obvious that any one of these may be a contributing or even a major factor in the individual case of law violation.

5. The home, despite the pressures to which it has been subjected, still exerts a powerful influence in the lives of children, and a firm, effective, and viable family system continues to be our strongest bulwark against crime and delinquency.

6. The possibility of a child's becoming involved in delinquency is increased—although such behavior is certainly not made inevitable—when he is reared in a broken home, a functionally inadequate home, a socially, morally, or culturally abnormal home, or an economically insecure home.

7. Lack of love and of affection, and faulty discipline (especially when it is highly permissive, excessively severe, or grossly inconsistent), appear to be particularly detrimental to the sound development of the child, leaving him sometimes cruel and aggressive, sometimes insecure, confused, and anxious, and always unprepared to cope with life's problems and disappointments.

8. The relationship between the home and delinquency now appears to be much more complex than it was formerly assumed to be, and other factors, such as age, sex, social class, neighborhood, offense, and race, must always be taken into consideration.

9. What appears to be very important as a cause of delinquency, regardless of whether the home is broken or not, is the relationship among the members of the family—the meaning of the home to them and their reactions to what the community thinks of it, to what happens in it, and to the behavior of one another.[17]

10. The neighborhood, like the family, has declined as an agency of social control, but despite this, it still exerts an important influence in the development of the child, contributing to crime and delinquency by blocking basic desires, engendering culture conflicts, and fostering antisocial values.

11. As a factor in the causation of crime and delinquency, the neighborhood is at its worst in areas where constructive neighborhood influences are weak or absent and various forms of lawlessness tend to be traditional and transmitted through neighborhood groups and institutions.

12. Theorists have tended to reify the concept of the delinquent gang, exaggerating its independence, its solidity, and its homogeneity, but even so, it does constitute an important factor in the causation of crime and delinquency.

[17] Caldwell, p. 261.

13. The influence of the gang is especially strong in delinquency areas, where participation in its activities often provides the only opportunity that a youth can find for the satisfaction of his fundamental wishes and desires.

14. The general influence of religion on human behavior—law-abiding or law-violating—cannot be appraised, for no way has been devised by which this influence can be disentangled from the many others that operate in the lives of persons. This, of course, is not to deny that religion can be a major force in the life of a particular individual, and certainly it seems unreasonable to assume that social norms, including the law, cannot be greatly strengthened by being given the support of religion and associated with the regular inculcation of religious principles.

15. Although formal education, of itself, may bear an important causal relationship to delinquency and crime in the individual case, this cannot be shown to be so in general. In fact, the extent to which the school, as an educational agency, prevents or contributes to delinquency and crime in general remains a highly controversial subject.

16. The mass media do affect the lives of millions of people and unquestionably contribute to crime and delinquency in some cases, but the extent to which they are *directly* involved in the causation of these problems is not clear. Nevertheless, this much is certain: To the extent that these media are creating a cynical indifference to questions of morality and an irresponsible permissiveness, they are producing changes that, in turn, will ultimately contribute to crime and delinquency.

Efforts to find a single cause of crime and delinquency have failed. Furthermore, the complexity of these problems and the limitations of our knowledge firmly counsel the rejection of theories that offer an all-inclusive explanation of delinquent and criminal behavior. Such theories, whether by design or not, may do much to promote certain ideologies, but they can accomplish little in providing criminology with the facts and explanations that it so urgently needs.

# III

# CORRECTION AND PREVENTION

# 11

# The Police

## IMPORTANCE OF THE ROLE OF THE POLICE

The primary duty of the police is to maintain order and enforce the law so that the persons and property of the members of the community may be protected against acts of both adults and children. Clearly, then, no other public agency is of greater importance than the police, whose activities so significantly affect the lives of everyone, whether he be law-abiding or law-violating. Furthermore, the increasing complexity of our society, with its urbanization, industrialization, technological improvements, and migrations and mobility of population, has brought greater need of law and efficient police protection. This, as we have shown earlier, is strongly reflected in the rising crime and delinquency rates. The problem of delinquency is not only a serious one for the police, but it has been growing more and more serious.

The authority and organization of the police, moreover, place them in a strategic position not only to detect crime and delinquency but also to initiate preventive action. That this is so is attested by the estimate that about 75 per cent of the delinquency cases appearing before the juvenile court are brought there by police agencies.[1] And what is perhaps even more significant is the estimate of the United States Children's Bureau that about three-fourths of the total number of children dealt with by the police are not referred to the juvenile court but are handled in some other way.[2] In other words, the police act as an important screening agency. Criteria to guide the police in their screening of juveniles can be established by the police administrator or the legislature.

[1] Richard A. Myren and Lynn D. Swanson, *Police Work with Children*, U.S. Children's Bureau Publication, No. 399 (Washington, D.C.: Government Printing Office, 1962), p. 39.
[2] Quoted by Herbert A. Bloch and Frank T. Flynn, *Delinquency: The Juvenile Offender in America Today* (New York: Random House, 1956), p. 251.

The President's Commission task force report on juvenile delinquency concludes that the range of police dispositions through screening is considerable, that "the criteria for selection of disposition are seldom set forth explicitly, ordered in priority, or regularly reviewed for administrative purposes," and that although the police need to exercise discretion in their disposition of juvenile cases, they should have written standards to guide them in doing this.[3] In effect, each time a police officer has to deal with a child, he "holds court." He may do any of the following: let the child go after a word of warning; conduct him to the police station, where he may be turned over to a juvenile officer or to the juvenile bureau or reprimanded and released; take him home and have a talk with his parents; escort him back to school; refer his case to a clinic, a family society, a welfare agency, or the juvenile court; or take some similar action. Furthermore, we should understand that the police need these discretionary powers in order to give maximum protection to both the juvenile and the community. Thus the police officer largely determines how society will react to the child's behavior and often takes the first and basic step in a corrective program which may eventually involve many agencies and professions. Obviously, then, the way in which the police officer acts in each case can have a great effect on the child, his response to authority and the efforts made to help him, and the ultimate chances for his success and happiness.

Moreover, we must remember that the police, in addition to their contacts with delinquents and other children who need their immediate attention, have a continuous relationship with the entire community. In the exercise of their authority to maintain order and enforce the law, they supervise, protect, regulate, direct, order, and instruct many persons every day and thus represent the law in all kinds of relationships and situations. In fact, for many persons, the police are the law. Consequently, how the officer looks, how he conducts himself, and what he accomplishes are important, for they can do much to build better understanding between the police and the community and create greater appreciation of and respect for the law.[4]

[3] See The President's Commission on Law Enforcement and Administration of Justice, *Task Force Report: Juvenile Delinquency and Youth Crime* (Washington, D.C.: Government Printing Office, 1967), pp. 12–14, 19; Nathan Goldman, *The Differential Selection of Juvenile Offenders for Court Appearance* (New York: National Council on Crime and Delinquency, 1963); Robert M. Terry, "Discrimination in the Handling of Juvenile Offenders by Social-Control Agencies," *Journal of Research in Crime and Delinquency,* IV (July, 1967), 218–30; Aaron V. Cicourel, *The Social Organization of Juvenile Justice* (New York: John Wiley and Sons, Inc., 1968).

[4] See John P. Clark and Eugene P. Wenninger, "The Attitude of Juveniles Toward the Legal Institution," *Journal of Criminal Law, Criminology, and Police Science,* LV (December, 1964), 482–89; Frank J. Remington, "The Role of Police

## LEGAL BASIS FOR POLICE ACTION

The police, as we have explained, are charged with the duty of maintaining and enforcing the law. Since the criminal law provides for action against *all* persons—not just adults—who violate its provisions, the police have the authority to take into custody juveniles who allegedly have committed acts which would have been crimes if they had been committed by adults. Of course, as soon as it is established that the alleged violator is a juvenile, his case is handled by a procedure different from that for an adult, but to that point the police operation is the same in all cases.

However, there is more to the question than this. The juvenile court laws of all the states provide that certain types of behavior, such as truancy, incorrigibility, and so on, constitute delinquency, although they are not covered by the criminal law and so are not crimes. It is in this area of possible police action that some questions regarding police authority have been raised. The *Standard Juvenile Court Act* and the juvenile court laws of some states, addressing themselves to this point, specifically grant authority to the police to act in cases involving such behavior. Where this has not been done, however, the authority of the police in these cases must be inferred from the general provisions of the law through the use of the doctrine called protective custody. The application of this doctrine causes no difficulty when the person involved agrees to cooperate, but when he objects to having the "benevolent assistance" of the state, the authority of the police is not clear. It appears, therefore, that those states that have not yet specifically given the police authority to act in cases of this kind should do so.

The police can often proceed in an investigation without getting a search warrant or without making an arrest, because the persons involved consent to waive their constitutional rights. In determining whether the consent of a juvenile is truly voluntary when he makes such a waiver, the courts have considered his immaturity as one of the factors that must be weighed.

The overall test is whether the young person has been treated with fundamental fairness.[5] This means that the police officer must decide in

in a Democratic Society," *ibid.*, LVI (September, 1965), 361–65; Robert L. Derbyshire, "Children's Perceptions of the Police: A Comparative Study of Attitudes and Attitude Change," *ibid.*, LIX (June, 1968), 183–90; Ellwyn R. Stoddard, "The Informal 'Code' of Police Deviancy: A Group Approach to 'Blue-Coat Crime,'" *ibid.*, LIX (June, 1968), 201–13. See also Orman W. Ketcham and Monrad G. Paulsen, *Cases and Materials Relating to Juvenile Courts* (Brooklyn: The Foundation Press, 1967), pp. 343–49.

[5] The law is not entirely clear on the meaning of the test of fundamental fairness, and future decisions may change the interpretation that is offered here.

each case whether the child is sufficiently mature and sophisticated to know what he is doing when he consents to be searched or to be taken to the police station to be questioned, without being taken into custody or arrested on the basis of probable cause. If the officer decides that he can accept the consent, then he must explain to the juvenile what his consent means, that he has the right to remain silent, that anything he says can be used against him in court, and that he has the right to contact his parents and to legal counsel.

Sometimes, however, the officer must take the juvenile into custody. In doing this, he has the same right to secure, search, and question a juvenile taken into custody as he has in the case of an arrested adult, but he has also the same responsibilities.[6] He must inform the juvenile about his legal rights, allow him to contact parents, friends, relatives, or counsel, insure his having a hearing before some judicial officer within a specified period of time, and abide by the general standards of fair treatment accorded to all citizens.

The *Standard Juvenile Court Act*, (Section 16) contains the following provision regarding the taking of children into custody:

A child may be taken into custody by any officer of the peace without order of the judge (a) when in the presence of the officer the child has violated a state or federal law or a county or municipal ordinance; (b) when there are reasonable grounds to believe that he has committed an act which if committed by an adult would be a felony; (c) when he is seriously endangered in his surroundings, and immediate removal appears to be necessary for his protection; (d) when there are reasonable grounds to believe that he has run away from his parents, guardian, or legal custodian. Such taking into custody shall not be deemed an arrest.

The laws of most states provide the officer with about the same authority for taking children into custody as that recommended by the *Standard Juvenile Court Act*, but the usual practice is to use the term "arrest" in situations involving items (a) and (b) listed above.[7]

If a case is referred to the juvenile court on an allegation that the juvenile has committed an act that would be criminal if committed by an adult, the police should understand that there must be proof of every element of the alleged offense. They should also recognize that a case may go to the criminal court, where there must be proof beyond a reasonable doubt and not just a preponderance of the evidence, which is the test usually employed in the juvenile court. This means that the investi-

---

[6] Here again the law is not entirely clear, but the interpretation given above seems to be a reasonable one.

[7] *The Standard Juvenile Court Act* (New York: National Probation and Parole Association, 1959), Section 16.

gation in such a case must seek evidence that will pass the test of the criminal court.

If the delinquent conduct is in progress, the officer must first stop the conduct and then decide what he should do with the juvenile. In this situation the officer has the authority to take the child into immediate custody when the child has violated a state or federal law or a county or municipal ordinance. If the delinquent conduct is not in progress, the officer, as in the case of an adult offender, must have reasonable grounds to believe that the person has committed a felony before he makes an arrest. When this situation does not exist, police action may have to wait until sufficient evidence is available to support a referral to the court. However, in minor cases, the juvenile is rarely referred to court and almost never taken into custody. Usually, he is left with his family or referred to some social service or welfare agency. Whenever the child is taken into custody, his parents should be notified.

In abuse and neglect cases, the officer has the authority to take the juvenile into custody immediately and then have the case referred to the juvenile court or to some welfare or social service agency. He may take this action whenever he believes that it is necessary to protect the child. Furthermore, criminal prosecution of the parents may be initiated if it appears that they have committed a harmful act against the child or exposed him to acute danger.[8]

The laws of most states provide the officer with about the same authority for taking children into custody as that recommended by this act, but the usual practice is to use the term "arrest" in situations involving items (a) and (b) under Section 16 (listed above).

## ORGANIZATION FOR JUVENILE WORK

The police have greatly expanded their activities in the handling of children in order to cope with the increasing problem of juvenile delinquency. However, here as elsewhere in the field of law enforcement, the quality of police work is greatly affected by the kind of organization within which it must be done. Since there are major differences between the handling of juveniles and that of adults, some degree of specialization is advisable except in the smallest law-enforcement agency. Even when a department has only a few members, however, some specialization may be initiated by having one officer spend part of his time in handling the juvenile cases. Furthermore, a department does not have to become very large before one officer will have to spend all of his time

[8] Myren and Swanson, *op. cit.*, pp. 20–76.

in such work. Naturally, the degree of specialization will vary from one department to another, and decisions regarding it will have to take into consideration such factors as the size of the force, the quality of personnel, the amount of work involved, the pressure of other duties, and so on.[9]

Apparently, the first woman to work with police in the prevention of juvenile delinquency was Mrs. Lola Baldwin, who was appointed, in 1905, to provide protection for girls at the Lewis and Clark Centennial Exposition in Portland, Oregon. Since, however, she was not called a policewoman, the first woman in the world to have that title was Alice Stebbins Wells, of Los Angeles, who was appointed to her position in 1910. A few years later, Portland, Oregon, created the first juvenile bureau in America.[10]

Today many police departments have such bureaus, staffed by both men and women who have received special training in juvenile work. A study made a few years ago estimated that 552 police departments in cities having a population of more than 10,000 had specialized juvenile officers or juvenile units.[11] In smaller departments the head of the juvenile bureau may report directly to the chief of police, but where too many persons report directly to the latter some other arrangement may be used. For example, the heads of the juvenile bureau and the detective bureau may report to an assistant or deputy chief, who in turn reports to the chief of police. The number of persons assigned to the juvenile bureau will vary from department to department; according to one rough rule that has been used, the number should be 5 per cent of the total force. But the question of proper staffing can be answered only by sound planning and an adequate review of the bureau's effectiveness.[12] However, one more point must be borne in mind. Work with juveniles is not limited to that done by officers in the juvenile bureau. Every police officer, regardless of his specific duties, has contacts with persons of all ages in many different situations, and so all officers should receive some training in the proper techniques and procedures to be used in dealing with children.

[9] The Institute for Training in Municipal Administration, *Municipal Police Administration* (Ann Arbor, Mich.; Lithoprinted by Cushing-Malloy, Inc., 1961), pp. 213, 214; O. W. Wilson, *Police Administration* (New York: McGraw-Hill Book Co., Inc., 1963), pp. 36–45, 326–37.

[10] Edward Eldefonso, *Law Enforcement and the Youthful Offender: Juvenile Procedures* (New York: John Wiley and Sons, Inc., 1967), pp. 108, 109. The juvenile unit is sometimes given some other name, such as juvenile aid bureau, crime prevention bureau, youth division, and so on, but in this text it will be called the juvenile bureau.

[11] Myren and Swanson, p. 22.

[12] The Institute for Training in Municipal Administration, pp. 214, 215.

## SELECTION AND TRAINING OF PERSONNEL

The success of the juvenile bureau depends in large measure on the competence of its personnel. Their selection, therefore, should be based on written examinations, background and character investigations, and thorough interviews. Policemen for the juvenile bureau are usually drawn from the patrol division in accordance with the promotion policies of the department, but policewomen must almost always be found through outside sources. If the candidate has never had any police experience, he should first receive regular police training and serve a six-month probationary period in general police work before his assignment to the juvenile bureau. In this way he will become familiar with police problems, the organization, operation, and procedures of the department, and sufficient training for work in other branches of the service if his reassignment becomes necessary.

Juvenile officers should have all the qualifications of a good police officer. They should be in excellent physical condition and above the average in character, intelligence, personality, and appearance. In addition, they should have a special interest in juveniles, and an eager desire and an unusual ability to work with them.

After their selection, juvenile officers should be given special training, both on the job and in classes conducted by the department, the police academy, or by colleges and universities, some of which offer short courses in juvenile work. Their program of training should include such subjects as these: the philosophy of police work with children, with its emphasis on protection, guidance, and education; laws regarding juveniles; causation of crime and delinquency; functions, procedures, and techniques of the juvenile bureau and its relationship with other parts of the department; investigation in juvenile cases; interviewing; community organization and resources; records; public relations; and prevention of crime and delinquency.[13]

## OPERATION OF THE JUVENILE BUREAU

The juvenile bureau should be located in attractive quarters in the building that houses the police department. It should have at least two rooms—one for office space and one for interrogation—and should have an informal and noninstitutional appearance, so that it does not make

---

[13] *Ibid.*, pp. 215–18; John P. Kenney and Dan G. Pursuit, *Police Work with Juveniles* (Springfield, Ill.: Charles C. Thomas, 1965), pp. 91–121.

the child feel that he has taken "the first step to prison" when he goes through the door. Since relatives, witnesses, and others who have little knowledge of police work and often wish to remain as inconspicuous as possible will have to go to the bureau, it should be so situated that it can be easily found with a minimum of public attention.[14]

Policewomen usually specialize in the handling of girls and young boys, whereas policemen work with older boys. In every case, however, the officer should treat the child with consideration and try to gain his confidence and respect and discover and understand his problems. This does not mean, however, that the officer should be ingratiating or coaxing. On the contrary, he should be firm, positive, and definite, so that the child will clearly understand that he must behave himself and obey the law. On the other hand, the officer should never resort to profanity, vulgarity, or obscenity and should avoid harsh and loud language and excessive force. Often the child is afraid, antagonistic, and resentful. Clumsy, inept, or cruel treatment may drive him beyond the reach of guidance and counseling and even solidify the hostile feelings that he has for the police and the law.

The juvenile bureau has five basic functions. They are:

1. The discovery of delinquents, potential delinquents, and conditions contributing to delinquency.
2. The investigation of cases of juveniles who are delinquents or involved as accessories or victims with adults.
3. The protection of juveniles.
4. The disposition of juvenile cases.
5. The prevention of juvenile delinquency.

Delinquency or the conditions contributing to it may be discovered as a result of a complaint made by such persons as parents, neighbors, teachers, and social workers, or as a result of tips supplied by cab drivers, waitresses, bartenders, bellhops, theater doormen, and so on. Many discoveries, however, are made through patrolling and inspection, both by juvenile officers and other police officers, especially of places where children may be exposed to harmful conditions, such as dance halls, pool rooms, playgrounds, penny arcades, skating rinks, bus stations, railroad depots, cheap hotels, all-night restaurants, taverns, bars, drive-ins, motels, and theaters.

The investigation of juvenile cases is often more difficult than that of adult, requiring special techniques to deal with the mental and emotional immaturity of children and their changing relationships with various gangs and other groups. Furthermore, it should be based on carefully planned and generally understood policies, so as to avoid friction and

[14] The Institute for Training in Municipal Administration, p. 218.

conflicts with detectives who also may be involved in certain aspects of juvenile cases. During the investigation, the child may be held by the police or released to his parents.

Interviewing is the most important method that the officer can use in an investigation of juvenile cases. It is desirable to conduct at least part of the interview with the juvenile when he is alone, so as to free him from the influence of others, but this may not be possible in some cases. Since all kinds of children, including the frightened, confused, bewildered, hardened, and arrogant, as well as many adults, such as parents, teachers, employers, and so on, must be questioned, the interview has to be adjusted to fit the individual case, but a realistic balance between the rights of the individual and those of the community must always be maintained. In interviewing a child, the officer should be tactful, considerate, and patient but at all times firm and positive. He should try to gain the confidence and respect of the child, and in simple, definite language encourage him to tell his own story. Although the purpose of the interview is to learn as much as possible about the child, prolonged questioning should be avoided. Usually the interview of juveniles is more fruitful than that of adults, and often it reduces the fears, tensions, and hostilities of the child and helps to lay the foundation for later treatment in his case.

Frequently the police find children to be in need of protection. Many of these children are neglected or even abused by their own parents and are inadequately clothed and nourished. Others, for example, are runaways or are being exploited, or in danger of being exploited, by adults. Sometimes the police must take immediate action to help these children, in some cases obtaining food, clothing, and shelter for them, or returning them to their homes. Usually, however, they refer children who need protection to schools, churches, welfare departments, and other such agencies and institutions, or to the juvenile court. Even so, if the police are not careful, they will find themselves assuming more and more responsibilities in welfare service. This possibility should always be guarded against, for welfare work is not a legitimate police function and can drain off money and personnel that are needed in the performance of basic police duties.

The juvenile cases that are handled by the police are disposed of in various ways. Some are referred to schools, churches, welfare agencies, and probation departments. Some are disposed of by releasing the child to his parents or by dropping the charges, because of insufficient evidence or exoneration of the child. Some, however, are sent to the juvenile court, or, if, for example, certain offenses are involved, to the criminal court. There is, of course, no magic formula which can automatically decide for the police officer whether a case should go to the juvenile court.

Even so, the presence of certain conditions, such as any of the following, indicates that this action should be taken: (1) the alleged offense is a serious one; (2) the alleged act is not intrinsically serious but the facts point to the need of protective action; (3) the child has a record of numerous delinquencies; (4) the child and his parents have been unable or unwilling to cooperate with other agencies; (5) casework with the child by other agencies has failed; (6) the services needed by the child can be obtained most adequately through the court and its probation department; (7) the child denies the offense, but sufficient evidence exists to warrant referral and judicial determination is called for; and (8) the child is to be placed in detention. However, the juvenile court does not always take jurisdiction in a case, just because the case has been referred to it by the police. Instead, through its intake process, the court may send the case to some other agency.

When the police send a case to the juvenile court, they should provide the court with the following information:

1. The alleged facts that give the court jurisdiction over the case and the pertinent personal data about the child.
2. Information about any co-delinquent.
3. Information about the complainant or the victim, including a statement regarding injuries or damages.
4. Any explanation of the request for juvenile court action other than the present alleged offense, such as previous police contacts with the child that did not result in a court referral.
5. A brief summary of any significant factors revealed in the investigation, such as court records of parents, that point to the need of action by the juvenile court.[15]

## SOME POLICY QUESTIONS

### Fingerprinting and Photographing

In the handling of juvenile cases, the police must establish definite policies with respect to some important questions. One of these is the fingerprinting and photographing of children. In general, the police are in favor of doing this, but many persons have advanced arguments against the practice, except in extreme cases. Those who oppose fingerprinting contend that (1) it is a stigma that affects both the attitude of the juvenile and that of others toward him, sometimes giving him the impression that he has become a "tough guy" and so must measure up to his new label; (2) it is contrary to the philosophy of the juvenile court, since it treats him as a criminal, and (3) it is a threat to his future, since, even

---

[15] The Institute for Training in Municipal Administration, pp. 219–24; Myren and Swanson, pp. 28–30; Kenney and Pursuit, pp. 55–83; Eldefonso, pp. 88–107.

after many years, it may interfere with employment or security clearance. Those who favor fingerprinting argue that (1) it is the best method of identification, (2) it is no longer a criminal stigma, since it is now so widely used for noncriminal purposes, (3) it is not any more objectionable than the practice of asking for the child's name, age, place of birth, and so on, which is now generally accepted, (4) it is a good method not only of protecting the child against unjust accusations when fingerprints are found at the scene of the alleged act but also of identifying him in cases of injuries that produce unconsciousness or amnesia, and (5) it is a deterrent, since many children are afraid to take chances when their fingerprints are on file. Although the controversy over the photographing of children is not so intense, the arguments for and against it are about the same as those that have been used in the dispute about the fingerprinting of juveniles.

Although this controversy continues, most authorities in the field of law enforcement believe that the police should have the power to formulate their own policy regarding the identification of juveniles, and that, without first having to secure the permission of some other agency, like the juvenile court, they should fingerprint and photograph the juvenile (1) when he is suspected of having committed a felony or has admitted that he has done so, (2) when he has a long history of delinquencies and will probably continue to be a "repeater," and (3) when identification is specifically needed, as, for example, when his fingerprints might be compared with those of a known offender, or he is unable or unwilling to identify himself. Still, other authorities believe that the fingerprinting and photographing of juveniles by police should take place only upon the specific consent of the court in each instance, and that after the fingerprints and photographs have served their immediate purpose, they should be destroyed.[16]

## Use of the Term "Arrest"

There has been also some opposition to the use of the term "arrest" in connection with juveniles. It is claimed that this term clashes with the principles of the program of treatment which should be used in dealing with children, and that therefore the term "taken into custody" should be used instead.[17] The police, however, explain that the term "arrest" is universally employed to refer to the taking into custody of a person

[16] See, for example, Advisory Council of Judges of the National Probation and Parole Association, in cooperation with the National Council of Juvenile Court Judges, *Guides for Juvenile Court Judges* (New York: National Probation and Parole Association, 1957), pp. 32, 33.

[17] See, for example, the *Standard Juvenile Court Act* (New York: National Council on Crime and Delinquency, 1959), p. 37.

on a charge of violation of a law or ordinance, that it will continue to be so used, and that the mere changing of the term would not alter in any way what happens when an arrest is made or reduce the responsibilities of those who are involved. In fact, they insist, this change in terms would cause a great deal of confusion in police reports and records, and that they must follow the instructions of the Federal Bureau of Investigation in the preparation of records for the *Uniform Crime Reports*, so that the data received from all agencies will remain comparable. There seems to be no sound reason why a situation that amounts to an arrest should not be called an arrest. The best way to provide a solid basis for change in persons is to have them clearly understand that what they have done is wrong. To shield them from reality with euphemistic language is to weaken their sense of responsibility and foster their attitudes of dependence. This is not to deny that some children are mentally or physically ill, but the shield of euphemism will be of little help to them. They need special care and treatment.

## Other Questions

On another question, however, there is more agreement. Almost all juvenile officers work in plain clothes and use unmarked cars, and this appears to be a wise policy. A uniform or a marked car may give warning to those who are being inspected or investigated and may cause antagonism or hostility if the officer has to talk to the juvenile in his home or at a playground or school. Yet, there are exceptions, and in some situations a uniform or a marked car may be needed so that there may be no mistake about the identity of the officer or his authority.

Some other questions of policy have attracted widespread attention. Thus there has been considerable discussion about the release of the names and photographs of juvenile offenders to the news media. Some states have enacted laws which forbid this, and many news services have voluntarily adopted a policy against publishing the names of juveniles. Still, some writers hold the opinion that the press should be free to publish the names of all offenders, and that the public is entitled to know about them. The general view, however, appears to be that usually the names of juvenile offenders or of juvenile victims of adult acts should not be revealed, since the resulting notoriety might unnecessarily complicate or even ruin their lives, but that the name of the juvenile should be released when he has committed a serious offense or when he is highly dangerous and the publication of his name, description, and photograph will assist in his apprehension.

When should the juvenile be detained and how long should he be held? These are two more questions that have caused some controversy.

Few investigations can be completed immediately, and often the juvenile must be held until some progress has been made in an examination of his case. On the other hand, detention should not be used as a form of punishment, and the child should not be detained just because this will enable officers to investigate his case at their convenience. Even so, the child must be detained in cases like the following:

1. His presence will greatly facilitate the completion of the investigation.
2. He is so incorrigible that he is beyond the control of his parents.
3. His parents cannot be located or probably will not assume responsibility for him.
4. He has no home or his home cannot be located.
5. His previous record indicates that he should be kept in custody.

Furthermore, the juvenile may have to be detained for a short time at the station house instead of being sent to a regular detention facility. This may happen, for example, when the investigation is moving so fast that it would be highly inconvenient to go back and forth to the detention facility in order to question the juvenile or confront him with witnesses or accomplices.

Obviously, the length of time that the child will have to be detained will depend upon the nature of the case. One policy for the police to follow when they must detain a child for more than a few hours is to hold him in a proper place until the juvenile court judge (or someone who is authorized to act for him) is available and can be informed of the facts of the case. The judge can then decide on where and how long the juvenile should be detained.

The National Council on Crime and Delinquency has suggested the following standards for the detention of juveniles:

Children apprehended for delinquency should be detained for the juvenile court when, after proper intake interviews, it appears that casework by a probation officer would not enable the child to control his own behavior. Such children fall into the following groups: (a) Children who are almost certain to run away during the period the court is studying their case, or between the disposition and transfer to an institution or another jurisdiction. (b) Children who are almost certain to commit an offense dangerous to themselves or to the community before court disposition or between disposition and transfer to an institution or another jurisdiction. (c) Children who must be held for another jurisdiction; e.g., parole violators, runaways from institutions to which they were committed by a court, or certain material witnesses.[18]

But should the police do welfare or correctional work when they are dealing with juveniles? Although the police generally support programs

---

[18] *Standards and Guides for the Detention of Children and Youth* (New York: National Council on Crime and Delinquency, 1961), p. 15.

of rehabilitation for juveniles, they tend to resist efforts to push them into correctional or welfare work; and their resistance is justified. This kind of work is not a police function, and the police are not selected or trained to do casework. Nevertheless, sometimes the police are tempted to act as "unofficial probation officers" or as recreational workers in order to reduce or prevent delinquency and to improve the attitude of the public toward law enforcement. However, they should not assume this responsibility, for it is clearly beyond their official duties. Furthermore, after they begin this work, they may find that they are expected to continue, even though the responsibility becomes an increasing load on an already over-burdened police budget. The proper solution in this situation is the employment of more probation officers and recreational workers.

One more question of policy remains to be examined here and that has to do with the keeping of juvenile records. These records must be maintained because (1) they assist in the investigation of cases, (2) they help to locate conditions that contribute to delinquency and thus facilitate its prevention, (3) they provide a basis for the evaluation of police work with juveniles, and (4) they furnish information that the police must have if they are to dispose of juvenile cases in the proper way. However, the police should limit juvenile records to those that are necessary for law-enforcement purposes and should not expand them merely for the convenience of other agencies. Moreover, juvenile records should be kept in the regular centralized record system of the department and not in a separate unit like the juvenile bureau, although they should be segregated from adult records, and access to them should be open to police officers on a "need-to-know" basis through the same procedures that are followed in the use of other records. A definite policy, however, should be established to protect juvenile records from indiscriminate and harmful use by others.[19] In this regard, the United States Children's Bureau recommends that juvenile records should be kept at an absolute minimum, that the files containing them should be purged at regular intervals, and that they should be closely guarded against unauthorized access. When the files are purged, records of defined categories of juveniles should be removed and destroyed. This should be done, the Children's Bureau explains, so that the files will not become overloaded with outdated and useless information and young persons can begin their adult lives with a clean slate.[20]

---

[19] The Institute for Training in Municipal Administration, *op. cit.*, pp. 229–34; Kenney and Pursuit, *op. cit.*, pp. 122–47; Eldefonso, *op. cit.*, pp. 112–17.

[20] See Myren and Swanson, *op. cit.*, pp. 77–94.

# 12

# Juvenile Detention

## NATURE OF DETENTION

Usually children who come into contact with the law are permitted to remain in their own homes, but sometimes they must be detained in order (1) to protect the community, because of the seriousness of their alleged offenses, or because they cannot be controlled by their parents or guardians; (2) to protect them, because otherwise they may be harmed by themselves or others, or because they are in physical or moral danger in their own homes; or (3) to insure their availability for future action by the court, because this cannot be accomplished in any other way. Detention, therefore, is not a form of punishment, but rather the holding of a juvenile for a comparatively short period of time until some disposition can be made of his case.

Many writers, however, now make a distinction between detention and shelter care. According to this view, detention is the temporary care of alleged or adjudged delinquents who require secure custody in physically restricting facilities pending court disposition or transfer to another jurisdiction or agency. Any place for temporary care that has locked outer doors, a high fence or wall, and screens, bars, detention sash, or other window obstruction designed to prevent escape is a detention facility. Shelter care, on the other hand, is the temporary care of children—usually those who are neglected or dependent—in physically unrestricting facilities, such as boarding homes or group homes, pending return to their own homes or placement for longer-term care. Neither detention nor shelter care, however, is commitment, which involves sending a juvenile to a correctional or welfare agency or institution for a longer period of time.

The juvenile court laws of most states provide for the protective custody and care of children while their cases are pending before the court and usually prohibit the detention of any person under sixteen years of age in jails and lockups; but often officials do not enforce these laws or their provisions do not cover all children. At present, children who require detention or shelter care are being kept in a variety of places, including lockups, jails, boarding houses, orphanages, hospitals, almshouses, detention homes, and correctional institutions.[1]

## HISTORY OF JUVENILE DETENTION

Since 1899, when the first juvenile court was established in Chicago, the separate detention of children has come to be considered an essential part of its operation. As juvenile court laws were enacted in state after state, detention homes, most of which were converted private homes, were established in the larger cities of the United States. By 1915, Milwaukee, Newark, and Chicago had specially designed buildings for the detention of children, but most jurisdictions continued to rely upon the jail for this purpose. Nevertheless, some jurisdictions began to make other arrangements for the detention of children, sometimes putting them into an old, remodeled residence, called a detention home, or into a workhouse, a county infirmary, or even a hospital. Other jurisdictions, like Massachusetts, Connecticut, and New York, went beyond this and subsidized boarding homes for the care of children who were fifteen years of age and under, thus keeping most of them out of the jails. Even so, at the conclusion of World War II, only a few of the larger jurisdictions had constructed specially designed buildings for the detention of juveniles. Since then the number of such units has increased, so that we now have well over a hundred of them in the United States, and many communities use separate quarters for the shelter care of neglected and dependent children. Furthermore, regional detention centers have been established in eight states.[2]

However, progress has been slow, and many children are still being kept in jails and lockups. As a matter of fact, most of the other facilities

[1] The President's Commission on Law Enforcement and Administration of Justice, *Task Force Report: Corrections*, Appendix A (Washington, D.C.: Government Printing Office, 1967), p. 119; *Standards and Guides for the Detention of Children and Youth* (New York: National Council on Crime and Delinquency, 1961), pp. 1–9, 33–43; Sherwood Norman, "A Nationwide Survey of Juvenile Detention," *Proceedings of the American Prison Association, 1945*, pp. 244, 245; National Conference on Prevention and Control of Juvenile Delinquency, *Report on Juvenile Detention* (Washington, D.C.: Government Printing Office, 1947), pp. 18, 19. See also Sherwood Norman *Detention Practice: Significant Developments in the Detention of Children and Youth* (New York: National Probation and Parole Association, 1960).

[2] The President's Commission on Law Enforcement and Administration of Justice, pp. 119, 120.

that are being used for the detention of juveniles are far from satisfactory. In 1946, Sherwood Norman, field consultant for the National Probation Association, reported that he had visited and intensively studied forty-three detention facilities in twenty-nine communities. He found that two-thirds of them were overcrowded, that even those which offered reasonably good physical care frequently did not provide the kind of life that was conducive to mental health, that none had a building which could be considered a model for the special demands of detention care, and that only four had an adequate program for children and a sound in-service training program for the staff.[3] Over a decade later, in 1960, at the annual meeting of the American Society of Criminology, Sherwood Norman again looked with disapproval at the conditions in juvenile detention facilities in the United States. He reported that, with rare exceptions, these facilities were depressingly inadequate. Staffs were poorly selected, paid, trained, and supervised; overcrowding made rehabilitative programs ineffectual; inadequate classification and segregation converted some institutions into veritable "crime schools."

## SURVEY OF 1966

During 1966, the National Council on Crime and Delinquency conducted a survey of the correctional agencies and institutions operated by states and communities throughout the United States, including the facilities for the detention of juveniles.[4] All the data presented in this section are taken from that survey.

### Juveniles Detained

More than 409,000 alleged and adjudged delinquents, or approximately two-thirds of all those who were apprehended, were admitted to detention facilities during 1965. The average daily total of these children kept in places of detention was more than 13,000; and their average stay in detention was 12 days at a total cost of $53,000,000—an average cost of $130 per child. These estimates include all children who were held in 242 juvenile detention homes, 4 training schools, and an unknown number of county jails and jail-like facilities in 2,766 jurisdictions, but they do not include any children who were detained in police lockups.

---

[3] Sherwood Norman, "Detention Facilities for Children," *Yearbook, 1946* (New York: National Probation Association, 1947), pp. 86–99. See also Sherwood Norman and Helen Norman, *Detention for the Juvenile Court: A Discussion of Principles and Practices* (New York: National Probation Association, 1946).

[4] The President's Commission on Law Enforcement and Administration of Justice, pp. 115–29.

## Places of Detention

The survey revealed that 93 per cent of the country's juvenile court jurisdictions, covering about 2,800 counties and cities and having 44 per cent of the nation's population, had no place of detention other than a county jail or police lockup and detained too few children to justify the establishment of a detention home. If the number of children who were held in police lockups are added to the 87,951 children who were held in county jails, the total number admitted to jails and jail-like facilities in the United States during 1965 exceeded 100,000.

Of the 242 detention homes in the country in 1966, only 48 per cent had been constructed for the purpose of detaining children; and, of these, some were given a low rating by the survey. Many of the other homes, which were usually remodeled residences or other makeshift facilities, were found to be neither fire-resistant nor designed for proper supervision. Since they were usually located in urban communities, detention homes served over 50 per cent of the nation's population but only 7 per cent of its counties. About half of the detention homes were over 20 years old, but facilities with a total capacity of more than 1,700 were under construction, and additional construction with a capacity of more than 5,300 had been either authorized or projected. If all these plans materialize, by 1975, the detention facilities in the United States will have accommodations for about 7,000 more juveniles than in 1965.

## Personnel of Detention Homes

About 7,900 persons were employed in the country's detention homes to care for an average daily population of 13,113 juveniles. The educational level of these employees had risen considerably during the preceding decade; but, in spite of this, only 39 per cent of the counties visited during the survey claimed to have any in-service training program. Furthermore, only one-third of these had this kind of training as frequently as once a week, and in many instances, the so-called training period was only a staff meeting at which training rarely took place. However, 71 per cent of the counties visited maintained a workweek of 40 hours or less; 43 per cent of them employed their superintendents and staff supervisors through a civil service or merit system; and except in a few cases, the personnel in the detention homes were not subject to political interference. With the improvement of the educational qualifications of the staffs had come an increase in salaries and an expansion of the programs in some of the homes. Nearly half conducted school programs; nine used group techniques; twelve had special education activities, including remedial reading; and six taught vocational training.

Nevertheless, over half of the detention homes did little more than provide a place where children could be "stored" until their final disposition by the court.

## State's Role

Thirteen states had assumed some or all of the responsibility for the detention of juveniles. These states were Alaska, Connecticut, Delaware, Georgia, Massachusetts, Maryland, Michigan, New Hampshire, New York, Rhode Island, Utah, Vermont, and Virginia. Eight states had established regional detention centers, and two others had promoted regional detention by state subsidy. However, not all of the regional facilities measured up to recognized standards of building design and staffing, and all but two of the states with these facilities had to use jails for some of their overnight detention. Twenty states provided that their counties might receive state consultation services regarding detention, but little of this was actually being given. Although fifteen states claimed that they had an inspection service for detention homes, most consultation was given only when it was requested.

## Use of Detention

More than 409,000 alleged and adjudged delinquents, or about two-thirds of all the juveniles who were apprehended on delinquency charges, were admitted to detention facilities in the United States during 1965. In a scientifically selected sample of 250 counties, the range of stay in jails and detention homes was from 1 day to 68 days, the average stay being 18 days. Nearly all of the smaller county jails reported that they usually detained children from 1 to 3 days. Longer average periods of detention were found in the detention homes and other facilities.

### SOME DETENTION PROBLEMS

## Existing Facilities

Many jails and some detention homes are hardly more than storage bins where homeless and neglected children are indiscriminately mingled in enforced idleness with the hardened, the delinquent, the feebleminded, and the emotionally disturbed, and where juveniles are often exposed to brutal treatment, exploitation, and the degrading practices of vice and crime. Furthermore, in many places of detention, children are kept indefinitely, simply because judges, probation officers, and social workers do not know what else to do with them or have neglected to find a satisfactory way to dispose of their cases. Thus the detention of children is characterized by confusion, misuse, ignorance, neglect, and indifference, and those who are interested in its improvement are confronted with a series of difficult problems, some of which will be indicated here.

Every year more than 100,000 children are being detained in the jails of the United States. In this connection, it should be emphasized that less than 20 per cent of the jails in which children were detained during 1965 were rated as suitable even for adult federal offenders. In fact, it is generally agreed that even the best jails are not proper places for the detention of children, and many tragic experiences can be cited to support this point of view. For example, during 1965, four teenage boys, jailed on suspicion of stealing beer, died of asphyxiation from a defective gas heater when they were left alone in the jail for eleven hours, and a thirteen-year old boy hanged himself in a jail, where he was being held in segregated quarters until he could be given a court hearing. Near where his body was found, there was this penciled note: "I don't belong anywhere." Like this boy, many children are frightened, anxious, and demoralized when they are detained; others are hostile and rebellious; some are pleased at the prospect of increased status among their peers. Regardless of what their feelings may be, however, children need care, supervision, and guidance during their detention. These they rarely receive in a jail or lockup.

Although there has been improvement in many American jails and lockups during the past decade—and in some cases this has been considerable—the average jail or lockup is still characterized by poor administration, low sanitation and medical standards, poor food, idleness of inmates, little or no segregation, and untrained personnel. Certainly, such a place has nothing to recommend it as a detention facility for juveniles, and every effort should be directed toward keeping children out of it. If for any reason children have to be kept in a jail or lockup, they should be segregated from adults, preferably in quarters designed especially for them.[5]

## Special Detention Homes

The better solution, of course, is to be found in the construction of facilities that are especially designed for the detention of children. These facilities should be safe, healthful, and homelike, under the administration of competent persons, subjected to regular inspection service, and required to meet specified standards of operation. That this solution has been used by only a few of our cities and counties is evidenced by the fact that 93 per cent of the country's juvenile court jurisdictions

[5] *Ibid.*, pp. 121, 122.

detain their children in jails and lockups, and that most of the detention homes that we do have are converted residences or makeshift facilities.[6]

Sherwood Norman, an authority on the detention of juveniles, has written that the average jurisdiction that wants to abandon the use of the jail or jail-like building as a place for the detention of children has the following choices: [7]

1. The specially built detention home, which, in the opinion of Norman, "is the best solution, because it combines secure custody, home-like appearance, varied indoor activity areas designed to secure constant supervision, and other important features." He recognizes these three types of the specially constructed detention home:
   a. The family-type home, which is designed as a home for a man and wife and has facilities for up to eight children.
   b. The single-unit home, which may or may not have a resident staff and is designed for from eight to sixteen children.
   c. The two-unit or multi-unit home, which has separate living and sleeping quarters for two or more groups of children, each group not exceeding a maximum of fifteen.
2. The converted residence, which is a house owned or rented by the administering agency and remodeled for detention purposes.
3. Boarding homes for detention, which can be used for most children who need to be detained, provided skillful boarding parents can be found and given adequate financial support and supervision. When these homes are used, however, there are always some children who will have to be held elsewhere in a more secure detention facility.
4. The combination of detention with other facilities by providing space for detention in a courthouse, county office building, hospital, county home, training school, or other institution. Although this may be better than using a jail, it should be considered only a stopgap measure.

## Amount of Detention

Not only are many children being kept in unsuitable places, but too many of them are being needlessly detained. As the survey of 1966,

[6] *Ibid.*, p. 122.

[7] Sherwood Norman, "New Goals for Juvenile Detention," *Contemporary Correction*, ed. Paul W. Tappan (New York: McGraw-Hill Book Co., Inc., 1951), pp. 340–42. For a detailed discussion of the planning and construction of juvenile detention homes, see Federal Bureau of Prisons, *Handbook of Correctional Institution Design and Construction* (Washington, D.C.: Federal Bureau of Prisons, 1949), pp. 154–67. See also, Sherwood Norman, *The Design and Construction of Detention Homes for the Juvenile Court* (New York: National Probation Association, 1947); *Standards and Guides for the Detention of Children and Youth*, pp. 105–44.

quoted above, discovered, about two-thirds of all the juveniles who were apprehended on delinquency charges during 1965 in the United States were placed in detention.[8] This was far in excess of the standard for such children recommended by the National Council on Crime and Delinquency in 1961. According to this standard, the number of children admitted to a detention facility normally should not exceed 10 per cent of the total number of alleged delinquents apprehended by law enforcement officers, excluding traffic cases and cases outside of the court's jurisdiction, such as out-of-county runaways and federal court cases.[9]

Clearly, the majority of the juveniles who are being detained at present could be left in the community without danger to themselves or others and without in any way delaying or interfering with the proceedings of the court. Detention should be avoided whenever it is possible to do so, not only because of the deleterious effect it may have on the children, but also because of the expenditure of money that might be used to greater advantage elsewhere. And the detention of juveniles is expensive even when it is administered in the unsatisfactory way that it is in most jurisdictions today: as already noted, the total cost of detaining alleged and adjudged delinquents in the United States during 1965 amounted to more than $53,000,000, representing an average cost of $130 per child.[10] In fact, in 1965, the total of these juvenile detention costs was more than two-thirds of the entire cost of probation service for children. In commenting on this, the survey of 1966, cited above states, "If the detention volume could be halved, which it might well be if effective intake services and resources were available, and the savings were diverted to probation, funds available for probation services would be increased by about one-third, with no additional appropriations." [11]

## Length of Detention

Furthermore, the cases of many children are unnecessarily complicated by the fact that they are detained too long. Sometimes this happens because the judge uses detention to punish the child or needlessly prolongs his detention to keep him "out of trouble" and easily available for court action. Often it is because no specific time has been set for the child's release or because the agency or institution to which he is to be sent is not ready to receive him. Whatever the cause may be

---

[8] The President's Commission on Law Enforcement and Administration of Justice p. 121.

[9] *Standards and Guides for the Detention of Children and Youth,* p. 18.

[10] The President's Commission on Law Enforcement and Administration of Justice, p. 121.

[11] *Ibid.,* p. 23.

efforts should be made to eliminate it, for detention, no matter how ideal, can never be a substitute for normal life in the community, and the child's relation with his home should be restored as quickly as possible. Good practice dictates that juvenile detention should not ordinarily exceed two weeks.[12] Yet, despite this, in 1965, in a scientifically selected sample of 250 counties, the period of juvenile detention in the United States ranged from 1 day to 68 days, and its average length was 18 days.[13]

## Guidelines for Improvement

Some of the problems of detention could be solved by an improvement in the policies and programs of the detention facilities. For example, adjudged and alleged delinquents should be segregated from dependent, neglected, homeless, emotionally disturbed, and mentally ill nondelinquents, as well as from juvenile witnesses who are being kept in custody, all of whom should be cared for in other kinds of institutions or in foster homes. Furthermore, children should not be placed in detention just to study or punish them, and those who are being held until they can be transferred to correctional institutions should be removed from detention as soon as possible. When a child is admitted to a detention home, he should be given a physical examination in order to prevent the spread of disease, and then he should be classified and segregated according to the type of his case. During the period of his detention, he should receive adequate medical, religious, educational, recreational and counseling services, and to provide these, the resources of the community should be utilized whenever they are needed. And the public should not be forgotten, for as they are educated to appreciate the importance of juvenile detention through regular public relations work, the moral, financial, and legislative resources of the state and the community can be marshalled in support of the operation and improvement of detention facilities.

## STANDARDS FOR JUVENILE DETENTION

In November, 1965, a special committee on correctional standards was appointed by the staff of the President's Commission on Law Enforcement and Administration of Justice. These standards for juvenile detention were prepared by that committee: [14]

---

[12] *Standards and Guides for the Detention of Children and Youth*, p. 30.
[13] The President's Commission on Law Enforcement and Administration of Justice, p. 128.
[14] *Ibid.*, pp. 210, 211.

1. No child of juvenile court age should be admitted to a jail or police lockup. Local or regional detention homes for children should be provided.
2. No child should be placed in any detention facility unless he is a delinquent or alleged delinquent and there is a substantial probability that he will commit an offense dangerous to himself or the community or will run away pending court disposition. He should not be detained for punishment or for someone's convenience.
3. When the child denies the offense or when parents question the need of detention, a court hearing on detention should be held forthwith.
4. The release of a child should depend not on his family's ability to secure a bail bond, but on the personal recognizance of the parent, guardian, relative, attorney, or other responsible person.
5. Delinquent or allegedly delinquent children who must be removed from their homes temporarily but do not require secure custody should be placed in shelter care.
6. An appropriate state agency should be given statutory responsibility for statewide detention planning and the operation of regional detention homes.
7. The juvenile court is responsible for providing the policies and procedures governing conditions under which a child may be placed in temporary care (detention or shelter). Such policies and procedures provide the necessary legal safeguards for police, parents, and child regarding admission, case processing, and release from temporary care. They should be set forth clearly in writing, with specific delegation to appropriate personnel for implementing them at all times.
8. Detention construction requires complete separation from jail or any place of adult confinement, foolproof security features (psychiatrically secure and nonjail-like), provisions for auditory and visual control, fireproof materials, and 100 square feet of living area and program space per child in addition to individual sleeping rooms.
9. Sleeping rooms in detention should be individually occupied, should have a minimum floor dimension of 8 by 10 feet, and should be provided with toilets and lavatories protected by semi-partitions.
10. Sleeping units and activity groups should be of a size that encourages individual attention within one person's ability to supervise. Under no circumstances should groups exceed 15 children under 1 employee's supervision.
11. Group workers in direct contact with children should possess physical stamina, personality, and resourcefulness to conduct program and relate constructively to detained children. They should have sufficient intelligence and education (a B.A. degree in one of the social sciences) to participate effectively in the process of helping the child.
12. Staff should preferably work an 8-hour day and a 40-hour week.
13. Provisions should be made for medical, religious, and clinical services to meet needs promptly and competently to avoid prolonging detention.
14. Detention should provide care that will offset the danger inherent in confinement, enable observation and study, and enhance any later treatment.
15. Children in detention should be under direct supervision at all times to

assure their own safety, protect them from one another, and minimize further delinquency contagion.

16. Constructive activities should be provided to meet individual and group needs, including a full school program, preferably on a 12-month basis, and a balance of quiet and vigorous recreation, creative crafts, and work details.

17. Length of stay should be as short as possible, consistent with prompt processing of the case.

18. Children, including those committed to institutions or ordered placed in foster care, should be removed from detention immediately upon court disposition.

# 13

# The Juvenile Court: Origin and Development[1]

On July 1, 1899, the first juvenile court in the world began its legal existence in Chicago, Illinois. This claim, however, has not gone entirely without challenge. It is said, for example, that children's courts were introduced by ministerial order in South Australia in 1889, and later legalized, in 1895, by a state act, which provided, among other things, for probation and separate hearings of charges against children under eighteen years of age. But this court did not have all of the essential characteristics of a juvenile court, and it is generally agreed that the United States should be given credit for having the first real one.

Even so, there is also some dispute as to whether Chicago, Illinois, or Denver, Colorado, had the first juvenile court in the United States. Denver's claim is based on the fact that, two months before the Illinois law went in to effect and a few days prior to its passage, the Colorado legislature passed a so-called "school law." The county court had jurisdiction over cases arising under this law, and by its authority, Judge Lindsey, a pioneer in the juvenile court movement, held that a child under sixteen, who had committed any act which would technically constitute a crime, would be charged with improper conduct and therefore subject to the law's provisions. Nevertheless, preference is given to Chicago's claim, since the law approved in Colorado on April 12, 1899, was

[1] Some of the material presented in this and the next two chapters is adapted from that contained in Caldwell's article "The Juvenile Court: Its Development and Some Major Problems," *Journal of Criminal Law, Criminology, and Police Science*, LI (January–February, 1961), 493–511.

essentially a truancy law, although it did contain some of the features of a juvenile court law.[2]

The establishment of the juvenile court has been widely acclaimed as a revolutionary advance in the treatment of delinquent and neglected children and as the beginning of a new era in the cooperation of law, science, and social work in the field of child welfare. In fact, according to some writers, it foreshadows the time when all offenders, both juvenile and adult, will be treated individually through scientific and casework processes instead of punished by the methods of criminal law.[3]

## LEGAL ROOTS

The juvenile court owes a great deal to American ingenuity and enterprise, but it also has legal roots that can be traced back to principles that are deeply embedded in English jurisprudence. These principles are to be found in the differential treatment given to children by the English courts through the application of common law and equity doctrines for the protection of innocence and dependency.

One of the legal roots of the juvenile court is the principle of equity or chancery that originated because of the rigidity of the common law and its failure to provide adequate remedies in deserving cases. Eventually the chancellor, who was the head of England's judicial system, was held responsible for giving greater flexibility to the law in such cases and for balancing the interests of litigants in a more equitable manner as measured by the merits of the individual case. Since equity was thus dispensed by the Council of Chancery, the terms "equity" and "chancery" came to be used interchangeably. Through this system of equity, the king acted as *parens patriae*, or as "father of his country," in exercising his power of guardianship over the persons and property of minors, who were considered wards of the state and as such entitled to special pro-

2 Herbert H. Lou, *Juvenile Courts in the United States* (Chapel Hill: University of North Carolina Press, 1927), pp. 13–23; Ben B. Lindsey, "Colorado's Contribution to the Juvenile Court," *The Child, the Clinic, and the Court*, ed. Jane Addams (New York: New Republic, Inc., 1925), pp. 274–89; Helen I. Clarke, *Social Legislation* (New York: Appleton-Century-Crofts, Inc., 1957), 375–77. For easy reference to the first juvenile court act, see Grace Abbott, *The Child and the State* (Chicago: University of Chicago Press, 1938), Vol. II, pp. 392–401.

3 Lou, p. 2; Roscoe Pound, "The Juvenile Court and the Law," *Yearbook, 1944* (New York: National Probation Association, 1945), pp. 1–22; Charles L. Chute, "Fifty Years of the Juvenile Court," *Yearbook, 1949* (New York: National Probation and Parole Association, 1950), pp. 1–20; Nochem S. Winnet, "Fifty Years of the Juvenile Court: An Evaluation," *American Bar Association Journal*, XXXVI (May, 1950), 363–66.

tection. Although originally equity was used chiefly to protect dependent or neglected children who had property interests, its action prefigured the protective intervention of the state through the instrumentality of the juvenile court in cases of delinquency.

The other legal root of the juvenile court is the presumption of innocence thrown about children by the common law. According to its doctrines, a child under the age of seven is conclusively presumed incapable of entertaining criminal intent and therefore incapable of committing a crime. Between the ages of seven and fourteen, a child is presumed to be incapable of committing a crime, but the presumption may be rebutted by showing that the offender has enough responsibility to know the nature of his act. After the age of fourteen, children, like adults, are presumed to be responsible for their actions. Thus the creation of the juvenile court involved the extension of the principle that children below a certain age cannot be held criminally responsible—a principle that has had a long history in the common law.[4]

## HISTORICAL BACKGROUND

In America, where English jurisprudence was introduced by the early colonists, such tendencies as the increase in the complexity of social relationships, the growth of humanitarianism, and the rise of the social sciences contributed to the expansion of the area in which the child received differential treatment by law.[5] Thus in order to protect children from confinement in jails and prisons, special institutions for juvenile offenders were established in the United States during the third decade of the nineteenth century. The first of these, the New York House of Refuge, was opened in New York City in 1825. It developed out of the efforts of Edward Livingston, John Griscom, James Gerard, and other enlightened philanthropists to train the young in cities to seek a life of honest industry. Similar institutions were soon opened in Boston, in 1826, and in Philadelphia, in 1828, and gradually thereafter constructed in other states throughout the country.

Agencies for free foster-home care likewise developed during the years

---

[4] Lou, pp. 1–12; Clarke, pp. 372–74; Frederick B. Sussman and Frederic S. Baum, *Law of Juvenile Delinquency* (Dobbs Ferry, New York: Oceana Publications, 1968), pp. 5, 6; Pound, pp. 4–8. See also Roscoe Pound, "The Rise of Socialized Criminal Justice," *Yearbook, 1942* (New York: National Probation Association, 1942), pp. 1–22.

[5] Robert G. Caldwell, *Criminology* (New York: The Ronald Press Co., 1965), pp. 385, 386.

immediately before and following the War Between the States. The New York Children's Aid Society, founded by Charles Loring Brace in 1853, specialized in the placement of children on farms in the Midwest and in upstate New York and did much to popularize this method of care, significantly contributing to the spread of the foster-home movement to other states.

Other efforts were directed to the modification of court procedure in children's cases, and some important changes in this procedure were effected. For example, Chicago, as early as 1861, provided for a commissioner to hear and determine cases of boys between the ages of six and seventeen brought before him on charges of petty offenses. By the enactment of a statute in 1869, Massachusetts stipulated that an agent of the Board of State Charities should attend the trials of children, protect their interests, and make recommendations regarding them to the judge. The next year, another law passed in Massachusetts instituted separate hearings for juvenile offenders in Suffolk County (Boston), and in 1872, the state extended the requirements of this law to the police, district, and municipal courts of the state and authorized the governor to designate and commission as "trial justices of juvenile offenders" as many justices of the peace as the public interest and convenience might demand to handle children's cases. Still another law, enacted in Massachusetts in 1877, not only authorized separate trials for children, but also specified that a separate record and docket should be kept for their cases. New York, joining the reform movement, established separate hearings for children in 1877, and, in 1892, created separate dockets and records as well as separate trials for juveniles under the age of sixteen. By a law passed in 1891 and amended in 1893, Indiana authorized the Board of Children's Guardians to file a petition in the circuit court if it should have probable cause to believe that any child under fifteen years of age was one whom we usually designate now as dependent, neglected, truant, incorrigible, or sometimes delinquent. If the findings of the court supported the petition, the child was to be committed to the custody and control of the Board of Children's Guardians until he became of age. In 1898, Rhode Island, following the general pattern created by the laws of Massachusetts, enacted a statute providing for separate hearings of juvenile offenders, the presence of state and private agencies at their trial, and separate detention before trial.

Meanwhile other important reforms were taking place. Between 1878 and 1898, Massachusetts established a state-wide system of probation and thus initiated a movement that eventually carried this method of correction into every state in the United States. The years of the nineteenth century also saw the enactment of laws for the regulation of child labor, the development of special services for handicapped children, and the growth of public education.[6]

As this brief summary of some of the important changes in the field of child welfare indicates, there was a growing acceptance of public responsibility for the protection and care of children, but as yet there was no legal machinery by which juvenile offenders could be handled not as criminals according to the regular procedure of the criminal court, but as wards of the state who were in need of special care, protection, and treatment. Meanwhile, however, Chicago welfare and civic organizations, notably the Chicago Woman's Club and the Catholic Visitation and Aid Society were setting the stage for the appearance of exactly this kind of machinery.

Not that the conditions in the state of Illinois differed fundamentally from those in other states, but they were bad enough to evoke a concerted movement that carried the state to leadership in the reform of the procedure used in the handling of children's cases. During the closing years of the nineteenth century in Illinois, the juvenile offender between the ages of ten and sixteen was still considered a criminal as far as arrest, detention, and trial were concerned, and might be sent to a house of correction (city prison), to a county jail, or to a state reformatory. In fact, during the year 1898, a total of 575 children charged with offenses were confined in the Cook County Jail, and for the twenty months ending November 1, 1898, a total of 1,983 boys were committed to the house of correction of the city of Chicago. These children were tried for such offenses as petty theft, disorderly conduct, killing birds, fighting, truancy, stealing rides on the railroads, and so on. Twenty-five per cent of them were charged with truancy. The situation in Chicago became so bad that in March, 1897, the board of education created a school district in the house of correction and named it the John Worthy School. Boys were compelled to attend this school during certain hours of the day and kept in prison cells during the rest of the time.

Stirred into action by this state of affairs, which they considered to be deplorable, a body of socially minded men and women who had given earnest study to the problem of juvenile delinquents initiated a spirited campaign for the establishment of a juvenile court. Despite some early disappointments, their persistent efforts finally produced results. In 1898, at the request of the State Board of Charities, the Chicago Bar Associa-

---

[6] Chute, pp. 2, 3; Sussman, pp. 11–14; Negley K. Teeters and John Otto Reinemann, *The Challenge of Delinquency* (Englewood Cliffs, N.J.: Prentice-Hall, Inc., 1950), pp. 282–86; Paul W. Tappan, *Comparative Survey of Juvenile Delinquency*, Part I, North America (New York: United Nations, Department of Economic and Social Affairs, 1958), pp. 14–16; Lou, pp. 15–19; Enoch Cobb Wines, *State of Prisons* (Cambridge, Massachusetts: University Press, John Wilson and Son, 1880), pp. 125–29; Abbott, pp. 7, 8.

tion appointed a committee to conduct a thorough survey of the situation. Judge Harvey B. Hurd was selected as the committee's chairman and Dr. Hastings H. Hart as its secretary. Prepared principally by Dr. Hart, revised by the committee, and strongly endorsed by various organizations, a juvenile court bill, with some amendments, was passed by both houses of the Illinois legislature and became law on July 1, 1899.[7]

An examination of the historical background of this court shows that many varied influences helped to produce the climate in which it had its origin. Indeed, its establishment may well be considered a logical and exceedingly important development in a much broader movement for the expansion of the specialized treatment given to children in an increasingly complex society. Although the idea of the juvenile court combined already existing elements—institutional segregation, probation supervision, foster-home placement, separate judicial hearings, and an approach that emphasized the rehabilitation of the juvenile offender— even so, as Tappan explains, it did constitute a significant achievement in judicial integration by providing for a more systematic and independent handling of children's cases.[8]

## THE FIRST JUVENILE COURT

The Juvenile Court of Cook County, the first of its kind in the world, was established in Chicago in accordance with the provisions of the state law approved on July 1, 1899. This law, entitled "An Act to Regulate the Treatment and Control of Dependent, Neglected, and Delinquent Children," provided for the setting up of a juvenile court in all counties with a population of over 500,000, but since only Cook County had a population of that size, it alone received such a court. In other counties, circuit and county courts were to handle cases arising under the law. The juvenile court was given jurisdiction over children under the age of sixteen who were adjudged to be dependent, neglected, or delinquent, and it was to have a special judge (chosen by the circuit court judges from among their number at such times as they should determine), a separate court room, separate records, and an informal procedure, which meant that such important aspects of the criminal court trial as the indictment, pleadings, and jury (unless the jury was demanded by an interested party or ordered by the judge) were to be eliminated.

If any reputable resident of a county believed that a child in his

---

[7] Julia C. Lathrop, "The Background of the Juvenile Court in Illinois," and Timothy D. Hurley, "Origin of the Illinois Juvenile Court Law," *The Child, the Clinic, and the Court,* pp. 290–97, 320–30; Abbott, Vol. II, pp. 330, 331; Chute, pp. 3, 4; Lou, pp. 20, 21; Sussman and Baum, pp. 3, 4.

[8] Tappan, pp. 14, 15.

county was neglected, dependent, or delinquent, he might file with the court a written petition, setting forth the facts, verified by affidavit. However, a summons, unless it proved to be ineffectual, was to be used instead of a warrant in all cases, and the court was given authority to appoint probation officers, who were to serve without compensation. It was the duty of the probation officer to make such investigations as were required by the court, to represent the interests of the child during the hearing, to furnish the court such information and assistance as the judge might require, and to take charge of the child before and after the trial in accordance with the directions of the court. The court might continue the case of a delinquent from time to time, place him on probation, put him in a suitable family home, or commit him to an institution. In no case, however, was a child under the age of twelve to be committed to jail: he was to be kept in a suitable place outside of the inclosure of a jail or police station, and all children committed to institutions were to be segregated from adult offenders. The juvenile court act was to be construed liberally so that the case, custody, and discipline of the child should approximate as nearly as possible that which should be given by his parents.[9]

If one bears in mind the following facts about the first juvenile court law, it may help him to acquire a better perspective of the juvenile court movement in the United States:

1. The first court was not to be a new or independent tribunal but merely a special jurisdiction in the circuit court.

2. The juvenile court was to be a special court and not an administrative agency. As Dean Pound has said, "It was set up as a court of equity, with the administrative functions incidental to equity jurisdiction, not as a criminal court, and not, as might have happened later, as an administrative agency with incidental adjudicating functions."[10]

3. The law did not stipulate that juvenile delinquents should be "treated" and not punished. It merely provided that the child should receive approximately the same care, custody, and discipline that his parents should give to him.[11]

4. A juvenile delinquent was simply defined as "any child under the age of 16 years who violates any law of this State or any city or village ordinance."[12] It was not until later that this simple definition was modified to include other types of behavior which are illegal only for children

[9] Abbott, Vol. II, pp. 392–401.
[10] Pound, "The Juvenile Court and the Law," p. 5.
[11] Abbott, Vol. II, pp. 400, 401.
[12] *Ibid.*, p. 393.

such as incorrigibility, growing up in idleness or crime, waywardness, and so on.

5. In all trials under the law any interested party might demand, or the judge might order, a jury of six to try the case.[13]

In effect, then, the first juvenile court law established the status of delinquency as "something less than crime."[14] In doing this, it made two fundamental changes in the handling of juvenile offenders that are especially noteworthy. First, it raised the age below which a child could not be considered a criminal from seven to sixteen and made a child who was alleged to be delinquent subject to the jurisdiction of the juvenile court. Secondly, it placed the operation of the court under equity or chancery jurisdiction and thereby extended the application of the principle of guardianship, which had been used to protect neglected and dependent children, to all children, including juvenile delinquents, who were in need of protection by the state. These two changes, in modified form, remain as essential characteristics of all juvenile court legislation.[15]

## TRENDS IN THE JUVENILE COURT MOVEMENT

### Geographical Expansion

After Illinois had taken the initiative, other states soon followed her example and established juvenile courts. In fact, within ten years, twenty states and the District of Columbia enacted juvenile court laws. By 1920, all except three states had done so, and in 1945, when Wyoming took action, the list of states having juvenile court laws was finally complete. Today all states, the District of Columbia, and Puerto Rico have some kind of juvenile court legislation.[16] In addition, the movement has had considerable success in other countries.[17] There are, however, no federal

---

13 *Ibid.*

14 Tappan, p. 14.

15 Caldwell, pp. 360, 361.

16 Sussman and Baum, pp. 5, 77–87; Caldwell, p. 361.

17 See Anna Kalet Smith, *Juvenile Court Laws in Foreign Countries,* U.S. Children's Bureau Publication No. 328 (Washington, D.C.: Government Printing Office, 1951); Clarke, *op. cit.,* pp. 377–83; International Committee of the Howard League of Penal Reform, *Lawless Youth: A Challenge to the New Europe* (London: George Allen and Unwin, Ltd., 1947.); John A. F. Watson, *British Juvenile Courts* (London: Logman's Green and Co., 1948); Basil L. Q. Henriques, "Children's Courts in England," *Journal of Criminal Law and Criminology,* XXXVII (November–December, 1946), 295–99; Thorsten Sellin, "Sweden's Substitute for the Juvenile Court," *The Annals of the American Academy of Political and Social Science,* CCLXI (January, 1949), 137–49; C. Terence Pihlblad, "The Juvenile Offender in Norway," *Journal of Criminal Law, Criminology, and Police Science,* XLVI (November–December, 1955), 500–11.

juvenile courts. Children under eighteen who violate a federal law not punishable by death or life imprisonment may be transferred to a state juvenile court or proceeded against as a juvenile delinquent in a federal district court.[18]

## Jurisdictional Extension

While the juvenile court movement was spreading, the jurisdiction of the court itself was being extended. In general, the definition of juvenile delinquency was broadened, and the types of nondelinquency cases (such as those involving illegitimacy, mental and physical defectives, and so on) under the jurisdiction of the court were increased. Furthermore, the tendency was to raise the upper age level of the children subject to the authority of the court from sixteen to seventeen or eighteen, and for some cases in a few states, to twenty-one. In addition, the juvenile court was given jurisdiction over adults in certain cases involving children—for example, those in which an adult had contributed to the delinquency of a juvenile.[19]

## Increase in Court's Influence

Then, too, after the creation of the juvenile court, it began to exert an increasing influence on the principles and methods used in the adjustment of many other family problems and in the handling of adolescent and adult offenders. For example, some cities, like Cincinnati, Philadelphia, and Wilmington, Delaware, established special courts, called family or domestic relations courts, with jurisdiction over cases involving all kinds of family problems, such as delinquency, dependency, neglect, adoption, illegitimacy, nonsupport, and crimes by members of a family against one another. In effect, the operation of these courts means that many of the principles and methods of the juvenile court are being applied to an increasing variety of social problems. Moreover, special courts for adolescents have been set up in certain cities, like Chicago, Philadelphia, and New York, in which an attempt is being made to combine some of the principles and methods of the juvenile court with those of the criminal court in proceedings against youthful offenders who are above the juvenile court age but below the age of twenty-one. A much more systematic and inclusive program for dealing with this type of offender is represented by the various youth authorities that have been created in such states as California and Minnesota. In their emphasis upon individual diagnosis and treatment, these programs, too, reflect to some extent the spreading influence of the philosophy of the juvenile

[18] Sussman, *op. cit.*, p. 76.
[19] Caldwell, *op. cit.*, p .361.

court.  Finally, it may be said that this influence can also be seen in the use of presentence investigation and probation in the cases of adult offenders in our criminal courts.

The increasing complexity of American society has contributed significantly to these trends in the juvenile court movement.  Such interrelated factors as industrialization, urbanization, the unprecedented movement of populations, the amazing utilization of natural resources, the rapid accumulation of inventions and discoveries, and the acceleration of transportation and communication have tended to undermine the family and the neighborhood and, forcing our communities to find additional means of social control, have given considerable impetus to the establishment of juvenile courts and sent into them an increasing number and variety of cases.  In the meantime, other influences have more specifically affected the philosophy and methods of the juvenile court.  Thus social workers, under the aggressive leadership of such organizations as the United States Children's Bureau, the National Probation and Parole Association, and various other associations now united into the National Association of Social Workers, have joined with psychiatrists in stressing the importance of casework training and treatment services in the operation of the juvenile court; and the efforts of a comparatively few well-organized, big-city juvenile courts at conventions and conferences have served to focus and intensify these influences.  The resulting tendency has been to picture juvenile delinquency as symptomatic of some underlying emotional condition, which must be diagnosed by means of the concepts and techniques of psychiatry, psychology, and social work, and for which treatment, not punishment, must be administered through the efforts of a team of psychiatrists, psychologists, and social workers.  Surprisingly enough, the legal profession, also, has contributed to this tendency through court decisions regarding the juvenile court that have stressed its social service functions and minimized its legal principles.  The total effect of all this has been to place increasing emphasis on the treatment of the individual and to give decreasing attention to his legal rights and the security of the community.  Thus the balance between rights, on the one hand, and duties and responsibilities, on the other, which every court must seek to maintain, has been upset as the court has been pushed more and more into the role of a social work agency.

## CHARACTERISTICS OF THE JUVENILE COURT

Although the juvenile court has had an uneven development and has manifested a great diversity in its methods and procedures, certain characteristics have appeared which are considered essential in its operation.

As early as 1920, Evelina Belden of the United States Children's Bureau listed the following as the essential characteristics of the juvenile court:

1. Separate hearings for children's cases.
2. Informal or chancery procedure.
3. Regular probation service.
4. Separate detention of children.
5. Special court and probation records.
6. Provision for mental and physical examinations.[20]

Of course, many so-called juvenile courts have few of these characteristics, and others possess them only to a degree. However, in the opinion of many observers, if a court does not have them, it cannot claim to be a juvenile court.

Several decades ago, Katharine Lenroot, then chief of the United States Children's Bureau, presented a summary of standards for the juvenile court which indicate the characteristics that many now believe the court should have. These standards call for the following:

1. Broad jurisdiction in cases of children under eighteen years of age requiring court action or protection because of their acts or circumstances.

2. A judge chosen because of his special qualifications for juvenile court work, with legal training, acquaintance with social problems, and understanding of child psychology.

3. Informal court procedure and private hearings.

4. Detention kept at a minimum, outside of jails and police stations and as far as possible in private boarding homes.

5. A well-qualified probation staff, with limitation of case loads, and definite plans for constructive work in each case.

6. Availability of resources for individual and specialized treatment such as medical, psychological, and psychiatric services, foster family and institutional care, and recreational services and facilities.

7. State supervision of probation work.

8. An adequate record system, providing for both legal and social records and for the safeguarding of these records from indiscriminate public inspection.[21]

These standards form much of the basis of the *Standard Juvenile Court Act* (the latest edition of which was issued by the National Pro-

[20] Evelina Belden, *Courts in the United States Hearing Children's Cases,* U.S. Children's Bureau Publication No. 65 (Washington, D.C.: Government Printing Office, 1920), pp. 7–10.

[21] Katharine F. Lenroot, "The Juvenile Court Today," *Federal Probation,* XII (September, 1949), 10.

bation and Parole Association in 1959),[22] and to a great extent they have been incorporated in the *Standards for Juvenile and Family Courts*, which was prepared by the United States Children's Bureau in 1966.[23]

## COMPARISON OF THE JUVENILE AND CRIMINAL COURTS

In order to emphasize the essential characteristics of the juvenile court, it is sometimes compared with the criminal court. This can be helpful; but care must be exercised to avoid an exaggeration of the differences between the two courts, for juvenile courts vary greatly from place to place, and most of them differ very little from criminal courts.

The purpose of the criminal court is to determine whether there is sufficient evidence to convict the accused of a specific crime as defined by the law. The trial, usually a public one, is conducted in accordance with the technical rules of procedure, and it is primarily concerned with questions regarding the motive and the intent of the defendant and with the facts directly related to the alleged crime. If the defendant is convicted, he is sentenced to punishment as prescribed by law, but if he is acquitted, he is released from the authority of the court.

The purpose of the juvenile court, on the other hand, is not only to determine whether the child is delinquent, but also to learn why he has behaved as he has. Its chief objective, in fact, is the welfare of the child: his protection, guidance, and rehabilitation. The hearing is as private as possible, and flexibility of procedure is stressed, so as to prevent technicalities from interfering with the securing of all the pertinent information about the personality, the background, and the social situation of the child. If the court finds the child delinquent, it can use its broad discretionary powers to act as his guardian, and in doing this, it places emphasis on the specific needs of the child and on his rehabilitation rather than on the possible deterrent effects of its decision. If it does not adjudge the child delinquent, it does not necessarily release him from its authortiy, but may decide that it must act in some other way to promote his welfare. Thus, for example, the court may place the child in a foster home, put him under the care of some agency, or commit him to an institution.

---

[22] *Standard Juvenile Court Act* (rev. ed.; New York: National Probation and Parole Association, 1959).

[23] *Standards for Juvenile and Family Courts*, U.S. Children's Bureau Publication No. 437 (Washington, D.C.: Government Printing Office, 1966). This was a revision of an earlier publication, *Standards for Specialized Courts Dealing with Children*, issued by the United States Children's Bureau in 1954, Children's Bureau Publication No. 346 (Washington, D.C.: Government Printing Office, 1954).

## THE STANDARD JUVENILE COURT ACT

The sixth edition of the *Standard Juvenile Court Act*, published in 1959, was prepared by the National Probation and Parole Association, in cooperation with the National Council of Juvenile Court Judges and the United States Children's Bureau. Like the previous editions, this one was issued in the hope that it might be used as a model in the preparation and amendment of juvenile court laws throughout the United States.

This act states that its provisions are to be liberally construed, so that the child coming within its jurisdiction will receive the care, guidance, and control that will conduce to both his welfare and the best interests of the state. The child should remain in his own home if this is possible, but if he must be removed, then the court should try to provide him with the same kind of care that he should have received from his parents. In order to secure adequate prestige, status, and financial support, the juvenile court should be a division of the highest court of general trial jurisdiction. The judge should be chosen in the same way as the other judges of the highest court of general trial jurisdiction, or (as provided in an alternative section), he should be appointed by the governor for a term of six years from a list submitted to him by a nominating commission. The nominees on this list should be members of the bar and well-informed regarding the problems of family and child welfare, juvenile delinquency, and community organization. All the juvenile court judges of the state are to constitute a board of juvenile court judges, who are required to establish general policies and uniform rules for the state's juvenile courts and to publish annual reports regarding their work. The juvenile court judge may appoint referees to assist him in the performance of his duties.[24]

The court is to have exclusive original jurisdiction over all children under eighteen years of age who (1) are alleged to have violated any law or ordinance, (2) are neglected, (3) are in an environment which is injurious to their welfare or are behaving in such a way as to injure their own welfare or that of others, or (4) are beyond the control of their parents or other custodians. The court is given exclusive original jurisdiction also in proceedings (1) to determine the custody of any child or to appoint a guardian for him, (2) to arrange for the adoption of any person of any age, (3) to terminate the legal parent-child relationship, (4) to obtain legally required consent to the marriage, employment, or enlistment of a child, and (5) to provide for the treatment or commitment of a mentally defective or mentally ill minor. The act avoids

[24] *Standard Juvenile Court Act* (New York: National Probation and Parole Association, 1959), Article I, Sections 1–7.

the use of the "delinquency" and "neglect" labels, on the assumption that
such labels may be harmful to the child and interfere with his future
development and acceptance in the community.   Instead of using these
labels, the act merely describes the categories of children over whom
the court has jurisdiction.   Furthermore, the court is not given jurisdiction over dependent children who are not neglected.   These cases, it is
believed, should be dealt with by administrative agencies without court
action.   Jurisdiction obtained by the court in the case of a child is to
be retained by it until he becomes twenty-one years of age.   The court
is given exclusive original jurisdiction also over all cases involving a
parent or guardian accused of a crime against a child, or involving any
adult charged with deserting, abandoning, or failing to support a person
in violation of the law.   If the adult is entitled to trial by jury and
demands it, the court "may" transfer his case to a criminal court.   No
section on "contributing to delinquency" is included in the act, since
those who prepared it believed that many of the cases covered by such
a section should be prosecuted under specific provisions in the criminal
code, for example, those regarding assault, battery, impairing the morals
of a minor, and so on.[25]

Whenever a complaint is filed with the court, it should make a preliminary investigation to determine whether the interests of the public
or the child require further action.   If the court decides that further
action is necessary, it may authorize the filing of a petition.   The petition
should set forth (1) the facts which bring the child within the purview
of the act, (2) the name, age, and residence of the child, and (3) the
names and residence of his parents or guardians.

If the admitted facts appear to establish *prima facie* jurisdiction and
the parents and the child, if he is of sufficient age and understanding,
give their consent, the court may make whatever informal adjustment
it deems practicable without a petition.   However, efforts to effect informal adjustment should be continued no longer than three months
without review by the judge.   This limitation is contained in the act to
guard against the abuse of "unofficial casework."   On the other hand,
no preliminary investigation and petition are required in traffic cases.
In these cases, the court takes jurisdiction simply on the basis of the
issuance of a summons or citation.   In any case involving a child who
was sixteen years of age or older at the time he allegedly committed an
act which would be a felony if committed by an adult, the court, after
a full investigation and a hearing, may, in its discretion, transfer the
child to the criminal court if it deems this to be in the best interest of
the child or the public.   After a petition is filed, the court is directed

[25] *Ibid.*, Article II, Sections 8–11.

to issue summonses for the persons whose presence in court is required, unless they appear voluntarily. When the summons is served, the child may be taken into custody at once if this seems necessary for his welfare. If a person is summoned to appear in the juvenile court and, without reasonable cause, he fails to appear, he may be held in contempt of court and a warrant may be issued for him.[26]

The hearings of the juvenile court should be separate from those for adults, informal, without a jury, and as private as possible. The judge should explain to the child and the parents that they have a right to counsel, that if they cannot afford an attorney, the court will appoint one for them, and that they have a right to appeal in the event of an adverse decision. No disposition of the case, other than a discharge, should be made without a prior investigation, unless this requirement is waived by the judge. However, if the allegations of the petition are denied, the investigation should not be made until after the allegations have been established at the hearing. In disposing of the case, the court may discharge the child, place him on probation or in a foster home, order him examined and treated by a physician, psychiatrist, or psychologist, or placed in a hospital or some other institution or agency for whatever care may be considered necessary for his best interests, or commit him to a correctional institution. Separate legal and social records of all cases should be maintained by the court and protected against indiscriminate inspection.[27]

[26] *Ibid.*, Article III, Sections 12–15.

[27] *Ibid.*, Article V, Sections 19–28, Article VI, Sections 29–38. The above statement regarding the *Standard Juvenile Court Act* is only an abbreviated account of some of its specifications.

# 14

# The Juvenile Court: Structure and Function

## THE PRESENT STATUS OF THE COURT

In the United States the juvenile court varies greatly from one jurisdiction to another, manifesting at present all stages of its complex development. And it should not be overlooked that its philosophy, structure, and function are still in the process of evolution. Seldom is the court a distinct and highly specialized one, and in the more rural counties it is largely of a rudimentary nature. Usually it is part of a court with more general jurisdiction, the judges holding sessions for juveniles at regular or irregular intervals.[1] Since there is this great diversity, no simple description of the juvenile courts of the United States can be given. It is possible, however, to indicate in general terms their present status with respect to certain important features.

### Philosophy of the Court

In the words of Tappan, the juvenile court and its methods are "by no means a mere direct borrowing from chancery and common law," but, on the contrary, have emerged largely from "the philosophy and techniques of modern case-work and, more particularly, the ideologies of the child-welfare movement concerning the rights of children and the devices that should be used to meet their needs." In fact, "the operations of the specialized juvenile court reflect the contemporary impact of case-work

[1] Paul W. Tappan, *Comparative Survey of Juvenile Delinquency*, Part I, North America (New York: United Nations, Department of Economic and Social Affairs, 1958), pp. 15, 24; The President's Commission on Law Enforcement and Administration of Justice, *Task Force Report: Juvenile Delinquency and Youth Crime* (Washington, D.C.: Government Printing Office, 1967), pp. 3, 4.

oriented probation officers, administrative social agency procedures, and other non-legal (if not distinctly anti-legal) forces far more than they do the influence of either chancery or common law, modern or ancient." [2]

Although generalizations about anything as complex as the juvenile court are always hazardous, it appears that the following are important elements in the court's philosophy:

**1. The Superior Rights of the State.** The state is the "higher or ultimate parent" of all the children within its borders. The rights of the child's own parents are always subject to the control of the state when in the opinion of the court the best interests of the child demand it. If the state has to intervene in the case of any child, it exercises its power of guardianship over the child and provides him with the protection, care, and guidance that he needs. This is an adaptation of the ancient doctrine of *parens patriae*, by which all English children were made wards of the Crown.[3]

**2. Individualization of Justice.** A basic principle in the philosophy of the juvenile court is the recognition that people are different and that each must be considered in the light of his own background and personality. The court, therefore, must adapt its actions to the circumstances of the individual case by ascertaining the needs and potentialities of the child and coordinating the knowledge and the skills of law, science, and social work for the promotion of his welfare. This means the balancing of interests in an equitable manner by administrative rather than adversary methods within a flexible procedure such as that provided by chancery. Dean Pound has called this "individualized justice." [4]

---

[2] Tappan, p. 9. There is a difference of opinion regarding the extent to which the principles of equity and the criminal law contributed to the origin of the juvenile court. The sound interpretation, however, seems to be the roots of the juvenile court can be traced to both the common law and equity. See Julian W. Mack, "Legal Problems Involved in the Establishment of the Juvenile Court," *The Delinquent Child and the Home*, Sophonisba P. Breckinridge and Edith Abbott (New York: Charities Publication Committee, 1912), pp. 181–201; Roscoe Pound, *Interpretations of Legal History* (New York: Macmillan Co., 1923), pp. 134, 135; Sheldon and Eleanor T. Glueck, "Historical and Legislative Background of the Juvenile Court," *The Problem of Delinquency*, ed. Sheldon Glueck (Boston: Houghton Mifflin Co., 1959), pp. 258, 259; Herbert H. Lou, *Juvenile Courts in the United States* (Chapel Hill: University of North Carolina Press, 1927), pp. 2–7.

[3] Mack, pp. 181–87; Lou, pp. 2–9; Gustav L. Schramm, "Philosophy of the Juvenile Court," *The Annals of the American Academy of Political and Social Science,* CCLXI (January, 1949), 101–8.

[4] Roscoe Pound, "The Future of Socialized Justice," *Yearbook, 1946* (New York: National Probation Association, 1947), pp. 6–18; Schramm, 103, 104; Lou, pp. 2–5; Herbert A. Bloch and Frank T. Flynn, *Delinquency: The Juvenile Offender in America Today* (New York: Random House, Inc., 1956), pp. 317, 318; *Standards for Specialized Courts Dealing With Children*, U.S. Children's Bureau Publication No. 346 (Washington, D.C.: Government Printing Office, 1954), pp. 1, 2.

**3. The Status of Delinquency.** The state should try to protect the child from the harmful brand of criminality. In order to accomplish this, the law created the status of delinquency, which is something less than crime and is variously defined in different states. However, this still does not satisfy some students of the court who advocate the removal of even the "delinquency tag," which they claim is just another harmful label, and, furthermore, they assert that delinquency acts have no significance except as symptoms of conditions that demand investigation by the court.[5]

**4. Noncriminal Procedure.** By means of an informal procedure, the juvenile court functions in such a way as to give primary consideration to the interests of the child. In general, the courts have held that the procedure of the juvenile court is not criminal in nature, since its purpose is not to convict the child of a crime, but to protect, aid, and guide him, and that, therefore, it is not unconstitutional if it denies him certain rights which are guaranteed to an adult in a criminal trial.[6]

**5. Remedial, Preventive, and Nonpunitive Purpose.** The action of the juvenile court is to save the child and to prevent him from becoming a criminal. It seeks to provide him with about the same care and protection that his parents should give him. Although, as we have explained, the first juvenile court law did not stipulate that the child should not be punished, many subsequent court decisions and most of the literature on the subject insist that the substitution of treatment for punishment is an essential element in the philosophy of the court.[7]

## Geographical Area Served by the Court

The county is the geographical area served by most juvenile courts in the United States, but for some, the jurisdictional unit is the town, the city, the borough, or the judicial district. Since the county is the conventional unit of state government and of many private organizations,

---

[5] Mack, p. 189; Frederick B. Sussman and Frederic S. Baum, *Law of Juvenile Delinquency* (Dobbs Ferry, N.Y.: Oceana Publications, 1968), p. 11; Tappan, pp. 14, 15.

[6] Helen I. Clarke, *Social Legislation* (New York: Appleton-Century-Crofts, Inc., 1957), p. 410; Lou, p. 10. For a convenient digest of some of the important cases regarding the constitutionality of the juvenile court, see Glueck, pp. 334–506.

[7] Mack, p. 190; International Committee of the Howard League for Penal Reform, *Lawless Youth: A Challenge to the New Europe* (London: George Allen and Unwin, Ltd., 1947), pp. 9–21; *Standards for Specialized Courts Dealing With Children*, p. 1; Charles L. Chute, "Fifty Years of the Juvenile Court," *Yearbook, 1949* (New York: National Probation and Parole Association, 1950), p. 1; Lou, p. 7; Timothy D. Hurley, "Origin of the Illinois Juvenile Court Law," *The Child, The Clinic, and the Court*, ed. Jane Addams (New York: New Republic, Inc., 1925), p. 328; Clarke, pp. 410–15.

its use as the jurisdictional area for the court has obvious advantages in the coordination of its work with that of other agencies interested in child welfare. Most counties, however, cannot afford to maintain courts at modern standards, and even if they could, the volume of work would not justify the necessary expense.[8] In some states, this problem could be solved by making the area served by the juvenile court the same as the judicial district served by other courts in the state and thereby enable one juvenile court to take care of the cases of two or more counties. Utah, Connecticut, and Rhode Island have pushed beyond this and, by establishing state systems of juvenile courts, have created larger jurisdictional districts within their borders.[9]

## Types of Juvenile Courts

There are about 3,000 juvenile courts in the United States, although actually many are only slightly different from criminal courts. Several decades ago, Lowell Carr, in referring to the inferior quality of many juvenile courts, said, "In well over 2,000 counties in the United States nobody has ever seen a well-staffed, modern juvenile court in action." [10] About a decade ago, Tappan observed that even New York City, a wealthy community with relatively high welfare standards, had fallen considerably short of the ideal level of performance set for the juvenile court.[11] And in 1967, the President's Commission on Law Enforcement and Administration of Justice reported:

Studies conducted by the Commission, legislative inquiries in various States, and reports by informed observers compel the conclusion that the great hopes originally held for the juvenile court have not been fulfilled. It has not succeeded significantly in rehabilitating delinquent youth, in reducing or even stemming the tide of juvenile criminality, or in bringing justice and compassion to the child offender.[12]

Juvenile courts in the United States may be classified into these three types:

1. "Designated courts," such as municipal, county, district, and circuit courts which have been selected or designated to hear children's cases and while so functioning are called juvenile courts.

[8] Lowell Juilliard Carr, "Most Courts Have To Be Substandard," *Federal Probation*, XIII (September, 1949), 29–33.
[9] Sussman and Baum, p. 15; John Farr Larson, "Utah's State-Wide Juvenile Court Plan," *Federal Probation*, XIII (June, 1949), 15–17.
[10] Carr, p. 31. See also Harrison Allen Dobbs, "Realism and the Juvenile Court," *Focus*, XXXI (July, 1952), 104–8.
[11] Tappan, pp. 15, 16. For a careful study of New York's juvenile courts, see Alfred J. Kahn, *A Court for Children* (New York: Columbia University Press, 1953).
[12] The President's Commission on Law Enforcement and Administration of Justice, p. 7.

2.  Independent and separate courts whose administration is entirely divorced from other courts.
3.  Coordinated courts, which are coordinated with other special courts such as domestic relations or family courts.

The great majority of the juvenile courts are "designated courts," and even some of the separate and independent ones are presided over by judges from other courts, so that their separateness and independence may be more nominal than real.[13]

## Jurisdiction of the Court

All juvenile courts have jurisdiction in delinquency cases, and almost all of them have jurisdiction also in cases of dependency and neglect. In addition, some have authority to handle other problems, like feeble-mindedness, adoption, illegitimacy, and guardianship.  Although the definition of delinquency varies from state to state, in most states the violation of a state law or municipal ordinance (an act which in the case of an adult would be a crime) is the main category of delinquency. Yet in all states delinquency is more than this, including such items as habitual truancy, incorrigibility, waywardness, and association with immoral persons.

Juvenile court laws differ also with respect to the age of the children over whom the court has jurisdiction.  The laws of most states do not specify any lower age limit, merely providing that children under a certain age are subject to the jurisdiction of the court.  About two-thirds of the states make eighteen the upper age limit; some set it at sixteen or seventeen; and a few put it as high as twenty-one.  In some states the upper age limit differs according to the sex of the child.  However, about forty states provide for waiver or transfer by the juvenile court to the criminal court, thus giving the juvenile court some discretion and flexibility in exercising its jurisdiction.  Many states permit the juvenile court, after it has once acquired jurisdiction over the child, to retain it until he has reached twenty-one.

In many states the juvenile court does not have exclusive jurisdiction over all delinquency cases, but has only concurrent jurisdiction with the criminal court, delinquency cases being handled by either court.  Often, however, such concurrent jurisdiction is limited by law to cases of children above a specified age or to cases involving certain offenses or to certain counties.  Furthermore, in many states certain offenses, for example, murder, manslaughter, and rape, are entirely excluded from the

---

[13] Negley K. Teeters and John Otto Reinemann, *The Challenge of Delinquency* (Englewood Cliffs, N.J.: Prentice-Hall, Inc., 1950), pp. 295–97; The President's Commission on Law Enforcement and Administration of Justice, p. 4.

jurisdiction of the juvenile court, and in these states children charged with such offenses are tried in the criminal court.

The jurisdiction of the court is affected in still another way by the provision in most states that it may exercise authority over adults in certain cases involving children. Thus in many states the juvenile court may require a parent to contribute to the support of his child, or it may try adults charged with contributing to the delinquency, neglect, or dependency of a child.[14]

## The Judge and the Probation Officer

Although the effectiveness of the juvenile court depends to a very large degree upon the efficiency of its personnel, relatively few courts have staffs that are especially qualified for their work. In most juvenile courts the judges have been appointed or elected on the basis of their general qualifications for judicial work, and they divide their time between adult and juvenile cases. Only in a very few courts has the judge been selected because he has some specialized training or experience in the handling of children's problems. Often, however, a referee is appointed to assist the judge in the performance of his juvenile court duties. Even though considerable progress has been made in improving the quality of probation in some parts of the country, the great majority of courts are still without the services of a sufficient number of well-qualified and adequately paid workers.[15]

Some light was thrown on the inadequacy of the court's personnel in 1963, by a biographical survey of its judges, which was conducted under the sponsorship of the National Council of Juvenile Court Judges. In this survey, responses were received from 1,564 judges, who represented an estimated 70 per cent of those appreciably involved in juvenile matters. Of the total number of judges who responded, 71 per cent had received law degrees (95 per cent of those serving jurisdictions with a population of over 1 million had such degrees), but 48 per cent had received no undergraduate degree, 19 per cent had received no college education at all, and the most prevalent previous occupation (73.7 per cent) was the practice of law, for an average of nine years. Over 93 per cent

---

[14] Sussman and Baum, pp. 8, 9, 16–18; The President's Commission on Law Enforcement and Administration of Justice, p. 4.

[15] Katharine F. Lenroot, "The Juvenile Court Today," *Federal Probation*, XIII (September, 1949), 14, 15; Frederick W. Killian, "The Juvenile Court as an Institution," *The Annals of the American Academy of Political and Social Science*, CCLXI (January, 1949), 92–97; Teeters and Reinemann, pp. 313–19; Tappan, p. 13; F. James Davis, "The Iowa Juvenile Court Judge," *Journal of Criminal Law, Criminology, and Police Science*, XLII (September–October, 1951), 338–50.

of these judges were males; their average age was fifty-three; and their average salary was $12,490. Almost 75 per cent had been elected to officer (a third of them after an initial interim appointment), and 62 per cent had previously been elected to another public office. Of the full-time judges covered by the survey, 72 per cent spent a quarter or less of their time on juvenile matters. Often judicial hearings are little more than attenuated interviews, lasting only about ten or fifteen minutes. Furthermore, a third of the full-time judges reported that there were no probation officers or social workers available for their courts, and 83 per cent said that there were no regularly available psychologists or psychiatrists. This survey, then, indicates that, in general, our juvenile courts are presided over by a group of part-time, inadequately compensated judges, many of whom have not had enough professional preparation or opportunity for in-service training, have excessive case loads, and do not have access to sufficient resources in the performance of their duties.[16]

## Procedure of the Court

Police action initiates the procedure in most delinquency cases, but often it begins with action by a parent or by some other private person or with a referral by a social agency or another court. It is noteworthy that extensive screening and informal adjustment by the police on the street and in the police station significantly reduce the number of apprehended juveniles who are referred to the court. The police favor this screening of juveniles on the grounds that it not only offers an opportunity for helping the child but also provides fertile ground for cultivating friendship and understanding between juveniles and the police. Many writers, however, believe that the police, in this exercise of their discretion, should be guided by a set of written rules and standards.

Many juvenile court statutes provide that the court should make a preliminary inquiry of all complaints received by it to determine whether the interests of the child or the public require court action. This inquiry may vary from a cursory investigation to a full-fledged social study, involving a hearing and contact with numerous persons and agencies. In many juvenile courts, especially in those located in large metropolitan areas, this preliminary screening, known as "intake," is conducted by a special division of the probation department. As a result of the pre-

---

[16] The President's Commission on Law Enforcement and Administration of Justice, pp. 6, 7. See also Shirley D. McCune and Daniel L. Skoler, "Juvenile Court Judges in the United States—Part I: A National Profile," *Crime and Delinquency*, XI (April, 1965), 121–31; Regis H. Walther and Shirley D. McCune, "Juvenile Court Judges in the United States—Part II: Working Styles and Characteristics," *Crime and Delinquency*, XI (October, 1965), 384–93.

liminary inquiry, the case may be dismissed, the filing of a petition may be authorized, or the case may be disposed of by some "informal adjustment," such as the referral of the case to another agency or the placing of the child on "informal probation." In recent years, about fifty per cent of the delinquency cases have been handled informally or unofficially, that is, without an official record or hearing, the judge or someone else, such as a probation officer, taking the necessary steps to dispose of the case. The type of cases that are handled in this way vary greatly from court to court, but the tendency seems to be to reserve official hearings for older children and those brought before the court on serious charges.

When a case is not handled unofficially, a petition (which is merely a statement containing important facts of the case, such as the names and addresses of the child and his parents or guardians and the cause of the action) is filed in the court and the case is then scheduled for a hearing. If the child is not being held in detention and his presence is required, a summons ordering him to appear, or in some cases a warrant for his arrest, is issued. In some jurisdictions a prehearing investigation is conducted so that both the hearing and the disposition of the case can be based on the facts so obtained. Other jurisdictions, however, require that the child must be adjudged delinquent before his case is investigated. In these jurisdictions the hearing is held first, and if the child is found to be delinquent, the court is adjourned, the investigation is completed, and the information is then used by the court in the disposition of the case. Unfortunately, inadequacy of personnel and excessive case loads often prevent the investigation from being more than a superficial inquiry.

Juvenile court hearings are usually less formal than trials in the criminal court, but the degree of informality varies considerably throughout the country. In cases where the juvenile is charged with an act that would constitute a crime if committed by an adult, the adjudication of delinquency (as ordered by the United States Supreme Court in the *Winship* case on March 31, 1970) requires the same standard of proof as that used in the criminal court, that is, proof beyond a reasonable doubt. In other types of delinquency cases, however, this standard varies, but almost always it is less than proof beyond a reasonable doubt. Even so, privacy characterizes most hearings, only persons who are definitely connected with the case being permitted to attend. Where newspaper reporters are admitted, they are usually requested to refrain from using names or otherwise making the juvenile publicly identifiable. Seldom is a prosecuting attorney present during the hearing, although in some courts the case is presented by a police or probation officer. However, as a result of some recent decisions handed down by the United States Supreme Court, the child and his parents must now be given notice of the charges, be advised of their right to counsel or, if they are unable to afford counsel, to have one appointed for them, be permitted to confront and cross-examine witnesses, and be protected against self-incrimination. Although jury trials are permitted in some jurisdictions, usually juries are not used. Furthermore, appeals form the decisions of juvenile courts are rarely made, despite the fact that the right of appeal in one form or another is available in most jurisdictions.[17]

## Disposition of Cases

In arriving at a decision in a case, the juvenile court judge relies to a great extent on the social, or predisposition, report, which the probation officer prepares after he has made a study of the physical and mental conditions of the child and his social background and development. Since most jurisdictions give the judge broad discretionary powers, usually he may hand down one of a variety of decisions. He may, for example, dismiss the case, warn the juvenile, fine him, place him on probation, arrange for restitution, refer him to a social agency, clinic, or hospital, put him in a foster or a group home, commit him to an institution, or, perhaps, combine some of these possibilities. Even so, after a child has been adjudicated a delinquent, the judge has these three major choices:

1. He may leave the child in his own home under a suspended sentence without official supervision, under a probation plan and the supervision of a probation officer officer, or under some program of assistance or treatment directed by a public or private agency.
2. He may place the child in a foster home or a group home under any one of the same conditions.
3. He may commit him to an institution.

Usually, the length of institutional commitment is indefinite, but in most states it cannot extend beyond the juvenile's twenty-first birthday. Thus the period of institutionalization for a young child may be long, but in the opinion of many authorities, it should not be more than three years, unless a longer term is deemed necessary for the promotion of the child's welfare or the protection of the community's interests.

About ten states authorize their juvenile courts to commit juveniles

---

[17] Sussman and Baum, pp. 19–30; National Conference on Prevention and Control of Juvenile Delinquency, *Report on Juvenile Court Laws* (Washington, D.C.: Government Printing Office, 1947), pp. 6, 7; The President's Commission on Law Enforcement and Administration of Justice, pp. 4, 5.

directly to institutions for adult offenders. Furthermore, about a third of the states permit a child who has already been committed to an institution for juvenile delinquents by a juvenile court to be transferred administratively to an institution for adults who have been convicted of a crime. More than five hundred children were so transferred during 1962. State appellate court decisions are in conflict on the constitutionality of this practice. However, the Standard Juvenile Court Act opposes the commitment or transfer of a juvenile delinquent to an institution for adult offenders—and for sound legal reasons. Juvenile delinquency is a legal status created by a juvenile court through the use of a noncriminal procedure, during which the child is denied certain rights guaranteed to the adult in a criminal trial. Consequently, the delinquent should not be treated as if he were an adult offender, whose legal status is different, and should not be kept in an institution designed for an adult offender without first having his day in a criminal court.

The structure and function of the agencies which administer services and facilities for delinquent children vary as much as do those of the juvenile courts. As a result, the responsibility for a child may shift back and forth among courts and a variety of public and private agencies, on both state and local levels. One plan that has been developed to overcome these difficulties—one already adopted by about a third of the states—vests the responsibility for the administration and expansion of a state's control and treatment program in a single state agency to which all children adjudged in need of care are committed.[18]

## Cooperation With Other Agencies

The success of the juvenile court depends in great part on the work of other agencies, such as the police, schools, clinics, churches, welfare organizations, and correctional institutions; in turn, it can contribute significantly to their success. It should be obvious, then, that the court should play an important part in promoting greater coordination among the law-enforcement and welfare agencies of the community and in the establishment of a delinquency prevention program. Some courts have coordinated their work very closely with other agencies, but many have done very little to foster this relationship.[19]

---

[18] Sussman and Baum, pp. 43–48; The President's Commission on Law Enforcement and Administration of Justice, pp. 5, 6; Standard Juvenile Court Act (New York: National Probation and Parole Association, 1959), p. 57.

[19] Schramm, pp. 104, 105; National Conference on Prevention and Control of Juvenile Delinquency, Report on Juvenile Court Administration (Washington, D.C.: Government Printing Office, 1947), pp. 18–20; Sophonisba P. Breckinridge, Social Work and the Courts (Chicago: University of Chicago Press, 1934), pp. 231–40.

## CRITICISMS OF THE JUVENILE COURT [20]

Since the establishment of the juvenile court over seventy years ago, it has been severely criticized by both its friends and enemies. For example, in 1967, the President's Commission on Law Enforcement and Arministration of Justice—certainly not an enemy of the court—felt compelled to conclude that juvenile courts had failed to achieve their goals. Instead of being rehabilitative and helpful, they had been punitive and sometimes harmful. Instead of being protective, they had stigmatized and labeled the child as a "junior criminal." Instead of providing an informal procedure in the best interests of the child, they had frequently done nothing more than deprive him of his liberty without due process of law. Instead of utilizing the best of current social science learning, they had rejected the innovative and the progressive in order to protect their own vested interests. And this harsh indictment was directed against the court by some of its best friends! [21]

At first, much of the criticism of the juvenile court questioned its constitutionality, but as one judicial decision after another supported the court, the attack against it shifted toward its modification or improvement. In fact, today few critics would have the temerity to advocate the abolition of the court, and it seems, as Dr. William Healy said, that "the juvenile court is here to stay." [22] However, since so many well-informed persons have joined in the criticism, several of the important questions raised by them require our examination.

### Degree of Effectiveness

1. Has the juvenile court dealt effectively with juvenile delinquency? This question is so complex that perhaps any discussion of it can succeed in only raising other perplexing questions. It is true that various statistical attempts have been made to evaluate the effectiveness of the juvenile court, several of these showing that from about one-fourth to over two-fifths of older juveniles and adult offenders had previously been dealt with by the court.[23] Another, made by the Gluecks, revealed that 88.2

[20] Much of the discussion of the criticisms of the juvenile court presented here is an adaptation of that contained in Robert G. Caldwell, *Criminology* (New York: The Ronald Press Co., 1965), pp. 396–404.

[21] The President's Commission on Law Enforcement and Administration of Justice, 7–9.

[22] William Healy, "Thoughts About Juvenile Courts," *Federal Probation,* XIII (September, 1949), 18, 19.

[23] Edwin H. Sutherland, *Principles of Criminology* (Philadelphia: J. B. Lippincott Co., 1947), pp. 316, 317.

per cent of the juveniles included in their analysis again became delinquent within five years after the end of their official treatment by the
juvenile court of Boston, and that 70 per cent of them were actually
convicted of serious offenses.[24]

Studies like these, however, have not been conclusive. Not only have
comparatively few courts been carefully studied, but the findings of the
investigations have not been consistent. Besides, there are all kinds of
juvenile courts, many being such in name only, and an evaluation of one
is hardly a fair appraisal of others. Then, too, often the cases covered
by the investigations do not constitute a representative sample of those
coming before the court, and the recidivism noted is only that of which
there is a record. Actually no one knows how much undetected possible
delinquency and crime there is among those who have been previously
handled by the court. Furthermore, the court is only one part of a very
complex culture, with which it is inextricably and functionally related;
and no one, therefore, knows to what extent influences other than (and
perhaps even in spite of) that of the court caused the improvement in
those who subsequently did not become recidivistic.

But suppose it could be proved that the juvenile court has failed,
should delinquents be tried in the criminal court? Certainly no informed
person would be in favor of this. Is the solution then, "bigger and better"
juvenile courts? To this question, also, no simple answer can be given.
Most counties have too few people to justify better juvenile courts, others
too little wealth to afford them. Besides, large segments of our populations are already restive under the burden of heavy taxation. Should
taxpayers be asked to contribute more for the improvement of our juvenile courts? Should some of the funds that are now being spent for
other purposes, for example, for the operation of public schools, be
diverted to the development of the juvenile courts? [25]

But even the "biggest" and the "best" court could do little to change
the conditions that are causing crime and delinquency. No systematic
science of human behavior exists, and the knowledge that we do have
requires the support of public opinion if it is to be used most effectively.
Furthermore, how much judicial regulation will a community tolerate?
If a community is to preserve certain rights and privileges, how much
regulation should it tolerate? Obviously, questions of this kind can be
considered only as they are related to other values in our culture.

[24] Sheldon and Eleanor T. Glueck, One Thousand Juvenile Delinquents (Cambridge: Harvard University Press, 1934), p. 167. For opposing views regarding
this study, see Sheldon Glueck's and Harry L. Eastman's articles in Yearbook, 1934
(New York: National Probation Association, 1934), pp. 63–103.

[25] Robert G. Caldwell, Criminology (New York: The Ronald Press Co., 1965)
pp. 397, 398.

Still other questions must be raised. What is meant by a "better" or the "best" juvenile court? What criteria should be used to measure the quality of a court? There is considerable disagreement regarding these questions. Some claim that the provisions of the *Standard Juvenile Court Act* should be used as the criteria for evaluating a juvenile court, but others would refuse to endorse such a proposal. However, in spite of the fact that so many difficulties interfere with attempts to evaluate the effectiveness of the juvenile court, certain steps can be taken now to improve the quality of its work. Some of these will be mentioned later in connection with the discussion of the problems of the court.

## Types of Cases To Be Handled

2. What types of cases should be handled by the juvenile court? Like the first question, this one is too broad to be examined thoroughly here, but reference to a few specific situations will indicate why it has been raised.

After the juvenile court was established, it became the one agency in most communities which could provide some kind of social service for the increasing number of children who needed care and prtoection, and so it tended to assume responsibility for a growing volume of cases. Moreover, this tendency was accelerated by the passage of laws that stipulated that certain types of children were to be cared for at public expense. In general, the court did not resist this tendency, and in some communities court officials actually encouraged it so that they might gain in power and influence. And once the court assumed responsibility for certain cases, it tended to keep this responsibility even after the need of doing so had disappeared. As a result, the juvenile court became a catchall for a great variety of cases requiring public attention.

However, as educational facilities and child welfare services have developed throughout the country, there has come an increasing demand for the transfer of certain cases from the jurisdiction of the court to that of the schools and the welfare agencies. Just how this is to be accomplished is not always clear, but some who speak for the welfare agencies say that the transfer could be made on the basis of having the juvenile court exercise functions that relate to primarily judicial and law-enforcement areas, and of having the welfare agency exercise functions that are primarily administrative. But this suggested standard is not sufficiently precise to indicate exactly where the line is to be drawn. Undoubtedly it would mean the transfer of many neglect and dependency cases to welfare agencies, but opponents have stressed the complexity of the situation. Neglect, dependency, and delinquency are often interrelated, and delinquency cases involve much administrative work. Besides, many neglect and dependency cases require the exercise of authority supported by the law. In many instances only the court has sufficient authority to enforce decisions and to protect the rights of children and parents, and depriving the court of its administrative duties would unnecessarily complicate the handling of every delinquency case.

**The Court and the Schools.** The suggestion that certain cases, like those of truancy and incorrigibility, be transferred from the juvenile court to the school has likewise stirred up a controversy. Those in favor of the transfer have argued that schools are in close contact with children and their families, have a great deal of information about them, and are already doing a considerable amount of work through the efforts of visiting teachers, counselors, clinicians, and parent-teacher associations, that children should not be exposed to court experience, with its stigmatizing and traumatic implications, except as a last resort, and that schools would develop more effective programs for the prevention of delinquency if they were not permitted to shift so many of their responsibilities to the court. On the other side of the controversy many have contended that the personnel of the schools are already overworked and underpaid and should be relieved of some of their responsibilities instead of being given more, that the schools do not have enough authority to handle many of the cases, that the stigma of a law-enforcement agency would be attached to the schools if they had to handle delinquency cases, and that many children are not attending school or are in private and parochial schools and thus beyond the authority of public educational officials.

There is much merit in the arguments on both sides of this controversy. Some of the work of the court can be safely transferred to educational and welfare agencies, but many administrative duties must be retained by it. Just where the line will be drawn will probably have to be worked out on a local basis through the judicious balancing of needs and resources and the development of greater cooperation among courts, schools, and welfare agencies.

**Serious Offenses by Older Juveniles.** Apart from this, however, other critics of the court have insisted that older juveniles who commit serious crimes, such as murder, manslaughter, rape, and robbery, should not be dealt with in the juvenile court but should be tried in the criminal court. In fact, many states have laws giving the criminal court either original or exclusive jurisdiction over such cases. Opponents of this have branded it as reactionary and in violation of the philosophy of the court. According to this philosophy, they explain, the court should have exclusive jurisdiction over all children requiring judicial action, should guide and protect those who come before it, and should not stigmatize or punish them or hold them up as examples for others.

In reply to this argument, those who believe that older juveniles charged with serious offenses should be tried in the criminal court contend:

1. The upper age limit of children, especially those charged with serious crimes, over whom the juvenile court should have jurisdiction is a debatable subject.
2. Although the juvenile court uses words like "guidance," "care," and "protection," the fact is that it, too, resorts to punitive methods in handling children.
3. The public, regardless of what the philosophy of the court may be, looks upon the court as a place where violators of the law are sentenced and punished.
4. One measure of the support that courts and the law receive is the intensity of the feeling that law-abiding citizens have against law violators.
5. Failure to punish serious violators not only encourages others to commit crimes but also discourages law-abiding citizens from supporting law-enforcement agencies.

In this controversy, also, there is much to be said in favor of both sides. Certainly, no court can exist apart from the community in which it functions and to which it must look for support, and for the court to try to ignore the deep feelings and strong desires of the people whose values it is called upon to enforce is a highly unrealistic and arbitrary attitude. It is partly because of this fact that the *Standard Juvenile Court Act* includes a provision that juveniles sixteen years of age or older charged with serious crimes may be tried in the criminal court if the juvenile court deems this to be in the best interests of the children or the public.[26] However, if the case of a youthful serious offender is heard in a juvenile court, then this should be done according to clearly defined rules of procedure, and he should be protected from arbitrary action and abuse of authority just as the defendant is in the criminal court.

There has also been some recognition of the limitations of the juvenile court for dealing with older and more serious offenders by states when the pressure has been to raise the upper age limit of the court and to give it exclusive jurisdiction over all children. For example, in California, where the court had exclusive jurisdiction to the age of eighteen and concurrent jurisdiction to the age of twenty-one, a special study commission in 1949 recommended that the juvenile court judge should be required to decide specifically whether a juvenile over sixteen charged with a crime could be better handled by the juvenile court or by a criminal court.[27]

---

[26] *Standard Juvenile Court Act,* Article III, Section 13.
[27] Tappan, p. 8.

## Protection of Rights

3. Does the court protect the rights of the child and his parents? As the juvenile court has developed it has become increasingly dominated by the ideas and methods of child welfare and case-work authorities. Contributing to this tendency have been the occupancy of many juvenile court positions by persons who have been trained in social work or who are in agreement with its principles, the infrequent presence of attorneys in the court, the inadequate legal training of many of its judges and referees, the general exclusion of the public and the press from its hearings, and the rarity of appeals from its decisions. As a result of this departure of the juvenile court from some of the most basic concepts of justice in our culture, there has appeared a growing controversy over whether the rights of the child and his parents are being endangered by the increase in the authority and administrative functions of the court.[28] In fact, during the past few years, some legislatures and courts, including the United States Supreme Court, have initiated certain changes, and now more lawyers are going into juvenile court and an increasing number of its decisions are being appealed. In this controversy, criticism has been directed especially against (1) broad definitions of delinquency, (2) unofficial handling of cases, (3) prehearing investigations, and (4) extreme informality of procedure.[29]

In general, these have been defended by the claim that they facilitate preventive and nonpunitive action by the court. Thus advocates of a broad definition of delinquency contend that it permits the court to act in situations which warrant its intervention without becoming entangled

---

[28] *Ibid.*, p. 2. Administrative functions of the court include such activities as investigation of cases, planning of the care of children, supervision of probationers, and foster-home placement. These are to be contrasted with the court's judicial functions, which refer to such matters as adoption and guardianship and decisions regarding custody and commitment.

[29] See Paul W. Tappan, *Juvenile Delinquency* (New York: McGraw-Hill Book Co., Inc., 1949), pp. 195–223; Roscoe Pound, "The Rise of Socialized Criminal Justice," *Yearbook, 1942* (New York: National Probation Association, 1942), pp. 1–22; Edward F. Waite, "How Far Can Court Procedure Be Socialized Without Impairing Individual Rights?," *Journal of Criminal Law and Criminology*, XII (November, 1921), 339–47; Sol Rubin, "Protecting the Child in the Juvenile Court," *Journal of Criminal Law, Criminology, and Police Science*, XLIII (November–December, 1952), 425–40; Kahn, pp. 95–135; Henry Nunberg, "Problems in the Structure of the Juvenile Court," *Journal of Criminal Law, Criminology, and Police Science*, XLVIII (January–February, 1958), 500–16; Stephen M. Herman, "Scope and Purposes of Juvenile Court Jurisdiction," *Journal of Criminal Law, Criminology, and Police Science*, XLVIII (March–April, 1958), 590–607; Lewis Diana, "The Rights of Juvenile Delinquents: An Appraisal of Juvenile Court Procedures," *Journal of Criminal Law, Criminology, and Police Science*, XLVII (January–February, 1957), 561–69; The President's Commission on Law Enforcement and Administration of Justice, p. 9.

in technical disputes over the meaning of terms. As an expression of this view, some states have broadened the definition of delinquency by substituting a few general categories of delinquency for a number of specifically defined acts. The laws of some other states and the *Standard Juvenile Court Act* [30] have gone beyond this and do not define delinquency at all. Instead, without using the term "delinquency," they merely describe certain situations and classifications of children over which the court has jurisdiction. This avoidance of the "delinquency tag," it is argued, enables the court to help and protect the child without stigmatizing him in any way.

The unofficial handling of cases has been justified on the grounds that official court action is not needed in many situations, that it enables the court to assist children who, although not yet within its jurisdiction, are in danger of becoming so, and that the official label of delinquency should be avoided as much as possible. Prehearing investigations should be used, it is asserted, because they provide important facts for the hearings and thus allow the hearings themselves to be utilized as part of the treatment process. Extreme informality of procedure is favored by those who believe that only by minimizing all rules can the philosophy of the juvenile court gain full expression, and that the rules are not important anyway, since the state is not bringing action against a defendant, as it would be in a criminal trial, but rather acting as a guardian of the child, and that, therefore, we need not be concerned about protecting the child from possible harm.

However, a number of important points have been stressed on the other side of the controversy, and an examination will now be made of some of these. Broad definitions of delinquency and the unofficial handling of cases, it is contended, channel an increasing number of children not having serious problems into courts which, by general admission, are overloaded, understaffed, and inadequately equipped for preventive work. This not only gives such children the appearance of being seriously delinquent in the eyes of the public, and thus actually defeats the alleged purpose of this process, but also exposes them to the danger of being handled as if they were serious delinquents, or, what is worse, of being indiscriminately committed to correctional institutions when perhaps they are only suffering from neglect or dependency. Moreover, even when the court can engage in extensive preventive activities, this may discourage the development of other agencies better organized and equipped to do this work.

Besides, it is argued, where is the child who does not have a problem? With little effort hundreds of children who have problems can be found

[30] *Standard Juvenile Court Act,* Article II, Section 8.

in any community and brought into court. And if the court is not vigilant, it may be used by parents as a weapon against children in situations where the parents themselves are to blame. Thus the family is given a crutch at a time when it should be encouraged to strengthen itself through its own efforts—and other agencies can assist the family to do this far more effectively than can the court.

Furthermore, it is asserted, the situation is not improved by the use of the prehearing investigation. Too often this tends to become the hearing itself—a process during which the facts are gathered and the decision regarding disposition is reached even before the court has determined whether the child is delinquent. Indeed, his mere presence in court may be interpreted as presumptive evidence of his delinquency, and this may be easily inflated to conclusive evidence if some personal problem in his history can be discovered and dilated upon by the probation officer. And if the hearing has been conducted with an extremely informal procedure, the child will find that the decision can be overturned only with great difficulty. If, as its advocates claim, the prehearing investigation is not to be used to acquire evidence against the child, then there is no sound reason why the investigation should not be postponed until after the child has been adjudged delinquent. And here another point needs to be stressed. The court cannot be certain that a problem child will become a delinquent child, and besides, its own ineptitude may convert a problem into delinquency.

Moreover, it is urged, the rights of the child and his parents are especially endangered if the case is handled with extreme informality, because then there is no attorney to guard against the abuse of authority, no rules to ward off hearsay and gossip, no way of breaking through the secrecy of the hearing, and often no appeal from the court's decision. The child and his parents have even less protection if the case is handled unofficially, for in such a procedure very few legal checks limit the court's discretion, and redress at law becomes difficult, since no official record exists upon which the child can plead his case. And the situation can be worse if broad definitions of delinquency are used, because these leave the term vague and fuzzy, and under them all children tend to be pooled indiscriminately as wards of the state without an opportunity to marshal evidence against a specific charge. Then, if these children are processed through unofficial handling or informal hearings from which many, if not most, of the limitations of due process have been removed, they are largely at the mercy of the court's discretion, which too frequently is only the expression of the judge's prejudice. How ironical it is that this has been done and justified in the name of equity! Especially since the court of equity has always had its rules and formality and for the same reason that rules and formality must be present in the juvenile court, that is, to check the abuse of power and to protect the rights of the individual.

Finally, it is protested, euphemistic terminology, such as "hearing" instead of "trial," or "disposition" instead of "sentence," should not be allowed to conceal the fact that the nature of the entire procedure in the juvenile court may be little different from that of a criminal court. In fact, it may be worse, for it may abandon the principle upon which justice is based under the guise of promoting a superior justice. It is understandable, therefore, that Carr has said, "No man is wise enough or good enough to be trusted with arbitrary power—even the arbitrary power to prejudge the case of some delinquent child in the juvenile court." [31]

These, then, are some of the points that have been stressed by those who are opposed to broad definitions of delinquency, unofficial handling of cases, prehearing investigations, and extreme informality of procedure. That they are impressive ones is evidenced by the fact that an increasing number of thoughtful writers have demanded greater protection for the child and his parents in the juvenile court. And Tappan, in dismay over the seriousness of the situation, has asked, "Who is to save the child from his saviors?" [32]

## Summary of Criticisms

This analysis of the criticisms of the juvenile court clearly shows that we are dealing with questions of emphasis and the making of fine distinctions in a process which involves the balancing of the best interests of both the individual and society. It also indicates some of the social, philosophical, legal, and operational problems that confront the juvenile court. In the consideration of these problems, we shall be able to maintain a better sense of proportion if we remember these facts:

1. Although the general tendency has been toward the operation of the juvenile court as an administrative agency with great emphasis on social service functions, this type of operation has not been reached to any great extent except in the comparatively few highly organized, independent courts in our large cities; but, it must be added, these courts have been exerting a disproportionate influence in the establishment of standards and goals in the juvenile court movement.
2. Many courts, instead of taking action in a large number of cases, are already referring them to schools and welfare agencies.
3. Many courts that have few of the essential characteristics of a

---

[31] Carr, *Delinquency Control* (New York: Harper and Row, 1950), p. 240.
[32] Tappan, *Juvenile Delinquency*, p. 208.

juvenile court are nevertheless effectively handling cases because of the wisdom of the judge and the support of interested citizens.

4. Many courts, regardless of what can be done in their behalf, will remain "substandard courts" even when measured by the most moderate criteria—a fact which becomes increasingly apparent since these courts have shown little improvement despite the unprecedented prosperity of this country.

5. Many communities will have to continue to send their neglect and dependency cases and some of their truancy cases to the juvenile court simply because they do not now have, and may never have, any other agency able to assume this responsibility.

6. The great majority of the alleged delinquents appearing in the juvenile court do not contest the allegations brought against them and are actually delinquent, although, of course, this does not mean that these children are not entitled to all necessary legal protection.

Since the juvenile court in the United States is a functioning part of an increasingly complex culture, it must share in all the social problems, including delinquency, that this type of society tends to produce. To the extent that the juvenile court operates effectively to express and support the social norms, to rehabilitate juvenile offenders, and to deter others from becoming delinquent, it functions as an agency of prevention and contributes somewhat to social organization. But obviously it can remove only some of the conditions that are causing the delinquency with which it is dealing, and it has virtually no control over industrialization, urbanization, and other such powerful forces that are transforming and disorganizing American society—and along with it, the juvenile court itself—and piling up social problems faster than we can handle them.

## RECENT UNITED STATES SUPREME COURT DECISIONS

### The *Kent* Case

Eventually, the controversy over the juvenile court reached the Supreme Court of the United States. In *Kent* v. *United States* [33] the Court examined one aspect of the question of whether the rights of the child and his parents are given adequate protection in the juvenile court. Morris Kent, a sixteen-year-old juvenile, first came under the authority of the Juvenile Court of the District of Columbia in 1959. He was on probation under the jurisdiction of that court when, in 1961, he was

[33] 383 U.S. 541 (1966).

apprehended on several charges which again brought him into the juvenile court. At that time, the juvenile court waived its exclusive jurisdiction over him and directed that he be held for trial under the regular procedure of the United States District Court for the District of Columbia. The jury found Kent not guilty of rape by reason of insanity but convicted him on six counts of house-breaking and robbery. The United States Court of Appeals for the District of Columbia Circuit upheld this verdict, but the United States Supreme Court found that the order of the juvenile court waiving its jurisdiction was invalid and, therefore, reversed the decision. Furthermore, since Kent had passed the age of twenty-one and the juvenile court could no longer exercise jurisdiction over him, the Supreme Court removed his case to the United States District Court for the District of Columbia for a hearing *de novo* on waiver, which was to be consistent with the requirements laid down by the Supreme Court. As directed, the United States District Court for the District of Columbia held a hearing *de novo* on the merits of the waiver of jurisdiction by the juvenile court, and on March 22, 1967 (five and a half years after the original waiver), Judge Corcoran filed his findings, which ended with this statement: "We reiterate our conclusion that the waiver of Morris A. Kent, Jr., was, on the merits, appropriate and proper and entirely consistent with the purposes of the Juvenile Court Act."

In its decision in the *Kent* case, the Court stated that much evidence indicates that "some juvenile courts, including that of the District of Columbia, lack the personnel, facilities, and techniques to perform adequately as representatives of the State in a *parens patriae* capacity, at least with respect to children charged with law violation." In fact, said the Court, there may be grounds for concern that "the child receives the worst of both worlds," getting neither the protections accorded to adults nor the solicitous care and regenerative treatment postulated for children.

The Court then explained that the hearing of the juvenile court did not have to conform with all the requirements of a criminal trial or even of the usual administrative hearing, but that it had to measure up to the essentials of due process and fair treatment. The juvenile court, in waiving its jurisdiction in the *Kent* case, had not met this test. In order to do so, the juvenile court, as a condition to a valid waiver order, must grant the child these rights:

1. A full hearing on the issue of transfer to an adult court.
2. The assistance of counsel at such a hearing.
3. Full access to social records used to determine whether transfer should be made.
4. A statement of the reasons why the juvenile court judge has decided to waive jurisdiction.

Although the *Kent* decision applied only to the District of Columbia, it called into question procedures in juvenile courts everywhere in the United States. In addition, it must be remembered that this decision applies only to procedure and does not raise the question of the validity of laws providing for the transfer of cases from the juvenile court to an adult court.

## The *Gault* Case

In the *Gault* case [34] the Supreme Court returned to an examination of the rights of the child and his parents in the juvenile court. This time, however, the case came from a state juvenile court, and the Supreme Court made a more extensive examination of the question. The *Gault* case involved an appeal from a judgment of the Supreme Court of Arizona, which had affirmed the dismissal of a petition for a writ of habeas corpus and had found that requirement of due process had not been violated. A divided United States Supreme Court, however, reversed this judgment and remanded the case for further proceedings not inconsistent with its opinion.

In this case, Gerald Gault, who was fifteen years of age and already on probation, and a friend, Ronald Lewis, were taken into custody by the sheriff of Gila County, Arizona, on the complaint of a neighbor, Mrs. Cook, who alleged that they had made a telephone call to her and used lewd and indecent language. No notice that Gerald Gault was being taken into custody was given to the parents, although they later learned of this. They were told, however, that there would be a hearing of the case the next day in the juvenile court, but a copy of the petition was not served on them. The mother and older brother appeared at the hearing; Mrs. Cook, the complainant, however, was not there. At the hearing, no one was sworn; no transcript or recording was made; no memorandum or record of the substance of the proceedings was prepared. Even though Gerald said that he had only dialed Mrs. Cook's number and then handed the telephone to his friend, Ronald, the probation officer recalled that Gerald had admitted making the lewd remarks. At the conclusion of the hearing, the juvenile court committed Gerald to the state industrial school for the period of his minority, that is, until twenty-one, unless sooner discharged by due process of law.

In its majority opinion, the Supreme Court emphasized that it was not considering the entire process relating to juvenile delinquents but only the problems presented in the *Gault* case. It then decided that the proceedings to determine delinquency which may result in commitment to an institution must measure up to the essentials of due process and

[34] 87 Sup. Ct. 1428 [1967].

fair treatment,[35] and that those in the *Gault* case did not do this. The majority opinion stated that it was of no constitutional consequence that the institution to which Gault was committed is called an industrial school, because the fact is that "however euphemistic the title, a 'receiving home' or an 'industrial school' for juveniles is an institution of confinement in which the child is incarcerated for a greater or lesser time." Furthermore, said the court, if Gault had been an adult, he would have been only fined from five to fifty dollars or imprisoned in jail for not more than two months, instead of being committed to an institution for a maximum of six years.

If such proceedings are to meet the requirements laid down by the Court, the child and his parents must (1) be notified regarding the charges sufficiently in advance of the hearing to provide them with a reasonable opportunity to prepare for it, (2) be informed of their right to be represented by counsel retained by them, or be provided with counsel if they cannot afford to employ one, and (3) be granted the right to confront and cross-examine witnesses who are under oath and be given protection against self-incrimination.

Although the *Gault* case has been called a victory for those who claim that the rights of the child and his parents are not adequately protected in the juvenile court, it has also been subjected to adverse criticism. Some critics, for example, argue that there is nothing in the Constitution or in its historical background to justify the application of the Bill of Rights to the states through the Due Process Clause of the Fourteenth Amendment, and that, therefore, the *Gault* case is just one more in a long series of cases which usurp the powers of the states, contribute to the centralization of power in the federal government, and thus actually threaten the rights which the Court claims it is seeking to protect. Other critics contend that the application of the requirements of due process to the juvenile court will excessively formalize its procedure and convert it into a "junior criminal court." A third group of critics claim that the *Gault* decision is highly unrealistic and very superficial. In support of this claim, they explain that, although the Supreme Court limited its decision to those delinquency cases which may result in a commitment to an institution, the need for such a disposition can become apparent only after the hearing has been held, and thus virtually all delinquency cases and some cases that originally involve neglect charges will in prac-

---

[35] In *Haley* v. *Ohio*, 332 U.S. 596 (1948), which involved the admissibility of a confession by a fifteen-year-old boy in a state criminal court of general jurisdiction, the United States Supreme Court held that the Fourteenth Amendment applied to prohibit the use of the coerced confession. To the same effect is *Gallegos* v. *Colorado*, 370 U.S. 49 (1962). The decisions in these cases indicated that, whatever may be their precise impact, neither the Fourteenth Amendment nor the Bill of Rights is for adults alone.

tice be included within the scope of the *Gault* ruling. Moreover, they insist, by failing to provide comprehensive guidelines the Supreme Court has actually increased the problems of the juvenile court and raised more questions than it has answered. Just what impact the *Gault* case will have on the juvenile courts of the United States is not yet clear, but it does seem certain that an increased number of cases involving alleged delinquency will now reach the Supreme Court.

### The Winship Case

Whether juvenile courts may constitutionally decide guilt by a "preponderance of the evidence," that is, only in terms of the quantity of evidence without regard to its effect in convincing the mind of the truth of the proposition asserted, rather than by "evidence beyond a reasonable doubt," was considered by the Supreme Court in the *Winship* case.[36] Samuel Winship, when he was twelve years of age, entered a locker and stole $112 from a woman's pocketbook. The New York family court, in accordance with state law, adjudged him delinquent on a preponderance of the evidence and sent him to a training school for an initial period of eighteen months, subject to annual extensions of his commitment until he reached the age of eighteen. This meant that Winship might have been confined in a training school for six years. This decision was affirmed by the Appellate Division of the New York Supreme Court and by the New York Court of Appeals.

The United States Supreme Court, however, by a five-to-three vote, reversed this decision and ruled that, when a juvenile is charged with an act which would constitute a crime if committed by an adult, adjudication of delinquency requires proof beyond a reasonable doubt. This standard of proof, the Court explained, is among "the essentials of due process and fair treatment." Citing the *Gault* case, it also stated that civil labels, like delinquency, and good intentions do not in themselves obviate the need of criminal due process safeguards in juvenile courts, "for a proceeding where the issue is whether the child will be found to be delinquent and subjected to the loss of his liberty for years is comparable in seriousness to a felony prosecution." In the dissent, Chief Justice Burger said that the Court's decision was just another step in eroding the differences between the juvenile court and the criminal court, and Justice Black insisted that the United States Supreme Court had never clearly held that proof beyond a reasonable doubt was either expressly or impliedly commanded by any provision of the Constitution.

It should be clearly understood that the ruling in the *Winship* case applies only to cases where a juvenile is charged with an act that would

[36] *In re Winship*, March 31, 1970, *The United States Law Week*, Vol. XXXVIII.

constitute a crime if committed by an adult. Thus, it appears that adjudication of delinquency in other types of cases, such as truancy, incorrigibility, waywardness, and so on, will continue to require only a preponderance of evidence or some other standard less than proof beyond a reasonable doubt.

Criticism against the *Winship* case has been similar to that directed against the *Gault* case, stressing, for example, that it is another step in the usurpation of the powers of the states and a continuation of the process of converting the juvenile court into a criminal court. Regardless of the effect that this criticism may have, it now seems that the *Winship* case has opened the door wider for the admission of more legal questions about the operation of the juvenile court.

# 15

# The Juvenile Court:
# Its Improvement
# and Influence

There has been considerable debate about how the juvenile courts can improve their staffs, lower their case loads, and reduce their other operational problems, but most students of the court agree that certain changes can be made now to accomplish this. Many communities can and should spend more money on their courts, and others should use their present expenditures more effectively. Many courts should have judges who are better trained in both the law and the social sciences, larger jurisdictional areas, and a stronger position in their state's judicial system so that their judgeships will enjoy a higher status in the eyes of the bar. All courts should closely coordinate their operations with those of welfare and law-enforcement agencies. And everywhere the public should be told more about the court and encouraged to support its work.[1] The way in which the position of the juvenile court in the state's judicial system is to be strengthened will be affected by the surrounding social and political conditions. According to the *Standard Juvenile Court Act*, if the court is not part of a state system of juvenile courts, it should be set up within the existing judicial structure as a separate division at the level of the highest court of general trial jurisdiction.[2]

---

[1] The President's Commission on Law Enforcement and Administration of Justice, *Task Force Report: Juvenile Delinquency and Youth Crime* (Washington, D.C.: Government Printing Office, 1967), pp. 7–9.

[2] *Standard Juvenile Court Act* (New York: National Probation and Parole Association, 1959), Article I, Section 3. See also Frederick B. Sussman, *Law of Juvenile Delinquency* (New York: Oceana Publications, 1959), p. vii; Sol Rubin, "State Juvenile Court: A New Standard," *Focus*, XXX (July, 1951), 103–07.

It is recognized, of course, that all of the problems of the court are interrelated and interacting, and that many of them are beyond its control. However, there are major problems of a philosophical and legal nature with which the court can deal directly and which are contributing materially to its operational difficulties. The juvenile court, like all courts, must try to balance the interests of the individual and society in the adjudication of its cases. In the United States social relationships are being torn apart by conflicts, and agencies of social control are subverted by divisive influences. The ensuing confusion is blurring the sense of right and wrong, diluting basic loyalties, endangering many cherished rights, and sweeping away duties and responsibilities essential for the security of the community. The juvenile court can help to reduce this confusion if its philosophical and legal foundations are strengthened. The proposals advanced below are designed to do this by casting the court in a more realistic role, protecting the rights and clarifying the duties of those coming before it, and enabling it to effect a better balance between the rights of the child and his parents and the security of the community.

## PROPOSALS FOR STRENGTHENING THE COURT

### Philosophy of the Court

The roots of most of the controversy over the juvenile court are to be found in the dual role that it plays in attempting to function both as a court of law and as a social service agency. In fact, many writers on the subject believe that the basic problem confronting the court involves a decision as to which of its two functions, the legal or the social service, is to predominate.[3]

The juvenile court was established as a court, albeit a special one, and in structure, function, and procedure it remains essentially a court.[4] Therefore, efforts should be made to strengthen its true, or judicial, nature

---

[3] See, for example, Herbert M. Baker, "The Functions of the Juvenile Court," *Case and Comment*, XXIV (November, 1917), 449–52; Donald E. Long, "The Juvenile Court and Community Resources," *Yearbook, 1940* (New York: National Probation Association, 1940), pp. 24–33; Harry L. Eastman and A. M. Cousin, "Juvenile Court and Welfare Agency: Their Division of Function," *American Bar Association Journal*, XXXVIII (July, 1952), 575–77, 623; Henry Nunberg, "Problems in the Structure of the Juvenile Court," *Journal of Criminal Law, Criminology, and Police Science*, XLVIII (January–February, 1958), 500.

[4] See, for example, Roscoe Pound, "The Juvenile Court and the Law," *Yearbook, 1944* (New York: National Probation Association, 1945), p. 5; and Alice Scott Nutt, "The Responsibility of the Juvenile Court and the Public Welfare Agency in the Child Welfare Program," *Yearbook, 1947* (New York: National Probation and Parole Association, 1948), p. 212.

and to retain and develop only that part of its social service function that is necessary for the administration of individualized justice.

As a court, even in the administration of this type of justice, it must not only express the values of the society in which it functions but also reinforce these values. Dean Pound, a friend of the juvenile court, clearly recognized this when he said:

> If we work out a system of making penal treatment fit the crime, we risk losing sight of the individual delinquent in pursuit of system. If we look only at the individual delinquent, we risk losing system in pursuit of individual treatment and lose objectivity which is demanded when we are constraining the individual by the force of politically organized society. It comes down to the reconciling of the general security with the individual life, which as I have said, is a fundamental problem of the whole legal order.[5]

In other words, no court, not even the juvenile court, can be just a therapeutic agency. It is, and must be, also a moral agency. And when a child is adjudicated a delinquent by the court, he is, and of necessity must be, stigmatized as a violator of the moral values of his society. This judgment is what the people want and expect of any agency like a court, which is established to protect and strengthen their values. In fact, the court must act in this way if it is to promote the rehabilitation of the child. If it did otherwise, it would flout the very values to which the child must learn to adjust and for which he must develop a loyalty.

In modern society, punishment is the penalty inflicted upon a person adjudged guilty of crime or delinquency. Its principal purposes are retribution, reformation (or rehabilitation), and deterrence, but these must be seen as they relate to one another, for each affects and strengthens the others. Reformation must be conducted and deterrence exerted in terms of the values of organized society, whatever they may be. Retribution, which the law proportions to the gravity of the harm done as measured by these values, is designed to support reformation and deterrence. Thus, reformation and deterrence to be effective need retribution, which in turn is facilitated when they are effective. And in this interaction, deterrence must be seen as involving more than the instilling of fear in those who might be tempted to commit an offense. It involves, also, the positive moral influence that the law exerts in the educational and training processes, where, by stigmatizing certain acts in terms of prescribed penalities, it helps to engender attitudes of dislike, contempt, disgust, and even horror for these acts and thereby contributes to the development of personal forces hostile to crime and delinquency. "Thus some may abstain from murder because they fear the penalty, but many

---

[5] Roscoe Pound, "The Rise of Socialized Criminal Justice," *Yearbook, 1942* (New York: National Probation Association, 1942), p. 15.

others do so because they regard the act with horror." [6]  In a similar manner, retribution must be viewed as constituting more than an "eye for an eye" response to socially harmful conduct.  It provides a basis for distinguishing among varying degrees of seriousness of delinquent and criminal acts.  "Borrowing" a car, maliciously destroying the property of others, smoking "pot," and other forms of delinquency are not regarded with the same degree of seriousness as murder.

This is not to ignore the fact that values change and that considerable confusion regarding moral standards exists in the United States.  The point is that the court cannot avoid its responsibility as a moral agency. It must do what it can to reduce this confusion.  It must devote itself to the interests of the delinquent and respect his rights, but it must also take its stand with the community and insist that he learn to discharge his duties and assume his responsibilities as a member of society, thus giving encouragement and support to law-abiding citizens and helping to maintain the public sense of justice.  The way in which the court does this will, of course, depend upon the facts of the case as they are revealed and evaluated in the process of "individualized justice."

Furthermore, in the disposition of the delinquency case the court forces the child to submit to its authority by placing him on probation, by committing him to a correctional institution, or by dealing with him in some other similar way.  And by no stretch of the imagination can what actually happens to the child during this process be called merely "treatment."  Thus in the action of the court there are both community condemnation of antisocial conduct and the imposition of unpleasant consequences by political authority—the two essential elements of punishment.  It is, therefore, highly unrealistic to say that the court treats, but does not punish, the child.  What it really does is to emphasize treatment in a correctional process which includes, and of necessity must include, both treatment and punishment.  Treatment is a process during which causes in the individual case are studied and the knowledge thus obtained is used to produce the desired effects.  In treatment the experience of pain may be deliberately utilized, but often no such pain is sought, or if it is caused, it is merely incidental to action which is directed to other goals.  Always, however, the emphasis is on the individual, his nature, his problems, and his interests, whereas in the process of punishment the emphasis is on the group and its moral code.  Nevertheless, just as punishment cannot disregard the individual, whose reformation is one of its goals, so treatment cannot ignore the group, to which the "treated" individual must be returned.  Furthermore, the two processes

[6] Robert G. Caldwell, *Criminology* (New York: The Ronald Press Co., 1965), pp. 419–33.

of treatment and punishment must operate in terms of values—the values of organized society, which, if it is to survive, must establish and preserve its norms.  Therefore, although both the interests of the individual and the group must be considered in the handling of offenders, the interests of the group are always paramount, and treatment and punishment must be administered within the limits imposed by the moral code, the values of which must be guarded by retribution.  It is not, then, a question of whether there should be retribution, or reformation, or deterrence, or whether there should be treatment or punishment, but rather how both treatment and punishment can be most judiciously balanced to produce the best results in the control and modification of behavior.[7]

This conclusion tends to be supported by several other facts.  There is no systematic science of human behavior, and the concepts and techniques of treatment are still largely inadequate.  Moreover, as Dunham has explained, neither the child nor his parents are inclined to view his behavior as symptomatic of a sickness that needs treatment, but instead "are committed to the view that the court is there for justice and for punishing a person who has done something that is wrong." [8]  Besides, the stipulation that the court should act as a parent in providing care, custody, and discipline for the child, which was contained in the first juvenile court law and has been repeated by many authorities since then, does not rule out the necessity and desirability of punishment.  Here again Dean Pound has a clear understanding of the court:

> Juvenile probation is not a mode of penal treatment nor a substitute for punishment.  It is a mode of exercising the authority of the state as *parens patriae*.  It may be conceded that the parent may have at times to administer what common law called reasonable correction to the child.  No doubt there is often a corrective element in judicial treatment of juvenile offenders.  But the spirit is that of the parent rather than that of the ruler.[9]

This modification of the philosophy of the juvenile court is superior to the philosophy which is generally accepted in several important respects.  First, it clearly recognizes the necessity of balancing the interests of the delinquent and the community in the process of "individualized justice."  Second, it provides a practical basis of action which can be accepted without conflict by both law-enforcement officers and court personnel.  Third, by honestly admitting that the court must not only treat but also punish, this modification of the philosophy dispels the cloud of

---

[7] Caldwell, pp. 433–35.  See also Henry M. Hart, "The Aims of the Criminal Law," *Law and Contemporary Problems,* XXIII (Summer, 1958), 401–41.

[8] H. Warren Dunham, "The Juvenile Court: Contradictory Orientations in Processing Offenders," *Law and Contemporary Problems,* XXIII (Summer, 1958), 520.

[9] Pound, "The Rise of Socialized Criminal Justice," p. 16.

hypocrisy now enveloping the juvenile court, and gives it a position in society where it can be respected by all law-abiding citizens. Finally, by revealing the true nature of court, this modification of the court's philosophy brings the possibility of the abuse of power out into the open where it can be clearly understood and effectively controlled.

## Jurisdiction of the Court

The jurisdiction of the juvenile court should be limited to (1) delinquency cases and (2) dependency and neglect cases where a decision must be made affecting the legal status of the child, his custody, or the rights of his parents. All other dependency and neglect cases should be handled by administrative agencies without court action, and truancy should be dealt with by the schools.[10] This proposal is made in recognition of the fact that the juvenile court is essentially a court and not an administrative agency, and that, therefore, it suffers from inherent limitations in welfare work. Furthermore, the considerable increase in the number of welfare agencies and public services during the past few decades not only makes this transfer of responsibilities possible but also leaves the court with a greater capacity to handle the growing volume of delinquency cases.

The court should deal with children who can be shown to be delinquent by the application of specific, sharply defined criteria, and not with children who have problems according to the opinions of teachers, clergymen, and social workers—however sincere these may be. Juvenile delinquency, therefore, should be defined as the violation of a state law or city or town ordinance by a child whose act if committed by an adult would be a crime. This simple, specific definition eliminates all the references to such vague conditions as "being ungovernable" or "growing up in idleness" which clutter up our statutes on delinquency and invite loose interpretation and abuse of authority. Thus it will prevent the juvenile court from moving into areas where other agencies can render more effective service and at the same time protect children and their parents from indiscriminate handling by the court without regard for the cause of action in the case.

The *Standard Juvenile Court Act* and some states avoid using the terms "delinquency" and "neglect" and merely describe the various cate-

---

[10] This is essentially the proposal made by Sol Rubin in his book, *Crime and Juvenile Delinquency* (Dobbs Ferry, N.Y.: Oceana Publications, Inc., 1958), pp. 60–63. See also Nutt, "The Responsibility of the Juvenile Court and the Public Welfare Agency in the Child Welfare Program," p. 213; Agnes K. Hanna, "Dependency and Neglect Cases in the Juvenile Court," *Yearbook, 1941* (New York: National Probation Association, 1941), pp. 136–52; *Standards for Juvenile and Family Courts* (U.S. Children's Bureau Publication No. 437, Washington, D.C.: Government Printing Office, 1966), pp. 7, 8.

gories of children over which the juvenile court has jurisdiction. This avoidance of the delinquency and neglect "tags," its advocates contend, accords with the philosophy that classifying or labeling the child is "always unnecessary, sometimes impracticable, and often harmful." Opponents, however, maintain that the use of labels clarifies the basis on which the court moves into the life of a child and his family, and that it thus checks the abuse of authority, provides information necessary for defense against charges, and promotes better public relations. Moreover, this so-called avoidance of "tags" is highly unrealistic, for it fails to recognize that, no matter what language is used, the public (including employers and prospective employers) tends to equate it with delinquency and neglect, and so the children are labeled and stigmatized anyway. Besides, any word gets nasty when it is rubbed in the dirt. And if euphemisms are used to mislead the public, later discovery of the deception may actually cause the euphemism to become a word of opprobrium. The point is that the importance of labels has been greatly exaggerated. The nature of the act, as measured by the moral values of the community, is of much more importance in the stigmatizing of the perpetrator—both in his own eyes and in those of the community—than the name by which it is called. In fact, if this were not true and if all relationships were built upon the uncertain and shifting meanings of words, the possible depth of loyalty for any set of values could never be very great, and little hope could be held out for any process of education or rehabilitation.[11]

But there is more here than meets the eye. Everywhere our age appears to be frantically avoiding the truth. Pleasure-seeking and materialistic, it prefers to cover the evil, the ugly, and the unpleasant with platitudes and euphemisms. One must have courage, conviction, and a sense of responsibility to call something by the name that it deserves, for this carries the implication that he is ready to fight for his stand. But the very thought of this can be painful to a pleasure-loving people. It is so much easier to pretend that the problem does not exist and to avoid a showdown on the real issues. And this seems to be the course our age prefers. As history clearly shows, euphemisms are always a refuge for the effete.

Nevertheless, a child who is adjudged a delinquent is certainly not the recipient of any honors. It is true that he is not a criminal but, on the other hand, he is not a law-abiding person. He should be called what he is—a delinquent. This is what the people want the court to do, so that

---

[11] See the *Standard Juvenile Court Act,* Article II, Section 8; *The Future of the Juvenile Court: Implications for Correctional Manpower and Training* (Washington, D.C.: Joint Commission on Correctional Manpower and Training, 1968), pp. 8–10; Erwin Schepses, "A Note on Labels," *Crime and Delinquency,* XI (April, 1965), 162–66.

the moral code will be supported and the law-abiding will be vindicated. To do otherwise is to say, in effect, that the moral code, in terms of which the child must be "treated" and rehabilitated, is really not very important after all. Thus the removal of the stigma from delinquency can become an invitation to more delinquency. Call the child what he is so that all the facts are out in the open. He will then clearly understand that he is a violator of the law and is expected to change, and neither he nor his parents will be given an opportunity to shift their moral and legal responsibilities to others and to employ rationalizations in support of their law-violating behavior.

The juvenile court should have original and exclusive jurisdiction over all children between the ages of seven and eighteen who are alleged to be delinquent, except in cases where a child is charged with a minor traffic offense or where a child of sixteen or over is charged with a serious felony, such as murder, manslaughter, aggravated assault and battery, rape, and armed robbery. In the cases involving minor traffic offenses, there is no need of special handling. They can be adequately dealt with by a police or traffic court, and thus the burden on the juvenile court can be reduced.[12]

In cases where children sixteen or over are charged with serious felonies, the criminal court should have original jurisdiction but with authority to transfer such cases to the juvenile court if in the opinion of the judge this would be in the best interests of the child and the community.[13] The criminal court should have the authority to act first in these cases, because it, more than the juvenile court, is held responsible for the security of society and the public sense of justice and is organized and administered especially for this purpose. As Ludwig has emphasized, "Making treatment of all criminal behavior of young offenders, regardless of its seriousness or triviality, depend solely upon the individual need of the offender for rehabilitation may well lead our impressionable young community to conclude that fracturing someone's skull is no more immoral than fracturing his bedroom window."[14] This point is particularly important since a large and increasing percentage of serious crimes are being committed by young people. Thus the handling of a large percentage of these young offenders in the juvenile court—a court which is not primarily concerned with the public sense of justice and security—

---

[12] See *Standards for Juvenile and Family Courts*, pp. 37, 38.

[13] The *Standard Juvenile Court Act* gives the juvenile court exclusive original jurisdiction over all children under eighteen years of age who are alleged to have violated any law. However, the juvenile court may transfer the case of a child sixteen years of age or older charged with a felony to the criminal court if it deems this to be in the best interest of the child or the public. See Sections 8 and 13.

[14] Frederick J. Ludwig, *Youth and the Law* (Brooklyn: The Foundation Press, Inc., 1955), p. 311.

will make the criminal law increasingly inoperative and cause additional confusion regarding our official code of morality and the importance of vigorous law enforcement. This in turn may contribute to the growth of indifference and cynicism regarding the duties and responsibilities of citizenship and to an already alarming trend toward the centralization of power in the hands of a few, who under the guise of science and treatment often seek to impose their own values upon an increasingly disorganized people. And, to make matters worse, what is hailed as humanitarianism may become just public indifference regarding the way in which delinquents and criminals are handled.

The cases of adults charged with crimes against the child or the crime of contributing to the neglect or delinquency of a child should be handled not in the juvenile court but in the criminal court. This will place these cases in a court better designed to assure protection of all fundamental rights in a criminal proceeding [15] and will help the public to understand that the juvenile court is a special court for children and not in any sense of the word a criminal court. This recommendation is contrary to that in the *Standard Juvenile Court Act*, which stipulates that the juvenile court should have exclusive original jurisdiction over offenses against a child by his parent or any other adult having his legal or physical custody, and over any adult charged with deserting, abandoning, or failing to provide support for any person in violation of the law. In such cases, the juvenile court may transfer the adult to a criminal court.[16]

## Procedure of the Court

Through its intake procedure the juvenile court should carefully screen all cases brought to its attention so as to eliminate those that do not require the attention of the court or any other agency and to insure the referral of as many other cases as possible to agencies that are better equipped to provide curative and preventive treatment. The intake procedure is essentially an office, and not a field, procedure. It involves a review or evaluation of information which should be supplied by the person or agency seeking to file a petition, and thus it should be distinguished from the investigation of the case, which seeks to discover the causative factors in the child's behavior and to develop a plan of treatment. In order for a case to be accepted for action by the juvenile court, the intake procedure should show that the court has jurisdiction, and that there is sufficient evidence to justify the filing of a petition, but should not be used to dispose of cases unofficially. Juvenile court intake procedure is now provided for by statute in over half of the states, and

[15] Ludwig, *op. cit.*, p. 151.
[16] The *Standard Juvenile Court Act*, Section 11 and the comment on Section 11.

authorities generally agree that a separate intake unit is essential, especially in larger courts. Juvenile court intake differs from the screening process in adult criminal courts in that the selection of juvenile cases is court-sanctioned and pre-adjudicatory, whereas the screening of criminal cases is usually a function of the prosecutor's office.[17]

Whether cases accepted by the court should be handled on a formal or informal basis is an issue that has aroused considerable debate. It is not difficult to find recommendation for the unofficial or informal handling of cases. The *Standard Juvenile Court Act*, for example, provides for the informal handling of a case when the facts establish *prima facie* jurisdiction, are not controverted, and consent for such action has been obtained from the parents and the child. However, although it stipulates that efforts to effect informal adjustment may not continue longer than three months without a review by the judge or director of court services, it does not set an ultimate time limit for such efforts and so they may continue indefinitely.[18]

The President's Commission on Law Enforcement and Administration of Justice recommended that preliminary conferences, such as those now used in New York and Illinois, and consent decree negotiations might be used for the informal handling of cases by the juvenile court. Both of these would be conducted by intake officers and would involve the juvenile, his parents and lawyer (the presence of whom, unless waived, would be required), and the probation officer assigned to the case. Attendance at the preliminary conference would be voluntary, and regardless of its outcome, a petition might still be filed. The negotiations for a consent decree would be appropriate for cases in which adjudication appears unnecessary but some control, agreed to by the parents and the child, seems essential to assure community protection or the well-being of the juvenile. In addition to these methods for the informal adjustment of cases, the commission recommended the establishment of youth services bureaus, to which juveniles would be referred by the police, the juvenile courts, parents, schools, and other agencies. These bureaus would act as central coordinators of all community services for young people and would also provide services that might be lacking in the community, especially ones designed for less seriously delinquent juveniles.[19]

[17] See William H. Sheridan, "Juvenile Court Intake," *Journal of Family Law*, II (Fall, 1962), 139–56; *Standards for Juvenile and Family Courts*, pp. 53–55; *The Future of the Juvenile Court: Implications for Correctional Manpower and Training*, pp. 26–30. See also Council of Judges of the National Council on Crime and Delinquency, *Model Rules for Juvenile Courts* (New York: National Council on Crime and Delinquency, 1969).

[18] The *Standard Juvenile Court Act*, Section 12.

[19] *The Challenge of Crime in a Free Society* (Washington, D.C.: Government Printing Office, 1967), pp. 19–21, 22.

Our view is different from these. Too often unofficial or informal handling is merely the haphazard, ineffective disposition of cases by understaffed, overloaded courts, which is justified under the guise of avoiding the "delinquency tag."[20] The cases that are accepted by the court should receive official handling. If a case is not in need of formal or official handling, it should not be handled by the court at all, but should be referred to some other agency.

The court should establish the fact of delinquency in a case before the investigation of the case is made. In order to deal with this matter administratively, the President's Commission on Law Enforcement and Administration of Justice recommended that juvenile court hearings should be divided into an adjudicatory hearing and a dispositional one, and the evidence admissible at the adjudicatory hearing should be so limited that findings are not dependent upon or unduly influenced by hearsay, gossip, rumor, and other unreliable types of information.[21] Prehearing investigations are not only an encroachment upon the rights of the child who has not yet been proved delinquent, but also costly in time, energy, and money in the cases of those who are discharged as not delinquent.[22]

The procedure during the hearing should be informal but based upon sufficient rules to insure justice and consistency. The child and his parents should be fully informed about their legal rights. These should include representation by counsel, adequate notification of the charges, confrontation and cross-examination of hostile witnesses, the summoning of witnesses in the child's defense, protection against irrelevant and hearsay testimony and compulsory self-incrimination,[23] a hearing before a

[20] Paul W. Tappan, "Unofficial Delinquency," *Nebraska Law Review*, XXIX (1950), 547–58; Stephen M. Herman, "Scope and Purposes of Juvenile Court Jurisdiction," *Journal of Criminal Law, Criminology, and Police Science*, XLVIII (March-April, 1958), 596; Sussman, *op. cit.*, pp. 29, 30; Rubin, *Crime and Juvenile Delinquency*, pp. 66–68; *Standards for Juvenile and Family Courts*, pp. 57–60.

[21] *Challenge of Crime in a Free Society*, p. 87.

[22] According to the *Standard Juvenile Court Act*, the investigation of the case should begin after the petition has been filed unless the allegations of the petition are denied. If this happens, the fact of delinquency must be established before the investigation is made (Section 23). See also *Standards for Juvenile and Family Courts*, pp. 65–68.

[23] The *Gault* decision, 87 Sup. Ct. 1428 (1967), already guarantees the child representation by counsel, adequate notification of the charges, confrontation and cross-examination of witnesses, and protection against self-incrimination. See also Noah Weinstein and Corinne R. Goodman, "The Supreme Court and the Juvenile Court," *Crime and Delinquency*, XIII (October, 1967), 481–87; Spencer Coxe, "Lawyers in Juvenile Court," *ibid.*, 488–93; Lyell Henry Carver and Paul Anthony White, "Constitutional Safeguards for the Juvenile Offender—Implications of Recent Supreme Court Decisions," *ibid.*, XIV (January, 1968), 63–72; Peter R. Sherman, "'Nor Cruel and Unusual Punishments Inflicted,'" *ibid.*, 73–84.

jury if this is desired,[24] and access to a higher court for the purpose of an appeal. The President's Commission on Law Enforcement and Administration of Justice, whose report was issued a few months before the *Gault* decision, said in its recommendation regarding the right to counsel in the juvenile court, "Counsel should be appointed as a matter of course wherever coercive action is a possibility, without requiring any affirmative choice by child or parent." [25]

Members of the press should be admitted to the hearing but should not be permitted to publish the name of the child or any identifying data regarding him without the permission of the court. Their mere presence, however, should exert a wholesome and restraining influence on the court's operations.[26]

Whether juvenile courts may constitutionally deny minors the right of trial by jury and decide guilt by a "preponderance of the evidence" rather than by "evidence beyond a reasonable doubt" is still an unsettled issue. The *Standards for Juvenile and Family Courts* recommends "clear and convincing" proof of delinquency as a reasonable compromise between the majority position, which favors the preponderance-of-the evidence rule, and the minority view, which holds that delinquency should be proved beyond a reasonable doubt.[27] Illinois, in 1967, became the first state to require proof beyond a reasonable doubt in delinquency cases when the Illinois Supreme Court held that delinquency, when based on conduct that would be criminal for an adult, requires proof beyond a reasonable doubt. Critics claimed that this test would obstruct the adjudication of cases, but apparently conviction rates have not dropped significantly. However, the fear has been expressed that the new test is "beyond a reasonable doubt" in name only, and that delinquency is being established on the basis of less evidence.[28] In our opinion, delinquency

---

[24] For a similar view, see *The Standard Juvenile Court Act*, Section 19. In opposing trial by jury in the juvenile court, *The Standards for Juvenile and Family Courts* contends that this would be incompatible with the informal setting of the hearing (pp. 55–79). See also *The Future of the Juvenile Court: Implications for Correctional Manpower and Training*, pp. 13–20; George G. Newman (ed.), *Children in the Courts—The Question of Representation* (Ann Arbor: The Institute of Continuing Legal Education, 1967).

[25] See *The Challenge of Crime in a Free Society*, p. 87.

[26] Paul W. Tappan, "Treatment Without Trial," *Social Forces*, XXIV (March, 1946), 306–11; Isabelle R. Cappello, "Due Process in the Juvenile Court," *Catholic University of America Law Review*, II (January, 1952), 90–97; Gilbert Geis, "Publicity and Juvenile Court Proceedings," *Rocky Mountain Law Review*, XXX (February, 1958), 101–26; The *Standards for Juvenile and Family Courts*, pp. 76, 77.

[27] The *Standards for Juvenile and Family Courts*, p. 72. See also *Procedure and Evidence in the Juvenile Court* (New York: National Council on Crime and Delinquency, 1962).

[28] See *People v. Urbasek* (232 N.E. 2d 716, Ill., 1967); see also *Journal of Criminal Law, Criminology, and Police Science*, LIX (September, 1968), 398, 399.

should be proved beyond a reasonable doubt. Such a position is consistent with our earlier proposal that delinquency should be defined as the violation of a state law or a city or town ordinance by a child whose act if committed by an adult would be a crime.

## Disposition of Cases

The disposition of the case, including placement on probation, commitment to an institution, and so on, should be made by the judge after a study of the investigation report and consultation with the probation officer and other specialists who have worked on the case. However, simply because the judge must turn to specialists for assistance in his disposition of the case does not mean that it might be better to have the disposition made entirely by a panel of "experts." In the first place, this incorrectly suggests that there is a type of knowledge that the judge does not have, cannot understand, and can never acquire. This is not only grossly exaggerates the amount of knowledge that we now have about human behavior, but also greatly underestimates the intelligence and skill of the majority of our judges. If a particular judge is so incompetent or stubborn that he cannot, or will not, benefit by having the assistance of specialists, then the solution lies in his removal from office, not in unnecessarily complicating the machinery of the court by the creation of a panel of "experts." And if the judge is so overworked that he does not have time to analyze carefully the facts contained in the investigation report and to consult with specialists about various aspects of the case, then the answer is to be found in the appointment of more judges. There is no shortcut or cheap way to "individualized justice," and the mere existence of a juvenile court does not insure its achievement.

Furthermore, the facts of adjudication and those of disposition cannot be examined as if they existed apart from each other. These facts exist in the life of a single child who must be seen in his entirety—developing from what he was to what he will be. They must be assembled creatively in the mind of one person who has the authority to balance the interests of both the individual and the community and who is held responsible by the community for this. The facts of a case can be seen in a variety of ways, depending upon the relation of the examiner to the facts, and the mind is easily misled into seeing only one side of the picture. The judge who decides that a child is a delinquent should make this decision to intervene in the child's life not only in full knowledge of what will happen to the child as he is subjected to the available social services but also in deep awareness of being held responsible for the entire procedure. Only in such a process of sober deliberation can the knowledge of the facts be creatively transformed into a wise decision. The division of authority among the members of a panel fragments the facts of the case and dilutes the sense of responsibility regarding the interests of the child and his relationship to the community.[29]

These proposals are not advanced with any desire to convert the juvenile court into a criminal court but rather with full recognition of both its great potentialities and its inherent limitations. The juvenile court must be seen as a court—not as an administrative agency, but as a court —designed to protect the child from the traumatic experiences of a criminal trial and to provide more flexible machinery for balancing the interests of the child and the community in the light of the most recent knowledge regarding human behavior. It is not, however, especially equipped to do welfare work and so wherever possible it should be divested of jurisdiction over cases in which the child is simply in need of aid. On the other hand, it is a court, and its action does necessarily stigmatize the child. Therefore, its jurisdiction and procedure should be governed by simple, specific rules so that while the child is receiving guidance and protection, his rights and the interests of the community are not neglected.

The foregoing proposals have sought to strip away those excrescences that have interfered with the expression of the true nature of the juvenile court, but they have left it with all the characteristics which are essential to its functioning and growth. Delinquency as a status different from that of a crime, judges carefully selected on the basis of both their legal and social science training and knowledge, separate hearings as informal and private as are consistent with the protection of rights, availability of resources, such as medical, psychological, and psychiatric services, that can be used to make the investigation of cases more effective, regular probation service by an adequate number of well-trained officers, separate detention of children, special and confidential court and probation records—all these and more remain intact and are given a deeper meaning by a more realistic philosophy. It is recognized that not all of these proposals can immediately be put into effect everywhere. It is believed, however, that they do represent desirable goals toward which all juvenile courts should be directed so that they will become more effective agencies of social control.

But, as Dean Pound wisely counseled:

The law is not equal to the whole task of social control. . . . Delinquency presents a problem far too complex to be dealt with by any single

[29] Alfred J. Kahn, *A Court for Children* (New York: Columbia University Press, 1953), p. 277; Jerome Hall, "The Youth Correction Authority Act, Progress or Menace?," *American Bar Association Journal*, XXVIII (May, 1942), 317–21; Jerome Frank, *Courts on Trial* (Princeton, N.J.: Princeton University Press, 1949), Chapter 4.

method. Hence in this field cooperation is peculiarly called for and is called for in a very wide field. . . . If a socialized criminal justice is to achieve all that it may, we must be thinking about more than cooperation of judge and probation officer and social worker. These must cooperate, or at least be prepared to cooperate with the community organizer, the social engineer, the progressive educator, the social coordinator, the health officer, the clergyman, and the public-spirited promoter of legislation.[30]

## COURTS FOR ADOLESCENTS

Since the juvenile court was established in 1899, it has exerted an increasing influence on the principles and methods used in the handling of juvenile and adult offenders. Evidence of this influence, for example, is to be found in the movement to create special courts for adolescents, some of which have been established in several of the largest cities of the United States. The first of these courts appeared in Chicago when that city opened its Boys' Court in 1914. This court was made part of the municipal court and has jurisdiction over nonfelony cases involving boys between the ages of seventeen and twenty-one. In the following year, Philadelphia set up a similar court, giving it authority to handle certain minor offenders of both sexes who are over the juvenile court age but under twenty-one. In 1923, New York enacted the Wayward Minors Act, which provided for specialized treatment for offenders between the ages of sixteen and twenty-one who were charged with addiction to liquor or drugs, habitual association with undesirable persons, being found in a house of prostitution, being wilfully disobedient to parent or guardian, being "morally depraved" or in danger of becoming so, and other similar offenses. This act also substituted a "wayward minor" charge for the criminal charge. Under its authority, an adolescent court was established in Brooklyn in 1935 and in Queens in 1936.

In 1943, New York passed an act providing for a trial court for youth sixteen to nineteen years of age and indicted for felonies and a "youthful offender" category with a maximum probation span of three years and a maximum commitment of three years. This act also stipulates that

---

[30] Pound, "The Rise of Socialized Criminal Justice," pp. 13, 14. See also Orman W. Ketcham, "The Unfulfilled Promise of the Juvenile Court," *Crime and Delinquency*, VII (April, 1961), 97–110; Holland M. Gary, "The Juvenile Court's Administrative Responsibilities," *ibid.*, VII (October, 1961), 337–42; Thomas C. Hennings, Jr., "Effectiveness of the Juvenile Court System," *Federal Probation*, XXIII (June, 1959), 3–8; *Report of the Governor's Special Study Commission on Juvenile Justice*, Part I, Recommendations for Changes in California's Juvenile Court Law, Part II, A Study of the Administration of Juvenile Justice in California (Sacramento: California State Printing Office, 1960).

hearings may be private, that records of adjudication, fingerprints, and photographs should not be open to public inspection, that adjudication should not operate as a disqualification to hold public office or public employment, that no youth should be denominated a criminal, and that no adjudication should be deemed a conviction. A few years after this action by New York, another court for adolescents was created in Maryland. This agency was the Baltimore City Youth Court, for persons between sixteen and twenty-one, which was established in 1950 as a part of the criminal court of that city by rule of the Supreme Bench of Baltimore.

In general, the movement to establish adolescent courts represents an attempt to combine some of the principles and methods of the juvenile court with certain features of the criminal court in proceedings against youthful offenders who are above the juvenile court age but below the age of twenty-one and who, it is claimed, are in need of specialized treatment, because they have the peculiar problems of adolescence. During recent years, however, few efforts have been made to promote courts for adolescents in American cities, and although some authorities have recommended that laws like New York's Youthful Offender Act be adopted in all jurisdictions, little success along this line has been achieved.

Caldwell, in commenting on this movement, observed:

Since the adolescent court is neither a juvenile court nor a criminal court, it has been subjected to criticism from both sides, some critics condemning it as an agency for pampering tough young criminals, others ridiculing it as a timid, half-hearted gesture toward those who require full juvenile court treatment. A more realistic attitude toward them seems to be: (1) that such courts are needed in our larger cities, where many adolescents are being overwhelmed by the complexities of urban culture; (2) that there are neither funds nor justification for these courts in smaller cities and rural areas where improved juvenile courts should be able to handle the problems of most adolescent offenders; and (3) that the rights of the young person would be better protected in the court for adolescents by a more specific definition of its jurisdiction and a stricter application of the principles of criminal law and procedures.[31]

[31] Caldwell, p. 408. See Paul W. Tappan, *Juvenile Delinquency* (New York: McGraw-Hill Book Co., Inc., 1949), pp. 224–50; Negley K. Teeters and John Otto Reinemann, *The Challenge of Delinquency* (New York: Prentice-Hall, Inc., 1950), pp. 344–54; Sol Rubin, with Henry Weihofen, George Edwards, and Simon Rosenzweig, *The Law of Criminal Correction* (St. Paul, Minn.: West Publishing Co., 1963), pp. 446–57; Paul W. Tappan, "The Adolescent in Court," *Journal of Criminal Law and Criminology*, XXXVII (September–October, 1946), 216–29; J. M. Braude, "Boys' Court: Individualized Justice for the Youth Offender," *Federal Probation*, XII (June, 1948), 9–14; *The Future of the Juvenile Court: Implications for Correctional Manpower and Training*, pp. 11, 12.

## THE FAMILY COURT

The influence of the juvenile court has been shown also in the creation of special courts with jurisdiction over cases involving all kinds of family problems, such as delinquency, neglect, desertion, adoption, illegitimacy, nonsupport, alimony, divorce, separation, annulment, crimes by members of a family against one another, and commitment of an adult alleged to be mentally ill or defective. These courts, then, are really juvenile courts with extended jurisdiction, and where they have been established, they are usually called family courts or courts of domestic relations.

The first real family court was established in Cincinnati in 1914, as a division of the Hamilton County Court of Common Pleas, and since then it has been adopted in other counties in Ohio, and in some other states, chiefly in the larger urban areas, but even so, the number of adoptions has fallen far short of expectations. Agitation for it, however, has persisted, and during the past few decades, it has received strong support from the American Bar Association, which in 1948 went on record as favoring its establishment, and the National Probation and Parole Association (now the National Council on Crime and Delinquency), which in 1959 published the first *Standard Family Court Act*.

Wisely, this act does not call for the establishment of a *new* court. Instead, unlike the earlier *Standard Juvenile Court Act*, it provides that the family court be made a division in the "highest court of general trial jurisdiction." Thus, it seeks to give the proposed court a high status in the state judicial system, avoid the creation of another court of limited jurisdiction, and facilitate its passage, since this provision would not necessarily cause major changes in the existing organization of state courts. Estimates indicate that the passage of this act would mean that the family court would become a division of a circuit or district court in about two-thirds of the states. Because it would have jurisdiction over delinquency and neglect cases, as well as a number of other family problems, such as divorce, nonsupport, adoption, illegitimacy, and so on, its establishment would eliminate juvenile and domestic relations courts as separate tribunals. However, in the larger urban communities, the volume of cases would require that the family court be divided into various sections, so that each might specialize in different categories of family problems.

The act provides also for the creation of a state board of family court judges and a state director of the family court, who would have charge of the preparation of the budget, the compilation of statistics, the publication of reports, and the supervision of district staffs. Like the *Standard Juvenile Court Act*, it avoids the neglect and delinquency "tags" and its provisions regarding procedure and the maintenance and protection of records are similar to those included in that act.[32]  In fact, since the family court is built along the same general lines as the juvenile court, much of what has already been said about the improvement of the latter would be applicable to the former.

Those who advocate the extension of the juvenile court's jurisdiction, and thereby the establishment of the family court, argue as follows:

1. The creation of the family court is in keeping with the modern view regarding the causation of juvenile delinquency.  The family is very important in the moulding of a child's character.  He tends to reflect the forces that operate in the family situation.  In order to understand his behavior, one must understand his family.  The family court makes this possible, for under its jurisdiction the family, not the child, becomes the unit of study and supervision.

2. The establishment of the family court has deeper meaning than merely the treatment of delinquency.  The family is potentially a most effective agency in training responsible, loyal, and industrious citizens.  However, the family, like other parts of our culture, has been subjected to severe strains as a result of rapid social changes, and its influence in our national life, although still great, has declined.  The family court, through its supervision and guidance, is in a strategic position to strengthen the institution of the family and to aid in its reorganization.

3. The family court makes possible a unified policy of dealing with all phases of domestic relations.  There is not one theory or line of procedure regarding adults which may be nullified by another concerning juveniles.  On the contrary, since the family is treated as a unit, all methods reinforce and strength one another.

4. Much overlapping in court procedure is eliminated in the handling of cases in the family court, and through this centralization is achieved greater efficiency.  Whatever information is obtained regarding the problems of a particular family is immediately available for utilization in one court, and, consequently, whatever decision is made in a given case benefits by the direct knowledge of what has been done before.  To have all data concerning a family assembled in one court and all activities regarding that family coordinated under the jurisdiction of that court enables the judge and probation officers to work with an intelligence, economy, and unity of purpose that would not otherwise be possible.  The family

---

[32] Harriet L. Goldberg and William H. Sheridan, "Family Courts—An Urgent Need," *Journal of Public Law*, VIII (Fall issue, 1959), 337–50; *Standard Family Court Act* (New York: National Probation and Parole Association, 1959).  See Jacob T. Zukerman, "The Family Court—Evolving Concepts," *The Annals of the American Academy of Political and Social Science*, CCCLXXXIII (May, 1969), 119–28.

court thereby establishes a stronger basis for the treatment and prevention of family problems.

On the other hand, those who oppose the family court contend as follows:

1. The advocates of the family court assume that the juvenile court is an accomplished fact. This is not true, and it may be questioned whether the time, effort, and money that they would devote to "domestic-relations cases" should not be directed first to the improvement of the service rendered in children's cases. It is a mistake to regard the juvenile court as a solid foundation upon which to rear the structure of the family court before the juvenile court has been given sufficient attention and intelligent criticism to enable it to fulfill its aims. The fact is that the great majority of existing juvenile courts are overloaded, understaffed, and underfinanced and, therefore, in no position to assume the responsibilities which would be theirs if they were expanded into family courts.

2. It is evident that the procedure of the family court is not in harmony with the earlier demand for separate hearings for children. The purpose of the separate hearings was not merely to keep the adult audience from the courtroom during the hearing of children's cases, but also to produce a complete separation in the mind of the child and the public between juvenile delinquency and adult offenses. When the child is taken into a family court, this separation is destroyed.

3. The establishment of the family court would involve increased expenditures and perhaps heavier taxation.

4. No single court can effectively handle all of the complicated problems over which a family court is given jurisdiction, and thus it sacrifices the advantages of division of labor and specialization in a vain attempt to secure those of centralization and coordination.

In their rebuttal, those who favor the family court insist upon these arguments:

1. The juvenile court has not rendered a greater service partly because of the very obstacle which the family court would remove, that is, a limited jurisdiction. The juvenile court, therefore, can become a task accomplished through its enlargement into the family court.

2. The procedure of the family court can be made as flexible as may seem to be desirable, and so separate hearings for children can easily be arranged. In fact, it is no more necessary for adults to be present during children's hearings in a family court than in those held in the juvenile court.

3. Where the family court has to handle a heavy load of cases, it can be divided into various sections, each specializing in a different category of family problems.

4. The amount of money spent in operating the family court does not necessarily represent an additional expenditure. The cases that would come before the family court are already being handled in existing courts, that is, in such courts as the juvenile court, the circuit court, the municipal court, and the magistrate's court. It is apparent, therefore, that the only additional expense involved in the establishment of the family court is the possible difference between what is already being spent and what might be expended in the administration of the family court. Moreover, since the family court can supply a more efficient basis for the handling of family problems, the administrative costs and the number of cases coming before the court, and the number of persons referred to other agencies and committed to institutions, might be reduced in the future. Consequently, the family court should result not only in the reduction of public expenditures, but also in the building up of a more responsible and loyal citizenry.[33]

Strong points are thus raised on both sides of the controversy over the family court. In fact, the issues are so complex that a satisfactory conclusion can be reached only when the question of the establishment of the family court is related to the needs and resources of a particular community and a clear picture of the nature of the juvenile court, of which it is an extension, is kept in mind (see the analysis presented above). Nevertheless, apparently there will be a tendency for the family court to be adopted by the wealthier and more populous cities and counties, which can justify and finance its operation.[34]

## THE YOUTH CORRECTION AUTHORITY

The influence of the juvenile court is in evidence, too, in the *Youth Correction Authority Act*, which was published, in 1940, by the American Law Institute, an organization of prominent lawyers and professors of

---

[33] Caldwell, pp. 413, 414; *Ibid.*, "The Case for the Family Court," *Delaware Notes*, University of Delaware, Sixteenth Series, 1943; *Standards for Juvenile and Family Courts*, pp. 43–45.

[34] For further reading on the subject, see Alice Scott Nutt, "Juvenile and Domestic Relations Courts," *Social Work Year Book, 1949* (New York: Russell Sage Foundation, 1949), pp. 270–76; Atwell Westwick, "Wider Jurisdiction for the Juvenile Court," *Yearbook, 1939* (New York: National Probation Association, 1939); pp. 184–202; Walter H. Beckham, "One Court for Family Problems," *Yearbook, 1942* (New York: National Probation Association, 1942), pp. 80–93; Paul W. Alexander, "The Family Court of the Future," *Federal Probation*, XVI (September, 1952), 24–31.

criminal law and criminology. This represented an attempt to extend the philosophy and methods of the juvenile court to young adults, and, as a model act, it was recommended to the states for action by their legislatures.[35]

This act calls for the creation of a commission—a Youth Correction Authority, which is to consist of three full-time, well-qualified members appointed by the governor for a term of nine years and eligible for reappointment. All offenders up to the age of twenty-one, except those handled by the juvenile court, are to be committed to this commission, unless they are discharged or sentenced to a fine, a short term of imprisonment for a minor crime, life imprisonment, or the death penalty. The Youth Correction Authority has the power to determine what should be done with each offender sent to it, to employ all the facilities of the state for his correctional treatment, and to keep him under its control until in its judgment he can be discharged without danger to the public. However, if an offender is less than eighteen when committed, he must be released before he is twenty-one, or if he is more than eighteen at the time of commitment, he must be released within a period of three years unless an order to the contrary has been approved by the court. Every offender must be studied and examined upon commitment to the Youth Correction Authority and thereafter periodically at intervals not exceeding two years. In order to protect the rights of the offender, the act further provides that he may petition the court to review his case and to have counsel and witnesses in his defense.

Thus this act seeks to remove youthful offenders who are between the maximum year of juvenile court jurisdiction and their twenty-first birthday from the criminal court after their conviction but before sentencing and place them under a system designed especially for their care and treatment. The youth authority plan, however, has been subjected to severe criticisms. Important among these are: (1) The organization of facilities proposed by the plan is defective, for it seeks to unite essentially different functions under an excessively centralized authority, and then puts this authority in the hands of a multiple leadership instead of a single head; (2) the youth correction authority cannot perform the many duties with which it is charged; (3) the establishment and operation of a youth authority is more expensive than it is worth; (4) certain aspects

---

[35] The American Law Institute, *Youth Correction Authority Act* (Philadelphia: The American Law Institute, 1940). See also Joseph N. Ulman, "The Youth Correction Authority Act," *Yearbook, 1941* (New York: National Association, 1941) pp. 227–40; John F. Perkins, "Defect in the Youth Correction Authority Act," *Journal of Criminal Law and Criminology*, XXXIII (July–August, 1942), 111–18; John Barker Waite, "Judge Perkins's Criticism of the Y.C.A.," *Journal of Criminal Law and Criminology*, XXXIII (November–December, 1942), 293–96.

of the youth authority plan, such as the completely indeterminate sentence, may be unconstitutional; and (5) the main objectives of the youth authority plan can be achieved by other arrangements—as they have been in some states—without endangering constitutional rights and with less expense and disturbance to existing facilities.[36]

Since the publication of the *Youth Correction Authority Act*, the federal government and some states, notably California, Minnesota, Wisconsin, Massachusetts, and Texas, have enacted youth authority laws, but all of these differ in various ways from that which was recommended by the American Law Institute.   For example, California, which in 1941 became the first state to pass such legislation, includes juvenile delinquents in its plan, permits the courts to grant probation, and uses a limited indeterminate sentence.   In fact, only the plan adopted by the federal government deals exclusively with youthful offenders.   Following no unique or consistent pattern, what the existing youth authority laws really represent is a movement for the renovation of some of the machinery for handling juvenile delinquents and youthful offenders.

Shortly after the youth authority plan went into operation in California, its weaknesses became quite apparent.   The diagnostic facilities, which were the very essence of the plan, broke down under the heavy flow of cases, and the youth authority board had difficulty in performing the many duties with which it was charged.   To increase the effectiveness of the plan, the membership of the board was increased from three to six, case-hearing assistants were employed to aid the board in the hearing and disposition of cases, and the diagnostic and institutional facilities were expanded and improved.   At present the California youth authority is composed of six full-time, paid members appointed by the governor and confirmed by the state senate.   Under its administration, are ten institutions, four camps for youthful offenders, two separate reception center–clinics, and a reception center for girls at one of the institutions.   During recent years, it has placed considerable emphasis on the prevention of juvenile delinquency and youth crime.   Critics, however, insist that the state has wasted a great deal of money and saddled itself with a burdensome bureaucracy, and that greater progress in the

[36] Paul W. Tappan, "The Youth Authority Controversy," *Contemporary Correction*, ed. Paul W. Tappan (New York: McGraw-Hill Book Co., Inc., 1951), pp. 135–40; "The Correction of Youthful Offenders (A Symposium)," *Law and Contemporary Problems*, IX (Autumn, 1942); Joseph P. Murphy, "The Y.C.A. Act—Is It Practical and Needed?," *Yearbook, 1941* (New York: National Probation Association, 1941), pp. 247–59; John Barker Waite, *Twenty-Seven Questions and Their Answers About the Plan for a Youth Correction Authority* (Philadelphia: The American Law Institute, n.d.); Rubin, Weihofen, Edwards, Rosenzweig, pp. 439–46; Hall, 317–21; Kahn, p. 277.

improvement of the correctional program for juvenile delinquents and youthful offenders could have been accomplished without the creation of the complex and expensive structure of the youth authority plan. The future development of the youth authority plan in the United States is not yet clear. However, even its severest critics concede that it has stimulated agitation for the improvement of law-enforcement and correctional programs everywhere.[37]

## THE FUTURE OF THE JUVENILE COURT

Even the most devoted friends of the juvenile court now admit that it has not been able to achieve the great reforms dreamed about by its founders. It has not been significantly successful in rehabilitating juvenile delinquents. It has not contributed in any important way to the prevention of delinquency. It has not even been able to protect thousands of children from injustice and mistreatment. Is the answer, then, the abolition of the court? Few would be rash enough to recommend this. Despite its many failures, the juvenile court is firmly established in the laws and the customs and traditions of the American people. The great demand today is that it be improved, and future controversies about it will undoubtedly revolve about the question of how this is to be accomplished. Nevertheless, many authorities already agree on certain fundamental points. The true, or judicial, nature of the juvenile court must be recognized and strengthened, and it must be buttressed by a more realistic philosophy. The court can never be just a therapeutic agency

[37] Bertram M. Beck, *Five States* (Philadelphia: The American Law Institute 1951); John R. Ellingston, *Protecting Our Children from Criminal Careers* (Inglewood Cliffs, N.J.: Prentice-Hall, Inc., 1948); Karl Holton, "California Youth Authority: Eight Years of Action," *Journal of Criminal Law and Criminology*, XL (May–June, 1950), 1–23; Orie L. Phillips, "The Federal Youth Corrections Act," *Federal Probation*, XV (March, 1951), 3–11; James V. Bennett, "Blueprinting the New Youth Corrections Program," *Federal Probation*, XV (September, 1951), 3–7; Sol Rubin, "Changing Youth Correction Authority Concepts," *Focus*, XXIX (May 1950), 77–82; Will C. Turnbladh, "More about Youth Authority Concepts," *Focus* XXX (January, 1951), 23–25; Roy L. McLaughlin, "Is Youth Authority a Pattern for Children?," *Proceedings of the American Prison Association, 1948*, pp. 19–28. Harry Elmer Barnes and Negley K. Teeters, *New Horizons in Criminology* (New York: Prentice-Hall, Inc., 1951), p. 807; Paul W. Tappan, "Young Adults under the Youth Authority," *Journal of Criminal Law, Criminology, and Police Science* XLVII (May–April, 1957), 629–46; Department of the Youth Authority of the State of California, *California Laws Relating to Youthful Offenders* (Sacramento: California State Printing Office, 1963), *California Youth Authority*, Biennial Report for 1961–1962 (Sacramento: California State Printing Office, 1962); *The Youth and Adult Corrections Agency* (Sacramento: California State Printing Office, n.d.); Allen F. Breed, "Rehabilitation and Delinquency Prevention—The California Youth Authority in 1968," *American Journal of Correction*, XXX (July–August, 1968) 24–27.

It must be also a moral agency.    And its operation must be supported by an increased and better-trained personnel, larger and more wisely utilized appropriations, greater and deeper coordination with other agencies in the welfare and law-enforcement fields, and a stronger and more enlightened public opinion.    Action can be taken on these points immediately.

# 16

# Juvenile Probation

## NATURE OF PROBATION

Probation may be defined as a procedure whereby the sentence of an offender is suspended while he is permitted to remain in the community, subject to the control of the court and under the supervision and guidance of a probation officer. Thus, juvenile probation is a legal status created by a court of juvenile jurisdiction.[1] Since probation itself is a sentence, or, as it is called in juvenile cases, a disposition, and since commitment to an institution is always a possibility and is held in suspense, it would be more accurate to say that the commitment rather than the sentence is suspended in probation. For the suspension of the sentence may involve either the suspension of the imposition of the sentence or the suspension of the execution of the sentence. In cases where the sentence has already been imposed and its execution suspended, the court in revoking probation merely puts into effect this sentence. If the imposition of the sentence is suspended and revocation of probation becomes necessary, the judge can take this into consideration when he imposes the sentence. Sometimes courts suspend the sentence of an offender and release him into the community without supervision. Although this may be justified in the individual case, it should not be confused with probation, since one of the essential elements of probation is the supervision by which the offender is given assistance.

## ORIGIN AND DEVELOPMENT OF JUVENILE PROBATION

Probation began as a legal device for the mitigation of punishment—although it has come to mean more than this—and grew out of the prac-

[1] National Council on Crime and Delinquency, "Correction in the United States," *Crime and Delinquency,* XIII (January, 1967), 41. The National Council on Crime and Delinquency was formerly called the National Probation and Parole Association. It adopted its present name in 1960.

tice of suspending sentence subject to good behavior. Among the earlier precursors of probation, and related to it in various ways, were the benefit of clergy, judicial reprieve, provisional release on bail, and release of an offender on his own recognizance, all of which were devised to reduce the severity of the criminal law. Originally, benefit of clergy enabled members of the clergy to be tried by ecclesiastical courts instead of by lay courts and thus to be protected from the death penalty and other severe punishments of the criminal law. Later, not only the clergy, but also members of the laity who could read were given the right to claim benefit of clergy. Judicial reprieve was a device whereby the judge temporarily suspended the execution of a sentence and thus enabled the offender to apply for relief from the severity of the law.

Although juvenile probation has had its greatest development during the present century, its roots extend back through many years into European history. England, for example, introduced specialized procedures for dealing with youthful offenders as early as 1820, when the magistrates of the Warwickshire Quarter Sessions began the practice of sentencing the youthful criminal to a term of imprisonment of one day and then conditionally releasing him under the supervision of his parents or master. Soon this practice was further developed in Middlesex, Birmingham, and London, where at first probation supervision was supplied by police officers, then by volunteer and philanthropic organizations, and finally by public departments.

In the United States, juvenile probation developed as part of a social reform movement during the latter half of the nineteenth century, which produced a much wider acceptance of public responsibility for the protection and care of children. Thus this age not only extended and developed probation, but also enacted legislation against cruelty to children, organized philanthropic organizations for the health and welfare of dependent and neglected children, expanded and strengthened public education, adopted separate judicial hearings for children, established specialized institutions for juvenile delinquents, and finally created the world's first juvenile court, which, while receiving much nourishment and strength from probation, in turn contributed significantly to the growth and development of that procedure. And the interdependence of the juvenile court and probation is not surprising, for both are based on the conviction that children can be changed through education and treatment, and that the public has the responsibility to see that this is done.

The suspension of sentences produced the need of having some way of insuring the good behavior of the released offender. Sometimes this assistance was furnished by some kind of financial security, but more often it was achieved through the services of some reliable citizen who agreed to be responsible for the behavior of the offender and to assist him in his efforts to reform.  Thus, laws on probation merely formalized arrangements that were already in existence for the handling of those who were released under suspended sentences.

Massachusetts must receive credit for introducing probation into the United States, for it was in that state that probation began in this country after a period of experimentation under private leadership.  Among the early volunteers in Massachusetts who assisted offenders during the period of their suspended sentences was John Augustus, a prosperous shoemaker of Boston.  His efforts earned him the title of the "first probation officer," and by the time of his death, in 1859, he had assumed responsibility for about two thousand such offenders, including men, women, and children. In 1863, the Children's Aid Society of Boston was founded, and it immediately became active in the field of probation.  A few years later, in 1869, the State Visiting Agency of the Massachusetts Board of State Charities was established, and it was authorized to send its agents into any court, except the superior court, whenever the child faced commitment to a state reformatory, so as to protect the child and to promote the best interests of the community.  Then, from 1878 to 1898, Massachusetts, by passing a series of laws, created the first statewide system of probation in the United States and thus set an example for the other states to follow.[2]

The establishment of the first juvenile court in 1899 and its increasing influence contributed to the spread of probation, and by 1910, when 37 states and the District of Columbia had laws providing for a children's court, 40 states had also adopted probation for juveniles.  In fact, by 1925, every state had made probation available for juveniles, although this did not become true for adult probation until 1956.  Nevertheless, juvenile probation coverage is not complete within every state.  In 1966, for example, only 31 states had probation service for children in all of their counties.  Furthermore, although at that time 2,306 counties (74 per cent of all of the counties in the United States) had some kind of probation service for children, in a number of these counties this service

[2] See *The Attorney General's Survey of Release Procedures*, "Probation" (Washington, D.C.: Government Printing Office, 1939), Vol. II, pp. 1–16, 21–33; Frank W. Grinnel, "The Common Law History of Probation," *Journal of Criminal Law and Criminology*, XXXII (May–June, 1941), 15–34; Sol Rubin, Henry Weihofen, George Edwards, Simon Rosenzweig, *The Law of Criminal Correction* (St. Paul, Minn.: West Publishing Co., 1963), pp. 152–61, 176–83; Arne R. Johnson, "Recent Developments in the Law of Probation," *Journal of Criminal Law, Criminology, and Police Science*, LIII (June, 1962), 194–206; Fred E. Haynes, *Criminology* (New York: McGraw-Hill Book Co., Inc., 1935), pp. 442, 443; Robert G. Caldwell, *Criminology* (New York: The Ronald Press Co., 1965), pp. 463–67.

was probably only nominal, and 165 counties in 4 states had no juvenile probation service at all.[3]

During 1967, the juvenile courts of the United States disposed of about 811,000 juvenile delinquency cases (excluding traffic cases), 47 per cent of which were handled judicially or officially, that is, by filing a petition. Every year a large percentage of the judicially handled cases are placed on probation, and in 1966, approximately 223,800 children were under probation supervision for periods varying from three to thirty-six months. It is estimated that these juvenile probation services are costing the American people about $75,916,000 a year.[4]

## ADVANTAGES OF PROBATION

The advantages of probation can be most completely achieved only when these three elements are present: (1) an adequate presentence, or (as it may be called in juvenile cases) predisposition, investigation, (2) a careful decision by the court that probation is the best way to handle the offender, and (3) a systematic supervision by a probation officer who is not burdened with an excessive case load. The importance of these elements, therefore, must be kept clearly in mind when we examine the following advantages of probation:

1. The child remains in the community, usually in his own home, where he can live a normal life and thus, under the most favorable circumstances, learn to assume the responsibilities of a law-abiding member of society. That probation is advisable for many delinquents is evidenced by many reports and studies regarding it. One must admit, however, that a large number of probationers would probably make good without the help that supervision can provide, and that, perhaps, some are successful despite it.

2. He has the assistance of a probation officer who can counsel and guide him and help to correct the conditions in the home and community that may contribute to delinquency and crime.

3. In many cases, he may be kept out of an already overcrowded institution and perhaps from an experience that might leave him suspicious, bitter, and hardened against efforts to effect his rehabilitation.

---

[3] National Council on Crime and Delinquency, 49, 50; The President's Commission on Law Enforcement and Administration of Justice, *Task Force Report: Juvenile Delinquency and Youth Crime* (Washington, D.C.: Government Printing Office, 1967), p. 6.

[4] United States Children's Bureau, *Juvenile Court Statistics, 1967*, Statistical Series 93, pp. 1–3, 11; The President's Commission on Law Enforcement and Administration of Justice, p. 6.

4. He can, when the circumstances enable him to do so, discharge his obligations to his family and make restitution or reparation to those who have suffered from his delinquency.

5. He can be kept under probationary supervision at much less cost to the state than in an institution. At present, the average state spends about $3,400 a year (excluding capital costs) to keep a youth in a state training school, whereas it can keep him on probation at about one-tenth that amount. It must be conceded, of course, that probation would cost more if it were administered in accordance with the highest standards, but this would be true also of institutions, and there is no reason to believe that, even under the best conditions, probation would ever cost as much as institutionalization.[5]

Several more points should be made, however, before we leave this discussion of the advantages of probation. The mere suspension of a sentence (although it may be advisable in some cases) is not probation, and failures that can be attributed to it should not be cited to the detriment of probation. Furthermore, in some situations the existence of inadequate investigations, heavy case loads, and an insufficient number of trained personnel may make the use of probation highly questionable. The answer, then, is not the abandonment of probation, but, because of its many advantages, the removal of the conditions that make its use difficult or impossible.

## ADMINISTRATION OF JUVENILE PROBATION

Most juvenile probation services in the United States are administered by courts on a local basis. For example, in 1965, this was true in thirty-two states. Among the remaining states at that time, these services were administered by state correctional agencies in five, by state welfare departments in seven, and by other state or local agencies in six. However, in some of the states where local administration existed, the state participated in various ways, such as by setting certain standards, or by providing some financial support, or by the preparation and publication of statistical reports.

This diversity of operation has raised the question as to how juvenile probation services can be most effectively administered. Those who claim that this can be done by courts on a local basis see these advantages:

1. The court is responsible for determining which delinquents should be placed on probation and therefore should have the authority

[5] Caldwell, pp. 468–71; The President's Commission on Law Enforcement and Administration of Justice, *Task Force Report: Corrections* (Washington, D.C.: Government Printing Office, 1967), p. 28.

to select and control the probation officer, who functions as an arm of the court.

2. The working relationship between the judge and the probation officer requires freedom of consultation unhindered by the thought that what occurs in chambers may be revealed in a report to someone outside the judicial establishment.

3. Unless the judge has the authority to appoint and control probation officers, he may not have full confidence in them and so may reduce his use of probation.

4. The judge, by virtue of his position and influence in the community, can build strong public support for a service operating under his direction.

Other students of the problem, however, believe that juvenile probation services should be administered by a local, nonjudicial agency, and they present their case in this way. These services should be administered by those who are familiar enough with local conditions to function successfully in the communities where they work. Furthermore, local programs can develop better support from local citizenry and agencies and remain more flexible and less restricted by bureaucratic rigidity. The judge, however, has neither the time nor training to assume these administrative duties. This is especially true in large cities, where the probation department is a complex organization, often operating detention homes, psychiatric clinics, and foster homes, as well as performing investigative and supervisory functions. This type of organization requires continuous and intensive administrative attention by professional, full-time managers. Besides, if the court is composed of many judges, assignment to the juvenile court judgeship will rotate frequently and thus seriously interefere with the assumption of effective administrative leadership. Moreover, the judge should be an impartial arbiter. His administration of a probation department—an agency often party to the issues brought before him in the courtroom—may impair performance of his judicial functions.

A third group of authorities believe that the administration of juvenile probation should be handled by a state agency. They argue that a state agency is in a better position (1) to insure uniformity of standards and practice, including provision of service for rural areas, (2) to establish stable fiscal control, (3) to promote research and publish statistical reports, (4) to recruit qualified staff and to provide in-service training and staff development programs, (5) to permit staff assignment to regional areas in response to changing conditions, and (6) to facilitate relationships with other elements in the state correctional program. Furthermore, they claim, cooperation with local judges can be maintained by the preparation of a list of qualified probation officers from which each judge can select those who, in his opinion, can best serve him in his district.[6]

Although this controversy persists, there has been a tendency to blend both local and state administration and judicial and nonjudicial control, indicating that, perhaps, there is no one plan that is the best for every state, and that the variety of conditions in the different states will continue to require a diversity of administrative systems.[7] However, if juvenile probation services are administered on a local level, there should also be a state agency, such as a state probation commission, which can give support to the local agency in an advisory, supplementary, and educational way. This agency, for example, might educate the public regarding the advantages of probation, develop standards for employment, training, and promotion, conduct training courses for probation officers, collect, analyze, and publish statistics and other information about probation work, and furnish special services, such as psychiatric examinations, to those communities financially unable to provide such services for themselves. In addition, this agency might also administer interstate compacts which make it possible for juveniles placed on probation in one state to be transferred to another and there kept under supervision. By 1967, all but a few of the states had ratified these compacts.

## THE JUVENILE PROBATION OFFICER

One of the probation officers most exacting duties involves the preparation of a predisposition investigation report of the delinquent. One can appreciate the importance of this report when he understands that the judge depends on it to a great extent in making his decision in the case. The ideal investigation report, therefore, contains a large amount of information, covering such matters as the juvenile's delinquency record, his family situation, his neighborhood relationships and group associations, his religious background, his school and work history, his interests, activities, and personal habits, his physical and mental health, and so on. Obviously, the accumulation, analysis, and interpretation of all this information cannot be accomplished without much time and effort devoted to many interviews, conferences, and visits, much correspondence, pains-

---

[6] The President's Commission on Law Enforcement and Administration of Justice, *Task Force Report: Corrections*, pp. 35–37; National Council on Crime and Delinquency, 51–55, 60; Caldwell, pp. 471–73; Albert Wahl, "Federal Probation Belongs with the Courts," *Crime and Delinquency*, XII (October, 1966), 371–76.

[7] See *Standard Probation and Parole Act* (New York: National Probation and Parole Association, 1955); *Standard Act for State Correctional Services* (New York: National Council on Crime and Delinquency, 1966).

taking examination of numerous records, the careful preparation of reports and, in many courts, the setting forth of recommended action in the case. But this is only the beginning for the probation officer. He must also supervise probationers, counseling and guiding them, visiting their homes, often in the evenings, interviewing parents, relatives, clergymen, teachers, employers, neighbors, police, and other interested persons, utilizing the resources in the community, such as clinics, schools, recreational facilities, churches, police departments, sheriffs' offices, and so on, keeping detailed records, presenting cases in courts, collecting fines, and, in some cases, acting as a law-enforcement officer, in order to protect the interests and security of the community. Although in some large departments he specializes in either one or the other, usually a probation officer performs both investigation and supervision duties.

These, then, are the basic duties of the probation officer; but much more than this is expected of him. In many courts he must participate in the intake procedure, helping to screen and transfer cases to other agencies. Sometimes, too, he has significant auxiliary tasks to perform in connection with detention homes, mental health clinics, foster homes, forestry camps, group homes, and other similar facilities. And always he is expected to learn all that he can about the community and its resources and to work with public officials and community leaders in building good public relations and in creating and operating delinquency prevention programs.

Perhaps the foregoing will explain why the probation officer has been called the most important person in the whole process of probation. Indeed, so important is his position that it has been said that he should have good health, physical endurance, intellectual maturity, emotional stability, integrity, tact, dependability, adaptability, resourcefulness, sincerity, humor, ability to work with others, tolerance, patience, objectivity, capacity to win confidence, respect for human personality, and genuine affection for people.[8] Quite an array of qualities, one must admit—and ironical, too, in view of the probation officer's average salary!

And how should such a paragon be trained for his work? Some authorities believe that this can be done most effectively in a school of social work. Others, however, disagree, claiming that persons entering any kind of correctional work need a broad education in the social and behavioral sciences, knowledge of criminal law and procedure and the administration of justice, an understanding of the administration and operation of correctional and law-enforcement agencies and institutions, familiarity with the field of community organization and welfare services,

[8] Paul W. Tappan, *Juvenile Delinquency* (New York: McGraw-Hill Book Co., Inc., 1949), pp. 339–42.

and training and experience in interviewing, counseling, investigation, and case recording.  However, this kind of preparation is not available in a school of social work or in a graduate program of any of the social sciences.  Clearly, then, probation officers and other correctional workers must be trained in programs designed especially for them.[9]

But even the best of probation officers cannot perform their duties well if they are overworked, underpaid, and insecure in their positions. Yet these are the conditions under which many probation officers must function in the United States today.  In a 1966 survey, covering a sample of 235 agencies in 250 counties containing about fifty percent of the nations population (both rural and urban), the National Council on Crime and Delinquency found that the case loads averaged between 71 and 80 supervision cases (excluding work done on investigation studies, which take at least half the time of most probation officers). Of all the children on probation, 10.6 per cent were in loads where the number of supervision cases was over 100, the highest average supervision case load reported being 281.  Less than half (47 per cent) of these agencies had civil service or merit system coverage, and the median salary for their probation officers was between $5,000 and $6,000 (ranging from $1,500 to $11,000).

In view of these working conditions, we are not surprised to learn that probation departments cannot compete successfully for the best educated in the social service field, and that they cannot be too discriminating in their employment policies.  Although 74 per cent of the agencies included in the foregoing survey made a bachelor's degree a prerequisite for employment, only 4 per cent required their applicants for employment to have a master's degree in social work or in an allied social science. Despite this, however, resignations in the field of probation are frequent and vacancies difficult to fill.

How many cases a probation officer should carry is a difficult question to answer.  The amount of time devoted to traveling, the nature and

[9] For a discussion regarding the training of probation and parole officers, see Walter C. Reckless, "Training Probation and Parole Personnel," *Focus*, XXVII (March, 1948), 44–48; "Training Reconsidered" (comments on the article by Reckless), *Focus*, XXVII (November, 1948), 180–82; Walter C. Reckless, "The Controversy About Training," *Focus*, XXVIII (January, 1949), 23–25; Clarence M. Leeds, "Probation Work Requires Special Training"; and Loren J. Hess, "A Graduate School and Court Cooperate in Training for Probation Work," both in *Federal Probation*, XV (June, 1951), 25–32; Peter P. Lejins, "Professional and Graduate Training in Corrections," *Proceedings of the American Correctional Association, 1959*, pp. 35–50; *Standards for Selection of Probation and Parole Personnel* (New York: National Probation and Parole Association, 1954).  For a survey of college and university programs in corrections, see The United Prison Association of Massachusetts, "What's New in Education for Correctional Work?," *Correctional Research*, Bull. No. 13 (November, 1963).

number of the probation officer's duties, the kinds of cases to be handled —all these and many other factors have to be taken into consideration. Thus, what would be satisfactory in one situation might be excessive in another. The National Council on Crime and Delinquency, seeking to provide a minimal standard, recommends a case load of not more than fifty. This recommendation is based on "work units," each supervision case being counted as one work unit, and each predisposition investigation, as five. Since the maximum monthly load for a probation officer is placed at fifty work units, this may mean fifty supervision cases, or, for example, forty supervision cases and two completed predisposition investigations.

However, it is estimated that even this case load would give the probation officer only about one hour of close association with the child each month. Obviously, not much can be accomplished in such a short time. Besides, since some cases must be given more time, others will receive even less than one hour. As a matter of fact, of course, this minimal fifty-unit standard is seldom found in practice.

Many authorities now believe that the desirable case load average for juvenile probation officers should be only thirty-five. Since fewer than 4 per cent of these officers were carrying case loads of forty or less in 1965, the hiatus between the optimal and the actual levels of operation was depressingly great. At that time, there were 6,336 juvenile probation officers in the United States. In order to provide enough officers to conduct needed predisposition investigations and also reduce average case loads to thirty-five, it would have been necessary to employ an additional 5,300 juvenile probation officers and supervisors.[10]

## OPERATION OF JUVENILE PROBATION

The judge's decision to place the juvenile on probation should be based upon a thorough predisposition report, which, as we have seen, contains a great deal of information about the child's record of delinquencies, his social background, his mental and physical conditions, and other such matters, as well as the probation officer's opinion of the case and, perhaps, his recommendations. The predisposition report not only assists the judge in making his decision, but also provides a guide for the probation officer in his supervision of the delinquent and, if the child

---

[10] The President's Commission on Law Enforcement and Administration of Justice, *Task Force Report: Juvenile Delinquency and Youth Crime*, p. 6; *ibid.*, *Task Force Report: Corrections*, p. 30; National Council on Crime and Delinquency, pp. 60–64. See also John A. Wallace, "A Fresh Look at Old Probation Standards," *Crime and Delinquency*, X (April, 1964), 124–29.

fails on probation, valuable information for the institution to which he may be committed. Some authorities argue that the child and his counsel—and sometimes other interested persons—should have access to this report, explaining that this would act as a check on its accuracy and fairness and contribute to an understanding and acceptance of the disposition of the case. The majority of probation officers and legal experts, however, favor the confidentiality of the predisposition report. In support of their position, they contend that the guarantees of due process end with the child's adjudication as a delinquent, and that disclosure tends to dry up the sources of informaiton. Furthermore, they insist, when the child learns about the contents of the report, he may be unnecessarily disturbed, confused, and antagonized, and this may hamper the treatment process.[11]

## The Conditions of Probation

The assignment of probationers to probation officers is usually made by districts, which involves giving all probationers living in a certain geographical area to one probation officer, or according to the sex and race of the probationer. Sometimes, however, large departments make assignments by problems, that is, they give all probationers with a certain kind of problem to a probation officer who is an expert in dealing with that kind of problem.

Regardless of how case loads are assigned when probation is granted, the court imposes certain conditions, with which the child must comply during his period of probation, and makes certain that the child and his parents understand their duties and responsibilities. Usually the conditions include such matters as regular attendance at school, being home at an early hour, avoidance of undesirable companions and places of entertainment and recreation, payment of restitution, observance of the law, and making regular reports to the probation officer. Such conditions should be realistic and purposive, designed to help the juvenile become a law-abiding and self-respecting person, and should be so formulated that the probation officer can exercise his discretion in their application. Violation of the conditions, for example, should not necessarily result in revocation of probation but should be taken into consideration along with the needs and problems of the juvenile and the interests of the community. The conditions of probation serve an important function. They not only provide guides for the probationer and standards by which he can be judged, but also symbolize the authority of society, which must

---

[11] See Paul W. Keve, *The Probation Officer Investigates* (Minneapolis: University of Minnesota Press, 1960), pp. 3–15.

be recognized and respected if the rights of community life are to be enjoyed.[12]

## Supervision

The continuing relationship between the probation officer and the probationer is known as supervision. Essentially, this is individualized correction in the community setting and includes surveillance, counseling, and the use of community resources. Supported and restricted by the authority of the law, it strives to help the probationer to help himself toward an acceptable adjustment in the community. Although the probationer must be induced to trust the probation officer as early as possible during the period of supervision, he must also clearly understand that he is expected to obey the law, abide by the conditions imposed by the court, and assume increasing responsibilities in the modification of his own behavior. Furthermore, in the development of the supervisory relationship, the probation officer must be a leader, courageous and resourceful, and always in command of the entire correctional process. Able and willing to take the initiative whenever the situation requires him to do so, he must not hesitate to use his authority and to act decisively so as to protect the interests of the community.[13]

In order to inform himself regarding the effectiveness of the probation plan, the probation officer must continue his investigation of the child and his family and their relationships in the community. Such surveillance, of course, always carries the implication that probation may be revoked, but it also provides an opportunity for bringing the child and his parents into confrontation with the realities of life and the possible consequences of their failure to assume responsibilities. In addition, the probation officer, through individual or group counseling, must help the child and his parents to understand the nature of their problems and stimulate in them a desire for change. In this work, there is no substitute for the knowledge, skill, and good judgment of the probation officer, but he must go beyond this. He must work with the environmental forces that influence the life of the child, striving to modify them when this seems necessary, bringing into play all the educational, religious, medical, and welfare resources of the community, when this seems possible, and immersing the probationer in relationships that tend to evoke socially acceptable responses.

[12] David Dressler, *Practice and Theory of Probation and Parole* (New York: Columbia University Press, 1969), pp. 236–58.
[13] Caldwell, *op. cit.*, pp. 479, 480; Frank T. Flynn, "Probation and Individualized Justice," *Federal Probation*, XIV (June, 1950), 72; Alice Overton, "Establishing the Relationship," *Crime and Delinquency*, XI (July, 1965), 229–38.

Some writers, pointing to the compulsory nature of probation, have referred to the process of supervision as casework in an authoritarian setting. Other writers, however, insist that supervision should not be called casework at all. Unlike casework, they argue, supervision is strongly authoritarian and is not primarily interested in the personality adjustment and happiness of the individual but in the safety and welfare of the community. In fact, the inhibitions, repressions, and feelings of guilt of the probationer may have to be strengthened during supervision, and even though he may be successful on probation, he may not be any happier or better satisfied than he was before. A more realistic view of supervision, therefore, seems to require that it be called individualized correction in which punishment and treatment are balanced in the community setting.[14]

The relationship between the probation officer and the probationer is developed principally through office and family visits. Both of these are important, and neither should be considered as a substitute for the other. Office visits, which take place in accordance with a regular schedule, provide an opportunity for privacy and close association and tend to give the child a sense of responsibility and a feeling of participation in the correctional process. Home visits, on the other hand, permit the probation officer to see the home environment, correct unfavorable family influences, and enlist the cooperation of the members of the family in support of the probation plan.[15]

## Office Management and Record Keeping

However, probation cannot function satisfactorily without capable office management and competent administration. Case records must be compiled and properly maintained. Case loads must be regularly analyzed and evaluated to prevent their becoming excessive. Regular staff meetings must be scheduled for the formulation and reappraisal of policies and the discussion of agency problems. Careful research must be

[14] Richard A. Chappell, "Case Work," *Contemporary Correction*, ed. Paul W. Tappan (New York: McGraw-Hill Book Co., Inc., 1951), pp. 384–94; Kenneth L. M. Pray, "The Principles of Social Casework as Applied to Probation and Parole," *Federal Probation*, IX (April–June, 1945), 14–18; Elliot Studt, "Casework in the Correctional Field," *Federal Probation*, XVIII (September, 1954), 19–26; Ben Meeker, "Probation Is Casework," *ibid.*, XII (June, 1948), 51–54; Marilyn A. Blake, "Probation Is Not Casework," *ibid.*, 54–57; Sanford Bates, "When Is Probation Not Probation?," *Federal Probation*, XXIV (December, 1960), 13–20; Lewis Diana, "What Is Probation?," *Journal of Criminal Law, Criminology, and Police Science*, LI (July–August, 1960), 189–208.
[15] John Otto Reinemann, "Principles and Practices of Probation," *Federal Probation*, XIV (December, 1950), 28, 29; David F. Fike, "Family-focused Counseling: A New Dimension in Probation," *Crime and Delinquency*, XIV (October, 1968), 322–30.

conducted regarding the effectiveness of the probation services. Detailed reports must be prepared and published for the information of the public and the enlistment of its support. Volunteer workers, such as those who have been secured through cooperation with Big Brother and Big Sister organizations, should be encouraged to participate in probation services, although they should never be considered a satisfactory substitute for professionally trained probation officers. These and similar activities are an essential part of the modern probation program.[16]

## Length of Probation

And now we come to this important question: How long should probation last? Obviously, no definite answer can be given to this question, for the time required for probation varies from case to case. The laws of most states provide that the probationary period may last until the juvenile's twenty-first birthday, even though the juvenile court originally could not exercise jurisdiction over him up to that age. However, many authorities believe that the period of probation should be from eighteen months to two years in length, and the *Juvenile Court Standards*, published by the United States Children's Bureau, recommend a general minimum probationary period of from six months to one year for juvenile delinquents.[17]

The period of probation is terminated either by its revocation or by the discharge of the probationer. In cases where a definite time limit has been imposed—and usually this is done subject to review by the court —the probationer who has met all requirements is discharged when the time limit is reached and no extension is deemed necessary. When no time limit has been set, however, the probation officer and his supervisor, sometimes after consultation with the judge, must decide whether the discharge of the juvenile will be in the best interests of both the juvenile and the community. On the other hand, probation may be revoked because the probationer has violated the law or the conditions of his probation. But before this is done, the child and his parents must be duly notified, they must be represented by consul, and a hearing must be held, during which consideration is given not only to the nature of

16 John Otto Reinemann, "Research Activities in the Probation Department," *Proceedings of the American Prison Association, 1946*, pp. 39–48; Chappell, pp. 391, 392; Leonard Rosengarten, "Volunteer Support of Probation Services: An Experiment in the Philadelphia Juvenile Court," *Crime and Delinquency*, X (January, 1964), 43–51; Jewel Goddard and Gerald D. Jacobson, "Volunteer Services in a Juvenile Court," *Crime and Delinquency*, XIII (April, 1967), 337–43. See also U.S. Department of Health, Education, and Welfare, *Volunteer Programs in Courts* (J. D. Publication No. 478, Washington, D.C.: Government Printing Office, 1969).

17 Richard A. Chappell, "Federal Probation Service: Its Growth and Progress," *Federal Probation*, XI (October–December, 1947), 32.

the violation but also to what is best for the child, and the community. Usually, when probation is revoked, the child is committed to an institution.[18]

## SUPPORTING SERVICES

### Foster Family Care and Group Homes

Sometimes a child cannot be left in his own home, because of its harmful influences, and yet should not be committed to an institution. Such a child may be given probation and then placed in the care of a foster family or in a group home. If a foster home is chosen for the child, he may be legally adopted by the family, or his relationship with them may be based on some kind of financial or work arrangement. Usually, foster homes are used for neglected or dependent children, but to an increasing extent, delinquent children are being placed in them; and some of the results have been encouraging. However, good foster home placement is difficult to achieve, and great care must be exercised to protect the child from placement failures and the demoralization and emotional disturbance which they tend to cause.

Some states have begun to develop group homes, which are a variant of the traditional foster home, in order to care for youths who need a somewhat more institutional setting than it can provide or who cannot adjust to family life. Both Minnesota and Wisconsin, for example, are using group homes under financial arrangements with the home operators or intermediate agencies. The group home furnishes necessary external controls for a small group of adolescent offenders but without the emotional demands of the foster home, in which the juvenile may be expected to accept adults as "substitute parents." Such an acceptance is particularly difficult for the adolescent who is in the process of achieving emotional adjustment.

According to the 1966 survey conducted by the National Council on Crime and Delinquency, 42 per cent of the 233 agencies in the sample used foster homes for juvenile probationers. At that time, 4,967 juvenile probationers were in foster homes, although more than half of these were in three counties in California. Only 10 of the agencies, however, operated group homes, in which a total of 332 children were being cared for.

---

[18] Charles L. Newman, *Sourcebook on Probation, Parole, and Pardons* (Springfield, Ill.; Charles C. Thomas, 1968), pp. 139–45; *Standards for Juvenile and Family Courts* (U.S. Children's Bureau Publication No. 437, Washington, D.C.: Government Printing Office, 1966), pp. 90–92; *Guides for Juvenile Court Judges* (New York: National Probation and Parole Association, 1957), pp. 89–99; Eugene C. DiCerbo, "When Should Probation Be Revoked?," *Federal Probation*, XXX (June, 1966), 11–17.

## Psychological and Psychiatric Services

Probation departments use psychological and psychiatric services not only in staff development and in-service training but also in the diagnosis and treatment of some children. These services are available for the great majority of the probation departments in the United States, but apparently they are rarely adequate.

## Experimentation and Research

The field of probation is in need of experimentation and research, and some departments, recognizing this, are engaged in various research projects. For example, the probation department of Los Angeles County maintains a research division, which has made many studies that have proved of great practical value to that department and to the entire field of probation. Unforunately, however, efforts of this kind are still unusual.[19]

## THE EFFECTIVENESS OF JUVENILE PROBATION

Has probation been effective in the correction of juvenile offenders? Many authorities believe that it has been, but the evidence is not conclusive. Although the annual reports of probation departments throughout the United States generally show that more than 70 per cent of their cases succeed on probation, independent appraisals of probation have produced contradictory results. The Gluecks analyzed the careers of delinquent boys who had been on probation and found that only about 20 per cent had always succeeded in making a satisfactory adjustment.[20] In sharp contrast to the pessimistic conclusions of the Gluecks were the glowing estimates of Austin H. MacCormick, Executive Director of the Osborne Association. MacCormick expressed the belief that "a good juvenile court and probation service, operating in a community with adequate social resources and utilizing them fully, can put as high as 90 per cent of its juvenile delinquents on probation the first time around and 50 to

[19] National Council on Crime and Delinquency, pp. 64–66; The President's Commisison on Law Enforcement and Administration of Justice, *Task Force Report: Corrections*, p. 40; Arthur W. Witherspoon, "Foster Home Placements for Juvenile Delinquents," *Federal Probation*, XXX (December, 1966), 48–52; Sheldon Glueck (ed.), *The Problem of Delinquency* (Boston: Houghton Mifflin Co., 1959), 651–68; Edward J. Fischer and Nathan Farber, "The Psychologist in the Probation Department . . ." _____ *d Delinquency*, XII (January, 1966), 55–57; Olive T. Irwin, "Group _____ 'enile Probationers," *Federal Probation*, XXXI (September, 1967), _____ *Crime and Delinquency*, XI (October, 1965). This entire issue _____ ʼn group methods.
_____ ᴶ Eleanor T. Glueck, *Juvenile Delinquents Grown Up* (New _____ wealth Fund, 1940), pp. 153, 161.

75 per cent the second or third time around, and get as high as 75 to 80 per cent successes." [21] Studies of probation conducted by Albert J. Reiss, Jr., and others, however, fall somewhere between these two extremes, and tend to indicate that about 15 to 30 per cent of the juvenile delinquents fail on probation.[22]

A little thought will lead one to understand why the results of the studies of probation have been contradictory and why it is so difficult to measure its effectiveness. In the first place, the reports of the probation departments show only the violations that are detected. Furthermore, probation standards are not uniform throughout the country, and if the strict policies of supervision and revocation in effect in some departments were applied uniformly everywhere, the general averages of failure for the country as a whole would probably rise. Moreover, many probationers could—and actually do—"make good" without supervision, so their success can hardly be claimed as evidence of the effectiveness of probation.[23] In addition, it must be remembered that the reports of probation departments deal only with the behavior of juveniles while they are on probation. They leave unanswered this question: Does probation have a lasting effect in the lives of juveniles? Efforts have been made to answer this question by studying the careers of juveniles after their release from probation, but here, too, the evidence is meager and inconclusive, showing a wide range of successes and failures.[24]

But we are not yet finished with the difficulties that confront us, for there is still another question: Is probation more effective than some other method that might be used in dealing with delinquents—more effective, for example, than institutionalization? Actually, however, there is not enough evidence to give a satisfactory answer to this question. Standing in the way are considerable difficulties, for different kinds of

[21] See Austin H. MacCormick, "The Community and the Correctional Process," *Focus*, XXVII (May, 1948), 88.

[22] See, for example, Lowell Julliard Carr, *Delinquency Control* (rev. ed.; New York: Harper and Row, 1950), pp. 248, 249; Luther W. Youngdahl, "Give the Youth Correction Program a Chance," *Federal Probation*, XX (March, 1956), 3–8; Belle Boone Beard, *Juvenile Probation* (New York: American Book Co., 1934), pp. 147, 208, 209; Paul Schreiber, *How Effective Are Services for the Treatment of Delinquents?* U.S. Children's Bureau Report No. 9 (Washington, D.C.: Government Printing Office, 1960), pp. 5, 6; Albert J. Reiss, Jr., "Delinquency as the Failure of Personal and Social Controls," *American Sociological Review*, XVI (April, 1951), 200.

[23] Ralph W. England, Jr., "What Is Responsible for Satisfactory Probation and Post-Probation Outcome?," *Journal of Criminal Law, Criminology, and Police Science*, XLVII (March–April, 1957), 667–76; Diana, 202–04.

[24] See, for example, Edwin H. Sutherland, *Principles of Criminology* (Philadelphia: J. B. Lippincott Co., 1947), 403–04; Lewis Diana, "Is Casework in Probation Necessary?," *Focus*, XXXIV (January, 1955), 1; Jay Rumney and Joseph P. Murphy, *Probation and Social Adjustment* (New Brunswick, N.J.: Rutgers University Press, 1952), pp. 162, 163; Schreiber, pp. 6–9.

delinquents are handled by different methods. Thus, the "best prospects" tend to be placed on probation, whereas the "hard rocks" go to institutions. So, even if the records of probationers are better, this may be interpreted to mean that those who are sent to institutions are more resistant to change and not that institutionalization is less effective. Attempts have been made to overcome these difficulties by arranging to have the characteristics of the two groups, which are to be handled by two different methods, as similar as possible.[25] However, this procedure, which is called "matching," has not been very successful, and apparently little has been said about matching the characteristics of those who do the correcting. Obviously, this, too, must be done if we are to try to remove all factors except the correctional methods that are employed—otherwise, for example, the best application of one method may be compared with the worst application of the other.

On the basis of the foregoing, one can see how difficult it is to determine the effectiveness of probation. After all, the influence of probation—even at its best—is only one factor in a complex pattern of many interacting factors that affect the life of the juvenile. Parents, teachers, preachers, friends, employers, books, newspapers, moving pictures, television, radio—all these and more interweave and play upon the developing character of the child before, during, and after probation. Perhaps he is better—or worse—for having been on probation, but how can we know? This much is clear, however: Probation cannot be extolled or condemned solely on the basis of the existing reports and studies.

Nevertheless, authorities on the subject do not recommend the elimination of probation. On the contrary, they seek to improve it. They would inform the public regarding the advantages of probation; establish minimum qualifications for probation officers and select them on the basis of merit examinations, provide in-service training for all probation officers, reduce caseloads, make probation services available for juvenile delinquents everywhere, strengthen the organization and administration of probation, create closer coordination between the facilities of probation departments and those of such agencies and organizations as clinics, hospitals, welfare agencies, schools, churches, family societies, and businessmen's clubs, institute further research in order to develop new techniques and methods, and so on. Only in this way, they believe, can the potentialities of probation be clearly revealed and fully developed.

[25] See, for example, Sutherland, p. 403; The President's Commission on Law Enforcement and Administration of Justice, *Task Force Report: Corrections,* pp. 38, 39; Richard M. Stephenson and Frank R. Scarpitti, "Essexfields: A Non-Residential Experiment in Group Centered Rehabilitation of Delinquents," *American Journal of Correction,* XXXI (January–February, 1969), 12–18.

# 17

# Juvenile Institutions

Juvenile institutions provide custodial care and correction for juvenile delinquents who are committed to them by the courts—usually by the juvenile courts. Occasionally, however, other types of children, such as the neglected, the dependent, those awaiting trial, the feebleminded, and the emotionally disturbed are sent to them. Nevertheless, in general, they are used for delinquent children, especially those who are relatively hardened in their attitudes and habits or who for some reason cannot be cared for in any other way. The term "juvenile institutions," as employed here, includes training or industrial schools, camps, farms, and ranches, but not detention homes, which provide short-term custodial care for children who are awaiting final disposition by the court.

## HISTORICAL DEVELOPMENT

The juvenile institution in the United States is the direct descendant of the orphanage and house of refuge.[1] During the colonial period, children who were criminal, wayward, dependent, or neglected were pressed into the apprenticeship system, placed in orphanages or county almshouses, or kept in jails, where they were often exposed to the crudest kind of treatment. The first orphanage in the United States was established in New Orleans in 1729, and was known as the Ursuline Orphanage. Additional orphanages were soon opened elsewhere, and in 1853, Charles Loring Brace founded the New York Children's Aid Society, which devoted itself especially to the placement of many children on farms. Thus the idea of the foster home emerged and spread rapidly, being first applied to the care of neglected and dependent children and later to the handling of juvenile delinquents.

[1] Negley K. Teeters, "Institutional Treatment of Juvenile Delinquents," *Nebraska Law Review*, XXIX (1950), 577–604.

The first house of refuge was established in New York City in 1825, as a result of the work of the Society for Reformation of Juvenile Delinquents, which sought to protect children from vice, poverty, and neglect and to remove them from the degrading association with the hardened criminals in the county jails and state prison. Occupying a barracks leased from the government, it stood on a piece of ground that later became part of the present Madison Square Garden in New York City. Boston soon followed the lead of New York, opening a house of refuge in 1826, and Philadelphia became the third city to take such action when it founded its house of refuge in 1828. All these institutions, however, were founded by private reform societies, and private funds were employed in their maintenance. New Orleans created a municipal boys' reformatory in 1845, but the first state institution for juvenile delinquents was not established until 1847, which witnessed the opening of a state reform school for boys at Westborough, Massachusetts (now the Lyman School for Boys).

As the movement to establish institutions for juvenile delinquents advanced, different philosophies regarding their operation developed. For example, some emphasized training in trades and crafts; some, military training; some, academic studies. In each case, however, the purpose was to remove juveniles from association with hardened and adult criminals and to provide a place where young minds might be instructed and reformed. Even so, the new institutions for juveniles retained much of the atmosphere and many of the methods of the adult penal institution, and since their construction was limited to comparatively few areas, many children remained in the jails and prisons.

A promising step was taken in the movement to establish institutions for juvenile delinquents when the cottage system, which had originated in Europe, was introduced in this country in 1855, at the institution for girls in Lancaster, Massachusetts. Two years later, it was put into operation in the state reform school for boys at Lancaster, Ohio, and since these early adoptions, it has spread throughout the United States. It replaced the old, gloomy, and forbidding cell-block structure with a group of smaller buildings, called cottages, each under the direction of "cottage parents." Making possible more pleasant and homelike surroundings, greater ease of classification, and increased individualization of treatment, the cottage system has received general approval and is now used in most of our state institutions for juvenile delinquents. Unfortunately, however, in many institutions, the "cottage," lost in the welter of overcrowding and understaffing, has degenerated into a "junior prison."

By 1865, state institutions for juvenile delinquents were in operation in Massachusetts, New York, Pennsylvania, Maine, Connecticut, Michigan, Ohio, New Hampshire, and New Jersey, and by the turn of the century, there were sixty-five reformatories for juveniles in the United States, some of these being private and some, local public institutions. Today, every state has at least one public institution for juvenile delinquents, and many have private agencies which receive and care for such children.[2]

## THE PROS AND CONS OF COMMITMENT

In general, the juvenile delinquent should be left in his own home whenever this is possible, but if he must be removed, then foster home placement should be considered before he is committed to an institution. Since foster home placement is a possibility in many delinquency cases, some discussion of it should be included in any appraisal of commitment.

Those in favor of the foster home have argued that it provides the affection and emotional security needed by the child, permits him to remain in the normal relationships of community life, and avoids the more expensive regimen, the mass treatment, and the possible corrupting and stigmatizing influences of the institution. However, even the most ardent supporters of the foster home admit that—like all other methods designed for the handling of delinquent children—it has limitations. Good foster homes are not numerous and those that are available may not be suitable for the particular case in question. This is especially true in cases where the child has a strong attachment for his own home, has developed an independence of family life, has seriously violated the moral code of the community, has behavior patterns that threaten the interests of others, or has mental or physical conditions that require intensive treatment. Thus, many delinquent children cannot be disposed of by foster home placement. Furthermore, placement requires considerable skill, and if it fails, the child, in addition to all his other difficulties, may suffer another painful experience that deepens his suspicions and bitterness and makes him more resistant to rehabilitative efforts.[3]

On the other hand, we must remember that institutions have been severely criticized. For example, these shortcomings have been alleged:

1. They put too much emphasis on custody and not enough on treatment.
2. They tend to create an emotional dependence that unfits children for the competitive life of the outside community.

[2] O. F. Lewis, *The Development of American Prisons and Prison Customs, 1776–1845*. (Albany: The Prison Association of New York, 1922), pp. 40, 160, 302, 303, 316; Blake McKelvey, *American Prisons* (Chicago: University of Chicago Press, 1936), pp. 13–15, 37, 38; Paul W. Tappan, *Juvenile Delinquency* (New York: McGraw-Hill Book Co., Inc., 1949), p. 441.

[3] Carl R. Rogers, *The Clinical Treatment of the Problem Child* (Boston: Houghton Mifflin Co., 1939), pp. 97–101.

3. They do not sufficiently separate the young and the innocent from the hardened and the vicious and so tend to contaminate and corrupt many children.
4. They suffer from overcrowding, understaffing, inadequately trained personnel, and antiquated buildings and equipment.
5. They do not prepare the child emotionally, mentally, and physically for his re-entry into the community.
6. They do not put the child's family in readiness for his return to his home.
7. They have failed to enlist the support of public opinion in the reduction of their serious problems.
8. A high percentage of the young people continue to violate the law after their release from institutions.[4]

Furthermore, contend some investigators,[5] juvenile institutions have certain inherent limitations, which would exist even if these institutions were operated in accordance with the highest standards. This is true, they argue, because the very nature of institutional life tends to alienate the child and handicaps the treatment process. For him, the institution, despite its claims to the contrary, is an abnormal situation, filled with hostilities and frustrations, where he is forcibly separated from all loved ones and familiar associations, subjected to restraints which he resents, and compelled to associate with other equally resentful youths. Although the staff may seek to help him and modify his behavior, he tends to resist, throw in his lot with his fellows, find security and satisfaction in their approval and admiration, conform to their common beliefs and attitudes, and join with them in evading rules and annoying and deceiving custodians. Thus there emerges a subculture, which tends to unite institutionalized juveniles against the administration and to bring them under the domination and direction of their oldest, toughest, and most sophisticated companions.

However, it should not be assumed, explain these investigators, that all juveniles are assimilated into this subculture, or that juveniles and staff are solidly united against each other, but there are strong and persistent institutional influences that militate against rehabilitation. These influences can be counteracted to some extent by individualization of program and differential treatment, but they can never be eliminated.

In defense of juvenile institutions it has been argued:

[4] See, for example, Sheldon and Eleanor T. Glueck, *Criminal Careers in Retrospect* (New York: The Commonwealth Fund, 1943); *ibid., 500 Criminal Careers* (New York: Alfred A. Knopf, Inc., 1930; *ibid., Later Criminal Careers* (New York: The Commonwealth Fund, 1937).
[5] See, for example, Howard W. Polsky, *Cottage Six: The Social System of Delinquent Boys in Residential Treatment* (New York: Russell Sage Foundation, 1962), pp. 168–82.

1. They are compelled to accept a great variety of children, representing all ages, nationalities, races, and classes, possessing all types of personalities, and suffering from all kinds of mental and phyical problems.
2. They are required to take cases that no other agency will handle and in which many persons, including parents, teachers, clergymen, social workers, psychologists, psychiatrists, probation officers, and judges, have failed.
3. They are forced to operate with inadequate budgets, overloaded staffs, insufficiently trained personnel, and antiquated buildings and equipment and yet expected to work miracles in the rehabilitation of persistently delinquent children, whom they can keep for only a comparatively short time.
4. They are rendering a better service than an indifferent, uncooperative, and niggardly public deserves and are being improved as rapidly as the available resources will permit.

Although the controversy over the deficiencies of existing juvenile institutions continues, most authorities agree that institutionalization can guard the security of the community and provide intensive and consistent treatment and extended specialized care to a greater extent than any other method and that, therefore, it appears advisable in cases where the delinquent: (1) has serious mental or physical conditions; (2) has a history of serious and persistent delinquencies; (3) has entered adolescence and does not need the close attention and security of a foster home; or (4) has not responded to other methods of correction, and so institutionalization becomes the last resort.[6]

## THE INSTITUTIONS

In 1967 there were 307 public institutions for juvenile delinquents at the state and local level in the United States, including the District of Columbia, the Virgin Islands, and Puerto Rico. This figure included 212 training schools, 83 forestry camps and ranches, and 12 reception and diagnostic centers, but it did not include any detention homes or any institutions or camps used primarily for young offenders. Of the 307 public institutions, 78 per cent were operated by the states, 21 per cent, by city or county governments, and 1 per cent by the federal government.[7]

[6] Tappan, p. 429.
[7] United States Children's Bureau, *Statistics on Public Institutions for Delinquent Children, 1967*, Statistical Series No. 94 (Washington, D.C.: Government Printing Office, 1969), pp. 1–4.

The 1967 survey of juvenile institutions conducted by the United States Children's Bureau covered 97 per cent (298 institutions) of the 307 public institutions. This survey showed that 113 training schools (55 per cent) had capacities of 150 or more, 57 forestry camps (70 per cent) had capacities of 50 or more, and 8 reception and diagnostic centers (67 per cent) had capacities of 100 or more. In addition, many of the institutions were overcrowded. In fact, an analysis by types of institutions revealed that overcrowded conditions existed in 86 of the training schools (42 per cent), 25 of the forestry camps (31 per cent), and 6 of the reception and diagnostic centers (50 per cent). In this connection, it should be emphasized that administrators of juvenile institutions have found that, the smaller the facility, the more likely it is to enhance the impact of the treatment program, and that treatment in a training school tends to break down when the population rises above 150, because larger organizations tend to develop rigidity and formality.[8]

Many of the country's juvenile institutions are old, but improvements are being made, including the construction of smaller living units. Authorities believe that each living unit should have a maximum capacity of 20 for homogeneous groupings and of from 12 to 16 for heterogeneous groups or severely disturbed children, but that girls should have private rooms. Even so, of course, the handicap of oversized living units can be offset by the skill, ingenuity, and resourcefulness of the administration, although this does mean that the institution must carry an additional burden. In 1966, the National Council on Crime and Delinquency conducted a survey of 220 state-operated juvenile institutions in all states, Puerto Rico, and the District of Columbia. It found that of the 1,344 living units in these institutions, only 24 per cent had a capacity of 20 or less, 68 per cent, a capacity of from 21 to 50, and 8 per cent, a capacity of 50 or more.

In general, the size of the living unit is related to the age of the construction—the older the construction, the larger the unit. About 34 per cent of all living units in state-operated institutions for juvenile delinquents were 10 years of age or less, and 16 per cent were 50 years old or more. However, the increasing concern about the over-crowded conditions in public institutions for delinquents is evidenced by the fact that, when all the construction now under way, authorized, and planned is completed, the capacity of state-operated facilities will be increased by slightly over 42 per cent and over 90 per cent of the living units will have a capacity of 30 or less. In the meantime, many states are supplementing the capacity of their state and locally run facilities through the use of

[8] *Ibid.*, p. 2.

private ones, but although in some instances, these private facilities are receiving public funds, their programs remain in private hands.[9]

Juvenile institutions should not be located in inaccessible areas, for isolation aggravates problems of staff recruitment and housing and reduces the use of services offered by related agencies. Yet, training schools have often been located in isolated sections of states by legislatures that have been primarily interested in the bolstering of the economy of certain communities. In the National Council on Crime and Delinquency Survey, referred to above, 29 jurisdictions reported a bad location for one or more of their state-operated facilities, 46 per cent of them citing it as an obstacle in recruiting professional staff, and 15 per cent as a deterrent to visits by parents.[10]

## ADMINISTRATION

In the United States, the early institutions for juvenile delinquents, both private and public, were under the direction of local boards, often called boards of trustees. Gradually, however, the direction of state-operated institutions for juvenile delinquents has been transferred to some administrative agency on the state level, in order to promote better coordination with related agencies and more specialized use of facilities. This tendency toward centralized control is evidenced by the fact that, in 1966, these institutions were administered by some type of parent agency that had only correctional responsibilities in 21 states, by a state department of public welfare in 14 states, and by a state board of institutions in 6 states, and that the institutional programs were completely administered by the institutions themselves in only 3 states. The same tendency toward centralized control can be found in other aspects of the administration of juvenile institutions, for example, in the legal custody of the child during commitment, in the authority to order his release, in the setting of standards, inspection, and financial support, in research and in the collection and dissemination of statistics.[11]

Some correctional authorities are in favor of centralizing the control of all correctional institutions, both juvenile and adult, under the administration of a state department of correction. However, others, including

---

[9] National Council on Crime and Delinquency, "Correction in the United States," *Crime and Delinquency*, XIII (January, 1967), 89, 90. This survey covered 86 per cent of the juvenile training capacity in the United States. The remaining 14 per cent, which was not included, consisted of 83 locally operated programs located in 16 states.

[10] *Ibid.*, 90, 91.

[11] *Ibid.*, 91, 92.

the United States Children's Bureau, object to this arrangement on the following grounds:

1. It would tend to obscure the importance of handling children in a different way from adults.
2. It would cause juvenile institutions to be operated as if they were prisons.
3. It would stigmatize children as criminals, since they would be associated with adult offenders in the mind of the public.

Opponents of this view, however, offer these counters:

1. These conditions would not exist if the department of correction were well administered.
2. In any event, this view represents a great exaggeration of the conditions that might result.
3. Delinquents are offenders and should not be handled as if they were just neglected or dependent children.
4. Correction must include both punishment and treatment and its philosophy should not be diluted and distorted by those of welfare, social work, and psychiatry, which happens when delinquents are handled in a noncorrectional department.

In fact, the opponents continue, some of the worst abuses in training schools have occurred when these institutions have been administered by noncorrectional departments.[12]

During 1967, an estimated total of $209,000,000 was spent by public institutions serving juvenile delinquents, which represented a 13 per cent increase since 1966. The national average annual cost of keeping a delinquent in a public institution for 1967 was $3,896 (as compared with $3,345 in 1966), but this varied considerably from one state to another.[13]

## THE CHILDREN

Approximately 53,000 children were being cared for in public institutions for delinquent children on June 30, 1967—an increase of 4 per cent since 1966. The rate of commitment to these institutions during 1967 was 172 per 100,000 of the total child population (aged 10 through 17), as compared with 169 in 1966. Boys constituted about three-fourths

[12] *Standard Act for State Correctional Services* (New York: National Council on Crime and Delinquency, 1966), pp. 16–18. The act provides for the establishment of a state department of correction, but offers a choice as to whether or not institutions for juvenile delinquents should be placed under its administration. See Article II, Sections 2, 3.

[13] United States Children's Bureau, pp. 3, 13.

of these children—a proportion that had not changed since 1953. About 50 per cent of the institutions kept their children 8 months or less, whereas only 24 per cent retained them for a year or more. For training schools, the average length of stay in 1967 was approximately ten months; for forestry camps, six months; and for reception centers, 3 months.[14]

## PERSONNEL

If public institutions are to provide effective training, education, and rehabilitation for delinquents, they must recruit and retain an adequate number of well-qualified personnel. Unfortunately, the available data indicate that these institutions are having difficulties in doing this. In 1967, there was an estimated total of 25,000 full-time employees in the public institutions for juvenile delinquents, which represented an increase of about 11 per cent since 1966. Nevertheless, vacant positions in 1967 numbered about 1300.[15]

The National Council on Crime and Delinquency found that, in 1965, the 220 state-operated institutions covered by its survey employed 1,154 treatment personnel, including psychiatrists, psychologists, and case workers. The recommended standards call for a minimum of one full-time psychiatrist and one full-time psychologist for every 150 children, and a case load of not more than thirty children for each full-time case worker. However, the survey showed that these institutions needed 236 more psychiatrists, 100 more psychologists, and 487 more case workers to measure up to the recommended standards. In fact, more than half of the psychiatrists were in only 5 states, and almost 60 per cent of the psychologists were in 9 states. Furthermore, each of 37 states had less than the equivalent of one full-time psychiatrist, each of 21 states had the equivalent of not more than one full-time psychologist, and only 4 states had enough psychiatrists, and only 12 states enough psychologists, to satisfy the standards.

Moreover, the survey revealed that in these institutions the overall teacher-pupil ratio was 1:17 instead of the recommended 1:15 (36 states having higher than 1:20), that 32 state systems had less than the equivalent of one chaplain per facility (12 states having no chaplaincy staff at all), that while the majority of the state-operated institutions had merit systems for their employees, the superintendents were not included in 30 states, and that in 16 states the work week was more than 40 hours (in 7 of these states being more than 50 hours). The minimum starting

[14] Ibid., pp. 1, 2.
[15] Ibid., p. 3.

salaries for superintendent were from $5,000 to $15,000; for case worker, from $3,240 to $9,000; for academic teacher, from $2,400 to $8,640; for vocational teacher, from $3,600 to $8,640; and for cottage staff, from $1,600 to $8,592. Although the cottage staff in charge of the living unit is the backbone of the training facility program, the present salary schedules made it virtually impossible to secure even persons who had only a high school education. Indeed, some of the cottage staff in one state were on public welfare. After making a distinction between what services were available "on paper" and what were available "in fact," the National Council on Crime and Delinquency came to the conclusion that, with the possible exception of education, the "improvement of all types of services seemed badly needed." [16]

## PROGRAM

### Orientation

In some states, when a child is committed to an institution, he goes first to a reception and diagnostic center operated by a state administrative agency (sometimes called a youth authority or commission), where his case is studied, and he is then sent to some type of institution or assigned to some kind of program; but in other states, a child is committed directly to a juvenile institution. Regardless of the procedure that may be used, however, with the child should go a copy of his record, containing all the essential information that will be helpful to the institutional staff in providing for his custodial care, treatment, and training. When he arrives at an institution, he usually goes to a reception unit or cottage for a period of quarantine or orientation, which may last from one or two weeks to two months; although, of course, the length of this period is affected by the present tendency for many institutions to keep the child for only a short time. This period can serve three purposes: (1) it can segregate the child from the rest of the institution's population so as to determine whether he has any communicable disease; (2) it can give the staff time to acquaint the child with the policies, rules, and routine of the institution and to allay any fears, homesickness, hostilities, anxieties, and suspicions that he may have acquired prior to his admission; and (3) it can provide an opportunity to make a thorough study

[16] National Council on Crime and Delinquency, 80–89. See also, U.S. Children's Bureau, *Administration and Staff Training in Institutions for Juvenile Delinquents* (Washington, D.C.: Government Printing Office, 1959); Merritt Gilman, "Problems and Progress in Staff Training," *Crime and Delinquency*, XII (July, 1966), 254–60. This entire issue of *Crime and Delinquency* is devoted to articles on correctional manpower.

of the child by means of interviews, physical, psychiatric, and psychological examinations and tests, and an investigation of his social background and community relationships.

Thus, it can be seen that the period of orientation is a crucial one in the institutional experience of the child; for, if it is properly utilized, it can not only furnish essential information about the child but also prepare him mentally and physically for the institution's program. However, during the time that the child is in the reception cottage his medical, religious, educational, and recreational needs should not be neglected. In fact, a reception cottage is unnecessary in small institutions, although, of course, the various intake and orientation services should still be used in each case.

## Classification

With the period of orientation should begin what is known as classification in the field of corrections. It is a method by which all the resources of the institution are marshalled and brought to bear most effectively in the individual case for the purpose of promoting rehabilitation. This can be accomplished by (1) studying the child and analyzing his problems through the use of every technique and procedure, (2) formulating in a staff conference a program of custodial care, treatment, and training that is best suited to the child's particular needs, abilities, and potentialities, (3) assuring that this program is put into operation, (4) providing guidance for the child through interviews and counseling, (5) observing the progress of the child, and by modifying or changing his program from time to time when this is necessary, and (6) making recommendations with respect to the child's release at the appropriate time.[17]

All the information about the child that is obtained during his orientation should be compiled and submitted to the classification committee, which should be composed of representatives of the various services and departments of the institution, although it should not be so large as to be unweildly and cumbersome. After this committee has made a study of the case, it should assign the child to a cottage or living unit, formu-

---

[17] See Robert G. Caldwell, "Classification: Key to Effective Institutional Correction," *American Journal of Correction*, XX (March–April, 1958), 10, 26–28. See also Kenneth S. Carpenter and George H. Weber, "Intake and Orientation Procedures in Institutions for Delinquent Youth," *Federal Probation*, XXX (March, 1966), 37–42; George H. Weber, *A Theoretical Study of the Cottage Parent Position and Cottage Work Situations* (U.S. Children's Bureau Report No. 18, Washington, D.C.: Government Printing Office, 1962); Lamar T. Empey and Jerome Rabow, "The Provo Experiment in Delinquency Rehabilitation," *American Sociological Review*, XXVI (October, 1961), 679–95; Mayer N. Zald and David Street, "Custody and Treatment in Juvenile Institutions," *Crime and Delinquency*, X (July, 1964), 249–56.

late plans for the child's custodial care, mental hygiene, medical treatment, work assignment, vocational training, education, recreation, and religious instruction, and make whatever arrangements are necessary for extending social service to the child's family. But classification should not end here, for the study of the child should continue during his entire stay in the institution, so that his program can be modified to remove its inadequacies and adjusted to meet his changing needs.

Unfortunatly, in many institutions, classification remains hardly more than a gesture: inadequate budgets, incompetent personnel, antiquated facilities, persistent overcrowding, and other such obstacles keep it from being anything more. Classification, after all, is just a method; its fruitfulness depends on the strength and diversity of the institution's resources. For example, casework and clinical services can succeed in a juvenile institution only if there are enough competent social workers and clinicians to establish intimate and meaningful relationships with the children and thereby reduce personality maladjustments that may have contributed to the development of delinquencies. Certainly, caseworkers and clinicians can accomplish little if most of their time and energy are devoted to institutional routine and the keeping of records. And yet, thus far only a few states have enough psychologists, psychiatrists, and trained social workers to operate a first-class rehabilitation program in their juvenile institutions.

## Range of Activities

In general, the religious, educational, and recreational programs in juvenile institutions are stronger than the social work and clinical services, but they, too, face some serious obstacles. Many children are emotionally upset and hostile; most are retarded in their education and are in the institution for only a few months; all of them enter and leave their classes at irregular intervals during the year. Nevertheless, the children attend academic and religious classes, receive vocational training (boys, in such fields as woodworking, machine shop, shoe repairing, painting, auto mechanics, electrical work, agriculture, and so on, and girls, in such subjects as sewing and beautician's techniques), work in agriculture and maintenance activities and sometimes in nearby community stores and shops, participate in games and athletics, play in orchestras and bands, sing in choruses and choirs, engage in hobby and craft work and club activities, act in plays and skits, and go to religious services, picnics, plays, and motion pictures.

Although the potentialities of this program are great, usually the staff is too handicapped, the child too young, and his stay in the institution too short to effect any great change in his fundamental attitudes or to provide him with a solid foundation in any trade or craft. Nevertheless, sometimes his interest in some type of work is nurtured, his personal hygiene is improved, and new opportunities are presented to him after his release. It is a mistake, however, to assume that education in juvenile institutions takes place only in the classroom and the shop. The fact is that everything that happens to a child during his stay in an institution is part of his education, and in view of the neglect, brutality, sex perversions, incompetence, political corruption, and other similar conditions that still exist in some juvenile institutions, this is a sobering thought.

But it is in its disciplinary policy that the deficiencies of an institution are most clearly focused and most glaringly revealed. Caught in the vortex of underfinancing, overcrowding, and understaffing, the superintendent may be forced to resort to more and more authority and set up a tighter and tighter system of management. When this happens—and it does happen—emphasis shifts from the child to the routine, from understanding to rules, from rehabilitation to custody. However, although harsh methods and even brutality still persist in some institutions and disciplinary policies vary widely, the trend is toward the adoption of measures that relate discipline to rehabilitation and seek to motivate what is desirable rather than merely to suppress what is undesirable. Rewards and the deprivation of privileges are now favored over efforts to control through fear,[18] and in some institutions certain types of discipline may be administered through the juveniles' own self-government. For example, the George Junior Republic, a private school for juvenile delinquents at Freeville, New York, seeks to train children in the rights, duties, and responsibilities of citizenship through its system of self-government. The children help to formulate the rules by which they are governend and share in the administration of these rules and in the imposition of penalties for violations of them. Some other juvenile institutions, both private and public, have introduced similar plans.

## Goals

Although the institutional activities that we have been examining are important in themselves, we must remember their primary purpose: to prepare the child for his return to the community and to facilitate his adjustment there. They must, therefore, do more than provide care and comfort for the child or educate him to understand and obey the institution's rules. They must also increase his sense of responsibility, his desire to take the initiative in solving his own problems, his ability to function in the greater freedom of the community, and his willingness to accept the fact of authority. And the process by which this is accom-

[18] National Council on Crime and Delinquency, p. 76.

plished should be a gradual and progressive one, leading the child from the restrictions of the institution, through such steps as community visits, home furloughs, greater freedom within the institution, assignment of institutional tasks requiring more initiative and carrying more authority, and so on, to the freedom of the community. Furthermore, while this approach is being built toward the community, another should be constructed *from* the community by preparing the neighborhood and the child's own home or foster home, or perhaps, as an intermediate step, a halfway house or a group home, to receive him, by providing opportunities for the continuation of his religious training and education and sometimes for his employment, and, in some cases, by making arrangements for his treatment at a hospital or clinic. In this way, the bridge between the institution and the community can be completed and the possibility of the child's again becoming a delinquent, reduced.

However, if this—the goal of all institutional activities—is to be achieved, there must be adequate financing and staffing. These are certainly important in the operation of the modern institution for juvenile delinquents, but far more important is the vigorous leadership of a wise administration. Where such guidance is lacking, the program of an institution is deprived of its vitality, morale is undermined, competence is overwhelmed by pettiness, suspicion, and confusion, and children are sacrificed for the sake of appearances. Furthermore, classification, to achieve its greatest effectiveness, must function not only within the institution, but also on a statewide basis, so that all the resources of the state can be utilized, standards can be raised and made uniform, and the child can be transferred from one type of service or institution to another as his needs and potentialities so require. Some states now recognize the importance of this broader concept of classification and have begun to develop a system of diversified services and institutions, the ultimate goal of which is to match personnel, environments, and methods with types of delinquents in such a way as to individualize corrections and thus produce the maximum rehabilitative influence.[19]

## NEW ALTERNATIVES TO INSTITUTIONALIZATION

This recent development has been marked by: (1) an emphasis on community-based correctional services, including intensified and selective probation and parole caseloads, foster homes, trial furloughs, residential

[19] Mayer N. Zald and David Street, "Custody and Treatment in Juvenile Institutions," *Crime and Delinquency*, X (July, 1964), 249–56; Abraham G. Novick, "Institutional Organization for Treatment," *ibid.*, 257–62; Anthony Catalino, "A Prerelease Program for Juveniles in a Medium-Security Institution," *Federal Probation*, XXXI (December, 1967), 41–45.

correctional programs, and "day care" in specialized institutional programs that return children to their homes at night and on weekends; (2) the use of group treatment; and (3) the appearance of small, specialized institutions and agencies, such as reception and screening centers, forestry camps, group homes, and halfway houses.[20] Thus, there is offered a set of alternatives to regular probation and parole supervision, on the one hand, and mass institutionalization, on the other. Providing more guidance than the former, they are, in general, less costly and disruptive than the latter. They appear, therefore, to supply an important means for coping with the rising tide of juvenile delinquency. That they will be needed is clearly reflected in the estimate that the number of delinquents who will have to be institutionalized will increase by 70 per cent from 1965 to 1975.[21]

## Group Treatment

One of the new alternatives is group treatment, which, it is claimed, is not only more economical than one-to-one counseling, but also more effective in some cases. Various forms of this are being used, including the inspirational, the didactic, and the analytic, but all of them seek to change the individual by immersing him in guided group interaction, which is directed toward the acceptance of socially approved attitudes and behavior. The general theory holds that: (1) since juvenile delinquency is a group experience, efforts to change the delinquent should focus primarily on a group like that in which the individual functions; (2) through group interaction, a group "culture" can be developed that will encourage those involved to assume responsibility for helping and controlling one another; and (3) the participants will be more responsive to the influence of their fellow offenders—their peers—than to the admonitions of the staff and less likely to deceive and manipulate one another.[22]

On the basis of this theory, the advocates of group treatment allege that, by the process of revealing inner thoughts and feelings and of sharing common experiences, tensions are reduced, a greater feeling of security is achieved, new insights into behavior are gained, hope and confidence are restored, a better understanding of the common lot of man is acquired, and a deeper sense of responsibility is developed. The nature of this process is not entirely clear; but apparently its existence has been recognized since time immemorial, and it has always been utilized in the

20 National Council on Crime and Delinquency, 93, 94.
21 The President's Commission on Law Enforcement and Administration of Justice, *Task Force Report: Corrections* (Washington, D.C.: Government Printing Office, 1967), p. 38.
22 *Ibid.*, pp. 38, 39.

fields of politics and religion. Many cases do not respond to this type of treatment, however, and it should always be supplemented with some personal counseling. Furthermore, it lends itself to some abuses. The group meetings, unless skillfully planned and guided, can become the focal point of unrest, discontent, and conflict, provide a means whereby some juveniles can dominate and exploit others, and generate friction among members of the staff. Besides, even though we do not know how effective this type of treatment is, economy-minded administrators may rely upon it as a panacea and a cheap and easy solution for all the problems of rehabilitation.[23]

Nevertheless, the possible value of group treatment should not be overlooked, and, in fact, it is receiving more and more recognition. A survey, conducted in 1959, indicated that the use of group treatment was spreading in the United States, that 72 per cent of the federal correctional institutions and 50 per cent of the state correctional institutions were employing it, and that state reformatories and training schools were utilizing it more than the state prisons.[24]

The Highfields project in New Jersey is considered the pioneer attempt to use guided group treatment with juvenile delinquents. After its initiation in 1950, it became a model for correctional workers elsewhere, who employed its principles and techniques with both juveniles and adults in and outside institutions. At present, Highfields limits its population to twenty boys aged sixteen and seventeen, who are assigned directly to it from the juvenile court. However, boys who have been formerly committed to correctional schools or who are deeply disturbed or mentally retarded are not accepted. The goal of the program is to effect rehabilitation within three to four months, which is about half the average period of confinement in New Jersey's state training school. Housed in the old Lindbergh mansion, the boys work in a nearby mental institution during the day and participate in evening group counseling sessions five days a week. Weekends, however, are devoted to housecleaning, religious services, receiving visitors, play, and recreation.[25]

Efforts to evaluate this program have been the subject of considerable controversy. Although one early study showed that the rate of recidivism was lower for its former inmates ( 37 per cent ) than for boys released

---

[23] Robert G. Caldwell, *Criminology* (New York: The Ronald Press Co., 1965), pp. 603–07. See also, Frederic L. Faust, "Group Counseling with Juveniles—By Staff Without Professional Training in Group-work," *Crime and Delinquency*, XI (October, 1965), 349–54. This entire issue of Crime and Delinquency is devoted to articles on group methods.

[24] Lloyd W. McCorkle and Albert Elias, "Group Therapy in Correctional Institutions," *Federal Probation*, XXIV (June, 1960), 57–63.

[25] The President's Commission on Law Enforcement and Administration of Justice, pp. 38, 39.

from Annandale (53 per cent), a traditional state training school, located in New Jersey, critics have pointed out that the boys sent to Highfields were better prospects for rehabilitation and were more leniently treated after release than those sent to Annandale. The supporters of the High-fields program, however, argue that it was at least as effective as that at Annandale, and that its work was accomplished within a much shorter period of time and at a much lower cost.[26]

Two important variations of the Highfields project were developed at Essexfields, New Jersey, and at Pinehills in Provo, Utah. Like the one at Highfields, these programs were built around gainful employment in the community, school work, and daily group meetings, but there was this significant difference: at Essexfields and Pinehills, the boys continued to live at home.

Essexfields was located in a former private residence in a depressed area of a large city and was within commuting distance for boys who were placed on probation and assigned to it by county judges. However, only boys aged sixteen and seventeen who were not psychotic or severely retarded and had had no prior institutional commitment were eligible for admission. Furthermore, only twenty at a time were in the program, which was under the direction of a staff of four and consisted of super-vised work for five days a week on county hospital grounds, a cleaning of the center on Saturday mornings, and an evening session of guided group interaction five times a week. Nights and weekends, however, were spent at home. The boys participated in the program for about four or five months and then returned to regular probation. In order to determine the effectiveness of this program, a study was made of it for the three-year period 1962 to 1965. The study found that the recidivism rate for Essexfields was 48 per cent as compared with 15 per cent for boys on probation, 41 per cent for three group centers in New Jersey (Highfields and two other centers), and 55 per cent for Annandale. However, since boys in these four programs differed in ways likely to affect recidivism, the study attempted to match boys across the programs. Difficulties reduced this to a rather limited analysis, but it seemed to indicate that the recidivism rates for each program remained about the same after matching. The study concluded that a program of treatment patterned after Highfields and other residential group centers can be carried out successsfully in a nonresidental setting in the community.[27]

In the Pinehills project, all the boys were employed by the city on

[26] *Ibid.*, p. 39; H. Ashley Weeks, *Youthful Offenders at Highfields* (Ann Arbor: University of Michigan Press, 1958).

[27] Richard M. Stephenson and Frank R. Scarpitti, "Essexfields: A Non-Residential Experiment in Group Centered Rehabilitation of Delinquents," *American Journal of Correction*, XXXI (January–February, 1969), 12–18.

the golf course, in the cemetery—wherever needed—and were paid 50 cents an hour. During the late afternoon after the day's work was over, the boys returned to the program headquarters, where they met in daily group interaction sessions. After 7 P.M. they were free to go home; they were not at the center at all on Sunday. A study was made of the effectiveness of this program, and it found that its recidivism rate was lower than those of both probationers and the state training school (which was highest), even after arrangements were made so that all the boys studied in the three programs could be drawn at random from a common population of persistent offenders living in the same county. Here again, however, the difficulties of making the comparisons limited the analysis, although the study concluded that the results appeared to be significant.[28]

Several other guided group interaction projects have been developed in Louisville, Kentucky (the Parkland Project), in Richmond, California (the Girls' Unit for Intensive Daytime Education, called Guide), and in a girls' program in San Mateo, California. All three of these projects include a daily session devoted to a combination of educational activities, craft projects, center development and beautification, and group and individual counseling.[29]

## Halfway House Programs

Originally, halfway house programs were planned for offenders who were "halfway out" of institutions as a means of easing the stress of transition from institutional regimentation to community freedom. In the United States, the prerelease guidance centers of the Federal Bureau of Prisons, the first of which were opened in 1961, in New York, Chicago, and Los Angeles, are the best-known halfway house programs for offenders who are in the process of being released from correctional institutions. Recently, however, the halfway house has come to be thought of as a potential alternative to institutionalization, and thus a program for those "halfway in between" probation and institutional control. In the federal halfway houses, the offenders work in the community during the day and return to the center in the evening. As their parole date approaches, some may even be permitted to move out of the center, although they are still required to return to it for conferences several times a week. All offenders at these centers receive individual and group counseling, which is designed to relieve them of their anxieties and tensions and to help them handle their daily problems. Some of the offenders attend school on a part-time or full-time schedule, in addition to, or

---

[28] The President's Commission on Law Enforcement and Administration of Justice, p. 39.
[29] *Ibid.*

instead of, working. This is sometimes called "study release," and it is particularly appropriate for juvenile and youthful offenders. In fact, several states have developed this type of program in state centers, which resemble the federal prerelease guidance centers.[30]

## Intensive Community Treatment

The California Youth Authority's community treatment project is perhaps the best known of the country's efforts at controlled experimentation in the correctional field. Boys and girls committed to the California Youth Authority from Sacramento and San Joaquin Counties are screened at a reception center, in order to determine which ones should be used in the experimentation. Those who have committed serious offenses or have mental abnormalities, or whose immediate release would arouse strenuous community objections, are excluded, and the remainder are then either paroled and assigned randomly to the community project— the experimental group—or channeled routinely into an institution and eventually paroled—the control group. The boys and girls who go to the community project are interviewed, classified into offender subgroups, and admitted to a program, consisting of individual and group counseling, group and family therapy, group activities, and school tutoring services. The staff, which is composed of experienced and carefully selected persons, tries to fit the program to the needs of each type of offender, intensive treatment being made possible by the fact that there is a ratio of 1 staff member for every 12 youths. Afternoon and some evening sessions are held at the program center, which houses the staff and educational, recreational, counseling, and therapy facilities. Parolees in the program are frequently kept in detention at the agency's reception center for short periods, varying from a few hours to a few days, so as to assure compliance with the requirements of the program and "to set" limits on their behavior.

Two methods have been used to measure the results of this program: (1) psychological tests, which indicate that it has been more effective with some types of offenders than with others; (2) comparison of its "failure rate" with that of the control group, who had been institutionalized and then placed under regular parole supervision. This comparison showed that at the end of fifteen months, 28 per cent of the experimental group and 52 per cent of the control group had had their paroles revoked. In 1964, the California Youth Authority, after experimenting with this program for several years, extended it to the Watts area of Los Angeles and to a neighborhood in west Oakland.

[30] *Ibid.*, pp. 40, 41. See also Frances McNeil, "A Halfway-House Program for Delinquents," *Crime and Delinquency*, XIII (October, 1967), 538–44.

## Reception Center Parole and Short-Term Treatment Programs

Diagnostic parole is a procedure by which commitments from the juvenile court are referred to a reception center where they can be screened for eligibility for parole, either immediately or after a short period of treatment. Introduced in New York, Washington, Kentucky, and California in the early 1960's, in order to cope with the acute population pressures in overcrowded institutions, it is now considered one of the alternatives to mass institutionalization.

## Comprehensive Programing

Although the great majority of the states continue to use only supervision in the community under probation and parole or confinement in institutions, a few correctional systems have adopted alternatives to mass institutionalization, such as those described above. New York, for example, has developed a particularly comprehensive set of programs as alternatives to the incarceration of juveniles. For the more sophisticated delinquent there are a number of installations that replicate the Highfields model. In these, work during the day at some state facility is followed by daily group counseling in a nearby residence that houses twenty to twenty-five older adolescents. For the more immature and dependent juveniles, a small forestry camp provides a combination of work, academic instruction, and group counseling. The third type of program is for youths who have some stability and maturity and are not unduly involved in delinquency. The earlier projects of this type were located in houses that would accommodate twenty to twenty-five youths, but more recently the state has been using large apartments in conventional apartment houses. Under this plan, there is a cluster of three units, each of which accommodates seven or eight juveniles and house parents. All three units are supervised by a program director, and although the program is minimal, sessions of group counseling are held every day. In addition, education and employment are sought within the communities adjacent to the centers. An analysis of the postrelease performance of all of the program's graduates after seven and one-half months of exposure to the community indicated that 13 per cent had been again convicted of some offense, but that only 8 per cent had been again confined. Although it was not possible to compare this performance with that of a control group, the "failure rate" appears to be impressively lower than that of juveniles released from state juvenile institutions.

Advocates of the alternatives to mass institutionalization recognize that difficult problems must be solved if programs like that of New York are to be widely adopted. They explain that to accomplish this, these alternatives must be brought to the attention of legislators and administrators; they must be given adequate financing and staffing; they must be made an integral part of the state correctional system and not just an isolated experiment; they must be coordinated with allied services, such as those supplied by welfare and mental health agencies; and they must be supported by community interest and participation.[31]

## THE KENNEDY CLASSIFICATION PROGRAM

A brief description of the classification program in effect at the Robert F. Kennedy Youth Center, a federal institution at Morgantown, West Virginia, will demonstrate how personnel and methods are being matched with types of delinquency in order to provide differential treatment.[32] This program classifies juveniles into these four treatment-related behavioral categories: (1) inadequate-immature delinquency; (2) neurotic-disturbed delinquency; (3) unsocialized-psychopathic delinquency; and (4) socialized-subcultural delinquency.

The *inadequate-immature delinquent* is described as being sluggish, daydreaming, inattentive, lazy, preoccupied, drowsy, reticent, and generally uninterested in things. Much of his behavior seems to be that of a boy at an earlier stage of development. He feels that he is a victim of life and that others should take care of him. His relationship with adults is characterized by resentment and dependency and with his peers, by demands and jealousy. He behaves impulsively and "blows up" easily.

The *neurotic-disturbed delinquent* is described as being anxious, withdrawn, hypersensitive, self-conscious, fearful, and insecure. He may be willing to verbalize that there is, in fact, something wrong with him, but he cannot understand why he keeps getting into trouble. He has the capacity to form sincere, satisfactory interpersonal relationships, even though he may be demanding and unsure of himself. Since he has internalized a set of ideals, standards, and values, by which he judges his own and others' behavior, he feels remorseful or guilty when he does

[31] The President's Commission on Law Enforcement and Administration of Justice, 41–44. Some of the descriptions of the new alternatives to mass institutionalization given above have been adapted from this Commission's *Task Force Report: Corrections.* See pp. 38–44. See also George H. Weber, *Camps for Delinquent Boys* (U.S. Children's Bureau Publication No. 385, Washington, D.C.: Government Printing Office, 1960); Milton Luger, "Innovations in the Treatment of Juvenile Offenders," *The Annals of the American Academy of Political and Social Science,* CCCLXXXI (January, 1969), 60–70; Albert Elias, "Innovations in Correctional Programs for Juvenile Delinquents," *Federal Probation,* XXXII (December, 1968), 38–45.

[32] *Differential Treatment: A Way to Begin,* Handbook Prepared by Roy Gerard, Director, and Staff, May, 1969, pp. 1–29.

not measure up to it. He attempts to master immediate pressures without trying to come to terms with long-standing difficulties or fears.

The *unsocialized-psychopathic delinquent* is described as being aggressive, cruel, defiant, and malicious. He will become hostile when confronted with his misbehavior, blame others rather than accept responsibility for his own acts, and in general, views himself as always in the right and able to outwit others. For him, this is a "dog-eat-dog" world where "good guys finish last." He is extremely self-centered, wily, deceitful, and very untrustworthy. Tending to see himself as powerful, invulnerable, "cool," and "smooth," he tends to discount his past mistakes and sees his future as secure and successful. He rarely expresses any guilt and has little consideration for others, although other often think him "likable" and even "charming."

The *socialized-subcultural delinquent* is described as having been involved in gang activities or group delinquencies. He has intense loyalty to a delinquent peer group and behaves according to the code of ethics set by this group. His behavior usually exhibits a failure to abide by middle-class standards and values. He is "well adjusted" to a deviant or delinquent culture and sees himself as adequate, capable, independent, responsible, and mature. He takes pride in living up to his own values and principles and sees no need to change his views of the world or improve himself.

Each juvenile is assigned to staff members who are especially qualified to deal with his type of delinquency and who adapt the treatment program to his individual needs and potentialities. The basic treatment program is centered in the living unit. In each cottage there is a committee (treatment team) which has the responsibility of developing and implementing appropriate strategies. This cottage committee is interdisciplinary in composition and includes a caseworker, an educator, and a counselor. Once a youth is assigned to his permanent living unit, the continuing responsibility for classification rests with the treatment team or cottage committee. However, he may be transferred to another cottage if it becomes evident that he has been improperly classified. Thus an effort is made to prevent the individual inmate from being lost in the routine of classification.

## THE EFFECTIVENESS OF INSTITUTIONALIZATION

Many lurid stories have been told about the institutions for juvenile delinquents, and often they have been condemned as cesspools of corruption and dens of iniquity. Employees, inmates, judges, journalists, grand juries, legislators, women's clubs, newspapers, magazines, radio, and television—all at various times have joined the chorus, usually directing their barbs at a certain institution or superintendent. To support the charge that these institutions have failed, critics ordinarily point to personal experiences, damning evidence produced by some investigation, or general statistics on crime and delinquency. The rate of juvenile delinquency climbs higher every year. A large percentage of our juveniles are repeating their offenses. More and more of them are engaging in serious criminal activities. Many of them are developing into hardened criminals. And this is happening despite the fact that thousands of our boys and girls have been confined in juvenile institutions.

Some studies, however, have gone beyond this approach and have attempted to learn the rate of recidivism of those who have been in juvenile institutions. But these studies have given different results. Many of them report a rate of recidivism ranging from 30 to 40 per cent; others indicate that this rate is about 50 per cent.[33]

Although these studies have thrown some light on the subject, we really do not know how effective our juvenile institutions are. Obviously, so many variables are at work that no one can determine the effect of institutionalization on the rates of crime, delinquency, and recidivism in the United States. Furthermore, many acts which might be found to be delinquent are never detected. Besides, juvenile institutions get boys and girls after almost everybody else has failed in trying to change them, and they have acquired habits and attitudes that resist even the best of our rehabilitative techniques.[34] And here is a fact that many overlook. The influence of the institution is only one of the many influences that play upon the lives of the boys and girls who are committed to it and then released. The institutional correction that a boy receives may be the best that can be given and quite fruitful, but it may be completely counteracted by his later experiences in the community.

Nevertheless, juvenile institutions can—and should—be improved. They should be operated under a state department—preferably a separate department of correction which is not submerged in a larger division, so that its head will be given direct and unobstructed access to the governor, and its distinctive character and needs will not be distorted by the philosophies of other fields, such as those of welfare, social work, and psychiatry. They should be better financed and more adequately staffed. For example, minimal standards call for one full-time psychiatrist and

---

[33] Paul Schreiber, *How Effective Are Services for the Treatment of Delinquents?* (U.S. Children's Bureau Report No. 9, Washington, D.C.: Government Printing Office, 1960), pp. 9–13.

[34] See William McCord and Joan McCord, "Two Approaches to the Cure of Delinquents," *Journal of Criminal Law, Criminology, and Police Science,* XLIV (November–December, 1953), 442–67.

one full-time psychologist for every 150 children, one social case worker for every 30 children, one trained recreation worker for every 50 children, and one teacher for every 15 children. The capacity of a training school should be limited to 150 children, and living units should be designed for not more than 20 children.[35] Classification should operate both within each institution and throughout the state, so that different correctional units can be combined in various ways, and a diversity of resources can be used to fit correction to the needs and potentialities of each child. And all institutional policies, programs, and services should be directed toward preparing the child for a more successful life in the community. These, and similar recommendations, point the way to better juvenile institutions in the United States.

[35] The President's Commission on Law Enforcement and Administration of Justice, pp. 211, 212. See also *Institutions Serving Delinquent Children: Guides and Goals* (U.S. Children's Bureau Publication No. 360, Washington, D.C.: Government Printing Office, 1957); *Tentative Standards for Training Schools* (U.S. Children's Bureau Publication No. 351, Washington, D.C.: Government Printing Office, 1954); William E. Amos, "The Future of Juvenile Institutions," *Federal Probation*, XXXII (March, 1968), 41–47; National Conference of Superintendents of Training Schools and Reformatories, *Institutional Rehabilitation of Delinquent Youth* (Albany, N.Y.: Delmar Publishers, Inc., 1962); Leonard J. Hippchen, "An Exploration of Factors Related to Staff Vacancies and Separations among Public Institutions Serving Delinquent Children," Reprinted for U.S. Department of Health, Education, and Welfare, Welfare Administration, Children's Bureau, from *Criminologica* (Fall, 1966); *ibid., Personnel and Personnel Practices in Public Institutions for Delinquent Children: A Survey* (U.S. Children's Bureau Statistical Series No. 86, Washington, D.C.: Government Printing Office, 1966).

# 18

# Juvenile Parole

## NATURE AND DEVELOPMENT

Juvenile parole is different from juvenile probation in that it is a procedure by which a juvenile who has been in a correctional institution is conditionally released into the community and placed under the supervision of a parole officer. Thus, the major difference between the two is that probation occurs prior to incarceration, whereas parole takes place afterwards. While not all that glaring at first glance, such a distinction is crucial. Parole begins to operate subsequent to a time when numerous significant influences from the experiences of confinement in a correctional institution have been introduced into the delinquent's life. As a result, although entailing many of the same types of activities and problems encountered in probation, parole work merits special discussion.

Many social workers prefer the term "aftercare" instead of "parole" and call the parole officer a "counselor." In favor of this terminology, they argue that juvenile programs should be separated from the legalistic language and concepts of adult parole. But it should be clear that no mincing language will change the fact that juvenile delinquency is a legal status involving legal duties and responsibilities, that a juvenile delinquent is an offender as defined by the law, that a legal procedure is used to adjudicate his case and that his legal rights are guarded by it, that the process of correction in the juvenile case involves a balancing of treatment and punishment as prescribed by law, and that failure on probation carries with it the legal consequences of commitment to an institution.

Furthermore, this is the way that it must be, for, as in the case of the adult, society must not only concern itself with the interests of the individual, but also guard its dominant values, by which the individual's duties and responsibilities are defined, his rights are protected, and his rehabilitation is measured. All this cannot be glossed over by euphemisms.  Indeed, failure to understand the situation can lead to the frustration and disillusionment of the people, the concentration of power in a centralized bureaucracy, and the substitution of its values for the values of the people.

The roots of juvenile parole in the United States can be found in the system of indenturing children which existed during the Colonial period. Under this system, the child was bound out to a master for a certain period, during which time he was taught a trade and put into service for the master.  Although originally this system was used to provide care and training for dependent persons, in time, juvenile offenders, also, were indentured.  This meant that after a juvenile offender had served part of a term in a correctional institution, he might be released without supervision, placed in the employ of a private citizen to whom he was legally bound, and permitted to earn his final discharge from his employer, who had the authority to make the decision regarding this.  At first, the states assumed no responsibility for supervising this arrangement.  However, about the middle of the nineteenth century, New York set the beginning of a pattern by the appointment of a state agent to supervise indentured children and to guard them against abuse.  Nevertheless, it was not until 1876, when the Elmira Reformatory was opened in New York, that a modern parole program was established in the United States.  Since then parole has spread throughout the country, and today all states and the federal government have statutory provisions for the parole of both juveniles and adults.[1]  In fact, most juveniles are placed on parole when they are released from correctional institutions.  Although we do not know how many of these juvenile parolees there are at any particular time in the United States, it has been estimated that, at the beginning of 1966, they totaled 59,000 and their numbers ranged from 110 to 13,000 per state.[2]

## RATIONALE

Parole should not be regarded as an act of leniency, although it does shorten the term of confinement.  Its chief purpose is to bridge the gap between the closely ordered life of the institution and the freedom of normal life in the community.  Thus, it assumes that the period of confinement is only part of the correctional process, and that it should be supplemented by a period of supervision and guidance in the community.

[1] David Dressler, *Practice and Theory of Probation and Parole* (New York: Columbia University Press, 1969), pp. 72–76; Robert G. Caldwell, *Criminology* (New York: The Ronald Press Co., 1965), pp. 674, 675.

[2] National Council on Crime and Delinquency, "Correction in the United States," *Crime and Delinquency,* XIII (January, 1967), 101.

Parole, therefore, is not just a way of releasing offenders from an institution. It is an integral part of the correctional process.[3]

Plans for the parole of the juvenile should begin immediately after his commitment and should be developed to meet his needs and potentialities during the entire period of his confinement. Furthermore, these plans must take into consideration not only the effects of institutionalization on the child, but also the attitudes and conditions of the community to which he must return. Some children, for example, become more antisocial and hardened in their attitudes and habits as a result of their institutionalization, whereas others become dependent and timid. And the community settings into which these children must go vary widely. Some are the very ones that contributed to the delinquency of the children in the first place. In many, the children will be stigmatized and their adjustment made difficult. Clearly, then, the parole plans for each child must be highly individualized, and a variety of resources, both inside and outside of the institution, must be used in their implementation. Only in this way can the child's return to the community be made meaningful and productive, and a good foundation laid for his future success.[4]

The possible advantages of juvenile parole are manyfold. It provides a transitional period between institutionalization and the community, during which the parole officer can supervise the child and assist him in his efforts to become a law-abiding member of society. It permits the child to be released when he is mentally and emotionally ready for this and the community setting to be prepared for his return. It reduces the possibility that the period of institutionalization may be excessively extended to the detriment of the child, thus, for example, depriving him of his initiative and self-confidence—qualities which he needs for success in the outside world. It enables the parole officer to exert an influence for the prevention of crime and delinquency both in the child's family and in his neighborhood. It gives older children an opportunity to contribute to their own support and to make restitution to the victims of their delinquencies. It costs less to keep a juvenile on parole than to maintain him in a correctional institution. During 1965, the United States spent about $18,000,000 for the operation of juvenile parole programs, the state costs for that year ranging from $7,000 to over $4,000,000. This meant that the average cost for each juvenile parolee during that year was $320. But this cost was small in comparison with that of maintaining a juvenile in a correctional institution. During 1965, for example, it it cost over $144,000,000 to operate state institutions for juvenile delinquents, which had an average daily population of slightly over 42,000.

[3] Caldwell, p. 667.
[4] National Council on Crime and Delinquency, 99, 100.

Thus, the average cost of maintaining a delinquent in a state-operated institution during that year was about $3,400, or more than ten times that of keeping a juvenile on parole.

While economy should not be the primary reason for using parole for juveniles, certainly it cannot be disregarded when all other circumstances indicate that the juvenile should be placed on parole. However, it must be conceded that parole would cost more if it were administered in accordance with the recommended standards—and this should be done if we expect to realize fully all of its possible advantages—but this would be true also of juvenile institutions. And certainly, all of the available evidence indicates that both of these methods of correction need much improvement in the United States.[5]

Some objections against the parole of juveniles have been raised. For example, it has been claimed that it leads to the coddling of delinquents, permits discrimination against certain groups, encourages disrespect for the law, and exposes the community to additional acts of delinquency. These objections, however, are not fatal and can be deprived of whatever force they may have by the establishment of competent, honest, and responsible parole agencies, and by the careful selection and adequate supervision of parolees.

## ADMINISTRATION

The way in which juvenile parole is administered in the United States varies from state to state. Even so, regardless of the organization that is used, two major functions must be performed: (1) the granting and revoking of parole; and (2) the supervision and guidance of parolees. Since these two functions are so closely related, they should be administered by the same agency.

In about two-thirds of the states, the first function is performed by the staffs of the juvenile institutions, but in the rest of the states, decisions to grant and revoke parole are made by more or less independent boards or agencies, which are usually appointed by the governor. However, in many of the states where the latter arrangement exists, the members of the board or agency have had no special training for their work, serve only part-time, and receive no pay for their services.

The administration of juvenile parole is further complicated by the fact that the second function—the supervision and guidance of parolees—also, is handled in various ways. In about two-thirds of the states, the state department which administers the juvenile institutions also takes care of the supervision and guidance of the juvenile parolees. In the

---

[5] *Ibid.,* 101.

remainder of the states, however, this function is performed by a variety of agencies, including private and public welfare agencies, state youth correction authorities, state institution boards, state training school boards and so on. For example, in 1966, five states gave local probation departments the responsibility for juvenile parole, although these departments had no official relationship to the agency that administered the training schools.[6]

In support of having the institutions administer parole, it is argued that they are closer to the children and so are in a better position to understand them and to decide how they should be handled. But in opposition to this, it is claimed that a separate, independent board or agency can devote all its time to parole work, establish uniform standards for all institutions throughout the state, and handle all cases without being unduly influenced by such institutional problems as discipline and overcrowding, and, at the same time, inform itself about prospective parolees by examination of records, consultations, and parolee hearings.

Actually, however, there are only a few completely independent juvenile parole boards or agencies in the United States, and there appears to be little tendency to create additional ones. In fact, many authorities in the field of juvenile delinquency believe that neither the institution nor a separate, independent board or agency should administer parole, but that instead this should be done by a parole authority within the state correctional department, which, however, should take into consideration the reports and recommendations of the institutional staffs. In this way, it is urged, a state can have not only all the advantages claimed for a separate parole board or agency, but also the coordination of parole with the other juvenile correctional services.[7] Nevertheless, at present, it seems that a diversity of parole administration is required to meet the great variety of social conditions and customs in the various states. And certainly, no form of parole administration should be imposed upon a state regardless of whether it can or cannot adequately serve the needs and interests of its people.

## PERSONNEL

Those who administer juvenile parole should be qualified for their positions by character, personality, education, training, and experience, paid adequate salaries, and supported by sufficient clerical and field personnel. In addition, in states where separate juvenile parole boards or

[6] Ibid., 102–5.
[7] Ibid., 105; The President's Commission on Law Enforcement and Administration of Justice, Task Force Report: Corrections, pp. 65, 66, 70, 71.

agencies function, the members of these boards or agencies should be appointed by the governor for long terms, and given as much protection as possible from political influences. Some states now provide in-service training programs for their juvenile parole administrators, and this has proved helpful. Another development has been the addition of professional parole examiners, who conduct hearings and interviews for the parole board and make certain kinds of decisions within limits fixed by it. This permits the board to devote more of its time to policy making, eliminates the need of having to add to the membership of the board as its burdens increase, creates another resource of knowledge and skill, and makes possible the use of a part-time board in states where the dimensions of the delinquency problem do not justify elaborate administrative machinery. California employs parole examiners in both its adult and youth authorities, and the United States Board of Parole has added the position to its organization.[8]

The effectiveness of juvenile parole, however, is largely dependent upon the competence of its parole staff, which should have at least a chief parole officer, a sufficient number of parole officers to handle the investigation and supervision of parolees without excessive case loads, and an adequate clerical force. Although some of the larger parole systems assign one group of officers to investigation work, and another to supervision, it is better for the same officer to do both, so that two officers do not have to study the same parolee. How many cases should an officer carry? This is a difficult question to answer, for so many factors are involved. For example, one would have to take into consideration the degree of supervision required, the geographical spread of the load, the available transportation facilities, the number of visits made outside of regular working hours, and so on. Nevertheless, it has been recommended that an officer engaged in supervision should not carry more than fifty cases at one time, and that this maximum case load should be reduced by at least three cases for every preparole or parole investigation that the officer makes each month.[9] In fact, many authorities now believe that even this case load is too heavy, and that it should not be greater than about thirty-five cases per officer. This, they reason, would permit the officer to distribute his supervisory duties more effectively among the parolees in accordance with their needs.[10]

All parole officers and supporting personnel should be appointed

---

[8] The President's Commission on Law Enforcement and Administration of Justice, pp. 66, 67.

[9] *Manual of Correctional Standards* (New York: The American Correctional Association, 1959), pp. 541, 542; National Council on Crime and Delinquency, 107.

[10] The President's Commission on Law Enforcement and Administration of Justice, p. 70.

from lists of eligible candidates compiled on the basis of competitive examinations, and should have security of tenure as long as their work and conduct meet established standards. The parole officer should have a bachelor's degree with a major in the social or behavioral sciences, plus one year of graduate study in correction, social work, or a related field, or one year of paid, full-time case work in the field of correction. Lacking this, he should be given an intensive course of training when he enters the service, and every officer, regardless of his past education and experience, should have regular in-service training. Furthermore, salaries should be high enough to attract and hold qualified persons, and regular promotions and salary increases should be provided for on a merit basis.

However, an examination of the situation in the United States today shows how far we fall below these standards. A 1966 survey, which covered 40 states,[11] found that civil service or merit system coverage existed for the director of juvenile parole in 23 states, for the district supervisor in 26 states, and for the parole officer in 29 states, that many parole officers had less than a college education, that the opportunity for an officer to earn more than $6,000 a year was extremely limited in most states, that even if he advanced to a supervisory level, he could rarely earn more than $9,000 a year, that most states had done little to provide in-service training programs, and that the average case loads ranged from 30 to 125 cases, with the median in the 61 to 70 range, although the case load was really much heavier than this, since the figures shown here were not weighted for the number of investigations made or for the number of children worked with in juvenile institutions. Indeed, one fact stands out in this survey: There are simply not enough parole officers to do all of the work that is assigned to them. This is clearly revealed by the fact that there were only 1,033 juvenile parole officers in the 40 states covered by the survey, the number in each state ranging all the way from 2 to 273. As a result, in many states supervision usually consisted of a monthly report written by the juvenile himself and mailed to the state office, and parolees in rural areas sometimes never saw their parole officers. In short, as the survey concluded, supportive, sustained, and positive implementation of a parole plan was, "more often than not, rare."[12] Although volunteer workers can help in the improvement of this situation, their services should never be considered a satisfactory substitute for those of professional, full-time parole officers. Sometimes arrangements are made for a juvenile to have a sponsor dur-

---

[11] National Council on Crime and Delinquency, 106–9. The following states were not included in this survey, which was conducted by the National Council on Crime and Delinquency: Alabama, Arkansas, Illinois, Kansas, Maryland, New Mexico, North Carolina, North Dakota, Pennsylvania, and Virginia.

[12] National Council on Crime and Delinquency, p. 108.

ing parole. The sponsor may be a friend of the family, a clergyman, an employer, or some other interested person, but, whoever he is, he should be carefully selected, since he will be acting as confidant and counselor for the child over a period of many weeks.

## OPERATION

In the selection of juveniles for parole, the agency authorized to perform this function must, of course, operate within whatever limits the law or administrative regulations impose. In some states, this agency is not restricted by such limitiations and is entirely free to use its own judgment. In many other states, however, restrictions of various kinds do exist. For example, minimum terms that juveniles must serve before parole are fixed by administrative regulations in many states and by law in a few. Furthermore, in some other states the committing judge must be consulted before the child is paroled. Many authorities in the field believe that the paroling agencies should have broad discretionary powers, that only such limitations as are necessary to protect the rights and interests of the child, on the one hand, and the security and interests of the community on the other, should be imposed, and that in the great majority of cases, the child should not be kept in an institution for more than three years. Certainly the parole agency should not be completely free to use its discretion in paroling juveniles. No correctional agency should operate without legal restrictions.[13]

As we have emphasized, in every case, both the child and the community should be systematically prepared for his release; and the information that has been accumulated about him, both before and during institutionalization, along with recommendations regarding action in his case, should be submitted to the paroling agency in sufficient time for its proper consideration.

Usually, a juvenile does not appear in a hearing before an agency when he is being considered for parole. If no hearing is held, the decision in the case is based entirely on written reports and staff conferences, at which the offender may not be present. And yet a hearing can be helpful, for it provides an opportunity for the members of the agency to learn more about the child, to allay his fears, anxieties, and hostilities, and to instruct him regarding the nature of parole. In order to assist the parole agency in its work, prediction tables have been constructed. These are based on various factors, such as age, offense, education, work history, prior record, and so on, which appear to be associated with either success or failure on parole, and are designed to be used as a guide

[13] For a contrasting view, see *ibid.*, p. 103.

in the selection of parolees. Although these tables may offer clues—and they have been improved—they should never be used as a substitute for the careful study of the individual case. In any event, at present, prediction tables can give little help to those who are engaged in the selection of parolees.[14] Unfortunately, in practice, the selection of juvenile parolees is often superficial and almost meaningless. In fact, in some states, it is virtually automatic, since a certain number of juveniles must be released from overcrowded institutions to make room for new commitments.

When a child is placed on parole, he is expected to abide by conditions which are imposed by the paroling agency. These conditions serve as minimum standards of good conduct for the guidance of the juvenile, and violation of any of them exposes him to the possibility of recommitment to an institution. Although they vary from state to state and from case to case, for an older juvenile, they often require that he abstain from the use of intoxicants, submit written or personal reports at stipulated intervals, not violate any law, not associate with "bad company," and not change his address or employment, own or operate an automobile, marry, or leave the state or county without permission, and so on. One more point needs to be mentioned here. Interstate compacts now make it possible to place a juvenile on parole in another state, and this may be advisable, for example, when he should return to his home or avoid undesirable former associates.

The parole officer should never permit the conditions of parole to become an end in themselves. Designed to protect the community and to assist the parolee, they should be seen as tools of supervision to be used discriminatingly by the officer as he seeks to guide the child into law-abiding behavior. Too strictly enforced, they become self-defeating; too leniently used, they become meaningless. At their best, they constitute a few, simple, and flexible rules, which a sensitive, mature, well-trained officer skillfully applies in accordance with the needs of each case.[15]

Thus, the supervision of parolees, like that of probationers, should be seen as individualized correction within the community setting. Although supervision must begin with the development of a relationship of trust and confidence between the parole officer and the juvenile and must involve guidance and counseling, it must also operate within the limits of the law, and induce the parolee to respect the law, abide by the con-

[14] For a discussion of the criticisms of prediction tables, see Caldwell, pp. 688–90; Dressler, pp. 107–18; *Crime and Delinquency,* VIII (July, 1962), which is entirely devoted to articles on parole prediction tables.

[15] The principles governing the application of the conditions of parole are the same as those which we have already discussed with respect to probation.

ditions of parole, and assume increasing responsibility for the direction of his own behavior. Furthermore, all of this carries the implication that failure may return the juvenile to an institution. Supervision of parolees, therefore, like all elements in the correctional process, involves a balancing of treatment and punishment. As the process of supervision develops, and the parolee shows definite signs of progress, the conditions of his parole can be relaxed, thus allowing him greater freedom in such areas as employment, travel, and recreation.[16]

The length of time that a juvenile should remain on parole depends largely on the individual case. In fact, excessive statutory and administrative restrictions can impair the effectiveness of parole. The parole period of the juvenile in most states may last until his twenty-first birthday, even though the juvenile court originally could not exercise jurisdiction over him up to that age. Apparently, however, most states are keeping their juveniles on parole for an average of about one year or more.[17] Parole can be terminated either by its revocation or by the discharge of the parolee. Revocation may occur either because the juvenile has committed another act of delinquency or a crime or because he has violated the conditions of his parole. Even though the law may not require it, the juvenile should always be given a hearing before his parole is revoked, so that he is provided with an opportunity to defend himself,[18] and at this hearing, the juvenile should be represented by counsel.

## SUPPORTING SERVICES

Foster homes, group homes, halfway houses, and psychological and psychiatric services should be available for use in parole just as they should be in probation. However, thus far not a great deal has been accomplished in the development of these resources. This conclusion, for example, was indicated by a survey conducted by the National Council on Crime and Delinquency during 1966. The survey asked this question: Does the aftercare program also operate foster homes, group homes, and halfway houses? Of the forty states with statewide programs, twelve answered "yes," including two that reported that they did not pay for foster care but did use free home placements, and three that qualified their reply by stating that local child welfare departments found and

---

[16] The principles of supervision are the same in both probation and parole.

[17] See National Council on Crime and Delinquency, 105; Fred Cohen, *The Legal Challenge to Corrections: Implications for Manpower and Training* (Washington, D.C.: Joint Commission on Correctional Manpower and Training, March, 1969), pp. 59–61.

[18] The President's Commission on Law Enforcement and Administration of Justice, pp. 67–69.

supervised foster homes for aftercare placements. Individual foster homes were being used more frequently than group foster homes, and halfway houses for aftercare were in operation in only four of the forty states.[19]

## EFFECTIVENESS

At present, a reliable national study of juvenile parole is impossible, because many states do not have adequate statewide reporting systems.[20] Consequently, no one knows very much about the effectiveness of juvenile parole. Indeed, not a great deal is known about the violation rates of juvenile parolees, although it is estimated that in general, they are higher than those of adult parolees, which are estimated to be about 35 to 45 per cent.[21] Nevertheless, many authorities believe that juvenile parole is more effective when the following elements are included in its operation: (1) the responsibility for it is vested in the same state agency that administers the juvenile institutions; (2) its officers are selected on the basis of merit examinations, given in-service training, paid adequate salaries, and protected from excessive caseloads; (3) every child is placed on parole when released from an institution and prepared for this by classification and a pre-release program; (4) foster homes, group homes, halfway houses, and psychological and psychiatric care are provided as supporting services; and (5) a statewide statistical reporting system is maintained by the state correctional agency, so that data are available for planning, program development, and research.[22]

[19] National Council on Crime and Delinquency, p. 110.
[20] *Ibid.*, p. 111.
[21] The President's Commission on Law Enforcement and Administration of Justice, p. 62.
[22] See, for example, The President's Commission on Law Enforcement and Administration of Justice, pp. 207–9.

# 19

# Prevention: The Home, the School, and the Church

On any one day in the United States over one-third of a million juveniles—more than the population of the state of Wyoming—are under the jurisdiction of state and local correctional agencies and institutions. During 1965, about 18 per cent of these were in institutions, and the remainder were in the community under probation and parole supervision. Furthermore, during that year, it cost the United States about $315 million to operate state and local correctional services for juvenile delinquents. This amount represented about one-third of the total annual expenditures for all state and local correctional systems in this country.[1] Besides, the problem is getting worse and apparently will continue to do so. However, these figures point only to the externals of the situation. Who can estimate the amount and cost of the misery, shame, embarrassment, family disorganization, personal degradation, and loss of productivity involved in all the delinquencies that occur each year in the United States? Yet, these certainly must be included in any appraisal of the problem of juvenile delinquency.

Can there be any doubt, then, that the prevention of juvenile delinquency is vitally important? Obviously, there can be none, but it is far easier to demonstrate this than it is to show how prevention can be accomplished, for all kinds of obstacles are hindering our progress. The most serious of these is the meagerness of our knowledge regarding the nature

[1] The President's Commission on Law Enforcement and Administration of Justice, *Task Force Report: Corrections* (Washington, D.C.: Government Printing Office, 1967), pp. 192, 193.

and causes of human behavior. And this obstacle persists despite our most strenuous efforts, greatly interfering with the diagnosis, treatment, and prognosis in the case of every social problem. Furthermore, the available methods and techniques that are being used in the application of the existing knowledge are crude and largely unproductive. For example, attempts to develop techniques to identify potential delinquents have thus far met with little success. Moreover, the development of every program for the prevention of crime and delinquency always involves a balancing of values.

Questions like these confront us: How much deviance from preferred behavior should we tolerate so that we can enjoy the benefits of individual creativity, initiative, and enterprise? Since every type of society tends to produce its own kind of problems, how far can we go in reducing our problems without endangering our type of society? What can we do to increase the effectiveness of our laws and regulations and at the same time protect the constitutional rights of the individual? In other words, what price do we want to pay for prevention? And this question reaches directly into our pocketbooks. How much taxation do we want to bear in order to have enough money to implement our plans for the prevention of delinquency? And if we do not want to increase taxes, do we want to reduce the amount of money that we are now spending on the building and maintenance of our highways, or on some other public enterprise, in order to establish programs for the prevention of delinquency?

## THE NEED FOR PUBLIC SUPPORT

In the field of human relations, we do not solve problems as we do, for example, in mathematics. There is no final solution but rather a continuing adjustment—sometimes at the expense of creating new problems —during which the public must be persuaded to support prevention programs, even though at present little empirical evidence can be offered regarding their effectiveness.

In view of all these formidable obstacles, we should guard against excessive zeal in any move to prevent crime and delinquency and set realistic limits on the extent to which we intrude into the lives of individuals. If these guides are followed, our limited goals will be attainable, and our policies will be consistent with our ideals of freedom and individual responsibility and our principles of representative government, which emphasize a system of checks and balances and a distribution of power among federal, state, and local governments.

However, there are those who would give no heed to this advice, and despite the paucity of supportive evidence, propose one "remedy" after another for the "cure" of crime and delinquency. Thus, we are urged to give all children a high school education, provide organized recreation for every one, prohibit indecent movies, banish violence from television, keep marihuana out of the hands of juveniles, send all children to Sunday school, eliminate malnutrition, and so on. Although each of these items may be related in some way to crime and delinquency, none of them can be called *the* cause. And then there are those who would tear down the "establishment" and get rid of a system that is "not worth saving." But we are not told where we shall go from there, or how long the millennium will be in coming. Amid this babble and confusion, wisdom cautions that we keep these points in mind:

1. Delinquency is only a symptom—the product of the interaction of personal and environmental factors. We must, of course, deal with the symptom and try to alleviate it, but—and this is very important—we must also direct more of our attack against the underlying causes if we hope to produce any real reduction in delinquency.

2. Delinquency is both an individual and a social problem. We must include individualized correction as well as community action in our efforts to prevent it.

3. Delinquency is the product of many causes. We must organize a complex attack against it, employing the resources of all fields of human knowledge.

4. Delinquency is interrelated with all other social problems. We must subject it to a diversified attack, including measures specifically directed against it as well as those designed to deal with it indirectly by reducing unemployment, broken homes, and other social problems.

5. Delinquency is relative to time and place. We must have a dynamic attack against it—one that can cope with changing conditions and the peculiarities of different situations.

6. Delinquency is an old problem and probably will never be completely eliminated. We must have a continuing attack against it.

7. Delinquency is a pervasive problem, affecting many people of all classes throughout society. An attack against it must have widespread public support, developed through an educational program that informs the people about the nature and extent of delinquency and encourages them to participate in every way in the action against it.[2]

A complete discussion of delinquency prevention would have to range over a wide area of human relationships. For example, it would have to include an examination of all the programs that seek to reduce other

---

[2] Robert G. Caldwell, *Criminology* (New York: The Ronald Press Co., 1965), pp. 700, 701.

social problems, such as prostitution, divorce, and unemployment, since these programs also may tend to reduce delinquency. Obviously, we cannot undertake so expansive a discussion here. Instead, we shall content ourselves with an examination of some of the most important programs that are directly related to the prevention of delinquency.[3]

## THE HOME

The home—the citadel of family life—is so basic, so vitally important, that it must be placed first in any discussion of the prevention of delinquency. Although its strength as an agency of social control has declined, the home remains the very foundation of our society. In fact, without it all else is to no avail. In it, the biological, affectional, economic, recreational, religious, educational, and protective functions of the family contribute to the making of the citizen of tomorrow, laying down foundations of character, ingraining habits, instilling principles, molding attitudes, and providing techniques, all of which tend to endure throughout the life of the individual. This, of course, should not be construed to mean that the family functions alone. As a social institution, it is interrelated and interdependent with all other social institutions and so tends to reflect and contribute to their organization and disorganization. Therefore, if we are to strengthen the home as a viable and constructive agency in the rearing and training of children, we must understand that forces both within and without the home produce strains and tensions in it and reduce its effectiveness in the prevention of delinquency and crime. As we have seen, these forces tend to produce four types of homes that especially increase the possibility of crime and delinquency.[4] They are the broken home, the functionally inadequate home, the socially, morally or culturally abnormal home, and the economically insecure home. Conse-

[3] See Lowell Juilliard Carr, "Organization for Delinquency Control," *The Annals of the American Academy of Political and Social Science*, CCLXI (January, 1949), 69, 70; Harrison Allen Dobbs, "Getting at the Fundamentals of Preventing Crime and Delinquency," *Federal Probation*, XIII (April–June, 1949), 3–9; John M. Martin, "Three Approaches to Delinquency Prevention: A Critique," *Crime and Delinquency*, VII (January, 1961), 16–24; Walter A. Lunden, "The Theory of Crime Prevention," *British Journal of Criminology*, II (January, 1962), 213–28; James C. Hackler, "Evaluation of Delinquency Prevention Programs: Ideals and Compromises," *Federal Probation*, XXXI (March, 1967), 22–26; Charles V. Morris, "Crime Prevention and Control Around the World," *Federal Probation*, XXXIX (December, 1965), 8–19. For a selected, annotated bibliography of prevention, see Lincoln Daniels (compiler), *The Prevention of Juvenile Delinquency*, U.S. Children's Bureau Publication (Washington, D.C.: Government Printing Office, 1969).

[4] See Sheldon and Eleanor T. Glueck, *Unraveling Juvenile Delinquency* (New York: The Commonwealth Fund, 1950), pp. 257–71. For an evaluation of the Glueck's study, see "Symposium on the Gluecks' Latest Research," *Federal Probation*, XV (March, 1951), 52–58.

quently, we should seek to reduce the number and influence of such homes, while at the same time giving due consideration to the social, economics, and political values that, as a nation, we cherish. The prevention of crime and delinquency is important, but it should not be sought in such a way as to endanger the republic, for, as we have indicated, if a society of a particular type is to retain its vigor, a certain amount of social problems must be considered the price that has to be paid for having that type of society.

However, there can be no denial that every society owes its children the best that nature can provide. Unfortunately, eugenics, the science that deals with the improvement of the hereditary qualities of man, has been neglected. And, yet, biology has been making important advances in the study of heredity. Certainly, its knowledge should be put to use through educational programs and counseling services. Men and women should be informed of the importance of providing their children with strong hereditary traits and urged not to have offspring if serious defective hereditary traits persist in their families. To this end, the studies of family trees should be increased, and their methodology improved.

Furthermore, observation and study indicate that if we hope to increase the role that the home can play in the prevention of crime, we should give special attention to husband-wife relationships, discipline of children, parental affection or rejection of children, identification between father and son, and family income. If one parent is absent, if there are too many children, or if there is discord between parents, parental control and authority are reduced and the child may thus be exposed to delinquent influences. Indeed, many studies have demonstrated that unhappy homes tend to produce more delinquent children than do happy ones. But happiness in the home is becoming more difficult to achieve, for the swirling current of conflicting values in modern society is confusing many parents and blinding them to their responsibilities. Nevertheless, they should courageously establish moral standards in the home, set an example by adhering to them, and follow a firm and consistent policy in the training, guidance, and discipline of their children.

Bewildered by so formidable a task, some parents abdicate and seek relief through extreme permissiveness. Some, frustrated and angered by their own ineptitude, resort to extreme severity. And some, overwhelmed by confusion, blunder into a vacillation between these two extremes. In all these instances, the child is deprived of the leadership and guidance that he needs and often progressively alienated from his parents. Extreme permissiveness may leave the child without an understanding of authority and with little inclination to accept its restrictions. He becomes accustomed to making his own decisions, often without consideration for the rights of others, and tends to see in the demands of authority an unreasonable challenge to his established independence. On the other hand, extreme severity tends to confuse and anger the child. Convinced that he has been unjustly treated, he may strike back at all representatives and symbols of authority. And, finally, erratic, vacillating discipline may engender anxiety, uncertainty, contempt, and eventually rebellion in the child. Thus, as these examples indicate, the improper disciplining of children tends to leave the child unprepared to handle the problems of life and to create habits and attitudes which may lead him into serious acts of delinquency. Apparently, even more conducive to delinquency than improper discipline is the failure of parents to give their children adequate love and affection. Crucial, too, for the behavior of the son is the absence of a strong father image that commands respect and provides a model for law-abiding behavior. And low family income, frustrating and blighting in its effects, may undermine the child's respect for his parents, drive him into evil companionship, and expose him to conditions that dwarf and corrupt.

In 1967, the President's Commission on Law Enforcement and Administration of Justice, after a consideration of these and other similar factors that are affecting the home, recommended that efforts, both private and public, should be intensified along these lines:

1. Reduce unemployment and devise methods of providing minimum family income.
2. Reexamine and revise welfare regulations so that they contribute to keeping the family together.
3. Improve housing and recreation facilities.
4. Insure availability of family planning assistance.
5. Provide help in problems of domestic management and child care.
6. Make counseling and therapy easily obtainable.
7. Develop activities that involve the whole family together.[5]

Some students of the problem of prevention would have explicitly listed birth control in these recommendations and would have emphasized the need of moral training in the home and the importance of achieving greater efficiency in the administration of the existing welfare laws and programs. However, whether or not we agree with the Commission's views—and many persons have some serious reservations—we must admit that the American home is being subjected to severe pressures. Perhaps it is true that "good" homes are much more common than many people realize. And let us suppose that most parents do love their children and want to give them protection and provide for their needs in every pos-

---

[5] The President's Commission on Law Enforcement and Administration of Justice, *The Challenge of Crime in a Free Society* (Washington, D.C.: Government Printing Office, 1967), pp. 63–66.

sible way.  Nevertheless, we can still understand why today even the best parents can benefit from the advice and services of specialists and professional agencies, and why additional efforts should be made to enable more families to provide better care and training for their children.[6]

## THE SCHOOL

The school, quite obviously, is in an excellent position to prevent delinquency; only the home is in a better position to do this.  The school has authority over every child of school age.  It exercises its influence over him many hours every week during his most impressionable years, and the law, public opinion, and almost all parents support and reinforce its efforts.[7]  So it can play an important part in any attack against delinquency.

Nevertheless, we must not let this distort our view of the essential responsibilities of the school.  It is not a clinic, a hospital, a welfare agency, a police station, or a correctional institution.  It is, instead, a place of learning—an educational institution—and we must not forget this.  And as an educational institution, it must establish and steadfastly maintain its own professional standards, strongly insist that its students measure up to these standards, and reward them with promotion and graduation only when this is done.  But even so, while it is discharging its essential responsibilities, it can still function effectively in a program of prevention.

### A Program of Prevention

In the first place, the school should provide an adequate program of study that fits the needs of all children and results in their wholesome growth and development.  For this purpose, the program must be as meaningful, diversified, and individualized as the resources of the school permit.  In slum areas, special efforts should be made to relate the instructional materials to conditions in the homes and neighborhoods of the children, to overcome the inadequate preschool preparation, to raise

[6] Caldwell, 701–3; National Conference on Prevention and Control of Juvenile Delinquency, *Report on Home Responsibility* (Washington, D.C.: Government Printing Office, 1947), pp. 5–18; The President's Commission on Law Enforcement and Administration of Justice, *Task Force Report: Juvenile Delinquency and Youth Crime* (Washington, D.C.: Government Printing Office, 1967), pp. 45–47, 188–221; 389–96; Ruth S. Tefferteller, "Delinquency Prevention Through Revitalizing Parent-Child Relations," *The Annals of the American Academy of Political and Social Science,* CCCXXII (March, 1959), 69–78; M. Stanton Evans and Margaret Moore, *The Lawbreakers* (New Rochelle, N.Y.: Arlington House, 1968), pp. 69, 70, 90–96.

[7] Caldwell, p. 703.

the aspirations and expectations of students capable of higher education, to offer better courses in child development and homemaking, and to strengthen vocational and technical training for those who will, and should, leave school as soon as the law permits. In addition, some educators urge that the compulsory school-attendance laws be modified so that children who can no longer benefit by attending school may leave at an earlier age and enter some business, trade, or industry.[8]

## Sex Education

There appears to be little opposition to most of the proposals that have been made to improve the school's program, but some have become highly controversial. For example, some leaders in the field of education believe that sex education should be made an integral part of the curriculum from preschool to college. This, they maintain, would help to dispel ignorance and misconceptions regarding sex and tend to reduce promiscuity, illegitimacy, and venereal disease.[9] In 1969, it was estimated that at least 60 per cent of all the school systems in the United States had formal courses in sex education, but serious objections to the sex education program have been raised by an increasing number of persons. They argue that it gives too much information too soon, shocking, frightening, and embarrassing many children with its crude frankness, that it features sex apart from the life situation and thus distorts its meaning and exaggerates its importance, and that it severs sex from morality and religion, exciting curiosity without instilling self-control and a sense of responsibility, and so actually provokes predatory experimentation with sex. Furthermore, they insist, the best place to learn about sex is in the home, but if any instruction about sex is to be offered in the school, then it should be given as a normal, inconspicuous, and logical part of a course in anatomy and physiology. As a matter of fact, they conclude, ten years of this program have not kept the District of

[8] Robert M. MacIver, *The Prevention and Control of Delinquency* (New York: Atherton Press, 1966), pp. 104–23; Carl L. Byerly, "A School Curriculum for Prevention and Remediation of Deviancy," *Social Deviancy Among Youth,* ed. William W. Wattenberg (Chicago: The National Society for the Study of Education, 1966), pp. 221–57; Bernice Milburn Moore, "The Schools and the Problems of Juvenile Delinquency: Research Studies and Findings," *Crime and Delinquency,* VII (July, 1961), 201–12 (this entire issue of *Crime and Delinquency* is devoted to articles on the school and delinquency); Berthold Demsch and Julia Garth, "Truancy Prevention: A First Step in Curtailing Delinquency Proneness," *Federal Probation,* XXXII (December, 1968), 31–37.

[9] Sex education is presently being aggressively promoted by the National Education Association of Washington, and the Sex Information and Education Council of the United States (SIECUS), with headquarters in New York City. Dr. Ralph Eckert, Program Chairman of the National Council on Family Relations, has sharply criticized all opposition of sex education and has stated that compulsory legislation should be passed to force all children to take courses in sex education.

Columbia from having one of the highest rates of illegitimacy and venereal disease in the United States.[10]

## Compensatory Education

Many prominent educators strongly support another controversial approach, the movement for compensatory education—so called because it aims to compensate children for initial disadvantages. In 1969, as a result of this movement, more than 20,000 programs and projects in communities throughout the country were reaching over 9 million children in about 17,000 school districts, or in three out of every four of these school units. Although this work had been initially sponsored by foundations and state and local governments, at that time it was being financed by the federal government at a cost of over $1 billion a year and was involving virtually every aspect of education, including such matters as preschool training, intensified education in various subjects, counseling and tutoring, food and health services, physical fitness, drop-out prevention, college preparation, parent participation, and so on.

Opponents of this movement contend that it has not significantly narrowed the educational gap between those who have been helped and other children, that it has wasted billions of dollars of the taxpayers' money, and that it has unrealistically inflated the hopes of thousands of children and their parents and then cruelly crushed them beneath one disappointment after another, thus filling them with angry and belligerent feelings and increasing their susceptibility to revolutionary propaganda. In support of their position, these opponents point to the dismal failures of many compensatory programs throughout the country, especially of such prominent ones as "Higher Horizons" (H.H.) and "More Effective Schools" (M.E.S.) in New York City, and to the admissions of defeat by prominent persons in the field of education. For example, Assistant United States Commissioner of Education Joseph Froomkin stated, "We still have little evidence that the problem is being licked; in fact, we may even be falling behind." Later in 1968, Alice M. Rivlin, Assistant Secretary of Evaluation and Planning of the Department of Health, Education, and Welfare, admitted, "Federal funds so far have failed to stop the downward spiral of poor children's achievements." These statements merely echoed the words of David K. Cohen of the Joint Center for Urban Studies at Harvard–M.I.T., who stated[11] that

---

[10] For some of the criticism that has been directed against sex education in the schools, see American Education Lobby, *Newsletter*, II (March, 1969); *ibid.*, *Sex Education: Assault on American Youth* (Washington, D.C.: April, 1969); "Why the Furor over Sex Education," *U.S. News and World Report*, LXVII (August 4, 1969), 44–46.

[11] David K. Cohen, Conference on Equal Education, Washington, D.C., November 16–18, 1967.

compensatory programs in urban schools had "resulted in no substantial improvement in students' academic competence."[12]

## Busing

Stunned by the failures of compensatory education programs, many educators are now advocating the "busing" of children from one school district to another so as to give all children access to an adequate program of study. They contend that racial, ethnic, and economic barriers tend to deprive the children of minority groups of educational and economic opportunities and thus contribute to delinquency, and, they insist, only the "busing" of children will destroy these barriers, which, they claim, tend to exist when schools are socially and racially homogeneous. Although they admit that at first this will send children of the upper classes into the poorer schools of the slum areas, the long-run effect, they argue, will be the "rapid upgrading of poor schools" through the influence exerted by the parents of these children.[13]

Opposition to the "busing" of children, however, is growing,[14] and here are some of the arguments that have been advanced against it:

1. The Coleman Report, which was sponsored by the United States Office of Education and based on a study (made in 1965–66 under the direction of James S. Coleman of Johns Hopkins University) of 4,000 schools with 600,000 children in grades 1 through 12, showed that the differences in the physical and economic resources of schools attended by Negro children and white children are *not* significant and thus do not provide an explanation for the difference in pupil performance.

2. Extensive research demonstrates that forced mixing of the races downgrades the schools by lowering the general achievement level, decreasing discipline and morale, and increasing the difficulty of obtaining competent teachers.

3. Research also reveals that when teachers and children are of different races, there is greater difficulty in communication, less empathy, and less learning, and that the resulting situation turns slow learners into children who refuse to learn at all, thus contributing to "drop-outs" and compensatory antisocial behavior.

4. There is now evidence from research in the field of educational psychology that discrepancies between the performances of whites and

[12] As reported in Roger A. Freeman, "The Alchemists in Our Public Schools," *Human Events*, XXIX (July 26, 1969), 519–22.

[13] The President's Commission on Law Enforcement and Administration of Justice favored the "busing" of children. See *The Challenge of Crime in a Free Society*, pp. 72, 73.

[14] American Education Lobby, *Newsletter*, II (March, 1969), 1, 2. See also "Local Schools Under Siege," American Education Lobby, *Newsletter*, II (June, 1969), 1, 3.

blacks cannot be completely or directly attributed to discrimination or inequalities in education, and that genetic differences between the two races must be taken into consideration.[15]

5. The policy of "busing" is practical only when it is based on legally enforced integration and so is a threat to the local control of public education and a move toward the centralization of power in a huge educational bureaucracy.

## Identifying Problem Children

The school should also try to identify children who appear susceptible to delinquency and adopt remedial measures to promote their better adjustment. The earlier a child's problems can be observed, recognized, and treated, the greater the possibility there is to overcome them. Efforts at identification, therefore, should begin as soon as possible, preferably in the kindergarten. Furthermore, all members of the school staff, especially the teachers, should be trained to identify problem children and to provide preliminary help and guidance. In his class work, the teacher should be particularly watchful for symptoms of personality problems among children who come from broken or badly organized homes or poor neighborhoods, or who play truant, lie, cheat, destroy property, belong to destructive gangs, or seem unhappy, seclusive, or sullen. However, if teachers are to be of much assistance in the identification of children who have delinquency tendencies, the size of classes must be limited to about twenty or twenty-five pupils.

Attempts have been made to develop tools and techniques for the early identification of children who may become delinquent. The Gluecks, Hathaway and Monachesi, and Kvaraceus have been especially active in this work.[16] Obviously, if effective tools and techniques for

---

[15] Arthur R. Jensen, "How Much Can We Boost IQ and Scholastic Achievement?" *Harvard Educational Review*, 39:1 (Winter, 1969), 1–123. For reactions to this article see the series of articles in *Harvard Educational Review*, 39:2 (Spring, 1969), 274–356.

[16] See Sheldon and Eleanor T. Glueck, *Predicting Delinquency and Crime* (Cambridge: Harvard University Press, 1959); Maude M. Craig and Selma J. Glick, "Ten Years' Experience with the Glueck Social Prediction Table," *Crime and Delinquency* (July, 1963), 249–61; *A Manual of Procedures for the Application of the Glueck Prediction Table* (New York: New York City Youth Board, Office of the Mayor, October, 1964); New York City Youth Board, *Delinquency Prediction, 1952–60: A Progress Report* (New York: New York City Youth Board, Research Department, October 1961); Starke R. Hathaway and J. Charnley McKinley, *The Minnesota Multiphasic Personality Inventory* (New York: Psychological Corporation, 1943); Starke R. Hathaway and Elio D. Monachesi (eds.), *Analyzing and Predicting Juvenile Delinquency with MMPI* (New York: Psychological Corporation, 1954); William C. Kvaraceus, "Forecasting Juvenile Delinquency: A Three-Year Experiment," *Exceptional Children*, XXVIII (April, 1961), 429–35; Alfred J. Kahn, "The Case of the Premature Claims—Public Policy and Delinquency Prediction," *Crime and Delinquency*, XI (July, 1965), 217–28.

the prediction of delinquency could be perfected, they would be of great help to the schools, but as yet, this has not been accomplished. Furthermore, some critics have warned that such devices should be used with great caution, since, they contend, if a child is officially labeled "predelinquent," he may begin to live up to the delinquency tag. Moreover, even if predictive instruments are greatly improved, they should never be used to the exclusion of a careful study of the individual child, for at best they can only indicate probability of delinquency and never certainty of it.[17]

Early identification of children who have more serious delinquency tendencies or unusual problems of adjustment should be followed by systematic referral of these cases to guidance counselors. In order to insure this, many schools now provide a variety of services, including those of physicians, attendance officers, counselors, social workers, psychologists, specialists in reading problems, visiting teachers, and so on. In some areas, like Passaic, New Jersey, when juvenile problems have become especially acute, even police have been added to the staffs of schools. These police not only supervise yards, halls, and corridors, but also work with the school's guidance personnel in dealing with the problems of delinquent children.[18] Although the school can make important contributions to the prevention of delinquency through its own program of identification, counseling, and adjustment, it should also enlist the support of other agencies and refer its more serious cases to them.[19]

## Special Schools and Classes

In addition, a number of larger school districts have established special schools and classes for maladjusted and delinquency-prone children. Only a few of these can be mentioned here. Gary, Indiana, for example,

[17] William C. Kvaraceus, "Programs of Early Identification and Prevention of Delinquency," *Social Deviancy Among Youth*, pp. 189–220; Charles F. Willford, "The Prediction of Delinquency," *Delinquency Prevention: Theory and Practice*, eds. William E. Amos and Charles F. Wellford (Englewood Cliffs, N.J.: Prentice-Hall, Inc., 1967), pp. 22–36; C. Ray Jeffery and Ina A. Jeffery, "Prevention Through the Family," *ibid.*, pp. 86–91.

[18] National Conference on Prevention and Control of Juvenile Delinquency, *Report on School and Teacher Responsibilities* (Washington, D.C.: Government Printing Office, 1947), pp. 3–8; William C. Kvaraceus and Walter B. Miller, *Delinquent Behavior: Culture and the Individual* (Washington, D.C.: National Education Association of the United States, 1959), pp. 122–41; Arthur S. Hill, Leonard M. Miller, and Hazel F. Gabbard, "Schools Face the Delinquency Problem," *The Bulletin* (a publication of the National Association of Secondary-School Principals), XXXVII (December, 1953), 188–95. See also William C. Kvaraceus, *Juvenile Delinquency and the School* (New York: World Book Co., 1945); George C. Boone, "The Passaic Children's Bureau," *Crime and Delinquency*, VII (July, 1961), 231–36.

[19] National Conference on Prevention and Control of Juvenile Delinquency, *Report on School and Teacher Responsibilities*, p. 6.

has done this. Attendance in its program is not compulsory; sessions last only half a day; and counseling is provided for the parents. New York City operates its well-known "600" schools for problem and delinquent children and the "700" schools for those who have more serious and persistent problems. Kingston, New York, is attempting to change the behavioral patterns of children with poor family backgrounds by providing them with a special program which has such courses as reading, writing, language arts, and development of cultural interests. Milwaukee has a work-study program in which boys receive academic and vocational training as well as remedial work and guidance. Kansas City's work-study program has three stages. The first stage, lasting from one to two years, consists of half-day classroom activities and half-day work assignments. This is followed by a period of half-day paid employment, and finally, when the child has reached the age of seventeen or eighteen, by a period of full-time employment under the supervision of school personnel.[20]

The school should work closely with parents and neighborhood leaders so as to develop a deeper understanding of the child and to help them eliminate influences that are detrimental to his health and welfare. This is not to say that the school should try to take the place of the home and all the character-building and welfare agencies of the community, but certainly it should support and reinforce their efforts. Some school districts, seeking to put more of the resources of the school at the disposal of the community, have inaugurated extended school programs. School buildings are kept open during the afternoons and, in some cases, during the evenings, Saturdays, and summer months for the use of both parents and children, and various leisure-time activities and programs, including games, music, dramatics, arts and crafts, homemaking, and so on, are organized for their benefit and enjoyment.[21]

However, a far more intensive effort to help parents and children is necessary in slum areas. In these areas, for example, the school should cooperate with families and welfare agencies in giving special attention to the needs, difficulties, and potentialities of "drop-outs." In some of these cases, the school should urge the parents to keep their children in school. However, in others, involving children who have no interest

---

[20] William E. Amos, "Prevention Through the School," *Delinquency Prevention: Theory and Practice*, pp. 128–32; Hill, Miller, and Gabbard, pp. 196–98; Edward H. Stullken, "The Schools and the Delinquency Problem," *Journal of Criminal Law, Criminology, and Police Science*, XLIII (January–February, 1953), 570–72; William C. Kvaraceus and William E. Ulrich, *Delinquent Behavior: Principles and Practices* (Washington, D.C.: National Education Association of the United States, 1959), pp. 174–220.

[21] Hill, Miller, and Gabbard, 215–17; Adele Franklin, "The All-Day Neighborhood Schools," *Crime and Delinquency*, VII (July, 1961), 255–62.

in the regular academic curriculum or who have insufficient ability to continue with it, the school should give the children work-experience courses directly related to the types of jobs on which they have a reasonable chance of being employed. In addition, the school should develop curricula designed to meet the changing needs of the job market and assist in placing juveniles in suitable positions in the community.[22]

## Home-School Relationship

And here another point must be kept in mind. While the child is going to school, his home and family relationships continue to exert what is usually the most important influence in his life. The school, therefore, should endeavor to understand his home life and develop a close and meaningful relationship with his parents. In the smaller communities, much of the responsibility for doing this will have to be borne by the teacher, but in the larger ones this work can be done chiefly by such professionally trained persons as counselors, visiting teachers, or social workers. In order to give greater vitality to the home-school relationship, additional steps like these should be taken:

1. Establishment of a program of parent education in child development and family relations under the direction of competent personnel.
2. Frequent conferences between the school staff and parents.
3. Utilization of the special abilities of certain parents in the planning and development of the school's program.
4. Organization and operation of parent-teacher groups under professional leadership.

The objective of all these activities, of course, is to combine the influences of the home and the school into a single effective force for the wholesome growth and development of the child.[23]

## The School as Part of Prevention

Thus, by the introduction of an adequate curriculum, the identification of children with serious behavioral problems, the counseling and guidance

---

[22] See MacIver, pp. 110–23; Nelson S. Burke and Alfred E. Simons, "Factors Which Precipitate Dropouts and Delinquency," *Federal Probation*, XXIX (March, 1965), 28–34; Milton F. Shore and Fortune V. Manning, "The School Dropout Situation: An Opportunity for Constructive Intervention," *ibid.*, (September, 1965), 41–44; Mark C. Roser, "On Reducing Dropouts," *ibid.*, (December, 1965), 49–55; Daniel Schreiber (ed.) *Profile of the School Dropout* (New York: Random House, Inc., 1967).

[23] See Harry J. Baker, "The Visiting Teacher Program and Delinquency Prevention," *Federal Probation*, XI (January–March, 1947), 30–34; Rachel D. Cox, "The School Counselor's Contribution to the Prevention of Delinquency," *Federal Probation*, XIV (March, 1950), 23–28.

of these children, the utilization of supportive community services, the creation of special classes and schools for maladjusted and delinquency-prone children, and the development of a cooperative and understanding relationship with parents and neighborhood leaders, the school, without undermining its own professional standards, can accomplish much in the prevention of delinquency. Nevertheless, its work must be seen as only part of a much broader program of prevention in which such organizations and agencies as churches, police departments, sheriffs' offices, courts, correctional institutions, probation and parole departments, child guidance clinics, family societies, welfare agencies, visiting nurses' associations, labor unions, and service clubs are either directly or indirectly participating, and therefore the school should do what it can to coordinate its efforts with theirs so that the impact of all will be greater.[24] Moreover, the "moral climate" in which the school operates is most important. As Caldwell explained:

> In our society the increasing emphasis on material possessions, the permissive attitudes of parents, and the everlasting evasion of effective discipline in the home and the school are contributing to the "get-away-with-it" philosophy of youth. Parents and teachers might well direct more attention to moral conduct and show less concern for the "flowering of personality" theory of child development. Children need and want the sense of security that comes from being so loved that they are told what to do. A definition of responsibility and a consistent application of penalties in both the home and the school would help children to accept the authority to which they must adjust in community life.[25]

## THE CHURCH [26]

The teachings of the church stress the highest spiritual and moral values of life, and so can exert great influence against crime and delinquency. There can be little question about this. But can the church play a more specific role in the prevention of these problems?

The church, it is said, can do this by taking the following steps:

1. Urge its members to assume leadership in community programs for the prevention of crime and delinquency and to serve on boards and councils of secular agencies involved in law enforcement and correction.

---

[24] National Conference on Prevention and Control of Juvenile Delinquency, *Report on School and Teacher Responsibilities,* p. 8; Kvaraceus and Ulrich, pp. 244–339; Paul W. Keve and Kenneth R. Young, "School and Court Working Together," *Crime and Delinquency,* VII (July, 1961), 242–48; Samuel M. Greenstone, "Getting the Returnee Back to School," *ibid.,* 249–54; MacIver, pp. 124–38.

[25] Caldwell, p. 707.

[26] The term "church" is used here in a broad sense to refer to all religious sects.

2. Encourage its young people to seek their life's work in fields where they can deal with social problems.

3. Provide guidance, counseling, and instruction for young people to strengthen their spiritual and moral values and assist them in the handling of their personal problems.

4. Organize meaningful and wholesome activities and group discussion periods for its young people.

5. Offer educational programs designed to prepare young people for marriage and family life and to assist parents in the solution of their family problems.

6. Furnish funds for indigent boys and girls to attend its summer camps.

7. Analyze its own programs for children to make sure that they are sound and meeting real needs.

8. Operate youth organizations which stress Christian education, character development, recreation, and so on.

9. Establish missions, settlement houses, and welfare agencies in poverty stricken areas.

10. Strive to give religion a more dignified and influential position in the programs of correctional institutions.

11. Point the way to the development of more effective correctional programs by utilizing in its own correctional institutions and agencies the best that science and human experience have to offer.

12. Invite judges, correctional workers, and law-enforcement officers to its study groups and conferences.

13. Bring as many children and adults as possible into its membership and services.

14. Cooperate with neighborhood organizations and citizen groups in handling common community problems, including crime and delinquency.[27]

Suggestions like these have produced virtually no opposition, but they do not go far enough to satisfy some religious leaders. They would take the church into such fundamentally secular concerns as federal aid to education, civil rights, urban renewal, disarmament, higher minimum wages, forcible union membership (closed shop), and so on. These

---

[27] National Conference on Prevention and Control of Juvenile Delinquency, *Report on Church Responsibilities* (Washington, D.C.: Government Printing Office, 1947), pp. 15–19; Robert and Muriel Webb, "How Churches Can Help in the Prevention and Treatment of Juvenile Delinquency," *Federal Probation*, XXI (December, 1957), 22–25; Marshall E. Miller, "The Place of Religion in the Lives of Juvenile Offenders," *ibid.*, XXIX (March, 1965), 50–53; Jerry B. Hissong, "The Role of the Church in Preventing Crime and Delinquency," *ibid.*, XXXII (December, 1968), 50–54; George Edward Powers," Prevention Through Religion," *Delinquency Prevention: Theory and Practice*, pp. 99–127.

leaders, however, have not gone unchallenged. Their opponents have called them "incompetent evangelists of the structures of society," and have presented this argument: Action to alleviate existing social ills should be taken by *individual church members* through such secular organizations as political parties, chambers of commerce, labor unions, parent-teacher associations, and service clubs and not by committing *the church as a corporate body* to controversial positions on which its members are sharply divided into warring camps and thus "stirring dissensions in the one place where spiritual unity should prevail." Furthermore, the opponents contend, when church leaders maintain lobbies in Washington and try to dictate what legislation should be passed on almost every conceivable economic, social, and political subject, they are endangering the separation of church and state, a principle which is deeply embedded in our culture and one to which they themselves would appeal if Congress sought to interfere with church matters.

These opponents of extended secular activities by the church are particularly distressed when members of the clergy and other church leaders justify their violation of federal, state, and local laws on the grounds that these are "bad" laws and that the only way to change them is to break them. This is a disgraceful position for church leaders to take, insist these opponents, for it can result only in an increase in crime and delinquency and eventually in the end of rule by law and the onrush of anarchy. This frenetic devotion to "social action" by church leaders in the United States has caused a theologian of the Church of England to declare that "it would be tragically ironic if the church, grown skeptical about God's power to redeem society by transforming human nature, were to fall into the same ideological error as communism and attempt to transform man by altering his environment." [28]

[28] Quoted by J. Howard Pew, chairman of the board of Sun Oil Co. and former president of the board of trustees of the General Assembly of the United Presbyterian Church in the U.S.A. (now the United Presbyterian Foundation) in his article, "Should the Church 'Meddle' in Civil Affairs?," in the May, 1966, issue of the *Reader's Digest*. Pew's views have been extensively drawn on here in presenting the arguments of those who oppose "social action" by the church.

# 20

# Prevention: Other Agencies and Programs

## ORGANIZED RECREATION

Organized recreation, it is claimed, can make an important contribution to the prevention of juvenile delinquency. The term "organized recreation," as it is usually employed, refers to the programs of such agencies as camps, playgrounds, scout and ranger organizations, boys' clubs, settlement houses, and so on. Participation in these programs— so the argument goes—will not only keep juveniles away from delinquent activities, but also help them to acquire law-abiding attitudes, habits, and interests.[1]

Various studies have been made to determine whether organized recreation is effective in preventing juvenile delinquency. Thus, Frederic Thrasher studied the operation of the Boys' Club of New York City during its initial four years from 1927 to 1931. He found that the members of the club were more delinquent than other boys in the community who were not members, and that the boys were more delinquent while active members than before or after the period of their membership. It is true that the study covered only the four initial years of the club's existence, and that it drew largely on the poorer classes for its membership. Nevertheless, there can be no question that for the period studied the club was not an effective agency of prevention. Thrasher, however, remained steadfast in his belief that the boys' club is one of the most important and essential elements in any crime and delinquency prevention program. Furthermore, he insisted that we need many more boys'

[1] National Conference on Prevention and Control of Juvenile Delinquency, *Report on Case Work—Group Work* (Washington, D.C.: Government Printing Office, 1947), pp. 13–15, 22, 23.

clubs in order to increase the effectiveness of our preventive efforts.[2] Thrasher's study has been called "the most careful and intensive study of the effect of a boys' club on delinquency,"[3] and its findings tended to dampen the enthusiasm of those who were making extreme claims about the power of the boys' club in the field of prevention.

The faith that Thrasher had in the boys' club appeared to find support in a study that was made in Louisville, Kentucky. There, the delinquency rates decreased steadily during an eight-year period in an area where a boys' club operated but increased during the same period in two other areas where no youth-serving agencies existed. Even so, as this study admitted, influences other than those of the boys' club might have produced the decline in delinquency in the area when the boys' club operated.[4]

Over twenty-five years ago, the Chicago Recreation Commission made a study of five selected communities in the Chicago area in order to ascertain the relationship between recreation and juvenile delinquency.[5] This study revealed that a higher percentage of nondelinquents than delinquents participated in supervised recreation, that when delinquents took part in supervised recreation, they preferred competitive sports and activities such as those in the game room where there was little supervision, and that participation in supervised recreation appeared to reduce delinquency. Although the results of this study were far from conclusive —the significance of some of the findings being dubious—the Chicago Recreation Commission recommended that more supervised recreation should be provided in all the neighborhoods of Chicago, especially where the delinquency rate was higher than the average for the city as a whole, that recreational agencies should make an effort to reach and hold boys of fourteen years and over, that recreation programs should be designed to attract and influence delinquents and energetic adolescents, that "unofficial" delinquents should be given individualized treatment, and that the home and all community agencies should be organized into a coordinated attack against delinquency.[6]

A few years after this Chicago study, the crime-prevention associa-

[2] Frederic M. Thrasher, "The Boys' Club and Juvenile Delinquency," *American Journal of Sociology*, XLII (July, 1936), 66–80.

[3] Edwin H. Sutherland, *Principles of Criminology* (Philadelphia: J. B. Lippincott Co., 1947), p. 619.

[4] Roscoe C. Brown, Jr., and Dan W. Dodson, "The Effectiveness of a Boys' Club in Reducing Delinquency," *The Annals of the American Academy of Political and Social Science*, CCCXXII (March, 1959), 47–52. This entire issue of the *Annals* is devoted to articles on the prevention of juvenile delinquency.

[5] See Ethel Shanas and Catherine E. Dunning, *Recreation and Delinquency* (Chicago: Chicago Recreation Commission, 1942), pp. 236–44.

[6] Robert G. Caldwell, *Criminology* (New York: The Ronald Press Co., 1965), pp. 710, 711.

tion of Philadelphia conducted an investigation and concluded that the recreation programs in that city had caused a decrease in minor offenses but had failed to effect any change in the number of serious offenses. Even so, this association believed that when recreation is used properly, it "does have a therapeutic value in the adjustment of behavior cases." [7] Another study conducted in Cincinnati showed that the rate of delinquency among the clientele of the group-work agencies there was not so high as that of the city as a whole. However, it could not be demonstrated that this difference in the rates of delinquency was the result of the efforts of the group-work agencies, for other factors were involved.[8]

Organized recreation is not attracting many young people who might benefit by it. Consequently, in some cities, for example, in Boston, New York, and Chicago, efforts have been made to take recreation to young people. This has been done through the services of the "detached worker," who, as his name indicates, is not associated with any particular facility, like a playground or community center. Instead, he works in a neighborhood and makes his initial contacts with young people on the streets. After becoming acquainted with them, he tries to win the confidence of juvenile gangs, and then seeks to lead them into some program of organized recreation.[9] The "detached worker," therefore, might be called the missionary of organized recreation, and like all missionaries, his qualifications must be above the average. Thus far, however, it is not clear how successful his efforts have been, and more studies of this type of approach are needed.[10]

As the foregoing studies indicate, no one has been able to prove conclusively that organized recreation has prevented juvenile delinquency. Nevertheless, authorities generally agree that it can exert an important preventive influence if it is skillfully planned, adequately staffed, sufficiently attractive to lure young people from the excitement of delinquency, strongly supported with guidance facilities and individu-

---

[7] J. Francis Finnegan, "The Work of the Crime Prevention Units of Philadelphia," *Proceedings of the American Prison Association, 1949*, p. 265.

[8] Ellery F. Reed, "How Effective Are Group-Work Agencies in Preventing Delinquency?," *Focus*, XXVIII (November, 1949), 170–76.

[9] Sidney G. Lutzin and R. C. Orem, "Prevention Through Recreation," *Delinquency Prevention: Theory and Practice*, eds. William E. Amos and Charles F. Wellford (Englewood Cliffs, N.J.: Prentice-Hall, Inc., 1967), pp. 150–70.

[10] For some of the studies that have used this approach, see Paul L. Crawford, James R. Dumpson, and Daniel I. Malamud, *Working with Teen-Age Gangs* (New York: Welfare Council of New York City, 1950); Walter B. Miller, "Preventive Work with Street-Corner Groups: Boston Delinquency Project," *The Annals of the American Academy of Political and Social Science*, CCCXXII (March, 1959), 97–106; John M. Gandy, "Preventive Work with Street-Corner Groups: Hyde Park Youth Project, Chicago," *ibid.*, 107–16.

alized supervision and treatment, and closely coordinated with other agencies in a general attack on crime and delinquency.[11]

## COUNSELING AND GUIDANCE

Psychiatrists and psychologists, unlike sociologists, tend to emphasize the mental and emotional processes of individuals as the causes of problems like juvenile delinquency. Their treatment for these problems is called psychotherapy, during which a trained person seeks to remove, modify, or retard existing symptoms, to mediate disturbed patterns of behavior, and to promote positive personality growth and development. Psychotherapy may be divided into three types:

1. *Supportive therapy*, which aims to strengthen defenses and restore adaptive equilibrium, and which includes such approaches as guidance, environmental manipulation, persuasion, suggestive hypnosis, drug therapy, shock therapy, and inspirational group therapy.
2. *Reeducational therapy*, which seeks to develop insights into the more conscious conflicts and produce a definite personality readjustment, and which includes such approaches as therapeutic counseling, casework therapy, and reeducative group therapy.
3. *Reconstructive therapy*, which strives to achieve insights into unconscious conflicts and effect extensive alterations of character structure, and which includes such approaches as psychoanalysis, hypoanalysis,[12] and analytic group therapy.[13]

These types, however, do not remain distinct in the practice of the therapist, who uses whatever approach, skill, or technique seems best fitted to effect the desired results in the case.

The psychotherapeutic approach to the prevention of delinquency extends back to the early part of this century, developing out of the mental hygiene movement and the conceptions of dynamic psychology. The first psychiatric clinic for children in the United States was established by Dr. William Healy in 1909, in the juvenile court of Chicago, and it was operated exclusively for delinquents. Ohio followed in 1915, setting up a clinic for the treatment of juvenile delinquents in its department of public welfare, and shortly thereafter, Michigan took similar

---

[11] Caldwell, 711, 712.
[12] Hypnosis is used in hypnoanalysis to accelerate the process of psychoanalysis.
[13] Lewis R. Wolberg, *The Technique of Psychotherapy* (New York: Grune and Stratton, 1954), pp. 3–16.

action. By the middle of this century, there were about 500 full-time and part-time clinics for children in the United States, some of which functioned mainly for diagnostic purposes in connection with juvenile courts.[14]

Efforts have been made to determine the effectiveness of the child guidance clinics. A study by the Gluecks of 1,000 boys who had been referred by the juvenile court of Boston to the Judge Baker Guidance Center found that 88 per cent of them had become delinquent again within five years after the end of their official treatment, and the 70 per cent had been convicted of serious offenses during that time.[15] This research led to the conclusion that child guidance service of the kind provided for the juvenile court of Boston was ineffectual in reducing recidivism. Another study by Healy and Bronner showed that 70 per cent of the delinquents handled by a guidance clinic responded satisfactorily to treatment.[16] A third study conducted in Berkeley, California, revealed that problem children who were treated in school clinics during a two-year period improved, whereas some maladjusted children who were not so treated manifested little improvement.[17] In 1941, Nathaniel Cantor, writing about crime prevention, stated that an examination of the work done by child guidance clinics in the United States seemed to show that about one-third of all cases made satisfactory adjustment.[18] It must be emphasized, however, that the child guidance clinic cannot claim credit for all the improvement shown by children who have been treated by it, since other influences, like those of parents and friends, continue to operate in the lives of these children during and after treatment. Even so, in 1954, Witmer and Tufts concluded that although child guidance clinics could do little for children who had been subjected to very harmful environmental influences or who were suffering from extreme personality disorders, they could help most of the others that they were accepting for treatment.[19]

Those who have planned prevention programs have often expressed

---

[14] National Conference on Prevention and Control of Juvenile Delinquency, *Report on Mental Health and Child Guidance Clinics* (Washington, D.C.: Government Printing Office, 1947), pp. 2, 3; Helen L. Witmer and Edith Tufts, *The Effectiveness of Delinquency Prevention Programs*, U.S. Children's Bureau Publication No. 350 (Washington, D.C.: Government Printing Office, 1954), pp. 34–36.

[15] Sheldon and Eleanor T. Glueck, *One Thousand Juvenile Delinquents* (Cambridge: Harvard University Press, 1934), p. 167.

[16] William Healy and Augusta F. Bronner, *Treatment and What Happened Afterward* (Boston: The Judge Baker Guidance Center, 1939), pp. 42, 43.

[17] Nathaniel Cantor, "Organized Efforts in Crime Prevention," *The Annals of the American Academy of Political and Social Science*, CCXVII (September, 1941), 158.

[18] *Ibid.*

[19] Witmer and Tufts, p. 40.

the opinion that many boys and girls would not have become delinquent if they had received help, guidance, and counseling from wise, loving adult friends. In 1935, a program which put these ideas into effect was set up in Cambridge, Massachusetts, in such a way as to test their efficacy in the prevention of delinquency. This program, which is known as the Cambridge-Somerville Youth Study, was conceived, organized, and financed by the late Dr. Richard Cabot of Harvard. The working principles of this study differed from those of the usual social casework agency in several important respects. First, those directing the study were to seek out boys and their families and urge them to accept social services instead of waiting for applications or referrals of individuals. Second, work with each boy was to be continuous until late adolescence instead of being ended when the problems were "cleared up." Third, personal intimacy and friendship, rather than a "casework relationship," was to be the basis of the counselors' influence.[20] This ten-year research project in delinquency prevention involved the treatment of some 325 boys by counselors, who utilized whatever skills they were capable of applying, and the use of a carefully selected control group, the members of which received no help at all from the counselors.

The results of the Cambridge-Somerville Youth Study may be summarized as follows:

1. The work of the counselors was no more effective than the usual forces in the community in preventing delinquency.
2. Although the first stages of delinquency were not wholly averted when treatment was begun at the 8-11 year level, the later and more serious stages were averted to some degree.
3. In many cases, even those of many of the delinquent boys, emotional conflicts were alleviated, practical problems were dealt with successfully, and boys were given greater confidence to face life's problems.[21]

According to Witmer and Tufts, this study seems to indicate that the kind of friendly guidance and other services that it provided will not reduce delinquent acts or keep chronic delinquency from developing. However, this conclusion, they added, does not mean that such services are not useful to certain children, especially to nondelinquents, but that they were particularly ineffectual with the kinds of boys who became

---

[20] *Ibid.*, p. 27.
[21] Edwin Powers, "An Experiment in Prevention of Delinquency," *The Annals of the American Academy of Political and Social Science*, CCLXI (January, 1949), 77–88. See also Edwin Powers and Helen Witmer, *An Experiment in the Prevention of Delinquency: The Cambridge-Somerville Youth Study* (New York: Columbia University Press, 1951).

chronic delinquents, including "slum boys with indifferent, neglectful parents, seriously neurotic boys, from various kinds of neighborhoods, who had even more emotionally unfavorable homes, and feebleminded or neurologically handicapped boys whose homes, too, were poor." [22]

In a later appraisal of the Cambridge-Somerville Youth Study, the McCords, after a comparison of twelve "treated" with twelve "untreated" boys—which they admitted did not represent an adequate sample— concluded that "intimate, long-term 'supportive' counseling may prevent crime." Even so, they stated that the Cambridge-Somerville Youth Study was "largely a failure" when it was judged by the "standard of 'official' criminal behavior." [23]  Other recent studies of projects at Highfields and Essexfields in New Jersey, and at Pinehills in Provo, Utah, seem to indicate that counseling and guided group interaction can contribute to the rehabilitation of juvenile delinquents, but the results of these studies, as we have already explained, cannot be called conclusive.[24]

## COMMUNITY PROGRAMS

One of the most widely known community programs is the Chicago Area Project, which was begun in 1934 as an outgrowth of the "delinquency area" studies of Clifford Shaw and his colleagues.  By 1948, this project had grown until it included fourteen local neighborhood units, which were operating in ten areas of high delinquency in Chicago.  The Chicago Area Project is based on the assumption that much of the delinquency in slum areas can be attributed to the lack of neighborhood cohesiveness and the resulting indifference on the part of many residents about the welfare of children.  To counteract this situation, the project encourages local self-help enterprises through which a sense of neighborliness and mutual responsibility can develop.  This program, therefore, tends to reflect the basic needs, interests, and sentiments of the people themselves, although it does receive financial support from the outside as well as guidance from professionally trained workers, who, however, seek to function only as consultants and advisors and not as leaders.  Since it is the policy of the project to secure the cooperation of churches, schools, recreation centers, labor unions, industries, and other resources in each area in order to create a coordinated attack upon neighborhood

[22] Witmer and Tufts, p. 30.
[23] Joan and William McCord, "A Follow-up Report on the Cambridge-Somerville Youth Study," *The Annals of the American Academy of Political and Social Science,* CCCXXII (March, 1959), 89–96.
[24] See Chapter 17, "Juvenile Institutions."

problems, the Chicago Area Project has been called a coordinated community program.[25] Despite the fact that it has been functioning for over three decades, there is still little objective evidence about its effectiveness, and even those who have been associated with it are in disagreement as to its achievements. A number of years ago, Sutherland, in attempting to make an evaluation of it, wrote that "perhaps the best that can be said in appraisal of these Area Projects is that they are consistent with an important theory of criminal behavior and with the ideals of democracy."[26] In 1959, Kobrin stated that the project had probably reduced delinquency, although this could not be precisely measured, and Sorrentino, while conceding that it could not definitely claim credit for preventing delinquency, expressed the opinion that it had encouraged wider participation in democratic social action programs.[27] Regardless of what the Chicago Area Project has been able to accomplish in the past, its work in the future may be more difficult, for the composition of the population in its areas is rapidly changing and the new residents may be less inclined than their predecessors to participate in the program.[28]

Another coordinated community program that has attracted considerable attention is the Back of the Yards' Neighborhood Council, which is located in the area near the stockyards in Chicago. Established by the Industrial Areas Foundation—which began its work in 1939—it encourages the community to participate in the organization and operation of its own program. In this respect, it is like the Chicago Area Project; but unlike that project, it is not primarily interested in the prevention of crime and delinquency but rather in the development of a "democratically minded people," who are organized to promote their own welfare. The Back of the Yards' Neighborhood Council has been given credit for having improved the conditions in the local community and for having fostered better relations between organizations that had been

---

[25] Clifford R. Shaw and Henry D. McKay, *Juvenile Delinquency and Urban Areas* (Chicago: University of Chicago Press, 1942), pp. 442–46; American Prison Association, *Report of the Committee on Crime Prevention* (New York: The American Prison Association, 1942), pp. 8, 9; Clifford R. Shaw and Jesse A. Jacobs, *The Chicago Area Project: An Experimental Community Program for Prevention of Delinquency in Chicago* (Chicago: Institute of Juvenile Research [Mimeographed]), Cited by Walter C. Reckless, *The Crime Problem* (New York: Appleton-Century-Crofts, Inc., 1950), pp. 517, 518; Witmer and Tufts, pp. 11–17.

[26] Sutherland, p. 618.

[27] Solomon Kobrin, "The Chicago Area Project—A 25 Year Assessment," *The Annals of the American Academy of Political and Social Science*, CCCXXII (March, 1959), 19–29; Anthony Sorrentino, "The Chicago Area Project After 25 Years," *Federal Probation*, XXIII (June, 1959), 40–45.

[28] Anthony Sorrentino, *The Story of the Chicago Area Project*, mimeographed (Chicago: The Chicago Area Project, April, 1962).

in conflict, but it has been adversely criticized for its failure to recognize the importance of professional leadership and guidance.[29]

Within recent years, many types of community programs for the prevention of crime and delinquency have been established throughout the United States. Some of these have stressed employment; some, education, as for example in Head Start, Upward Bound, and Job Corps; some, slum clearance; many have sought to stimulate local coordinated action in various neighborhood projects.[30] Limitations of space, however, permit the mention of only the concentrated attack on multiproblem families, a program that has received wide-spread attention. This program grew out of the research efforts of the New York City Youth Board, the city's official agency for the prevention and control of juvenile delinquency. During 1957, it learned that 75 per cent of the delinquency in New York City had its source in an estimated twenty thousand multiproblem families which represented less than 1 per cent of all the families in that city. A citywide register of these families was created and used as a basis for a coordinated service plan for each of them. "Aggressive casework," a technique which is so called because it searches for the client instead of waiting for him to apply for help, is employed to provide intensive treatment for the multiproblem families. Similar programs are being used in Chicago and St. Paul.[31]

Some writers have claimed that this type of attack on juvenile delinquency has had some success, although they have submitted no definite proof of this. Others, however, have labeled it a failure. One reason for this alleged failure, it is said, is the splitting of the family into "many categorized problems" and then assigning a "different worker to each category as crises occur." This "fragmentation of responsibility among agencies leads inevitably to fragmentation of services to families, and even to fragmented perception of problems within one family." [32] Instead of following this procedure, we should, according to one critic, (1) assess the family situation in terms of what the city—not one agency—needs

[29] American Prison Association, *Report of the Committee on Crime Prevention*, 9, 10; Saul D. Alinsky, *Reveille for Radicals* (Chicago: University of Chicago Press, 1946), pp. 77–86.

[30] For an examination of some of these programs, see William E. Amos, Raymond L. Manella, and Marilyn A. Southwell, *Action Programs for Delinquency Prevention* (Springfield, Ill.: Charles C. Thomas, 1965). For a discussion of the Indianapolis Anti-Crime Crusade, see M. Stanton Evans and Margaret Moore, *The Lawbreakers* (New Rochelle, N.Y.: Arlington House, 1968), pp. 195–266.

[31] Ralph W. Whelan, *Annual Report to the Mayor by the Executive Director, 1957* (New York: New York City Youth Board, Jan. 10, 1958); Charles J. Birt, "Family-Centered Project of St. Paul," *Social Work*, I (October, 1956), 41–47; Sophia M. Robison, "Why Juvenile Delinquency Prevention Programs Are Ineffective," *Federal Probation*, XXV (December, 1961), 34–41.

[32] Nina B. Trevvett, "Treatment Planning for Multiproblem Families," *Crime and Delinquency*, XIII (April, 1967), 307–16.

to do, (2) survey the total family as a single unit, (3) decide on a plan of action, (4) assign one worker to the family and make him responsible for all the treatment given to the family, (5) stimulate neighborhood action for self-improvement, and (6) use community development as part of the treatment process so as to assimilate the problem family more quickly into the life of the neighborhood.[33]

## HOUSING

Most of the "bad housing" of the country is located in the slum areas of large cities, but some of it—in fact, some of the worst of it—can be found in smaller cities and towns and even in rural areas. "Bad housing" does not directly cause delinquency; rather, it contributes to it in various indirect ways. First, the low rentals tend to attract many persons who already have developed criminal and delinquent habits and attitudes, and who then make the neighborhood a breeding place for more crime and delinquency. Second, the dirt, the filth, the unsanitary conditions, the congestion and lack of privacy, the poor ventilation, the darkness, the dankness, the smells, the ugliness, the shabbiness, the rot and deterioration—all these and other similar conditions—conspire to undermine health, lower morale, destroy pride and self-respect, weaken ambition, depress the spirit, increase friction, exacerbate tensions, sharpen conflict, and thus reduce the individual's resistance to criminal and delinquent influences. Third, "bad housing" drives away many of the law-abiding, who seek better living conditions elsewhere and thus remove their beneficial influence from the old neighborhood.

Early slum clearance projects and public housing developments appeared to contribute significantly to the reduction of crime and delinquency. The improvement, however, was more apparent than real, for what actually happened in many cases was the replacement of criminal and delinquent persons with those who were already law-abiding, without having effected any change in the behavior of the former, who simply went elsewhere to continue their violations of the law. Furthermore, in many other cases, the criminal and delinquent persons remained in the new housing but did not change their behavior in any way. The lesson here, then, is clear. Better housing, *per se*, does not prevent crime and delinquency. It may help, but is certainly no panacea; and much of its effectiveness depends on the education, counseling, guidance, and welfare assistance that should accompany new housing developments. This, of course, is no argument against slum clearance and improvement of housing—for "bad housing" and slum areas do increase the possibility

[33] *Ibid.*, 314–16.

of crime and delinquency—but it does remind us of the difficulties involved in any prevention program.[34]

## THE POLICE

One of the basic objectives of the police is the prevention of crime and delinquency, and they are in a strategic position to do this work. Of all the agencies that are directly concerned with the control of these problems, the police have the most clearly defined legal authority to act, the strongest organization for quick and decisive action, the best local and national records on offenders and their methods, and the most adequately trained, equipped, and deployed personnel.[35]

The police prevention program should include at least the following elements:

1. The patrol, inspection, and investigation of establishments, dance halls, poolrooms, bowling alleys, swimming pools, skating rinks, parks, playgrounds, vacant lots, and other places where young people may gather and come into contact with unwholesome influences, so that persons, places, and conditions contributing to crime and delinquency can be detected and supressed or eliminated.

2. The identification of predelinquents and delinquents, the determination of their needs, and the referral of them to the juvenile court or other agencies.

3. The participation by law-enforcement personnel in the broader community program of crime and delinquency prevention.[36]

[34] Sydney Maslen, "Housing and Juvenile Delinquency," Federal Probation, XII (June, 1948), 40–44; Harrison E. Salisbury, The Shook-up Generation (New York: Harper and Row, 1958), Ch. 5, "The New Ghettos"; Harry Manuel Shulman, Juvenile Delinquency in American Society (New York: Harper and Row, 1961), pp. 256–62.

[35] National Conference on Prevention and Control of Juvenile Delinquency, Report on Role of Police (Washington, D.C.: Government Printing Office, 1947), pp. 7–9; O. W. Wilson, Police Administration (New York: McGraw-Hill Book Co., Inc., 1963), pp. 327–29.

[36] Wilson, pp. 331–42, 347–52; A. F. Brandstatter and James J. Brennan, "Prevention Through the Police," Delinquency Prevention: Theory and Practice, pp. 193–206; V. A. Leonard, Police Organization and Management (Brooklyn: The Foundation Press, Inc., 1964), pp. 250–54; John P. Kenney and Dan G. Pursuit, Police Work with Juveniles (Springfield, Ill.: Charles C. Thomas, 1965), pp. 6, 7, 56, 57, 63, 64; Edward Eldefonso, Law Enforcement and the Youthful Offender: Juvenile Procedures (New York: John Wiley and Sons, Inc., 1967), 56, 57; Richard A. Myren and Lynn D. Swanson, Police Work with Children, United States Children's Bureau Publication No. 399 (Washington, D.C.: Government Printing Office, 1962), pp. 1–19.

Many of the larger police departments now have juvenile bureaus, and where such bureaus exist, they should have the major responsibility for the operation of the prevention program. Obviously, however, every law-enforcement officer can accomplish a great deal in the prevention of delinquency, and he should, therefore, receive some special training for this purpose. Although police officials differ regarding the extent to which they should participate in a program for the prevention of crime and delinquency, they generally agree that they could do more if certain obstacles were removed. They are particularly concerned about the low salaries and inadequate personnel in law-enforcement agencies, the laws which interfere with the effective apprehension and prosecution of dangerous juvenile offenders, the insufficient public support of police work, and the inefficient administration of detention facilities, juvenile courts, probation departments, correctional institutions, and parole systems.[37]

### Relations With Parents

Some officials advocate the punishment of parents for the delinquent acts of their children. This, it is argued, would force parents to assume greater responsibility in the training and supervision of their children and enable the victims of delinquency to collect restitution. In opposition to this proposal, it has been explained that often parents are not entirely responsible for the delinquency of their children, that in many cases punitive action would be ineffective, that many parents could be influenced more through education and counseling than through punishment, that many families do not have enough money to make restitution payments, and that the punishment of the parents might destroy the home and cause the family to become a public charge. There does not appear to be any sound reason for the adoption of a general policy for the punishment of parents in delinquency cases. Of course, sometimes parents should be punished, but a decision to do this should be based on the facts of the individual case.

### Other Proposals and Programs

The use of the curfew is another favorite proposal of some law-enforcement officials, who contend that it provides both parents and the police with a clear and uniform basis for dealing with juveniles after a certain time in the evening. Undoubtedly, the curfew has been helpful in many communities, but its opponents insist that it suffers from many limitations. Thus they argue that the police are faced with the problem

[37] National Conference on Prevention and Control of Juvenile Delinquency, *Report on Role of Police*, pp. 15–17; Wilson, pp. 329–31, 336.

of ascertaining whether the juvenile is above or below the age set by the curfew law, that many parents resent having their children stopped and questioned by the police, that it does little to remove the causes of delinquency, and that it is most effective in the regulation of the juveniles who are carefully supervised by their parents and so the least likely to become delinquent.[38]

Less controversial is the proposal that the police establish school safety patrols, which utilize boys and girls for full traffic control at most intersections near schools. This type of patrol enjoys widespread support among both educators and police, since it provides an opportunity for the development of an extensive safety education program in the schools and the promotion of good relations between juveniles and the police. Some authorities, however, believe that the police should do more than merely participate in limited activities of this kind, and that instead they should actually occupy a position of leadership in the development and operation of broad community prevention programs. Even in rural areas, they contend, the police should assume responsibility in planning and developing services for young people and work through farm organizations, schools, churches, parent-teacher associations, and service clubs in marshaling public opinion in support of the improvement of rural police agencies.[39]

One of the most elaborately organized police prevention programs in the United States is in New York City. Important units in this program are: (1) the Juvenile Aid Bureau (JAB), which emphasizes the creation of a more favorable attitude on the part of youth toward law enforcement; (2) the Police Athletic League (PAL), which seeks to instill good character, a sense of responsibility, and the development of a friendly relationship between youth and police officers; and (3) Precinct Coordinating Councils, which strive to coordinate and promote the work of existing agencies and to educate the public to an awareness of their responsibility to youth.[40]

## Police Public Relations

The vigorous and efficient enforcement of the law by a police agency, in itself and apart from any special program of prevention, contributes in a significant way to the prevention of crime and delinquency. Even

[38] For an examination of the curfew question, see "Curfew Ordinances and the Control of Nocturnal Juvenile Crime," *University of Pennsylvania Law Review,* CVII (November, 1958), 66–101; John E. Winters, *Crime and Kids* (Springfield, Ill.: Charles C. Thomas, 1959), pp. 27–34.

[39] National Conference on Prevention and Control of Juvenile Delinquency, *Report on Role of Police,* pp. 9–11.

[40] James B. Nolan, "The Crime Prevention Work of New York City's Police," *Federal Probation,* XI (April–June, 1947), 18–21.

so, it must be remembered that all police work is greatly facilitated by the maintenance of good public relations. With the development of these relations come more effective reporting of offenses, more productive investigations, larger budgets, better personnel, more modern buildings and equipment, and, fewer crimes and delinquencies. However, the leadership in this development must come from those who know law enforcement best, that is, the police themselves, although, of course, prominent citizens in the community can certainly help a great deal.

A police program for the establishment of good public relations should have these objectives:

1. The avoidance of public resentment by the fair and reasonable enforcement of the law.
2. The development of good will through the performance of courteous, efficient, and economical services.
3. The education of the public regarding the work and the problems of the police.[41]

To reach these objectives a department must have police officers who are physically fit, neat, alert, courteous, and efficient and policies, procedures, and methods that are designed to establish and maintain high standards of operation and a firm, fair, and impartial enforcement of the law. Yet there must be more than this. The department must have also a program especially directed toward the establishment of good public relations—a program that should stress such matters as (1) the creating of harmonious relations with the press, radio, and television, (2) the giving of public talks, lectures, and demonstrations by officers on various aspects of police work, (3) the providing of special services for the distressed and the visitors to the city, (4) the making of surveys to facilitate the flow of traffic and reduce accidents, (5) the furnishing of advice to businessmen on the prevention of vandalism and other offenses against their property, and (6) the public granting of awards to officers for outstanding services.

But should there be a civilian board with power to review the activities of the police department? The answer is no if this board would interfere in any way with the department's authority over personnel management and discipline. To permit this interference would undermine and destroy the authority of the chief, open the door to the politics of pressure groups, and thus block the progress that is being made toward the professionalization of police services. This does not mean, however, that there might not be a board of distinguished citizens

[41] Wilson, pp. 182–224; G. Douglas Gourley, "Police Public Relations," *The Annals of the American Academy of Political and Social Science*, CCXCI (January, 1954), 135–42.

appointed by the chief or police commissioner to consider complaints about police work and to make suggestions regarding the improvement of the department.

According to the International Association of Chiefs of Police, a public relations program for the police should be constructed around the following main points:

1. The participation by the chief and, where appropriate, his immediate command staff in the deliberations of the highest councils of government in the community.

2. The organization of a truly representative city-wide police-community relations council.

3. The organization within the council of an advisory committee (steering committee).

4. The development and operation of a constructive program to involve the people in working for better law observance and crime prevention.

5. The extension of the city-wide program to the grass-roots level through precinct organizations.

6. The assignment of specific responsibility for the program. (This would involve the creation of a police-community relations unit or the appointment of a special officer, depending on the size of the department.)

7. The proper training of all officers in human relations.

8. The adequate training of supervisory personnel and their alertness to good community relations practices.

9. The proper functioning of the department's complaint review system and forthright action as necessary.

10. The assurance of constant attention to the whole program and of the entire department's commitment to making it work.[42]

## COORDINATION AND PUBLIC SUPPORT

The attack on juvenile delinquency must be coordinated if it is to achieve its greatest effectiveness. Here are four important devices that are being used to coordinate the work of community agencies, some of which are directly involved in the prevention of delinquency:

1. *The social service exchange*, which is a central clearing bureau for the recording of the names and addresses of persons who have received help from social and health agencies and of the names of the agencies that have rendered the services. The purpose of this is to facilitate the

[42] Nelson A. Watson, *Police-Community Relations* (Washington, D.C.: International Association of Chiefs of Police, 1966), pp. 39–62.

exchange of information among agencies so that they can coordinate their work, avoid duplication of services, and plan more effectively with persons who apply for help.

2. *The council of social agencies* (also called the community welfare council), which is composed of delegates from public and private agencies in the fields of health, welfare, and recreation. The purpose of this council is to promote better understanding and coordination among the agencies, eliminate duplication of services, achieve joint action in some cases, and improve public relations.

3. *The community chest* (also called community fund or community givers), which is a cooperative organization for the raising of funds for the support of the member agencies and the disbursement of the funds to these agencies in accordance with ascertained budgetary needs. The purpose of this organization is to eliminate the necessity of having separate fund-raising drives by the individual agencies and the ensuing expensive, and sometimes destructive, competition for the contributions of the public.

4. *The coordinating council*, which is composed of representatives of public and private agencies, as well as interested citizens. The purpose of this council is to promote cooperation among the participating agencies, to study conditions and resources in the community, to inform the public about its findings, and to secure democratic action in meeting local needs. It emphasizes the importance of citizen or lay participation and directs much of its attention to the prevention of delinquency, sometimes making this its principal objective.[43]

The coordination of the work of agencies secured through these and similar devices is vitally important in the prevention of delinquency, but it is not enough. It must have public support—public support given through interest in community affairs, participation in community programs, law observance, insistence on wholesome community conditions and abundant opportunity for young people, respect for law enforcement and effective court procedures, demand for an adequate number of well-qualified police officers, judges, probation officers, welfare workers,

[43] Negley K. Teeters and John Otto Reinemann, *The Challenge of Delinquency* (Englewood Cliffs, N.J.: Prentice-Hall, Inc., 1950), pp. 267, 268, 672–75; Ruth Shonle Cavan, *Juvenile Delinquency* (Philadelphia: J. B. Lippincott Co., 1962), pp. 210, 211; Kenneth S. Beam, *Coordinating Councils in California* (California Department of Education, Bulletin No. 11, pp. 7–10; Lowell Juilliard Carr, *Delinquency Control* (New York: Harper and Row, 1941), pp. 331, 343; Kenneth S. Beam, "Community Coordination," in Report of a National Survey of Coordinating and Neighborhood Councils, *Coping with Crime, Yearbook of the National Probation Association, 1937* (New York: National Probation Association, 1937), pp. 47, 48; National Conference on Prevention and Control of Juvenile Delinquency, *Report on Community Coordination* (Washington, D.C.: Government Printing Office, 1947), pp. 15–17.

institutional employees, and parole officers, and a willingness to pay for programs that can deal effectively with social problems.[44] Furthermore, such public support will benefit not only the delinquency prevention program, but also the citizens themselves, for only by assuming their community responsibilities can they preserve their political rights. Indeed, it has been well said that a government that does everything for its people can do anything to them. We must, then, have a coordinated attack supported by the public. This will not eliminate delinquency, for no program can do that, but it will do much to reduce it.

[44] Caldwell, p. 724.

# Selected Bibliography

The books and articles below represent a selected bibliography. Except for the following textbooks and readings which should be consulted on various aspects of delinquency, it is divided into the same three parts as the text. For additional references, the reader should consult the footnotes.

BARRON, MILTON L. *The Juvenile in Delinquent Society.* New York: Alfred A. Knopf, 1960.

BLOCH, HERBERT A., and FLYNN, FRANK T. *Delinquency: The Juvenile Offender in America Today.* New York: Random House, 1956.

CAVAN, RUTH SHONLE. *Readings in Juvenile Delinquency.* Philadelphia: J. B. Lippincott, 1969.

———. *Juvenile Delinquency.* Philadelphia: J. B. Lippincott, 1969.

GIALLOMBARDO, ROSE. *Juvenile Delinquency: A Book of Readings.* New York: John Wiley and Sons, Inc., 1966.

GIBBONS, DON C. *Delinquent Behavior.* Englewood Cliffs, N.J.: Prentice-Hall, Inc., 1970.

GLUECK, SHELDON (ed.). *The Problem of Delinquency.* Boston: Houghton-Mifflin Co., 1959.

MacIVER, ROBERT M. *The Prevention and Control of Delinquency.* New York: Atherton Press, 1966.

MARTIN, JOHN M., and FITZPATRICK, JOSEPH P. *Delinquent Behavior: A Redefinition of the Problem.* New York: Random House, 1964.

NEUMEYER, MARTIN H. *Juvenile Delinquency in Modern Society.* Princeton, N.J.: Van Nostrand Reinhold Co., Inc., 1961.

QUAY, HERBERT C. *Juvenile Delinquency: Research and Theory.* New York: Van Nostrand Reinhold Co., Inc., 1965.

ROBISON, SOPHIA M. *Juvenile Delinquency: Its Nature and Control.* New York: Holt, Rinehart and Winston, 1960.

SHULMAN, HARRY MANUEL. *Juvenile Delinquency in American Society.* New York: Harper and Row, 1961.

TAPPAN, PAUL W. *Juvenile Delinquency.* New York: McGraw-Hill Book Co., 1949.

TEETERS, NEGLEY K., and REINEMANN, JOHN OTTO. *The Challenge of Delinquency.* Englewood Cliffs, N.J.: Prentice-Hall, Inc., 1950.

THE PRESIDENT'S COMMISSION ON LAW ENFORCEMENT AND ADMINISTRATION OF JUSTICE. *Task Force Report: Juvenile Delinquency and Youth Crime.* Washington, D.C.: U.S. Government Printing Office, 1967.

WOLFGANG, MARVIN E., SAVITZ, LEONARD, and JOHNSTON, NORMAN (eds.). *The Sociology of Crime and Delinquency.* New York: John Wiley and Sons, Inc., 1962.


## Part I
## THE PROBLEM


ABRAHAMSEN, DAVID. *Who Are the Guilty?* New York: Grove Press, Inc., 1952.

ALEXANDER, FRANZ, and STAUB, HUGO. *The Criminal, the Judge, and the Public.* New York: The Free Press of Glencoe, Inc., 1956.

ARNOLD, WILLIAM R. "Continuities in Research: Scaling Delinquent Behavior," *Social Problems,* XIII (Summer, 1965), 59–66.

AUSUBEL, DAVID P. *Drug Addiction: Physiological, Psychological, and Sociological Aspects.* New York: Random House, Inc., 1958.

BECKER, HOWARD S. (ed.). *Social Problems: A Modern Approach.* New York: John Wiley and Sons, Inc., 1966.

CHAFITZ, MORRIS E., and DEMONE, HAROLD W., JR. *Alcoholism and Society.* New York: Oxford University Press, 1962.

CLARK, JOHN P., and TIFFT, LARRY L. "Polygraph and Interview Validation of Self-Reported Deviant Behavior," *American Sociological Review,* XXXI (August, 1966), 516–23.

CLINARD, MARSHALL B., and QUINNEY, RICHARD. *Criminal Behavior Systems: A Typology.* New York: Holt, Rinehart, and Winston, Inc., 1967.

COOLEY, CHARLES H. *Social Organization.* New York: Charles Scribner's Sons, 1929.

DAVIS, KINGSLEY. *Human Society.* New York: The Macmillan Co., 1948.

DYNES, RUSSELL R., CLARKE, ALFRED C., DINITZ, SIMON, and ISHINO, IWAO. *Social Problems: Dissensus and Deviation in an Industrial Society.* New York: Oxford University Press, 1964.

EISNER, VICTOR. *The Delinquency Label: The Epidemiology of Juvenile Delinquency.* New York: Random House, Inc., 1969.

EMERSON, HAVEN. *Alcohol and Man.* New York: The Macmillan Co., 1932.

FARIS, ROBERT E. L. *Social Disorganization.* New York: The Ronald Press Co., 1955.

FEDERAL BUREAU OF INVESTIGATION, UNITED STATES DEPARTMENT OF JUSTICE. *Uniform Crime Reports for the United States.* Washington, D.C.: Government Printing Office. Issued yearly.

FERDINAND, THEODORE N. *Typologies of Delinquency: A Critical Analysis.* New York: Random House, 1966.

FINESTONE, HAROLD. "Narcotics and Criminality," *Law and Contemporary Problems,* XXII (Winter, 1957), 69–85.

GIBBONS, DON C. *Changing the Lawbreaker: The Treatment of Delinquents and Criminals.* Englewood Cliffs, N.J.: Prentice-Hall, Inc., 1965.

GLUECK, SHELDON. "Theory and Fact in Criminology," *British Journal of Delinquency,* VII (October, 1956), 108.

GLASER, DANIEL. "National Goals and Indicators for the Reduction of Crime and Delinquency," *Annals of the American Academy of Political and Social Sciences*, CCCLXXI (May, 1967), 104–26.

HEALY, WILLIAM. *The Individual Delinquent*. Boston: Little, Brown and Co., 1915.

――――, and BRONNER, AUGUSTA F. *Delinquents and Criminals*. New York: The Macmillan Co., 1926.

――――, and ――――. *New Light on Delinquency and Its Treatment*. New Haven: Yale University Press, 1936.

HEWITT, LESTER E., and JENKINS, RICHARD L. *Fundamental Patterns of Maladjustment: The Dynamics of Their Origin*. Springfield: Illinois State Printer, 1947.

HIMES, JOSEPH S. "Value Analysis in the Theory of Social Problems," *Social Forces*, XXXIII (March, 1955), 259–62.

HIRSCHI, TRAVIS, and SELVIN, HANAN C. *Delinquency Research: An Appraisal of Analytic Methods*. New York: The Free Press of Glencoe, Inc., 1967.

HOMANS, GEORGE C. *The Human Group*. New York: Harcourt, Brace, Jovanovich, Inc., 1950.

HORTON, P. B., and LESLIE, G. R. *The Sociology of Social Problems*. New York: Appleton-Century-Crofts, Inc., 1960.

JELLINEK, E. M. "Phases in the Drinking History of Alcoholics," *Quarterly Journal of Studies on Alcohol*, VII (June, 1946), 1–88.

JENKINS, RICHARD L. "Diagnoses, Dynamics, and Treatment in Child Psychiatry," *Psychiatric Research Report*, 18, American Psychiatric Association (October, 1964), 91–120.

KOLB, LAWRENCE. *Drug Addiction*. Springfield, Ill.: Charles C. Thomas, 1962.

KRETSCHMER, ERNST. *Physique and Character*, trans. W. J. H. Sprott. New York: Harcourt, Brace, and Jovanovich, Inc., 1925.

LEJINS, PETER. "Uniform Crime Reports," *Michigan Law Review*, LXIV (April, 1966), 1011–30.

LEMERT, EDWIN M. *Human Deviance, Social Problems, and Social Control*. Englewood Cliffs, N.J.: Prentice-Hall, Inc., 1967.

LEMERT, EDWIN M. *Social Pathology*. New York: McGraw-Hill Book Co., Inc., 1951.

LINDESMITH, ALFRED R. "A Sociological Theory of Drug Addiction," *American Journal of Sociology*, XLIII (January, 1938), 593–609.

――――. "The Drug Addict: Patient or Criminal?," *Journal of Criminal Law and Criminology*, XXXI (January–February, 1941), 531–35.

LINDESMITH, ALFRED R., and DUNHAM, H. WARREN. "Some Principles of Criminal Typology," *Social Forces*, XIX (March, 1941), 307–14.

MCGEE, REECE. *Social Disorganization in America*. San Francisco: Chandler Publishing Co., 1962.

MCKINNEY, JOHN C. *Constructive Typology and Social Theory*. New York: Appleton-Century-Crofts, Inc., 1966.

MAURER, DAVID W., and VOGEL, VICTOR H. *Narcotics and Narcotic Addiction*. Springfield, Ill.: Charles C. Thomas, 1967.

MERTON, R. K., and NISBET, R. A. *Contemporary Social Problems.* New York: Harcourt, Brace, Jovanovich, Inc., 1966.

PESCOR, M. J. "The Problem of Narcotic Drug Addiction," *Journal of Criminal Law, Criminology, and Police Science,* XLIII (November–December, 1952), 471–73.

PET, DONALD D., and BALL, JOHN C. "Marihuana Smoking in the United States," *Federal Probation,* XXXII (September, 1968), 8–15.

PITTMAN, DAVID J., and SNYDER, CHARLES R. (eds.). *Society, Culture, and Drinking Patterns.* New York: John Wiley and Sons, Inc., 1962.

PRESIDENT'S COMMISSION ON LAW ENFORCEMENT AND ADMINISTRATION OF JUSTICE. *Task Force Report: Drunkenness,* Appendix B. Washington, D.C.: Government Printing Office, 1967.

———. *Task Force Report: Narcotics and Drug Abuse,* Appendix A-2. Washington, D.C.: Government Printing Office, 1967.

———. *The Challenge of Crime in a Free Society.* Washington, D.C.: Government Printing Office, 1967.

ROBISON, SOPHIA, "A Critical View of the Uniform Crime Reports," *Michigan Law Review,* LXIV (April, 1966), 1031–54.

ROEBUCK, JULIAN B. *Criminal Typology.* Springfield, Ill.: Charles C. Thomas, 1967.

SCHUR, EDWIN M. *Narcotic Addiction in Britain and America.* Bloomington: Indiana University Press, 1962.

SELLIN, THORSTEN, and WOLFGANG, MARVIN E. *The Measurement of Delinquency.* New York: John Wiley and Sons, Inc., 1964.

SHELDON, WILLIAM H., HARTL, EMIL M., and McDERMOTT, EUGENE. *Varieties of Delinquent Youth.* New York: Harper and Row, 1949.

SHELDON, WILLIAM H., and STEVENS, S. S. *Varieties of Temperament.* New York: Harper and Row, 1942.

SHELDON, WILLIAM H., STEVENS, S. S., and TUCKER, W. B. *Varieties of Human Physique.* New York: Harper and Row, 1940.

SHORT, JAMES F., and NYE, F. IVAN. "Reported Behavior as a Criterion of Deviant Behavior," *Social Problems,* V (Winter, 1957), 207–21.

STERNE, MURIEL W., PITTMAN, DAVID J., and COE, THOMAS. "Teen-agers, Drinking, and the Law," *Crime and Delinquency,* XI (January, 1965), 78–85.

STINCHCOMBE, ARTHUR L. "Institutions of Privacy in the Determination of Police Administrative Practices," *American Journal of Sociology,* LXIX (September, 1963), 150–60.

THOMAS, W. I., and ZNANIECKI, FLORIAN. *The Polish Peasant.* New York: Alfred A. Knopf, Inc., 1927.

UNITED STATES CHILDREN'S BUREAU. *Juvenile Court Statistics.* Washington, D.C.: Government Printing Office.

WHEELER, STANTON. "Criminal Statistics: A Reformulation of the Problem," *Journal of Criminal Law, Criminology, and Police Science,* LVIII (September, 1967), 17–24.

WIKLER, ABRAHAM. *Opiate Addiction*. Springfield, Ill.: Charles C. Thomas, 1953.

## Part II
## CAUSATION

AICHHORN, AUGUST. *Wayward Youth*. New York: The Viking Press, 1951.

ANDRY, R. G. "Parental Affection and Delinquency," *The Sociology of Crime and Delinquency*, eds. Marvin E. Wolfgang, Leonard Savitz, and Norman Johnston. New York: John Wiley and Sons, Inc., 1962.

*Annals of the American Academy of Political and Social Science*, January, 1949, entire issue.

BACON, SELDEN D. "Alcohol and Complex Society," *Society, Culture and Drinking Patterns*, eds. David J. Pittman and Charles R. Snyder. New York: John Wiley and Sons, Inc., 1962.

BARKER, GORDON H. "Family Factors in the Ecology of Juvenile Delinquency," *Journal of Criminal Law, Criminology, and Police Science*," XXX (January–February, 1940), 681–91.

BITTNER, EGON. "The Police on Skid-Row: A Study of Peace Keeping," *American Sociological Review*, XXXII (October, 1967), 699–715.

BLOCH, HERBERT A., and NIEDERHOFFER, ARTHUR. *The Gang*. New York: Philosophical Library, 1958.

BOSSARD, JAMES H. S., and BOLL, ELEANOR STOKER. *The Sociology of Child Development*. New York: Harper and Row, 1966.

BRILL, A. A. (trans. and ed.). *The Basic Writings of Sigmund Freud*. New York: The Modern Library, 1938.

BURGESS, ERNEST W. "The Economic Factor in Juvenile Delinquency," *Journal of Criminal Law, Criminology, and Police Science*, XLIII (May–June, 1952), 29–42.

BURT, CYRIL. *The Young Delinquent*. New York: Appleton-Century-Crofts, Inc., 1925.

CALDWELL, ROBERT G. *Criminology*. New York: The Ronald Press Co., 1965.

CARR, LOWELL JUILLIARD. *Delinquency Control*. New York: Harper and Row, 1950.

CLOWARD, RICHARD A. "Illegitimate Means, Anomie, and Deviant Behavior," *American Sociological Review*, XXIV (April, 1959), 164–76.

——, and OHLIN, LLOYD E. *Delinquency and Opportunity: A Theory of Delinquent Gangs*. New York: The Free Press of Glencoe, Inc., 1960.

COHEN, ALBERT K. *Delinquent Boys: The Subculture of the Gang*. New York: The Free Press of Glencoe, Inc., 1955.

COOLEY, CHARLES HORTON. *Human Nature and the Social Order*. New York: Charles Scribner's Sons, 1902.

COON, CARLETON S. *The Origin of Races*. New York: Alfred A. Knopf, 1962.

DOLLARD, JOHN, and DOOB, LEONARD, *et al. Frustration and Aggression*. New Haven: Yale University Press, 1939.

ECKLAND, B. K. "Genetics and Sociology: A Reconsideration," *American Sociological Review*, XXXII (April, 1967), 173–94.

FERDINAND, THEODORE N. "The Offense Patterns and Family Structures of Urban, Village, and Rural Delinquents," *Journal of Criminal Law, Criminology, and Police Science*, LV (March, 1964), 86–93.

FREUD, SIGMUND. *A General Introduction to Psychoanalysis*. New York: Boni and Liveright, 1920.

FRIEDLANDER, KATE. *The Psychoanalytical Approach to Juvenile Delinquency*. New York: International Universities Press, Inc., 1947.

GEORGE, WESLEY C. *The Biology of the Race Problem*. New York: National Putnam Letters Committee Reprint, 1962.

Glueck, Sheldon. "Theory and Fact in Criminology," *British Journal of Delinquency*, VII (October, 1956), 108.

————, and Glueck, Eleanor T. *One Thousand Juvenile Delinquents*. Cambridge: Harvard University Press, 1934.

———— and ————. *Five Hundred Delinquent Women*. New York: Alfred A. Knopf, Inc., 1934.

———— and ————. *Juvenile Delinquents Grown Up*. New York: The Commonwealth Fund, 1940.

———— and ————. *Unraveling Juvenile Delinquency*. New York: The Commonwealth Fund, 1950.

———— and ————. *Physique and Delinquency*. New York: Harper and Row, 1956.

———— and ————. *Family Environment and Delinquency*. Boston: Houghton Mifflin Co., 1962.

GOODSELL, WILLYSTINE. *A History of Marriage and the Family*. New York: The Macmillan Co., 1939.

HALL, CALVIN S., and LINDZEY, GARDNER. *Theories of Personality*. New York: John Wiley and Sons, Inc., 1957.

HATHAWAY, STARKE R., and MONACHESI, ELIO D. *Analyzing and Predicting Juvenile Delinquency with the MMPI*. Minneapolis: University of Minnesota Press, 1953.

HEALY, WILLIAM. *The Individual Delinquent*. Boston: Little, Brown, and Co., 1915.

————, and BRONNER, AUGUSTA F. *Delinquents and Criminals: Their Making and Unmaking*. New York: The Macmillan Co., 1926.

———— and ————. *New Light on Delinquency and Its Treatment*. New Haven: Yale University Press, 1936.

————, ————, and BOWERS, A. M. *The Structure and Meaning of Psychoanalysis*. New York: Alfred A. Knopf, Inc., 1930.

HERTZLER, J. O. *American Social Institutions*. Boston: Allyn and Bacon, Inc., 1961.

*Journal of Research in Crime and Delinquency*, IV (January, 1967), entire issue.

KEPHART, WILLIAM M. *The Family, Society, and the Individual*. Boston: Houghton Mifflin Co., 1961.

KIRKPATRICK, CLIFFORD. *The Family as Process and Institution.* New York: The Ronald Press Co., 1963.

KLEIN, MALCOLM W. *Juvenile Gangs in Context: Theory, Research and Action.* Englewood Cliffs, N.J.: Prentice-Hall, 1967.

KOBRIN, SOLOMON. "The Conflict of Values in Delinquency Areas," *American Sociological Review,* XVI (October, 1951), 653–661.

LANDER, BERNARD. *Toward an Understanding of Juvenile Delinquency.* New York: Columbia University Press, 1954.

LEES, J. P., and NEWSON, L. J. "Family or Sibship Position and Some Aspects of Juvenile Delinquency," *British Journal of Delinquency,* V (July, 1954), 46–65.

LINDESMITH, ALFRED, and LEVIN, YALE. "The Lombrosian Myth in Criminology," *American Journal of Sociology,* XLII (March, 1937), 653–71.

LINTON, RALPH. *The Tree of Culture.* New York: Alfred A. Knopf, 1959.

MacIVER, ROBERT M. *Society: Its Structure and Changes.* New York: Ray Long and Richard R. Smith, Inc., 1932.

MARX, MELVIN H. (ed.). *Theories in Contemporary Psychology.* New York: The Macmillan Co., 1963.

MATZA, DAVID. *Delinquency and Drift.* New York: John Wiley and Sons, Inc., 1964.

MEAD, GEORGE H. *Mind, Self, and Society.* Chicago: University of Chicago Press, 1934.

MERRILL, MAUD A. *Problems of Child Delinquency.* New York: Houghton Mifflin Co., 1947.

MILLER, WALTER B. "Lower Class Culture as a Generating Milieu of Gang Delinquency," *Journal of Social Issues,* XIV (1958), 5–19.

MONAHAN, THOMAS P. "Family Status and the Delinquent Child: A Reappraisal and Some New Findings," *Social Forces,* XXXV (March, 1957), 250–58.

MONTAGU, ASHLEY (ed.). *The Concept of Race.* New York: The Free Press of Glencoe, Inc., 1964.

MUNROE, RUTH L. *Schools of Psychoanalytic Thought.* New York: The Dryden Press, Inc., 1955.

MYRDAL, GUNNAR. *An American Dilemma.* New York: Harper and Row, 1944.

NYE, F. IVAN. *Family Relationships and Delinquent Behavior.* New York: John Wiley and Sons, Inc., 1958.

OGBURN, WILLIAM F., and NIMKOFF, MEYER F. *Technology and the Changing Family.* Boston: Houghton Mifflin Co., 1955.

RECKLESS, WALTER C. *The Etiology of Delinquent and Criminal Behavior.* New York: Social Science Research Council, Bulletin 50, 1943.

REDL, FRITZ, and WINEMAN, DAVID. *Children Who Hate.* New York: The Free Press of Glencoe, Inc., 1951.

REISS, A. J., JR. "Delinquency as the Failure of Personal and Social Controls," *American Sociological Review,* XVI (April, 1951), 196–208.

————, and RHODES, LEWIS. "The Distribution of Juvenile Delinquency in the Social Class Structure," *American Sociological Review,* XXVI (October, 1961), 720–32.

ROGERS, CARL R. *The Clinical Treatment of the Problem Child.* Boston: Houghton Mifflin Co., 1939.

SALISBURY, HARRISON E. *The Shook-Up Generation.* New York: Harper and Row, 1958.

SHAW, CLIFFORD R., and McKAY, HENRY D. *Social Factors in Juvenile Delinquency.* Report No. 13, Vol. II, National Commission on Law Observance and Enforcement. Washington, D.C.: Government Printing Office, 1931.

———— and ————. *Juvenile Delinquency and Urban Areas.* Chicago: University of Chicago Press, 1969.

SHELDON, WILLIAM H., HARTL, EMIL M., and McDERMOTT, EUGENE. *Varieties of Delinquent Youth.* New York: Harper and Row, 1949.

SHIBUTANI, TAMOTSU. *Society and Personality: An Interaction Approach to Social Psychology.* Englewood Cliffs, N.J.: Prentice-Hall, Inc., 1961.

SHORT, JAMES F., JR., and STRODTBECK, FRED L. *Group Process and Gang Delinquency.* Chicago: University of Chicago Press, 1965.

SHULMAN, HARRY M. *From Truancy to Crime.* Albany: New York State Crime Commission, 1928.

————. "Intelligence and Delinquency," *Journal of Criminal Law and Criminology,* XLI (March–April, 1951), 763–81.

SKOLNICK, JEROME. *Justice Without Trial: Law Enforcement in a Democratic Society.* New York: John Wiley and Sons, Inc., 1967.

STANFIELD, ROBERT EVERETT. "The Interaction of Family Variables and Gang Variables in the Aetiology of Delinquency," *Social Problems,* XIII (Spring, 1966), 411–17.

SUMNER, WILLIAM GRAHAM. *Folkways.* Boston: Ginn and Co., 1906.

SUTHERLAND, EDWIN H. *Principles of Criminology.* Philadelphia: J. B. Lippincott Co., 1939.

————, and CRESSEY, DONALD R. *Principles of Criminology.* Philadelpia: J. B. Lippincott Co., 1966.

THOMAS, WILLIAM I. *The Unadjusted Girl.* Boston: Little, Brown and Co., 1923.

THRASHER, FREDERIC M. *The Gang.* Chicago: University of Chicago Press, 1936.

TOBY, JACKSON. "The Differential Impact of Family Disorganization," *American Sociological Review,* XXII (October, 1957), 505–12.

U. S. CHILDREN'S BUREAU AND NATIONAL INSTITUTE OF MENTAL HEALTH. *Thinking About Drinking.* Washington, D.C.: Government Printing Office, 1968.

VOLD, GEORGE B. *Theoretical Criminology.* Fairlawn, N.J.: Oxford University Press, 1958.

WATTENBERG, WILLIAM W., and SAUNDERS, FRANK. "Sex Differences Among Juvenile Offenders," *Sociology and Social Research,* XXXIX (September–October, 1954), 24–31.

WRONG, DENNIS H. "The Oversocialized Conception of Man in Modern Sociology," *American Sociological Review,* XXVI (April, 1961), 183–93.

YABLONSKY, LEWIS. *The Violent Gang.* New York: The Macmillan Co., 1962.

## Part III
## CORRECTION AND PREVENTION

AMERICAN LAW INSTITUTE, THE. *Youth Correction Authority Act*. Philadelphia: The American Law Institute, 1940.

AMOS, WILLIAM E., and WELLFORD, CHARLES F. (eds.). *Delinquency Prevention: Theory and Practice*. Englewood Cliffs, N.J.: Prentice-Hall, Inc., 1967.

CALDWELL, ROBERT G. "The Juvenile Court: Its Development and Some Major Problems," *Journal of Criminal Law, Criminology, and Police Science*, LI (January–February, 1961), 493–511.

CICOUREL, AARON V. *The Social Organization of Juvenile Justice*. New York: John Wiley and Sons, Inc., 1968.

CLARKE, HELEN I. *Social Legislation*. New York: Appleton-Century-Crofts, Inc., 1957.

CLARK, JOHN P., and WENNINGER, EUGENE P. "The Attitude of Juveniles Toward the Legal Institution," *The Journal of Criminal Law, Criminology, and Police Science*, LV (December, 1964), 482–89.

COHEN, FRED. *The Legal Challenge to Corrections: Implications for Manpower and Training*. Washington, D.C.: Joint Commission on Correctional Manpower and Training, March, 1969.

COOLEY, EDWIN J. *Probation and Delinquency*. New York: Thomas Nelson and Sons, 1927.

"Correction of Youthful Offenders (A Symposium)." *Law and Contemporary Problems*, IX (Autumn, 1942).

CRAWFORD, PAUL L., DUMPSON, JAMES R., and MALAMUD, DANIEL I. *Working with Teen-Age Gangs*. New York: Welfare Council of New York City, 1950.

*Crime and Delinquency*, VIII (July, 1962), entire issue.

DANIELS, LINCOLN (compiler). *The Prevention of Juvenile Delinquency*, U.S. Children's Bureau Publication. Washington, D.C.: Government Printing Office, 1969.

DIANA, LEWIS. "The Rights of Juvenile Delinquents: An Appraisal of Juvenile Court Procedures," *Journal of Criminal Law, Criminology, and Police Science*, XLVII (January–February, 1957), 561–69.

DRESSLER, DAVID. *Practice and Theory of Probation and Parole*. New York: Columbia University Press, 1969.

DUNHAM, H. WARREN. "The Juvenile Court: Contradictory Orientations in Processing Offenders," *Law and Contemporary Problems*, XXIII (Summer, 1958), 508–527.

ELDEFONSO, EDWARD. *Law Enforcement and the Youthful Offender: Juvenile Procedures*. New York: John Wiley and Sons, Inc., 1967.

ELLINGSTON, JOHN R. *Protecting Our Children from Criminal Careers*. New York: Prentice-Hall, Inc., 1948.

FEDERAL BUREAU OF PRISONS. *Handbook of Correctional Institution Design and Construction.* Washington, D.C.: Federal Bureau of Prisons, 1949.

*Future of the Juvenile Court: Implications for Correctional Manpower and Training.* Washington, D.C.: Joint Commission on Correctional Manpower and Training, 1968.

GLUECK, SHELDON, and ELEANOR T. *Predicting Delinquency and Crime.* Cambridge: Harvard University Press, 1959.

GOLDMAN, NATHAN. *The Differential Selection of Juvenile Offenders for Court Appearance.* New York: National Council on Crime and Delinquency, 1963.

HART, HENRY M. "The Aims of the Criminal Law," *Law and Contemporary Problems,* XXIII (Summer, 1958), 401–41.

HATHAWAY, STARKE R., and McKINLEY, J. CHARNLEY. *The Minnesota Multi-Personality Inventory.* New York: Psychological Corporation, 1943.

HATHAWAY, STARKE R., and MONACHESI, ELIO D. (eds.). *Analyzing and Predicting Juvenile Delinquency with MMPI.* New York: Psychological Corporation, 1954.

HEALY, WILLIAM, and BRONNER, AUGUSTA F. *Treatment and What Happened Afterward.* Boston: The Judge Baker Guidance Center, 1939.

HERMAN, STEPHEN M. "Scope and Purposes of Juvenile Court Jurisdiction," *Journal of Criminal Law, Criminology, and Police Science,* XLVIII (March–April, 1958), 590–607.

KAHN, ALFRED J. *A Court for Children.* New York: Columbia University Press, 1953.

KENNY, JOHN P., and PURSUIT, DAN G. *Police Work with Juveniles.* Springfield, Ill.: Charles C. Thomas, 1965.

KOBRIN, SOLOMON. "The Chicago Area Project—A 25-Year Assessment," *The Annals of the American Academy of Political and Social Science,* CCCXXII (March, 1959), 19–29.

KVARACEUS, WILLIAM C. *Juvenile Delinquency and the School.* New York: World Book Co., 1945.

———, and MILLER, WALTER B. *Delinquent Behavior: Culture and the Individual.* Washington, D.C.: National Education Association of the United States, 1959.

LOW, HERBERT H. *Juvenile Courts in the United States.* Chapel Hills, N.C.: University of North Carolina Press, 1927.

LUDWIG, FREDERICK J. *Youth and the Law.* Brooklyn: The Foundation Press, Inc., 1955.

*Manual of Correctional Standards.* New York: The American Correctional Association, 1959.

MYREN, RICHARD A., and SWANSON, LYNN D. *Police Work with Children,* U.S. Children's Bureau Publication, No. 399. Washington, D.C.: Government Printing Office, 1962.

NATIONAL CONFERENCE ON PREVENTION AND CONTROL OF JUVENILE DELINQUENCY. *Report on Case Work—Group Work.* Washington, D.C.: Government Printing Office, 1947.

———. *Report on Juvenile Court Laws*. Washington, D.C.: Government Printing Office, 1947.

NORMAN, SHERWOOD. *Detention Practice: Significant Developments in the Detention of Children and Youth*. New York: National Probation and Parole Association, 1960.

NUNBERG, HENRY. "Problems in the Structure of the Juvenile Court," *Journal of Criminal Law, Criminology, and Police Science*, XLVIII (January–February, 1958), 500–516.

PRESIDENT'S COMMISSION ON LAW ENFORCEMENT AND ADMINISTRATION OF JUSTICE, THE. *Task Force Report: Corrections*, Appendix A. Washington, D.C.: Government Printing Office, 1967.

*Procedure and Evidence in the Juvenile Court*. New York: National Council on Crime and Delinquency, 1962.

RUBIN, SOL. *Crime and Juvenile Delinquency*. New York: Oceana Publications, 1958.

SCHREIBER, DANIEL (ed.). *Profile of the School Dropout*. New York: Random House, Inc., 1967.

*Standards and Guides for the Detention of Children and Youth*. New York: National Council on Crime and Delinquency, 1961.

*Standards for Juvenile and Family Courts*. U.S. Children's Bureau Publication No. 437. Washington, D.C.: Government Printing Office, 1966.

*Standards for Specialized Courts Dealing with Children*, issued by the United States Children's Bureau. Children's Bureau Publication No. 346. Washington, D.C.: Government Printing Office, 1954.

*Standard Juvenile Court Act* (rev. ed.) New York: National Probation and Parole Association, 1959.

SUSSMAN, FREDERICK B., and BAUM, FREDERIC S. *Law of Juvenile Delinquency*. Dobbs Ferry, N.Y.: Oceana Publications, 1968.

TAPPAN, PAUL. *Comparative Survey of Juvenile Delinquency*, Part I, North America. New York: United Nations, Department of Economic and Social Affairs, 1958.

———. "Treatment Without Trial," *Social Forces*, XXIV (March, 1946), 306–11.

———. "Young Adults Under the Youth Authority," *Journal of Criminal Law, Criminology, and Police Science*, XLVII (April–May, 1957), 629–46.

TERRY, ROBERT. "Discrimination in the Handling of Juvenile Offenders by Social Control Agencies," *Journal of Research in Crime and Delinquency*, IV (July, 1967), 218–30.

WILSON, O. W. *Police Administration*. New York: McGraw-Hill Book Co., Inc., 1963.

WOLBERG, LEWIS R. *The Technique of Psychotherapy*. New York: Grune and Stratton, 1954.

# Index